Secrets of the Tax Revolt

Secrets of the Tax Revolt

James Ring Adams

Harcourt Brace Jovanovich, Publishers
San Diego   New York   London

A Manhattan Institute for Policy Research Book

The author wishes to thank the following for permission to quote from the sources
listed:
A Nation Within a Nation: The Rise of Texas Nationalism by Mark E. Nackman. By
permission of Associated Faculty Press, Inc. Copyright 1975 by Kennikat Press. *California: The Great Exception.* Copyright © 1976 by Carey McWilliams. Reprinted by
permission of Peregrine Smith Books. *The Revolt of the Haves: Tax Rebellions and
Hard Times.* Copyright © 1980 by Robert Kuttner. Reprinted by permission of Simon
& Schuster, Inc. From "New Hampshire" from *The Poetry of Robert Frost* edited by
Edward Connery Lathem. Copyright 1923, © 1969 by Holt, Rinehart and Winston.
Copyright 1951 by Robert Frost. Reprinted by permission of Holt, Rinehart and Winston, Publishers. *Progress and Poverty* by Henry George. Centennial Edition copyright © 1979 by Robert Schalkenback Foundation. Reprinted by permission of Robert
Schalkenback Foundation. *The Muqaddimah: An Introduction to History* by Ibn
Khaldun, translated from the Arabic by Franz Rosenthal, Bollingen Series 43. Copyright © 1958 and 1967 by Princeton University Press. Excerpts from Vol. 11, pp. 89–
91, reprinted by permission of Princeton University Press. *The Stamp Act Crisis* by

Edmund S. and Helen M. Morgan. Copyright © 1953 by the University of North Carolina Press. By permission of the publisher. *The Puritan Dilemma: The Story of John
Winthrop* by Edmund S. Morgan. Little, Brown and Company, 1958. *Rockefeller of
New York: Executive Power in the Statehouse* by Robert H. Connery and Gerald Benjamin. Cornell University Press, 1979. *The Public's Business: The Politics and Practices of Government Corporations.* Copyright © 1978 by Annmarie Hauck Walsh.
Reprinted by permission of MIT Press.

The author also acknowledges the gracious consent of the Advisory Commission on
Intergovernmental Relations, Washington, D.C., to the reproduction of several of its
invaluable tables and charts. Some material in Chapter Seven, "Louisiana and the
Sunbelt," was originally prepared for a symposium at Tulane University, February
6 and 7, 1981, on journalistic perceptions of the South and subsequently published
in *Dixie Dateline: A Journalistic Portrait of the Contemporary South* (Houston: Rice
University Studies, 1983). The author thanks John B. Boles, editor and organizer of
the symposium, and Rice University Studies for their permission.

Library of Congress Cataloging in Publication Data

Adams, James Ring.
  Secrets of the tax revolt.

  Includes bibliographical references.
  1. Taxation—United States—States—History.
2. Taxation—United States—History. I. Title.
HJ2385.A635 1984   336.2'00973   84-3765
ISBN 0-15-179998-9

PRINTED IN THE UNITED STATES OF AMERICA

FIRST EDITION

A B C D E

To my mother
   and the memory of my father

Contents

I Background

   1 The Supply Side and the States   *3*

   2 The New-Old Landscape of the Tax Revolt   *24*

II The Three Phases

   3 Phase One. Massachusetts: Where It All
      Began   *43*

   4 Phase Two. Lessons of New York   *73*

   5 The Fall and Rise of New York   *91*

   6 Phase Three. California the Golden   *124*

III Applications and Limitations

   7 Louisiana and the Sunbelt   *179*

   8 Texas: The Jacksonian Nation-State   *208*

   9 Ohio: The Middle-aged "Middle Region"   *240*

   10 Michigan: Tax Revolts and Hard Times   *266*

IV   Vindication

   11   New Hampshire: The Oldest Frontier
         Revives   *291*

   12   Massachusetts: The Tax Revolt Continues   *307*

V   Implications

   13   Revealing the Secrets of the Tax Revolt   *337*

   Notes   *347*
   Index   *393*

Acknowledgments

It would be extremely difficult to name all the people who have helped this project in the decade in which material has been accumulating. To express my gratitude in the proportion which each deserves would be almost impossible. I hope the many friends and informants who have enlightened my travels around the country will accept my blanket expression of thanks.

Some contributions deserve special mention, however. They start with a bearded gentleman in the California State Library whose name I don't know who photocopied the pamphlet cited on page 143 for me two minutes before closing time. And they culminate in the extreme patience shown by my family. The project was first suggested by Les Lenkowsky. It was made possible by a leave granted by my employer, *The Wall Street Journal*, and by the support of Robert Bartley and George Melloan, who have made the *Journal* editorial page the outstanding place it is.

Midway through the project, a portion of the book was spun off into a belated Ph.D. thesis. Stern but just scrutiny by my dissertation committee at Cornell University brought an invaluable discipline to the work. My thanks to Myron Rush, Patricia Leeds, Martin Shefter, and especially to my chairman, Werner Dannhauser, who is an example of intellectual courage and integrity rarely encountered in the academy, or in any walk of life. I have been lucky in my education, and if this book has any merit, it is because of what I have learned, in my middling way, from Professor Dannhauser and his friends. The late Herbert J. Storing deserves special mention because his teaching about American government was so powerful that one can never be sure whether what seems like an original thought is really the result of one of his stray comments. Likewise, much of the history in chapter three comes from an undergraduate course with Edmund S. Morgan at Yale; I doubt that he remembers me from his lectures, and he might be appalled at the use to which I have put them.

I should thank, to single out some people from several years of travel and writing, Leon Wein and William Quirk for teaching me to start at the beginning; Conrad Jamison and Ann Weidel of Security Pacific Bank in Los Angeles for confirming the historical bent; Edmund G. Brown, Jr., and his true guru, Francis Kelly, for sharing insights about technology; and John Walker Mauer, for sharing an enthusiasm for state constitutions. I received great courtesy from Professor C. Eugene Lee of Berkeley's Institute for Governmental Studies, which holds what may be the largest collection of material on the California Tax Revolt, and Molly Sturges Tuthill, curator of the Reagan Archives at the Hoover Institute in Palo Alto, California. My thanks go to the staffs who helped me at the California State Library; the Barker History Center at the University of Texas in Austin; the New Orleans Public Library; the university libraries of Ohio State, Michigan, and Michigan State; the New Hampshire State Library; the public libraries of New Rochelle and Larchmont, New York; the libraries of Harvard Law School, the University of Massachusetts at Amherst, Westfield State College, and the Westfield Athenaeum. Without slighting my friends and colleagues Jude Wanniski, Paul Craig Roberts, and David Ranson, I must acknowledge a special debt to Arthur Laffer. Among other things, he helped bring me in touch with Harcourt Brace Jovanovich, which has given me the pleasure of working with my editor, Paul McCluskey, and his assistant, Johanna Jordahl. Work on the book was greatly enhanced by the staff of the Manhattan Institute, notably William Hammett and the outstanding Joan Kennedy Taylor. Help with the typing came from the ever-cheerful Beth Boswell and Kathy Oppenheim and the excellent Lynn Falcone. And Dot Meyer let me use her toolshed.

The ultimate thanks go to my family: to the ever-faithful research associate Miss Marple, to Jared, Jonathan, and Abigail, who kept asking when Daddy would finish his chapter so he could play, and above all to Laurel, without whose incessant encouragement the work would never have been done.

I

Background

1

The Supply Side
and the States

When the climate is right, political orthodoxy grips the land as tightly as an Ice Age glacier. Public opinion lives in its shadow. Television announcers, newspaper pundits, and opinion-makers from the right neighborhoods clamber to establish themselves on its mass. Opposing outlooks are smothered. Yet climates change and glaciers recede, leaving behind moraines of shattered doctrine and an altered landscape.

American politics in the last decade has been undergoing such an alteration. The 1980 election of Ronald Reagan may someday be seen as the landmark of this geological succession. His administration, even with its vagaries and compromises, clearly revealed a new political ecology. Yet some travelers had crossed the freshly sculpted valleys and newly melted rivers nearly a decade earlier. In state after state, excited taxpayers had risen in revolt against their established elites. Where states provided the ballot measures of initiative and referendum, citizens attacked the traditions of big spending and high taxes by voting for radical constitutional amendments. The politics of California and Massachusetts were badly shaken by the earthquakes of Propositions 13 and 2½, yet their economies survived intact. Where the taxpayers had no such recourse, the old state political habits lingered on. But the jobs and workers voted with their feet, leaving for better climates, and erosion wore the economies down.

This book describes the still-emerging political and economic protest called "the Tax Revolt." The action takes place at the state level. There the new political ecology was taking hold while national politicians were still saying that Ronald Reagan was "unelectable." Yet almost invariably in the country's climatic political shifts, state and local governments show what lies up the road, for the nation changes from the bottom up. Alterations in the federal landscape are prepared for years in town meetings, city halls, and state assemblies. The Abolition and Secession movements of the nineteenth century gathered strength at the grass roots until national politicians could no longer control them. As the century closed, Greenbackers, Grangers, and Populists merged their demands for economic reform into the prairie fire that was William Jennings Bryan. The Progressive movement of the early twentieth century, which rid cities of corrupt bosses and brought states the direct primary and the referendum, was primarily a triumph of state and local reformers. In its scope of activity, it has had no equal until the Tax Revolt.

The genius of the federal government lies in its ability to reach compromise and resolve the raw conflicts of family rivalries, neighborhood loyalties, and ethnic distrust. States and localities live with these conflicts daily. Places like Sacramento and Baton Rouge are more likely than Washington, D.C., to bear the mark of strong men and strange events. Louisiana taxation leads back to the warped genius of Huey Long; California's fiscal plebescites grow out of the turbulence of the Gold Rush.

Much of the nation's domestic history would be greatly enriched if it were retold as an aggregate of state experiences. Underneath the homogeneous surface of the Washington-oriented textbooks lie weird and wonderful landscapes. Many states have extensive histories that predate the United States and therefore they carry not inconsiderable traces of their earlier institutions. Two were independent republics (Texas and, yes, Vermont), and one was an absolute monarchy (Hawaii). Those formed after creation of the United States still remember the manner of their birth. The Constitution to the contrary, the states of the old Northwest Territory, ceded by the original colonies, entered on a more equal footing than the western states slowly carved out of post-Civil War territories. Two states, Texas and California, burst into the Union like wild mustangs. Others vividly recall protracted struggles with their neighbors to secure their identity.

The Tax Revolt was a challenge to the orthodoxy of centralized government. By successfully changing the rules of state government, the voters immediately made it the focus of experiment. They operated on the sometimes unstated assumption that life would be better with lowered taxes. If the states that followed this lead outperformed the high-tax states, then one would have to conclude that state-level policies could make a difference, indeed that the states still held a claim to independent vitality.

The Tax Revolt had more than an institutional point to make. If one state could do better than another because of its fiscal policies, then the theory behind those policies deserved serious attention. The "tax rebels" themselves may not have worked out this theory in full detail (although many of these grass-roots characters had sounder economic instincts than their critics). Yet others did have a coherent set of ideas. The prevailing orthodoxy came under pressure from a small group of theorists known as the supply-side movement, developing its ideas in tandem and sometimes in cooperation with the practical activists of the Tax Revolt. The two strands together were producing a new political ecology.

For the new ecology there was a new agenda, accumulated as the weight of Democratic liberalism scraped and scoured on the bedrock of Republican conservatism. The New Deal orthodoxy was melting away, yet the landscape had been vastly transformed by the glacier. The new political program rejected the statism of the previous majority party, yet it could not return to the *status quo ante*. The old Republican agenda began with balancing the budget, by tax increases if necessary. The new program concentrated on ending the growth in taxation and subordinated the budget.

THE GLACIER: BEFORE THE TAX REVOLT

The new attack on taxation was a reaction to a very simple situation. The American tax burden had risen sharply over the preceding decades and, up till 1980, seemed destined to rise at even steeper rates. Federal budget receipts averaged 18.3% of gross national product from 1959 to 1968. In the following decade, this rough measure of federal tax burden bounced up to 19%. The real surge began in the mid-seventies, however, with the administration of Jimmy Carter. Following the lead of his fellow engineer Herbert Hoover, President Carter tried to close a widening budget deficit by raising taxes. His first budget for fiscal year 1977 (actually prepared in 1975 under President Gerald Ford) counted on revenues totaling 19.1% of GNP. This was already the highest federal tax burden since the recession years of the fiscal 1969 and 1970 budgets. But Carter proceeded to adopt two of the largest tax increases in American history, the "windfall profits tax," thinly disguised as a populist soaking of the oil companies, and the Social Security tax increase of 1977, still the peacetime record. His budget estimates projected that the federal tax burden would climb steadily at an average rate of 2.3% a year. According to his fiscal 1981 budget, tax receipts were to have soared to 22.7% of GNP by fiscal year 1983. What a difference an election can make! The actual federal tax burden in 1983, after President Reagan's tax cuts, was 18.7% of GNP. The difference amounts to an impressive 4% of GNP.[1]

The problem of the federal tax burden was one of distribution as well as size. The seventies were years of high inflation as well as rising taxes, and they gave a painful one-two punch to the middle-class family. Paychecks swelled with inflated dollars, but standards of living actually worsened. Groceries, clothes, and gasoline soared in price, giving most workers the feeling they were simply running in place. In dollars adjusted for inflation up to 1981, the median family income in 1970 was $23,111. In 1980, it was $23,204. From 1950 to 1960, the real gain had been nearly $5,000. From 1960 to 1970, it had been around $6,000. But from 1970 to 1980,

1. Notes are on pages 347–392.

the family had furthered itself, in the only measure that counted, by merely $93.[2]

Yet none of this mattered to the Internal Revenue Service. "Indexing" for inflation was still a radical notion afloat in the hinterlands. As far as the tax bill was concerned, "nominal" (or inflation-swollen) income was all that mattered. This bite might not have been so painful if the same tax rate had applied at all levels of income. But in their quest for social justice, generations of reformers had made progressive taxation an article of faith. The more a man earned, the higher rate he should pay, whether or not the dollars were worth as much as before. This turn of the screw came to be called "bracket creep." Whatever it did to the average man, it was a wonderful godsend for the politicians. Revenue came rolling in as more and more people were pushed into higher brackets, and legislators did not even have to vote for higher tax rates.

The sheer impact of bracket creep is startling. H. C. Wainwright & Co. Economics, in Boston, the original supply-side consulting firm, traced the tax bill of a hypothetical family of four which, after a decade of exactly keeping pace with inflation, earned a 1978 income of $25,000. In 1965, this family paid a 19% federal tax on its last dollar of income; in 1978, for a last dollar that had exactly the same buying power, it paid 28%. A family earning $50,000 suffered even more, as it was pushed from the 28% bracket in 1965 to the 46% bracket in 1978. Yet a family at the top end of the scale felt almost nothing; it paid the highest rate in 1965 and the highest rate thirteen years later.[3]

This burden was oppressive enough, yet there was more. State and local taxes had also been growing rapidly, more rapidly even than the federal levy. In 1952, they took up 5.7% of the gross national product. In 1972, the peak year, their bite of GNP had expanded to 9.9%. State taxes more often than not intensified the bracket creep, as reformers across the country won adoption of the progressive personal income tax. In 1952, state and local individual income taxes took less than three-tenths of 1% of GNP. In 1972, this category had expanded more than fourfold.[4] Moreover, the steepest increases in progressivity were concentrated in a few states, with results that make them key examples for this study of the Tax Revolt.

Politicians who had been raising state levies sometimes attempted to minimize their impact on the ground that state and local taxes can be deducted from the federal tax bill. Howard Jarvis, of Proposition 13 fame, drove this argument to its absurd conclusion by observing that all should be in favor of a 100% state income tax because there would then be no federal tax at all! In truth, however, the deductibility of a state or local tax makes no practical difference. The real impact of a tax comes in take-home pay, not in the abstract adjustments to gross income recorded on the pay stub.

The size and distribution of the increasing tax burden might have been more tolerated if the people who bore it had been convinced that it was necessary. Taxes have always been resented, but republics seem willing to pay extraordinarily high rates if their survival depends on it. There is also a common-sense willingness to shoulder the cost of public essentials such as police and fire protection, garbage pickups, and education. Yet remarkably little of the last decades' increased spending went for such meat and potatoes. In 1960, 49% of the federal budget was devoted to national defense; in 1980, this figure was 23.6%. Yet spending for income security in the same period had increased from 19.8% of the budget to 33.5%.[5]

State and local taxes, too, have been going less for hard services and more for transfer payments. As a symptom of this shift in "own source" spending, highways, which took 18.2% of all state and local revenues in 1960, received only 9% in 1980. But the proportion for welfare rose from 8.5% to 12.4%. This ratio would change even more dramatically if one included the federal aid which grew so rapidly during these decades.[6]

National averages, moreover, tell only part of the story. Some states have led the shift from infrastructure spending to welfare while others have kept their emphasis on traditional services. As one might expect, leaders of the shift have been such bastions of liberalism as California, New York, and Massachusetts.

THE THAW: THE GLACIER RECEDES

According to the prevailing orthodoxy, the increase in tax burden should have made no difference. A vulgarized version of statist economics seemed to blanket the political consensus, so that Richard Nixon could say on the eve of the supply-side thaw, "We are all Keynesians now." Broadly stated, this consensus traced the cause of economic depression to the defects of the private sector and attempted to cure them by the intervention of the government. Since taxes gave the government the wherewithal to stimulate the flow of private capital, there was little reason to fear they could reach a point that would do more harm than good to the economy. Transfer payments increased the buying power of a deprived segment of the market and also invigorated the economy. These policies were concerned primarily with stimulating *demand* for goods, either through direct government spending or by placing money in the hands of private spenders. And so one sometimes heard them called "demand-side" economics.

But the basic law of economics deals with supply as well as demand. During this period, some economists began to worry about encouraging people to supply products as well as to demand them. The true way to stimulate economic growth, they said, was to remove the constraints on the entrepreneur and the barriers to production. Instead of the "demand" side of the equation, they emphasized the "supply" side. And so, in a coinage almost universally attributed to Herbert Stein, the Keynesian chairman of President Nixon's Council of Economic Advisers, they became known as "supply-siders."

The best-known supply-siders were the unorthodox economist Arthur Laffer, the ebullient Jude Wanniski, a former *Wall Street Journal* editorial writer, and the eccentric Berkshire dairy farmer George Gilder. Although they seized the public eye, a host of lesser-known figures, including the economists Paul Craig Roberts and David Ranson, pushed the work forward. And some older academics, including W. W. Hutt, who spent his teaching career in South Africa, kept the basic ideas alive through all the years of the Keynesian overburden.

The core of the supply-side revival is the Law of Markets enunciated by the nineteenth-century economist Jean Baptiste Say (1767–1832). Say's major work was the *Traité d'économie politique* (1803), his translation and systematic reorganization of Adam Smith. In it, Say set out the famous maxim that "products are given in exchange for products." This phrase, often criticized as superficial in the Keynesian era, in fact refuted the "glut theorists" such as the Keynesians, who worried that markets would collapse under the pressure of general overproduction. Replied Say, "Nothing can be more illogical. The total supply of products and the total demand for them must of necessity be equal, for the total demand is nothing but the whole mass of commodities which have been produced."[7]

In other words, the total cost of producing one set of goods, especially the wages for the workers, becomes the wherewithal for the purchase of other sets of goods, paying their costs of production, including their workers, who in turn are enabled to purchase yet more goods. This circulation keeps the market going. Say's Law of Markets, in short, is an extension of Adam Smith's "Division of Labor." As with Smith, it implies a laissez-faire economy. Glut, depression, and stagnation are still facts of life, but they arise from outside interference with the natural growth and circulation of the economy. Cartels can distort pricing; tariffs can frustrate free trade; manipulation of money (another commodity in the expanded view of the revived Say's Law) can destroy the equilibrium in the supply and demand for other products. Above all else looms the motive-crushing force of taxation. Economic health can be restored by the removal of these external restraints. Measures could range from expanding free trade to reducing government regulation, but the policy that has captured the public mind in our day is the cutting of excessively high tax rates.

The best concise statement of this tax theory comes from a study by Laffer and his associate Charles W. Kadlec.[8] Their starting point is the "essential tenet of classical economic analysis" that a change in economic incentives alters a person's behavior. If taxes go up on a paycheck, John Doe is less likely to spend the same amount of time on his job. If, by the same token, there is relatively less financial penalty for taking a vacation or working for unreported income, John Doe is more likely to do so. If his pay stub shows a bigger bite for income taxes, is he likely to run up overtime to make back the difference? An eighteenth-century mercantilist would have said yes, and so does the present Congressional Budget Office. Or is John Doe more likely to take his skills to the underground economy, where he can work "off the books" at a 0% tax rate? Might he even chuck the whole thing and go fishing? A spate of studies has confirmed the explosive growth of an untaxed, second economy, but a moment's use of intuition should be sufficient to conclude that the mercantilists are no closer to the right answer now than they were in 1750.

But the story goes beyond John Doe's bottom line, his take-home pay. The bottom line for the company that pays him is the total cost of compensation: his gross pay, including income taxes, local, state, and federal; Social Security; and other benefits. The difference between the money that John Doe takes home and the money that General Widget Company pays to employ him is, in Laffer's terms, "the Wedge." As taxes increase, John Doe gets less take-home pay. He will then put in less effort at his job or demand a higher gross salary to protect his net paycheck. Either way, General Widget faces a higher cost of keeping John Doe on the payroll. Either its productivity declines or its costs of production increase. So the company is forced to raise the price of widgets or to reduce its total work force. Both the supply of and demand for labor decreases. The result is reduced production of widgets, and the contraction ripples through the economy, according to Say's Law of Markets.

The Wedge leads logically to the phenomenon popularized as the Laffer Curve. As originally drawn at a Washington restaurant in 1974, this hyperbola resembles a McDonald's arch flipped on its side. (Laffer, incidentally, claims that the figure was actually drawn by his dinner companion, Jude Wanniski, and so should have been called "the Wanniski Curve.") The lower sweep of the curve describes the condition of under-taxation, in which rates can be raised without fear of triggering a flight to shelter. As rates increase, revenue for the government will also increase. Yet at a certain point the rates

The Laffer Curve

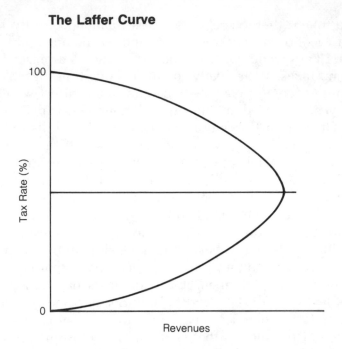

reach their optimum. Beyond it, John Doe and Widgco start to lose interest in production. As higher taxes force cutbacks in the Widgco work force and output, tax collections decrease. The curve sweeps back at the top, reaching zero revenue at 100% taxation, when all private activity ceases.

The Laffer Curve describes much more than production levels. Once tax rates rise above the optimum, the people who would pay the taxes resort to every device known, legal or illegal, to shelter their income. Enforcing a higher tax rate can easily eat up any potential increase in revenue. It is entirely conceivable that cutting excessive tax rates will produce more revenue, not less.

Most of the furor over the Curve has swirled around this truism, even though it is totally sound in theory. The less noticed flip side is even more important, however. That is, as taxes rise above the optimum point, the economy declines and government revenues fall.

THE NEW LANDSCAPE: THE STATES

While the supply-siders launched their theoretical assaults on the Keynesian glacier, their points were being made in practice almost behind their backs. Several states had begun to experience the negative impact of the Curve. Steep tax increases adopted in the certainty that taxes did not matter had unmistakably begun to hobble the economies of such commercial and industrial centers as New York and Massachusetts. This relationship began to show up not only anecdotally but also in formal statistical studies. Evidence was accumulating that the old order found increasingly difficult to ignore. Academics could always dispute the computer runs, but the political fact of the Tax Revolt showed that voters were reaching the same conclusions through everyday experience.

The Tax Revolt sparked the first attempt to do a statistical "cross section" of many states. In the heat of the Proposition 13 debate in California, Laffer and Kadlec compared twenty states to see how changes in their tax burdens affected growth in total state personal income. ("Tax burden" is defined as total state and local tax revenues expressed as a percentage of total state personal income.) Laffer and Kadlec chose the states with the largest property tax revenues and examined two types of tax burden: property tax and all others. In both cases they concluded that increases in the tax burden went hand in hand with a depressed rate of growth. Using this ratio, they predicted that if Proposition 13 passed, the state's personal income would increase $110 billion more than would be normal over the next ten years.[9]

Critics came down harshly on this study. One challenger complained that the sample was too selective; "Why did they not use all of the states?" he asked.[10] The next major study did just that. It came from two researchers at the Harris Trust and Savings Bank of Chicago, Robert J. Genetski and Young D. Chin.[11] They decided to see how the relative tax burdens of all fifty states related to personal income growth. Instead of trying to isolate the impact of an individual tax, they used the figures for total state revenue; this approach sacrificed Laffer and Kadlec's attempt at precision, but it made the numbers much easier to manage. On one axis, the state tax

Genetski-Chin Results

Relative Tax Burden Changes 1967 to 1974 (Ranked Highest to Lowest)	Relative Personal Income Changes 1970 to 1977 (Ranked Lowest to Highest)
Relative Tax Burden Growth Greater Than 10% of the U.S. Average {	1. Washington, D.C.	1. New York	} Relative Personal Income Growth Less Than 90% of the U.S. Average

Relative Tax Burden Growth Greater Than 10% of the U.S. Average

1. Washington, D.C.	1. New York
2. Illinois	2. Connecticut
3. Vermont	3. Massachusetts
4. Pennsylvania	4. Washington, D.C.
5. New York	5. Rhode Island
6. Michigan	6. Illinois
7. Rhode Island	7. New Jersey
8. Maine	8. Ohio
9. Massachusetts	9. Delaware

Relative Personal Income Growth Less Than 90% of the U.S. Average

Relative Tax Burden Growth near the U.S. Average

10. Alaska	10. Pennsylvania
11. New Jersey	11. Vermont
12. Connecticut	12. Maryland
13. Maryland	13. Missouri
14. Nebraska	14. Wisconsin
15. Ohio	15. Indiana
16. Wisconsin	16. Hawaii
17. Georgia	17. Minnesota
18. Virginia	18. California
19. Missouri	19. Maine
20. Indiana	20. Nebraska
21. Minnesota	21. Kansas
22. New Hampshire	22. Michigan
23. Nevada	23. Montana
24. California	24. Washington
25. Kentucky	25. Iowa
26. Texas	26. Georgia
27. Delaware	27. New Hampshire
28. Tennessee	
29. South Carolina	28. North Carolina
30. Washington	29. Virginia
31. North Carolina	30. Oklahoma
32. Louisiana	31. North Dakota
33. Montana	32. West Virginia
34. West Virginia	33. Tennessee
	34. Kentucky

Relative Personal Income Growth near the U.S. Average

Relative Tax Burden Growth Less Than 90% of the U.S. Average

35. Oregon	35. Alabama
36. Hawaii	36. Louisiana
37. Mississippi	37. Oregon
38. Florida	38. Mississippi
39. Alabama	39. South Carolina
40. Iowa	40. Colorado
41. Kansas	41. South Dakota
42. Arkansas	42. Utah
43. Colorado	43. Texas
44. New Mexico	44. Idaho
45. Utah	45. Arkansas
46. Oklahoma	46. Nevada
47. Arizona	47. New Mexico
48. South Dakota	48. Florida
49. Wyoming	49. Arizona
50. Idaho	50. Wyoming
51. North Dakota	51. Alaska

Relative Personal Income Growth Greater Than 5% of the U.S. Average burdens are expressed as a percentage of the average of all state tax burdens—in other words, as "relative" tax burdens. Taking this step eliminates factors such as general inflation that affect all the states: individual "relative state tax burdens" correlate very well with specific political decisions to raise or lower taxes. On the other axis, the Harris Bank researchers used "relative state personal income growth" to serve as a proxy for the more elusive notion of economic growth. Genetski and Chin kept their model simple and obtained surprising results.

For their first round, they took a static analysis, comparing the state's relative economic growth to its average tax burden from 1969 to 1976. In looking at the states thus frozen in time, they found no statistical relationship. Then they took what turned out to be the crucial step and compared the states for the *rate of change* in their tax burden. The dots started to fall into place, but the pattern still was not overwhelming. Finally, they allowed a three-year lag between the change in tax burden growth and the impact in personal income. This did the trick. The graph now showed an "extremely strong" fit. States with low tax increases or shrinking tax burdens showed the highest economic growth against the national average. States with the sharpest jumps in tax burden showed relative economic decline. Genetski and Chin concluded: "Much of the relatively slow or rapid economic development among particular states should not be attributed to climate, high union wages, or many of the other explanations which are frequently offered."[12] But it could and should be attributed to taxes. This study by no means settled the academic argument, since statistics are unlikely to end any dispute. Yet its appearance amid the aftershocks of Proposition 13 helped give the Tax Revolt respectability. It also gave a crucial insight into the mysterious workings of human nature.

The great revelation of Genetski and Chin's study was the importance of the *rate of change* in determining how people would react to the tax burden. Supply-side theory did not make it obvious why the change should have so much weight, yet the pattern fit a broader view of human nature. Tocqueville observed that revolutions occur when things are getting either rapidly worse or rapidly better. Humanity can adjust to a bad situation that seems to be an eternal fact of life. Nobody stages a rebellion against the weather. But if an oppressive condition no longer seems immutable, or a favorable situation begins to deteriorate, people are provoked into action. Once investors, workers, and entrepreneurs see their tax bills soaring with no halt in sight, they migrate elsewhere in a vast, silent revolution against a state government that attempts to claim too much personal property.

The basic human behavior described by Genetski and Chin was spelled out with much greater detail and, yes, statistical sophistication, in a study by Victor A. Canto and Robert I. Webb, associates of Arthur Laffer at the University of Southern California Graduate School of Business Administration. Using methods derived from the study of international trade, Canto and Webb constructed a model of economic movement among the states to test the impact of a state's taxation on its own economy. They assumed a "neoclassical world" in which differences in price and income should tend to even out as goods or "factors of production" (such as capital, labor, entrepreneurs) flowed like water away from the jurisdictions that penalized them most or rewarded them least. But states continued to have different levels of income growth. So Canto and Webb assumed two types of "production factors": those that could migrate and those that could not. Since the mobile factors by definition flee tax penalties, the immobile factors wind up bearing the burden of above-average state taxes. But these immobile factors have a choice, too: they may not be able to migrate, but they can shift activity from work to leisure, or, in the terms of the Canto and Webb study, from market income to household income. So *full* incomes may be equalized, according to the original assumption, but *market* incomes may not be. And it is the market income that is measured in official statistics. Hence the persistent differences in state economic performance could be laid to the impact of state government fiscal policies. This was the model at any rate, drawn from the ideas encountered earlier in the Wedge and the Curve. When it came to the test, Canto and Webb found that their model "is quite robust. For 42 states," they conclude, "there is strong evidence that the tax rates variable may have a significant and negative effect on the level of economic activity."[13]

The Canto and Webb study is by far the more sophisticated, but the work of Genetski and Chin remains more useful for this narrative. One reason is that Genetski and Chin worked with much more accessible data. Canto and Webb defined their tax variable in terms of the rate, not the burden (which reflects the total revenue collected). That approach fits more neatly into the Laffer Curve, yet it runs into serious problems in gathering data. Canto and Webb admit that their "effective average tax rates" understate the impact of state tax systems on the economy. On the other hand, the focus on the tax *burden* sacrifices clarity about the impact of the rate structure. It also leads to some distortions, since, as will be seen later, certain taxes can be much more harmful than others. There will be occasional attempts in the coming state case studies to refine this approach.

Another advantage of the tax burden figure is that the reader can readily get hold of it. For nearly a decade, a very useful state-by-state table of these figures and their rates of change has been published by the Washington-based Advisory Commission on Intergovernmental Relations (ACIR).[14] This work on tax burdens anticipated the Genetski-Chin study. But the ACIR had another agenda in mind. Not only did it decline to draw the implications of its figures, but it even refused to label them a "burden."

John V. Shannon, the mild-mannered head of the ACIR's public-finance staff, deserves mention as a pioneer in this field, even though he politely demurs from the direction in which it is heading. In 1976, he set out to improve the measurement of state and local fiscal stress, partly to help direct federal aid to places that needed it most. An implicit assumption was that states that heavily taxed themselves deserved more help than states that did not. (An even earlier report, dating to 1962, had attempted to measure each state's "fiscal capacity," and several federal-grant programs were subsequently revised to favor "poor" states over "rich" states.) But Shannon was dissatisfied with the existing comparisons of "tax loads," as the ACIR called them. He tried to measure how they changed over time, and came up with what he called a "fiscal blood pressure." The first reading, the "systolic," showed the state's relative tax load in a given year. The second, the "diastolic," showed the relative change in tax load since 1964. Shannon's index coincided rather well with the famous "Frostbelt-Sunbelt" division. The majority of the states with relatively high and rising pressure were located in the Northeast and Midwest, with the major exception of New Hampshire; those with low and falling pressure were primarily in the South and Southwest. Yet as an "objective" commission composed of several different viewpoints, the ACIR refrained from drawing conclusions.[15]

Some might take the high pressure reading as a warning to cut spending and taxes, said the ACIR, but others might find the low reading as evidence that taxes and services could safely be increased. Even the term "tax load," acknowledged the report, was a compromise between the phrase "tax burden," preferred by the taxpayer, and the phrase "tax effort," preferred by the people who levied the taxes.

In general, not many outside the world of supply-siders and tax rebels were eager to pay attention to the rather significant discovery that rapidly rising tax burdens did indeed hurt growth. Some attempted to dismiss the Genetski study on technical grounds, although these objections were almost never worked out in any detail. One report writer for the ACIR itself complained that the Genetski finding was "counterintuitive"; he could not see how government spending on infrastructure and the like could damage the economy.[16] Probably the most interesting rebuttal came from two researchers at the Minneapolis Federal Reserve Bank.[17] They ran through the figures again, using a more complicated set of variables and found that Genetski's conclusion did hold for the 1970s. But it did not work for the 1960s. Far from refuting the point, however, this never-published study underlined how radically the taxpayers' position had worsened by the 1970s. Weakened by inflation and oppressed by ever-increasing tax burdens, taxpayers were more than ever disinclined to let their reward for hard work disappear into the hands of the revenue officers.

The rapidity of this change left most of the academic researchers stranded in a strange new world. The professors had made it an item of faith in the sixties that state taxes did not

The ACIR "Fiscal Blood Pressure" Chart

A Two-Dimensional Measure of Relative State-Local Fiscal Pressure
Using the Representative Tax Method to Estimate Fiscal Capacity:
State-Local Systems More Than One Standard Deviation from the Median:
1964–1975

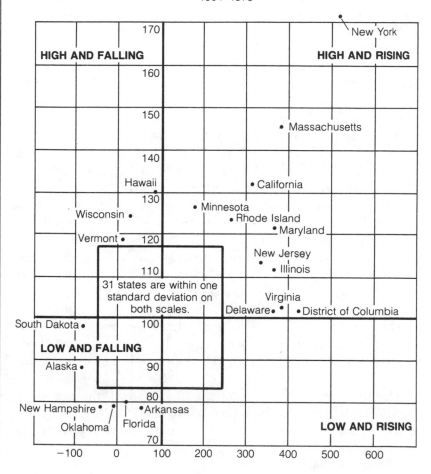

*To be within one standard deviation on both scales, a state's index number
would have to fall between 81.9 and 118.1 on the vertical axis and between
−49.5 and 249.5 on the horizontal axis.*

matter (thanks in part to a little manipulation of the data).[18] This doctrine was now largely irrelevant. Times had changed, of course, but in addition the "economic development" studies insisted on looking at the wrong things. They spent tens of thousands of dollars to research tax inducements and plant location when the real issue was general tax burden and economic growth.

Much of the talk about economic civil war portrays the Sunbelt and Frostbelt as waging a tug of war over corporate headquarters and large plants. If taxes are grudgingly allowed to have played a role (but only a small one), then it is derided as part of a "zero-sum" game. One region's gain is another's loss, and the economy grows not a whit.

But state economies simply do not work this way. However many headlines Mobil might make when it moves its corporate headquarters, the direct shift in employment will make only a minor impact on either the losing or the receiving economy. Furthermore, these migrations are relatively rare. It is even harder to relocate a working factory. Moving a plant lock, stock, and barrel involves a major loss of fixed assets, such as land, buildings, and skilled employees; it generally comes after the economic climate has already deteriorated to the point that the factory has become a major money-loser. More commonly, a multistate company in a losing situation will start to divert its new investments to greener pastures. In that case, the original property runs down and grows obsolete, and people start calling the region left behind a "mature" economy.

The most powerful engine of a state's economy is its native small and growing business. More than two-thirds of the nation's 75-million-strong work force is on the payroll of companies with fewer than 250 employees. It is almost a saw on Wall Street that the entrepreneurial skills that produce rapid growth flourish among the smaller personally run companies rather than among the management-bound behemoths. If a state wants to grow, it does not need corporate managers, it needs entrepreneurs. And these economically savvy individuals are extremely alert to the impact of taxation.

An entrepreneur, let us be clear, does not have to be Andrew Carnegie or Warren Avis. Some are neighborhood types who will work into the night and on weekends to open their own shops or build up their own businesses. If occasionally they come up with new products, so much the better.

The number of such people will expand or contract depending on the rewards. If the taxes take too much of their income, the most ambitious may migrate to a low-tax state; the rest may simply stay at home. When small entrepreneurs have reasons to work, they will start with whatever is at hand. The hardscrabble farmer in northern New Hampshire may turn mountain pastures into a ski trail. The Texas rancher may introduce Brahman crossbreeds on semiarid range. The California grower will experiment with off-season vegetables for shipping to East Coast markets. There is nothing zero-sum about this effort. With the right incentives, entrepreneurs will develop the obvious natural resources and geographical advantages of their surroundings and then find possibilities none had dreamed of. Without incentives, there will be no development.

A state with a low-tax policy could grow and prosper without luring any outside corporation. What matters is the way its own citizens allocate their energies, how they choose between work and leisure. That some states have reduced their tax burden while other states have raised theirs does not necessarily mean that one state is stealing the assets of the other; it means that the economic vitality of the "low and falling" tax states compensates in some degree for the induced decline of the "high and rising" tax states. If all states reduced their tax burdens simultaneously, the national growth would be all the greater.

If people miss this point—that entrepreneurs matter more than corporate headquarters—then they are likely to be sorely confused on another. The taxes most important to the economy are not necessarily the taxes on business. Quite the contrary. Much as Mobil resents New York State's efforts to tax its profits, it generally finds a way to pass the cost on to its customers. But the entrepreneur feels the income tax in his own shrinking wallet. The upper brackets take the largest bite, but *all* personal taxes eventually wind up hurting business. Remember the Wedge? The worker who watches his take-home pay diminish will very likely ask for higher wages. And so the personal tax burden quickly becomes an increased business cost. This buck-passing is known to the world of economics as the question of "incidence," and there are elaborate studies of the ways in which some tax burdens are passed on and others are not. But the basic principle was best stated by David Hume in 1752: "Every man, to be sure, is desirous of pushing off from himself the burden of any tax, which is imposed, and of laying it upon others."[19]

It stands to reason that the most general economic benefits come from reducing the most general taxes. Businesses have a variety of means for pushing off the impact of direct business taxes, but they encounter the indirect burden of the Wedge at every turn. It may be counterintuitive to help out business by limiting taxes on labor, but that is one lesson of the new economic landscape.

REQUIEM FOR THE GLACIER

Those comfortable in the old order have been understandably chagrined that the economic performance of the states coincides with the theories of the supply-siders. Could it be that the Keynesian consensus was wrong, that those who argued the virtues of limited government in defiance of fifty years of congealed statist opinion might have weighty evidence on their side? Resistance to this notion has been understandably tenacious.

Yet some protean form of these ideas has been suffusing the countryside. The ACIR calls it "the Great Slowdown." From 1942 to 1976, state and local spending grew almost three times as fast as the economy. Then, in the mid-seventies, this gravy train stopped in its tracks, falling behind both inflation and the sluggish economy. "Real" spending ceased to expand at the local level in 1974 and then peaked two years later at the state level.[20] State and local legislators evidently were responding to the same popular outcry that was beginning to reshape state constitutions. California Governor Ronald Reagan had unsuccessfully sponsored a spending-limit referendum in 1973, the famous Proposition 1. In spite of its failure, the idea had spread. On March 7, 1977, Tennessee approved a constitutional restraint on total state spending by a 64.7% margin. This relatively mild measure was completely over-shadowed the next year when, on a heady June 6, voters in California gave landslide approval to Proposition 13 and Republicans in their New Jersey primary unseated the veteran liberal U.S. Senator Clifford Case in favor of the young sup-ply-sider Jeffrey Bell.

The political climate seemed to be shifting, yet there were reverses. For a time the glaciers came edging back, as the Great Recession put a chill on the reception of supply-side ideas. Yet even at the depths of the recession, tax rebels and sup-ply-siders, including Richard Headlee in Michigan and Lewis Lehrman in New York, showed surprising popular strength. And now the winter of discontent is made spring by the bright sun of Recovery. The Tax Revolt is showing renewed vitality in the heart of the devastated Midwest. At the base of the ice, cracks and hollows are widening, feeding fast-running rivulets.

2

The New-Old Landscape
of the Tax Revolt

Many of the economic ideas of the postglacial world had walked the earth before. Some might say they had been preserved in ice like mastodons, miraculously to receive fresh vitality in supply-side economics. In a friendlier view, these principles had found congenial surroundings in the first age of American politics, and now the environment had again turned hospitable. "Supply-side" ideas had flourished among eighteenth- and nineteenth-century Americans, culminating in the phenomenon known as "Jacksonian Democracy." Just as the leaders of the current Tax Revolt often resemble the rough-hewn individuals of Old Hickory's frontier, the intellectual supply-siders are reviving the laissez-faire populism of Jacksonian political economy.

THE BEGINNINGS

A straight line can be drawn from the first principles of the Declaration of Independence to the first wave of fiscal limitations, sponsored by the Jacksonians. But the human traits at the heart of this development were no secret even at the beginning of political thought. Aristotle deplored the lack of limit to human acquisitiveness. Thucydides described the three springs of human conduct as "fear, honor, and interest" (or, in Thomas Hobbes's translation, "honour, fear, and profit").[1] But the ancients disdained the attempt to construct a political order on something so base as greed. "The City of Pigs," they called it. That effort was left to the political theorists of the "modern" period.

Governments do not wait for theorists to tell them how to collect taxes, however. Some of the greatest political writers gathered their material as practical politicians. They were well aware of the damage governments could do to themselves by foolhardy taxation. One of the greatest of the statesmen-philosophers was the fourteenth-century Arab, Ibn Khaldun. Surviving many hazards in his diplomatic career, including a month-long interview with Tamerlane, he wrote what is now considered the first attempt at a science of history, the *Muqaddimah*. In November 1377, he described the Laffer Curve as well as anyone would six centuries later: "At the beginning of the dynasty, taxation yields a large revenue from small assessments. At the end of the dynasty, taxation yields a small revenue from large assessments."[2]

The nomadic founders of a dynasty, he continued, had simple tastes and levied low taxes. Prosperity followed, promoting luxurious living. As the sons and grandsons of the founders raised taxes to support their extravagant needs, commerce and culture withered. Inevitably, their civilization died. Ibn Khaldun saw this progression as a tragic necessity, an integral part of the founding, flourishing, and fall of dynasties, in a cycle of three generations.

England's Stuart dynasty learned the lesson of tax policy the hard way. Its kings struggled constantly with Parliament over control of the purse. The chain of events that cost Charles I his head started with his need to get legislative consent to new taxes. These struggles reached their ultimate conclusion in the theory of John Locke (1632–1704). Locke's social-contract approach may not have been original, but he was the first to base it all on property. "Though the earth and all inferior creatures be common to all men, yet every man has a property in his own person; this nobody has any right to but himself. The labor of his body and the work of his hands, we may say, are properly his. Whatsoever then he removes out of the state that nature has provided and left it in, he has mixed his labor with, and joined to it something that is his own, and thereby makes it his property."[3] The transformation of something from nature into private property is the work of the individual, not the group, said Locke. People join together in civil society, in fact, to protect the fruits of their personal labor. The government is not the source of this labor, and the best thing the "godlike prince" can do for economic activity is to give it free rein. "This shows how much numbers of men are to be preferred to largeness of dominions; and that the increase of lands and the right employing of them is the great art of government; and that prince who shall be so wise and godlike as by established laws of liberty to secure protection and encouragement to the honest industry of mankind, against the oppression of power and narrowness of party, will quickly be too hard for his neighbors."[4]

It follows that the legislature would have only limited control over the property (including lives and liberty) of the members of the society. "The supreme power cannot take from any man part of his property without his own consent; for the preservation of property being the end of government and that for which men enter into society, it necessarily supposes and requires that the people should have property; without which they must be supposed to lose that, by entering into society, which was the end for which they entered into it—too gross an absurdity for any man to own."[5] But government must have resources to protect personal property. "It is fit every one who enjoys his share of the protection should pay out of his estate for the maintenance of it. But still it must be with his consent—i.e., the consent of the majority, giving it either by themselves or their representatives chosen by them."[6] From this logic came the first great statement of fiscal limitation, from which all the others derive: "They [the legislative] must not raise taxes on the property of the people without the consent of the people, given by themselves or their deputies."[7]

A great edifice is built upon this statement. Locke's brief *Second Treatise* laid out the principles of the liberal state, but it also stated the basic axioms of liberal economics. The separate but parallel tracks of tax revolt and supply-side economics begin here. They share the same junctions so frequently because of their common origin in John Locke.

An important step in drawing out these consequences came with Charles Louis de Secondat, later Baron de La Brède et de Montesquieu (1689–1755), born a year before publication of the *Second Treatise*. Locke had made the case for popular representation in tax policy, but Montesquieu spelled out just what that policy should be. Discussing the antithesis of Locke's "godlike prince," he states: "Nature is just to all mankind, and repays them for their industry: she renders them industrious by annexing rewards in proportion to their labor. But if an arbitrary prince should attempt to deprive the people of nature's bounty, they would fall into a disrelish of industry; and then indolence and inaction must be their only happiness."[8]

On the principle that excessive tax burdens will reduce productivity and even threaten the regime, Montesquieu makes an extended case for limited taxation. "Nothing requires more wisdom and prudence than the regulation of that portion of which the subject is deprived, and that which he is suffered to retain." State budgets should be restricted to the revenue produced by the economically optimum level of taxation. "The real wants of the people ought never to give way to the imaginary wants of the state."[9]

It is better, argues Montesquieu, to tolerate underassessment of property than to make people pay too much. If the citizens have a sufficient living, their prosperity will increase the public prosperity; if they are ruined, their loss increases public misery. The state should break the tragic cycle described by Ibn Khaldun by restricting its own fortune and allowing private individuals to make their own. After the people enrich themselves, the state will reap its reward. "All depends on the moment. Will the state begin by impoverishing the subjects to enrich itself? Or will it wait for the subjects to enrich it by their own prosperity? . . . Will it commence by being rich, or will it wind up that way?"[10] But Montesquieu never quite shakes the fatalism of the *Muqaddimah*. In a section explaining how republican regimes can carry heavier tax burdens than despotisms, he describes a kind of political Laffer Curve. "Because moderate government has been productive of admirable effects, this moderation has been laid aside; because great taxes have been raised, they want to carry them to excess; and ungrateful to the hand of liberty, of whom they received this present, they addressed themselves to slavery, who never grants the least favor.

"Liberty produces excessive taxes; the effect of excessive taxes is slavery; and slavery produces a diminution of tribute."[11]

There is a crucial but neglected link between the early modern philosophy of Locke and Montesquieu and the birth of classical economics. That link is David Hume (1711–1776). Famous as the philosophical Skeptic, Hume corresponded with Montesquieu and was Adam Smith's best friend. He receives scant mention in the histories of economics, yet his *Essays Moral, Political and Literary*, published in 1752, should be considered seminal to the work of his protégé and clubmate Smith. His essay "Of Taxes," drawing heavily on Montesquieu, contains this warning: "Exorbitant taxes, like extreme necessity, destroy industry, by producing despair; and even before they reach this pitch, they raise the wages of the laborer and manufacturer, and heighten the price of all commodities. An attentive disinterested legislature, will observe the point when the emolument ceases, and the prejudice begins: But as the contrary character is much more common, 'tis to be feared that taxes, all over EUROPE, are multiplying to such a degree, as will intirely crush all art and industry."[12]

Hume's connection to Locke goes even deeper. Although on the surface he attacked Locke's state of nature "as a mere fiction, not unlike that of the *golden age*, which poets have invented," he emphatically endorsed the centrality of the "avidity . . . of acquiring goods and possessions."[13] This "insatiable, perpetual, universal" passion could destroy society unless it were used to restrain itself by the consideration "that by preserving society, we make much greater advances in the acquiring possessions, than by running into the solitary and forlorn condition, which must follow upon violence and a universal license."[14]

Beyond its role in politics, avidity was crucial to Hume's

study of the nature of man. It is not accidental that both Locke and Hume wrote major works on what we now call "empirical psychology." The common elements in Locke's *An Essay concerning Human Understanding* and Hume's *A Treatise of Human Nature* point toward a science of economics. Following the Newtonian revolution, both men were seeking a science of human nature modeled on natural science, a logical structure whose first principles were based on observable phenomena and whose conclusions could be tested by experience. Hume described his *Treatise* as "the application of experimental philosophy to Moral Subjects."[15] This project, wrote one observer, required its advocates to "isolate in the human soul that feeling which seems to be the most easily measurable."[16] The political economists concluded that the passion to be studied was avidity, the pursuit of property.

This was the internal structure of the philosophy descended from Locke, Montesquieu, and Hume on the eve of the year of its greatest achievement, 1776. In this year, the year David Hume died, the American colonies issued the Declaration of Independence, and Adam Smith published the *Wealth of Nations*. Tax revolt and tax theory leapt forward together, propelled by the same philosophical tradition. The implications of John Locke would continue to unfold in both the intellectual and political realms until both arrived in tandem at the laissez-faire populism of Jacksonian Democracy.

ADAM SMITH AND THE CANONS OF TAXATION

The Inquiry into the Nature and Causes of the Wealth of Nations of Adam Smith (1723–1790) codified economic ideas that had been circulating among Smith's friends for at least three decades. It also established maxims destined to become deeply ingrained in American fiscal policy. Smith's four canons of taxation shaped American state tax systems on both technical and philosophic levels.

Adam Smith's first three canons dealt with mechanics, but with a touch of Locke. Taxes, wrote Smith, should be proportional to the revenue each subject enjoys under the protection of the state; like joint tenants of a great estate, each should contribute in the measure of his interest in the estate. The tax should be certain and not arbitrary; any discretion left to the tax collector makes room for extortion or oppression. Taxes should be levied in the time or manner in which it is most convenient to pay them.

The fourth canon, which for nineteenth-century Americans overshadowed the first three, embodied the principle of an incentive-oriented economy. Wrote Smith: "Every tax ought to be so contrived as both to take out and to keep out of the pockets of the people as little as possible, over and above what it brings into the public treasury of the state."[17] A tax, he continued, "may obstruct the industry of the people, and discourage them from applying to certain branches of business which might give maintenance and employment to great multitudes. While it obliges the people to pay, it may thus diminish, or perhaps destroy, some of the funds which might enable them more easily to do so."[18]

THE AMERICAN AUDIENCE

Smith's advice was widely followed in America. (One fiscal historian says that tax officials of the nineteenth century had little else to go on.) But Americans were fully aware of the rest of the tradition. On the eve of the Revolution, the thought of John Locke was as much a part of the colonists' background as the forests they cleared. Thomas Jefferson put a précis of the *Second Treatise* into the Declaration of Independence, modeling his defense of the American Revolution on Locke's apology for the Glorious Revolution of 1688.

In appealing to a candid world, Jefferson put a euphemistic face on the *Second Treatise*, but the drafters of the new American state constitutions were less circumspect. The Massachusetts Constitution of 1780, shaped largely by John Adams, stated in Article I of its Declaration of Rights: "All men are born free and equal, and have certain natural, essential, and unalienable rights; among which may be reckoned the right of enjoying and defending their lives and liberties;

that of acquiring, possessing, and protecting property; in fine, that of seeking and obtaining their safety and happiness."[19] Guarantees of the "life, liberty, and property" of the individual appear in every state constitution. On fiscal matters, they affirm that no tax can be levied without the consent of the people or their representatives in the legislature. The New Hampshire constitution drafted in 1783 states this provision in social-contract terms echoing both Locke and Montesquieu: "Every member of the community has a right to be protected by it in the enjoyment of his life, liberty, and property; he is therefore bound to contribute his share in the expense of such protection, and to yield his personal service when necessary or an equivalent. But no part of a man's property shall be taken from him, or applied to public uses, without his own consent, or that of the representative body of the people."[20]

The influence of Locke, Montesquieu, and their disciples was not exhausted in constitutional generalities. The American founders had fully digested their specific fiscal teaching about the dangers of excessive taxation and the possibility that increased rates would lower revenues.

Alexander Hamilton freely borrowed from Montesquieu and Hume in writing the string of *Federalist* papers defending the central government's power of direct taxation. (Hamilton regarded Hume's essays so highly that he used a direct quote from one in the rhetorical conclusion of *The Federalist*, and in an unusual gesture acknowledged the author in a footnote.) In part to mollify the advocates of stricter constitutional limits on the federal taxing power, Hamilton emphasized the lesson of Montesquieu, Smith, and Hume that excessive increases in taxation are self-defeating. "There is no part of the administration of government that requires extensive information and a thorough knowledge of the principles of political economy so much as the business of taxation. The man who understands these principles best will be least likely to resort to oppressive expedients, or to sacrifice any particular class of citizens to the procurement of revenue. It might be demonstrated that the most productive system of finance will always be the least burthensome."[21]

TOWARD THE TAX REVOLT

Perhaps no part of the Locke-Montesquieu-Hume-Smith tradition was more enthusiastically embraced by American politicians than its implied emphasis on reduced taxes. Hamilton's protestations about the self-limiting nature of taxation may have been designed to meet his contemporaries' suspicions that his own heart was not in the policy. As for Jefferson, there may never have been an American president, up to and including the present, who gained as much mileage from a policy of tax reduction. According to a British diplomat, this policy was the "great instrument" of his 1800 campaign. Continued this observer, "it must be owned that he has availed himself with great art of this powerful engine, and has afforded a complete triumph to his party."[22] The domestic imposts of George Washington and John Adams, even including a stamp tax, had already provoked two uprisings. So Jefferson in his first Annual Message boldly urged repeal of *all* internal taxation. "Considering the general tendency to multiply offices and dependencies and to increase expense to the ultimate term of burthen which the citizen can bear, it behooves us to avail ourselves of every occasion which presents itself for taking off the surcharge, that it never may be seen here that after leaving to labor the smallest portion of its earning on which it can subsist, Government shall itself consume the whole residue of what it was instituted to guard."[23] Furthermore, Jefferson followed through. His main opportunity to economize lay in putting much of the Navy in drydock; within a year its appropriation had fallen by half.[24] At the same time, Treasury receipts from external duties surged at the greatest rate yet seen. Jefferson wound up with a budget surplus, which he used to accelerate repayment of the debt.[25] This policy of "substituting economy for taxation" also produced a boom in Jefferson's popularity.

Jefferson's political heirs were even more thoroughgoing advocates of fiscal limitation and radical laissez-faire economics. The Jeffersonians did not endorse every byway of the theoretical tradition, but they certainly saw themselves as spiritual descendants of John Locke and Adam Smith.[26] This "free-market ideology" reached a peak in the remarkable social ferment of Jacksonian Democracy. Modern historians delight in Jackson's frontier-fighter egalitarianism, but they largely miss the classical economics behind his attack on corporate privilege and government-sponsored monopolies. These were the years, after all, in which the classics of laissez-faire were sweeping the mercantile system from the field. Jean Baptiste Say's *Treatise on Political Economy* was translated and published in Philadelphia in 1821 and spread rapidly through college curriculums. The intellectual triumph of laissez-faire was closely linked to the Jacksonian theme of popular control and fiscal limitation.

President Jackson was so averse to taxation that by the end of his tenure in 1836 he had cut internal tax receipts to less than $500. In his Farewell Address, he warned his fellow citizens: "Congress has no right, under the Constitution, to take money from the people unless it is required to execute some one of the specific powers intrusted to the Government; and if they raise more than is necessary for such purposes, it is an abuse of the power of taxation and unjust and oppressive."[27]

The Jacksonians devoted much of their energy to devising constitutional controls on government spending. Ironically, this issue came to a head as a result of Jackson's handling of bank reserves after he had destroyed the government's main financial arm, the privately owned Bank of the United States. In disbursing the reserves to state banks, he created a financial boom which collapsed in the Panic of 1837. State governments had vastly expanded their speculative involvement in projects of "internal improvement" and were caught short in the recession. They borrowed more money in the three years from 1835 to 1838 than they had for the previous fifteen.[28] A further irony came in the motives for this borrowing. Some of the increase was inevitable as population grew in the western states; some was necessary to cope with Jacksonian limits on federal spending, which threw more of the burden of providing services on the states. But another motive was the desire to reduce state taxation. In the first half of the 1820s, the states levied almost no direct taxation. This was possible in large part because of revenue from a variety of investments, such as bank stock and, in the case of New York, the Erie Canal. Many states hoped that borrowing for further profit-making ventures would provide them a revenue sufficient to eliminate direct taxation for the foreseeable future. When the investments went sour, the debt could be met only by a rapid increase in state tax burdens, tempered occasionally by repudiation or default.

The taxpayers' anger ultimately resulted in constitutional change. Before 1840, no state constitution limited the legislature's ability to contract debt; within fifteen years thereafter, starting with Rhode Island in 1842, nineteen of the thirty-two pre–Civil War states adopted debt-limiting amendments.[29] As will be seen later in New York, the Jacksonians who led the attack on debt saw it as merely a delayed form of taxation. The connection was all the more vivid because they had already been stuck with the bill.

LOCKEING THE BARN DOOR

The state debt crisis of 1839–42 ended forever the dream of eliminating direct taxation. Returning again to the principles of John Locke and Adam Smith, mid-nineteenth-century Americans reluctantly based their fiscal systems on what they concluded was the next-least-bad alternative, the general property tax. For the rest of the century it was the dominant source of state and local revenue.[30]

The classic justification for this tax came in the 1868 publication of Thomas McIntyre Cooley's immensely influential *Treatise on the Constitutional Limitations Which Rest Upon the Legislative Power of the States of the American Union.* Cooley wrote: "Taxation is the equivalent for the protection which the government affords to the persons and property of its citizens; and as all are alike protected, so all alike should bear the burden in proportion to the interests secured."[31]

Here we are once more at the altar of Locke's social contract, but with practical rules of conduct finally worked out and ready to be handed down. Locke said the state could demand a portion of each person's property as the means of preserving the rest; he did not specify how much it could demand, or whether some should pay proportionally more than others. Adam Smith settled one question with his first canon: taxation should be *proportional*. He must mean "proportional to property," figured the Americans, although Smith was ambiguous, since the social contract was to protect property, not simply income. Smith's second canon added the second element: a tax should be "certain, and not arbitrary," which the nineteenth century interpreted as *uniform*. These two terms, *proportional* and *uniform*, contained an entire ideology of taxation, which held sway over the century and still survives in some substantial retreats. Property must be assessed by a single standard and taxed at a single rate. All kinds of property should be taxed alike, since they all receive the same state protection. The ultimate purpose, drawn from Smith and Say, was to keep the tax burden low by speading it widely.

This ideology quickly collided with reality. Although the sum total of a man's property might have equal status in the view of the social contract, tax assessors had a hard time seeing things with the same certainty. Observed Viscount Bryce, the great nineteenth-century British historian and statesman, in his classic study of the American commonwealth: "Lands and houses cannot be concealed; cattle and furniture can be discovered by a zealous tax officer. But a great part, often far the largest part of a rich man's wealth, consists in what the Americans call 'intangible property,' notes, bonds, book debts, and Western mortgages. At this it is practically impossible to get, except through the declaration of the owner; and even if the owner is required to present his declaration of taxable property upon oath, he is apt to omit this kind of property."[32] Simply from the standpoint of enforcement, the general property tax was a failure.

Widespread evasion threw the weight of the tax burden onto real property. Under the general property tax, capital was not only lightly taxed, but it was subsidized to the extent that land and personal goods were assessed at a higher portion of their real value. The primary burden fell on land.

The principle of the general property tax was sound. The tax system by the late nineteenth century had come to favor large cities and large fortunes, fostering the growth of both. But the means of implementing this policy involved such a massive flouting of public morality that the situation became untenable. Bryce warned of "occasional bitterness of feeling among the American farmers as well as the masses against capitalists."[33] This bitterness provided the income tax movement with a constituency it might not otherwise have attracted.

The first significant push for the income tax came from the farms and countryside. Farmers paid a full measure of the general property tax on their land, but they had relatively little capital on which to reap the benefits of evasion. So the agrarian protest movements of the late nineteenth century began to demand the tax on incomes as a means of equalizing the burden. In the context of the attack on the general property tax, the first platform of the People's Party of Texas called for a graduated income tax.[34]

Dissatisfaction with the general property tax was not limited to farmers. Even before the personal income tax movement, reformers called for specific taxes on corporations, especially those enterprises that held property in a number of local jurisdictions. Railroads and utilities were among the first to be split off for separate taxation. They often welcomed the change, when it meant dealing with a single state collector rather than a horde of local assessors. (Once corporate property was taxed at the source, it was exempted from the general property tax.) This type of tax led to another innovation. The new revenues were often earmarked for the state government, rather than divided among all levels. The idea that separate revenue sources should be reserved to the different levels of government, now such a commonplace, was a major plank for late nineteenth-century tax reformers. Corporate taxes fell naturally to the state government, because of the convenience of centralized collection. The remainder of the general property tax by nearly universal agreement was kept a local tax and began to evolve into the real estate tax. The portion of the general property tax that still applied to personal property (as opposed to real estate) remained a sore spot for merchants. Retailers and wholesalers disliked the tax intensely because it imposed a large levy on their inventory no matter how strapped they were for cash.

BREAKDOWN OF THE LOCKEAN LIMITS

The collapse of the general property tax greatly weakened the idea of an inherent constitutional limitation on taxes. Cooley himself had admitted the protean nature of this basic legislative function: "The power to impose taxes is one so unlimited in force and so searching in extent, that the courts scarcely venture to declare that it is subject to any restrictions whatever, except such as rest in the discretion of the authority which exercises it."[35] Without the self-limiting aspects of the Lockean ideology, legislatures seemed free to impose as many taxes, at as high a rate, as the market would bear. In these circumstances, Chief Justice John Marshall had said, "the interest, wisdom, and justice of the representative body, and its relations with its constituents, furnish the only security against unjust and excessive taxation, as well as against unwise taxation."[36] By the mid-nineteenth century, this security was hardly reassuring. Taxpayers had enough experience with their legislators to know that more controls were needed. Future attempts to limit taxation now lay with the state constitutions.

THE THREE WAVES OF THE TAX REVOLT

Disenchantment with the general property tax weakened the one feature that most state finances held in common. In the search for alternatives, each state followed its own genius. The result is the current spectrum, ranging from states with almost no personal taxation, like New Hampshire, to those, like New York, that seem to have adopted nearly every tax imaginable. The Tax Revolt of the seventies complicated matters further, crosshatching the picture with yet another source of diversity. Later chapters will follow this story as it unrolled in individual states. This case-by-case approach reveals the connections and crucial details that often drop from sight in general histories, yet it also runs the risk of fragmenting the national pattern, shattering the overview into a heap of particulars. Still, a pattern does emerge from these histories. At the risk of great oversimplification, the Tax Revolt can be fit into three roughly chronological waves. Ripples from the first have persisted though the second and even into the third, and the dividing lines are not entirely clear. Yet they do illustrate the logical unfolding of the Lockean tax theory and its impact on popular politics.

THE FIRST WAVE

Locke himself generated the first wave of the Tax Revolt. American state tax policies bore the unmistakable imprint of his social-contract theory well into the twentieth century. The magic words *uniform* and *proportional* were to be a spell against excessive tax burdens. They were reinforced later by the legal doctrine that taxation could serve only a "public purpose."[37] But Locke's primary check on oppressive taxation was the requirement for consent. Property could be taken only through the votes of the people themselves or of their representatives. The importance of this limit should not be underestimated, even though it might seem a cliché. The American Revolution began with a slogan: "No Taxation without Representation." For three-quarters of a century after the Revolution, the issue of representation continued to bedevil Massachusetts politics. Yet Locke himself recognized that a legislature could come to have interests separate from those of the citizenry.

THE SECOND WAVE

A defect of representative assemblies soon became clear to American taxpayers. By borrowing instead of taxing, a legislature could amass a heavy financial burden for future generations, yet arouse no public outcry. So Jacksonians devised another form of fiscal control: they required direct voter consent, through bond referendums, for public borrowing. This second wave swept through the states in a series of constitutional conventions. It was one of the first attempts to shape the details of fiscal policy by rewriting the basic law. The intention was wise, but the controls were often futile.

THE THIRD WAVE

The Jacksonian revolt by and large relied on procedural controls, such as bond referendums and constitutional guidelines for tax structure. The third wave took to the state constitutions to dictate the actual details of a tax. It set specific tax rates, mandated spending limits, and even forced cuts in levies. The present Tax Revolt is part of this wave, but it could be traced back to the constitutional activity in the aftermath of the Civil War and Reconstruction, when the southern constitutional conventions imposed limits on property tax rates.

The crucial change came when the Progressive movement of the decade after 1910 sought direct democratic control over representative bodies. The new ballot measures of the initiative and the referendum spread through the West. This experiment in direct democracy made little difference in fiscal affairs at first, but the means were at hand. In the Great Depression, Midwestern voters used the ballot to cut their property tax rates. In the course of the economic catastrophe, voters in some twenty states adopted one form or another of constitutional tax limits. But it remained for our day to discover the full potential of the initiative. For its own reasons, this discovery came in California.

When the contemporary Tax Revolt burst onto the scene, it seemed like a sudden upheaval of the earth's crust, a political earthquake. A strange doctrine stalked the new terrain. Yet this geography had been well established in previous ages. The ideas and even the practice grew logically from the same source. The course of this development is clearest at the state level.

II

The Three Phases

3

Phase One
Massachusetts: Where It
All Began

The familiar story of the American Revolution becomes a rich and surprisingly strange saga when retold as the Massachusetts Revolution. The residents of this colony fought over taxation with the British, and when the Redcoats evacuated Boston, they continued to fight among themselves. The conflict turned on the slogan "No Taxation without Representation." Well into the nineteenth century, the commonwealth wrestled with the question "What is meant by representation?"

The debate began as early as 1632. Settlers of Watertown were felling trees and grubbing stumps when a message from the Massachusetts Bay Company directors in Boston interrupted their backbreaking labors. A portion of their hard-won profits would have to go toward a levy to build fortifications for nearby Cambridge. The Watertown settlers were furious, their outrage fanned by Pastor George Phillips and Elder Richard Brown. Don't pay, the local leaders warned, or the settlers would "bring themselves and posterity into bondage."

John Winthrop, governor of Massachusetts Bay, had been

confronted before with the independent thinking of Phillips and Brown. He summoned them before the colony's directors, and there ensued a discussion of crucial importance not only for the Cambridge stockade but also for the rest of American history. The Watertowners, argued Winthrop, had not understood the significance of his decision made just nine months earlier to give most settlers the right to elect their government. With the first election coming up in three months, the Massachusetts Bay Company would be transformed into a parliamentary government, before which they would have "free liberty . . . to declare their grievances."

The principle of taxation by representation was thus established on the American continent. The Watertowners "acknowledged their fault, confessing freely that they were in an error." And the first recorded American tax revolt came to an end.[1]

The Watertown protest cast a long shadow. Through the mid-nineteenth century, politics in the Commonwealth of Massachusetts revolved around the twin theories of taxation and representation. This chapter, which carries the story through Shays' Rebellion in 1786, explores the first phase of fiscal limitation: the insistence, drawn by John Locke out of the English tradition, that no tax be imposed without public consent. This insistence had the most serious consequences, for the colonial habit of tax revolt turned into tax revolution and finally into the American Revolution itself.

But Massachusetts was more than just the testing ground for the ideas of John Locke. Its original settlers, more than almost any other group of Americans, were fundamentally ambivalent toward his principles. Locke posited the social contract based on property, in which the individual accepted government to protect the fruits of his solitary labor. The Puritan commonwealths made their covenant with God, to subordinate their sinful selfishness to His commandments. If John Locke can be called the presiding genius of the American republic, the Puritans were his first and most persistent opposition. The tension between Lockean economics and Puritan civic virtue still lies deep within the American soul.

THE UNGODLY PILGRIMS

For the Massachusetts settlers, the tension was immediate. Were not the residents of this religious commonwealth strangely reluctant to surrender their individual property for the use of the general good? Did not their concern about taxation sit uneasily with the Puritan ideal of the moral community? Later Americans devoted to the pursuit of property worried about this conflict only subconsciously. But the Puritan generations faced it squarely, as they struggled to retain their belief in the Christian covenant and the sinfulness of greed.

To understand Puritan economics, one must abandon high-school notions about the *Mayflower*, Plymouth Rock, and "the Pilgrims" (a nineteenth-century label). Myths about the first settlers have obscured their very human nature, much of it not that godly. Along with the Brewsters and the Winslows were more prudent men, including William Ring, who left the expedition when it set into old Plymouth, England; he feared "to be meate for the fishes," recorded a friend. A more turbulent soul, Stephen Hopkins, completed the voyage; his family, the largest on board, has generated more descendants of the *Mayflower* than any other. This progeny owes its existence to the leniency of the leader of an earlier expedition, which took Hopkins to Bermuda. As a member of a mutiny there, Hopkins was sentenced to be hanged but spared because of his children. At Plymouth he became an assistant governor but also accumulated a series of fines for assault, for allowing his servants to drink on the Lord's day, and, significantly, for selling beer, wine, and "strong waters" above the ceiling price set by the colony's Christian price controls.[2]

Plymouth soon fell in the shadow of the far stronger Puritan colony at Massachusetts Bay and was eventually absorbed in the provincial charter that that colony obtained after the accession of William and Mary. Although more populous than Plymouth, the colony at Boston was equally addicted to economic regulation. The first official meeting of the Massachusetts Bay Colony, on August 23, 1630, set maximum wages for carpenters, joiners, and other builders. Later meetings of the General Court regulated the profit margin on imported goods.[3]

As the fining of Stephen Hopkins showed, the religious ethic of the early settlers gave little quarter to the free market. Those who sold goods for whatever price they could get had fallen victim to the deadly sin of greed. This belief exploded with surprising fury in the case of Robert Keayne. A prosperous merchant in Boston, Keayne was charged in 1639 with overcharging for a bag of nails. The accusations multiplied as the Puritans made him a scapegoat for the frustrations accumulated during years of inflation. He was tried and fined £200 by the General Court; his servants were abused in public; and the church elders admonished him severely "in the Name of the Church for selling his wares at excessive Rates, to the Dishonor of Gods name, the Offence of the Generall Cort, and the Publique scandall of the Cuntry."[4] Astonished by this treatment, Keayne devoted his last will and testament, fourteen years later, to refuting the charge that he was a sinner. His life was a model of what would later be called "the Protestant work ethic." Yet to his contemporaries, observes one scholar, "he had put the increase of his own wealth above the common good."[5]

Clearly, the Puritan attitude toward economics differed sharply from the later exaltation of avidity in Locke and Hume and from Adam Smith's more technical praise of the free market. On the question of taxation, however, the Puritans anticipated much of later doctrine.

One should be wary of reading too much of the social contract into the Puritan covenant. Following the Biblical model, the "chosen people" made a covenant with God and then made a second covenant among themselves to establish a government to enforce God's laws. "Consent of the governed" was not necessarily a continuing condition for the legitimacy of the government, which drew its authority from the Almighty.[6] Yet the doctrine of the covenant paved the way historically for the political invocation of the social contract.

In the New World, the Mayflower Compact, signed at anchor off Cape Cod, gave Plymouth Colony its first and only constitution; it was an extension of "the customary church covenant" to include the more turbulent unchurched

"Strangers," such as Miles Standish and Stephen Hopkins.[7] In Massachusetts Bay, John Winthrop transformed his colony's commercial charter into a constitution. The term *free-man* under the Massachusetts Bay Company charter referred to the corporation shareholders, who made rules for the company and its plantation in a quarterly meeting called "the Great and General Court." Winthrop and the other Bay Company officers who came with him to America radically altered this meaning of "freeman." In the first two meetings of the General Court in 1630, they turned the company's executive board into an elected assembly and extended the title and rights of freeman to all settlers who were members of the colony's Puritan churches.[8] In memory of this decision, the state legislature of Massachusetts is still called "the Great and General Court."

GOD'S COVENANT AND MAN'S TAXES

The implications of broadened representation became apparent as the Bay Company broached the question of taxation. When in 1632 Winthrop persuaded the error-prone settlers of Watertown to pay the levy for Cambridge, his talking point was the coming general election. Perhaps drawing a lesson from the incident, Winthrop enlarged the voting to ensure local representation. Each plantation was ordered to choose two men to confer with the governor on raising taxes, "so as what they should agree upon should bind all."[9] In 1634, the new freemen exploited the wording of the charter to demand the power of legislation. The General Court took over powers of government previously held by the Bay Company's Court of Assistants. Chief among these was taxation. The new ordinance declared "That none but the Genall Court hath power to rayse moneyes & taxes."[10]

Thus from its start the Massachusetts Bay legislature laid a claim to the power of the purse, for which the British House of Commons was at the same time waging its bitter struggle with the Crown. In England, this doctrine provided the mechanism by which the religious and political tensions under Charles I came to their final crisis. The Catholic king had attempted to rule without the Protestant Parliament for eleven years, when his bishops' attempt to introduce a new liturgy in Scotland provoked a riot in Edinburgh's St. Giles's church. (As the dean began to read the liturgy, a parishioner named Jenny Geddes was so offended she rose and hurled a stool at him.) To put down the spreading rebellion, King Charles needed more money than he could raise on his own. That required new taxes, and *that* required a session of Parliament. In 1640, he convened what was later known as "the Long Parliament." Before this body broke up, dispersed forcibly by Oliver Cromwell, the high Anglicans were impeached, King Charles had gone to the block, and England had entered its trauma of civil war and religious enthusiasm.

The New England colonies could scarcely have failed to note the immense leverage that control of the taxing authority had given their fellow Puritans. This leverage exerted its greatest force when wars and other calamities forced a rapid rise in government expenses.

By the end of the seventeenth century, Massachusetts settlers had already rough-hewn the building blocks that later came together in the doctrines of government based on compact and taxation drawn from consent. They had also devised a forerunner of the type of tax later to be the favorite of Lockean ideology. The first tax laws of the General Court were couched in language that to at least one later observer contained the embryonic principles of the general property tax. The 1634 ordinance defining functions of the General Court ordered "that in all rates and publique charges, the townes shall haue respect to levy *euy man according to his estate, &* with consideracion of all his other abilityes, whatsoever."[11]

Subsequent tax laws elaborated on the principle of obtaining "one genll rule & way of rateing throughout ye country." Nathan Matthews, the late-nineteenth-century mayor of Boston, argued that this colonial levy was the true origin of the general property tax; each settler was required to pay in proportion to the total market value of all his property. Matthews distinguished the American levy from the English tax system of the same period. The English, he said, applied their tax rates to the annual income of property rather than to its market value. The difference was significant. An English country estate might command a high sale price because of its value for prestige and sports, but its land might be worthless for agriculture. The tax based on the income from the English estate could amount to one-sixth of a tax based on its market value. There were no large estates in Massachusetts Bay, hence no constituency to shape the tax system in their favor. The general property tax as foreshadowed in colonial law reflected a preference for the small, nearly equal landholding of the American farms. Observed Matthews: "The effect of the English system is to make it possible to preserve the estate in the hands of a single family; the effect of the Massachusetts system is to make it unlikely that an estate of this size could be held together even for a single lifetime."[12]

In spite of its egalitarian premise, the colonial levy also foreshadowed the problems of the general property tax. "Easy, aequall & certaine" levies were easier to legislate than to procure in practice.[13] The way the levy was voted made it fall, perhaps unintentionally, more on the poorer colonials than on the rich. The General Court raised revenues by voting a "country rate" consisting of a head tax and a general property tax. As more money was needed, the General Court would vote additional "country rates," repeating those taxes at their fixed rates. A poor person with little spare cash or produce would have a harder time meeting repeated levies of the head tax than a propertied man.[14] Furthermore, the General Court had the same problem that nineteenth-century tax assessors would have in combating evasion. A 1651 statute of the General Court complained "that visible estates in land, corne, cattle, are, accordinge to order, wholly & fully taxed, but the estates of marchants, in the hands of neibours, staungers, or theire factors, are not so obuious to view, but upon search, little of theire estates doe appeare, beinge of great valew, so that the law doth not reach them by the rule of taxing visible estates."[15] The legislature responded by allowing assessors to estimate a taxpayer's property according to their "will and dome." Throughout the period of the Old Charter, the General Court continued to struggle with the task of providing "that all publicke charges may be aequally borne, & that some may not be eased & others burdened."[16] But the complaints of inequity reached an even higher pitch as new developments drove the colonial tax burden through the roof.

THE PURITAN CONSCIENCE: POOR LAWS AND SCHOOLS

Massachusetts taxation was much lighter in the first generation than it would later become but not because the Puritans believed in an inactive government. After listing examples of their severe Old Testament moral law, the source of so much hostile stereotyping, Tocqueville marveled at the extent of their social legislation. As early as 1650, vital statistics were being kept, roads were being maintained, the poor were tended to. "The ideas there formed of the duties of society towards its members are evidently much loftier and more comprehensive than those of European legislators at that time. . . . The law enters into a thousand various details to anticipate and satisfy a crowd of social wants that are even now very inadequately felt in France."[17]

The most significant charge was for public education. A statute of 1647 ordered localities to establish tax-supported public schools. Still famous among American educators as the "Old Deluder Satan Law," its language shows to what extent the expansion of public services under the Puritans derived from their religious impulse. The preamble reads: "It being one chief project of that old deluder, Satan, to keep men from the knowledge of the Scriptures, as in former times keeping them in an unknown tongue, so in these later times by persuading from the use of Tongues, that so at least the true sense and meaning of the Original might be clouded with false glosses of Saint-seeming-deceivers; and that learning may not be buried in the graves of our forefathers in Church and Commonwealth, the Lord assisting our endeavors: it is therefore ordered by this Court and Authority thereof . . ."[18] The religious motive has faded, but the descendants of the Puritans throughout their migrations have been leaders in urging taxation to support free public education.

THE FIRST DEFENSE BURDEN

The seventeenth-century school levies weighed lightly compared to the other great cause of public spending—war. The most bitterly resented tax levies were those required to support the colony's defense burden.

For the first generation of settlement, the Puritans by and large enjoyed peace with the American Indians. But as Puritan prosperity increased and Indian population declined, some Indian leaders foresaw doom. Foremost among these were the sons of Massasoit, the Wampanoag chief who had befriended the first settlers at Plymouth. The younger son, called "Philip" by the settlers after an earlier barbarian, determined to break the English power while there was still time. King Philip's War, from 1675 to 1676, was on its own small scale the most destructive Americans have yet fought. One out of every ten of the fighting colonials was killed or captured; a dozen of the eighty to ninety towns in the war zone were totally destroyed; and the cost of the war effort exceeded the total value of the colony's entire personal property.[19]

This cost produced a drastic change in the colony's fiscal life. In the course of the fighting, the General Court levied twenty-six separate country rates. The tax bill in Woburn, for instance, went from £30 to more than £530.[20] The rate of tax growth slowed with the end of the war, but the low-tax days of the first generation were over.

THE FIRST GENERAL TAX REVOLT

The rising tax burden profoundly changed the political culture of Massachusetts Bay. The postwar economy fell into depression. The selectmen of one town complained that taxes were so high they could not even afford "the maintaynance of the gospell."[21] Leaders of the older generation lost their credentials with their townsmen, and villagers demanded greater say in finances and tax levies.

This rising disaffection collided with the home government's first major intervention in New England's affairs. In 1684, fed up with colonial resistance to the Navigation Acts,

Charles II obtained a revocation of the Massachusetts Bay charter. He handed the government to a temporary appointee, the "place-seeking" son of the colony's second governor, who told the General Court that it had ceased to exist. The settlements were consolidated in the Dominion of New England. Sir Edmund Andros arrived to take charge, carrying a royal commission empowering him to "impose and assess and raise and levy such rates and taxes as you shall find necessary for the support of the government."[22] The dominion's government continued the tax structure devised under the Old Charter, but it was ample grievance to the colonists that any taxes were to be levied without the vote of the General Court. The General Court itself played on this grievance by repealing all of its revenue acts before dissolving, so that the new government had to pass them anew.

The dominion sent out tax warrants to the towns, which (following old practice) were to appoint the officers to collect the tax. In Essex County, a minister named John Wise rallied the town meeting of Ipswich to resist the levy; the meeting declared "that was not the townes Duties any wayes to Assist those ill Methods of Raising money without a General Assembly." Andros arrested Wise and five town leaders. At their trial they invoked Magna Carta and the rights of Englishmen. Andros in turn scoffed at the notion that "every Jack and Tom should tell the King what moneys he should have for the use of his government."[23] Wise emerged from jail a hero to the colony.[24]

Andros continued to drive his lesson home, abolishing town meetings except for annual elections. So many of his measures displayed such similar lack of tact that historians can debate indefinitely which it was that finally alienated his constituency among the Massachusetts Bay merchants. The colony was ripe for open rebellion when news arrived of the overthrow of James II. Within two weeks, hundreds of armed men from the countryside swarmed into Boston. Andros surrendered, the dominion collapsed, and Puritans and merchants alike joined in establishing a provisional government.

The new king, William of Orange, was slow to express appreciation for the colonial gesture of support. For three years the colony went through one of its unhappiest periods, while it awaited a new charter. The first of a long series of French and Indian wars had begun under Andros. After the overthrow, the ubiquitous Puritan leader Increase Mather hinted from London that the provisional government might further the negotiations for a new charter if it staged a dramatic display of loyalty. So Massachusetts launched several expensive expeditions against Canada. Their most lasting result was an increase in the tax burden that rivaled that of King Philip's War. By the end of 1690, the restored General Court had so vigorously practiced taxation with representation that it had voted thirty-seven country rates. Mather had to turn his pen from defending doctrine to defending taxation. "Tis true the Taxes are great and so is the Cause," argued the tract attributed to Mather. "The Taxes are to save your Lands and Lives from the Common Enemies."[25]

In the face of public grumbling, the government further undermined confidence by issuing paper currency. The new money depreciated rapidly. Without a legitimate government or a stable means of exchange, public anomie moved a tract writer in 1691 to ask "were not peoples Heads Idly bewhized with Conceits that we have no *Magistrates*, no *Government*, And by Consequence that we have no Security for anything, which we call our own (a *Consequence* they will be Loth to allow, though they cannot help it, If once we are Reduced to *Hobs* his state of Nature, which (says he) is a state of War, and then the strongest must *take all.*"[26] It was in this atmosphere that several adolescent girls in Salem sparked a general hysteria by accusing some neighbors of practicing witchcraft.

Some of the anxiety lifted when a new royal charter arrived in 1692, confirming the General Court's power to levy taxes. But the period of the Glorious Revolution in England marked a critical turning point for Massachusetts as well. In England the Protestant aristocracy had overthrown a Catholic king and also preserved the liberties of their rising commercial government. In New England, the Puritan clergy had been diverted from debating doctrine to defending the rights of Englishmen. According to Perry Miller, the great twentieth-century chronicler of the New England mind, Puritan other-worldliness was giving way to a practical concern for public finance and political rights. The colonists had made a dry run in defending their legislature's role in levying taxes. The mob in Boston that deposed Andros was still a reflex of European events, however. The colonists lacked the theoretical backbone for a direct challenge to British authority. Yet change was coming. Rhetoric after 1689 began to see government as "the great Buckler (when rightly managed) both of Religion and Property."[27] Continues Perry Miller, "One does not exaggerate" to see the events of 1689 as the forerunner of 1776.

THE ROLE OF LOCKE

What did colonial Massachusetts have left to learn from Locke? Did it not already believe that representative assemblies should vote the tax levies? Had it not already based its tax structure on the principle of proportional and equal contributions from all the property encompassed by the state?

The answers lie in understanding that institutions may be worked up by history into a nearly finished form before the theorist comes along to fit them into his explanation of human behavior. This is what Locke did with the Puritan tradition of the covenant, and the legislature's power of the purse. In working over the existing material, he gave it a new purpose and a new set of connotations. The practical doctrine of legislative consent to taxation took on new significance as a crucial mechanism of the social contract based on property. Before Locke, this consent derived from the historical rights of Englishmen; after him, it expressed a universal theory about the origin of government. Above and beyond Locke's social contract came his psychology. The attempt to reduce the visible world to the impact of sensation on the mind undercut the classical view that external qualities had an existence of their own, independent of perception. Passions now had the same status as rational ideas; both were sensations. Hence nothing was lost by reducing human behavior to the passion of greed.[28]

The impact of Locke on America went far deeper than his reinterpretation of the social contract. In spite of the wariness of the Puritan divines, the New Learning found its way to their younger generation. A student at Yale in 1715 recalled hearing "of a new philosophy that of late was all in vogue and of such names as Descartes, Boyle, Locke, and Newton, but they were cautioned against thinking of them because the new philosophy, it was said, would soon bring in a new divinity and corrupt the pure religion of the country." By 1717, in Wethersfield, Connecticut, a fourteen-year-old youth named Jonathan Edwards digested a copy of Locke's *Essay Concerning Human Understanding*. In his lifelong effort to reconcile the new psychology with Puritan theology, Edwards attained heights of thought that few Americans have equaled. But the practical impact was to destroy the old ground of Puritan theology.[29]

By degrees New Englanders passed from relying on religious convenant to invoking the rights of Englishmen to flirting with natural rights. The revolt against Andros had produced anguish over the dangers of Hobbesian anarchy. When the issue arose again, the colonists would have the benefit of both a historical precedent and a more heartening description of the state of nature.

THE SECOND TIME AROUND, FOR KEEPS

By the early eighteenth century, Massachusetts had one foot over the fence into a polity based on the protection of property. The Puritan commonweal was a fading ideal, but the sons of Mather and Winthrop kept their other foot on religious ground. When rising tax burdens took their economic toll, it was still possible to find spiritual descendants of Increase Mather reassuring a grumbling people that the levies were just and necessary. The Puritans had come to insist that taxes were illegitimate unless voted by the General Court. But this procedural point did not guarantee that taxation would remain low, as the General Court had demonstrated in the aftermath of the Glorious Revolution. To be sure, the insistence on the legislature's consent implied a judgment on the proper level of taxation; this procedure clearly was meant to provide protection against arbitrary, wasteful, and economically oppressive levies. But it was left to the second half of the eighteenth century to elaborate the economics as well as the procedures of taxation.[30]

It falls beyond our scope to recount the British effort to share the financial burden of the French and Indian War with the American colonies. The story of the Sugar Act (1764), the Stamp Act (1765), and the Townshend duties (1767) has been told exhaustively and well.[31] But it is worth noting that George Grenville, the architect of these measures, seems to have had in mind a remarkably consistent supply-side policy. When Grenville became head of the British government in 1763, holding the two offices of first lord of the treasury and chancellor of the exchequer, he already had a reputation for frugality in government.[32] His overriding concern was to restore control over the budget and the rapidly rising public debt. In the course of the war, Britain's national debt had nearly doubled. Its annual tax levies had more than doubled, producing a dangerously high tax burden of at least one pound sterling per capita. The rate of the land tax, the largest source of revenue, had doubled to four shillings per pound. In 1763, rioting broke out over new taxes on cider.[33] Moreover, the budget faced a continuing drain of £350,000 a year for the cost of defense and administration for the newly expanded American dominion. At the same time, Americans were lightly taxed, in part thanks to parliamentary subsidies extended during the war with France. From Grenville's viewpoint, it was natural to lighten the British tax burden by drawing revenue from the American colonies.

Grenville's first step could be described as the Laffer Curve in action. He found a series of customs duties for America already on the books, the most prominent of which was an impost of six pence a gallon on foreign molasses. Smuggling was so widespread that this levy brought in only £1,800 a year. Grenville calculated that the smuggler had to pay one and a half pence a gallon in bribes. So by reducing the duty on molasses and tightening enforcement he should be able to bring this trade within legal channels and sharply boost his revenue. His Sugar Act of 1764 cut the duty on molasses in half. Part of his problem, however, was that he had miscalculated the Laffer Curve effect. His three-penny duty was still too high. The historian Edmund Morgan speculates that if Grenville had listened to his Massachusetts advisers and cut the duty by five-sixths, the issue might have blown over. The three-penny rate did triple the revenue, but when the rate later was reduced to one pence, the revenues increased even more.[34]

The political impact of the Sugar Act was bad enough, but Grenville's next measure, the Stamp Act, was disastrous. To Grenville and his Treasury Office specialists, this measure seemed the least onerous of the alternatives. (Other measures being rumored were a direct poll tax and a tax on imports.) In soliciting information to help draft the tax, Grenville's assistant Thomas Whately wrote to a friend in Boston, "It will be a principal object of attention here to make this tax as little burthensome as possible."[35] In an able pamphlet defending the tax, this same Whately wrote: "This Mode of Taxation is the easiest, the most equal and the most certain that can be chosen; the Duty falls chiefly upon Property; but it is spread lightly over a great Variety of Subjects, and lies heavy upon none: The Act executes itself by annulling the Instruments that have not paid the small Sums they are charged with; and the Tax thus supported and secured, is collected by few Officers, without Expense to the Crown, or Oppression on the People."[36] The stamp tax thus satisfied the canons of taxation later enunciated by Adam Smith. It had the character of an indirect tax, as recommended by Hume and Montesquieu. Even more, the idea of a tax on legal paper had the explicit endorsement of Montesquieu.[37] These arguments made little impression on the colonials, and rightly so, because the provisions of the stamp tax proved more onerous in operation than they appeared to the bureaucrats of the imperial capital.

The furious American protests frustrated the tax; Grenville's government fell; and the new Whig government repealed the tax. But Grenville had far from ended his career as a supply-sider. Going into opposition in Parliament, he led a revolt against the first budget of Chancellor of the Exchequer Charles Townshend. With the support of members from the countryside, he won a vote to reduce the land tax rates by 25%. The vote, the first government defeat on a money bill since the Glorious Revolution, left a budget gap of £400,000. To close it, Townshend introduced the infamous duties on American imports of glass, lead, paper, paints, and tea that led straight downhill to the Boston Tea Party, the Coercive Acts against Boston, and the fighting at Lexington and Concord.[38]

Grenville's reputation in America should give ample warning that, when it comes to tax shifts, one man's supply-sider is another man's oppressor. One factor in the American fear of taxation by the British Parliament was that this shift would continue. If the precedent were set, no matter how innocuous the tax, future Parliaments would find it the course of least resistance to lighten the tax burden at home by passing as much of it as they could to the colonies. The New York petition to the House of Commons of October 18, 1764, stated this fear clearly: ". . . who, that considers the natural Reluctance of Mankind to burthens, and their Inclination to cast them upon the Shoulders of others, cannot foresee, that while the People on one Side of the *Atlantic*, enjoy an Exemption from the Load, those on the other, must submit to the most unsupportable Oppression and Tyranny."[39]

The Virginia Memorial to the House of Lords related this point to the question of representation: "Property must become too precarious for the Genius of a free People which can be taken from them at the Will of others, who cannot know what Taxes such People can bear, or the easiest Mode of raising them; and who are not under that Restraint, which is the greatest Security against a burthensome Taxation, when the Representatives themselves must be affected by every Tax imposed on the People."[40] To state this concern as the colonials themselves did is to lay bare the inner logic of the constitutional arguments that followed. It was irrelevant to say that the stamp tax was not a crushing tax. The Massachusetts General Court was willing to raise an amount equivalent to its share, provided it voted the tax itself, and other colonial assemblies seemed ready to follow suit. Nor was it sufficient to claim that colonials had the benefit of "virtual representation" in Parliament, as did the nine-tenths of the British population who were not electors. Unlike the residents of Britain, the Americans would not be sharing the experience of the new taxation with men who were electors. (And even if they did have actual representation, their M.P.s would form too small a minority to offer any effective resistance.) Without an institutional separation of the power to tax, the best one could expect was that the tax burdens on both sides of the Atlantic would even out, like water seeking its level. In the worst case, the Americans would bear the greater share, just as politically weak interests were doing at home.

The condition of Massachusetts shows just how great was the disparity of tax burden. While English taxes stood at one pound sterling per capita, the highest postwar levy in Massachusetts (in 1764–65) came in at only four shillings seven pence a head, less than one-quarter of the British burden. For much of the first half-century, the Massachusetts legislature had been putting off taxation by issuing paper money instead. (The province suffered the same inflation that is produced today by the more roundabout but essentially identical federal expedient of borrowing and monetizing the debt.)[41] Taxes surged when Parliament intervened to stop these issues, but in the decade before the Revolution, the tax burden had been steadily declining. In 1770, Governor Thomas Hutchinson could write in his History of the Colony and Province of Massachusetts Bay: "It is certain that there had been no period when the province . . . felt less of the ordinary burdens which must at all times be felt, more or less, by the people of every government. . . . From the surpluses of former funds and from debts due to the government for lands which had been sold, there appeared a fund sufficient to raise money not only for the service of the present year, but of some years to come, so as to render any tax unnecessary."[42] In 1773, Hutchinson announced that the province was "entirely free from debt." The lightness of this fiscal burden does not mean that the colonials were irrational to resist an increment of parliamentary taxation. On the contrary, they had a favored status to protect that was threatened, like a settlement at the foot of a leaking dam, in proportion to the disparity between the tax burden in England and in America.

LESSONS OF THE STAMP TAX

In defending their low-tax environment, the colonials went through a crash course in political theory. Taxation was not, of course, the only issue: denial of trial by jury, trade regulation, and even religious jealousy were other concerns troubling Massachusetts. But the progression of ideas following the Stamp Act crises led logically to independence.

The colonials insisted that they should pay no taxes to which they had not consented through their representatives. Remarkably, Grenville agreed; "May this sacred pledge of Liberty be preserved inviolate," his aide Whately wrote.[43] In a polemical point pregnant with unimagined offspring, Whately continued by saying that this principle applied to all new laws: "All other Acts that relate either to ourselves or to the Colonies, are founded upon no other Authority."[44] Parliament attempted to satisfy this principle through the doctrine of virtual representation. The members of the House of Commons acted on behalf of the whole realm, not for their local constituency.

This reply again forced Americans to inquire deeply into what was meant by representation. For material reasons as well as repeated incidents showing that the English administrators did not understand American circumstances, virtual representation was out. But if representation was the basis of all law, not just tax law, then the sole legal authority in Massachusetts was the General Court. According to this view, Parliament had no superior authority over the colonial legislatures; each one possessed the complete power of legislation. This conclusion meant that the only mortar holding the empire together was loyalty to the Crown. When that cement dissolved, in part through the pamphleteering of Thomas Paine, the colonies were intellectually independent. The Revolution was merely a matter of implementation.

The point of departure for this chain of thought was the formula "No Taxation without Representation." Although the colonials regarded that principle as a feature of the rights of Englishmen, rooted in English history, they were also beginning to derive it from the laws of nature. Thus the Massachusetts House of Representatives declared, in universal language: "That there are certain essential Rights of the British Constitution of Government, which are founded in the Law of God and Nature, and are the common Rights of Mankind, Therefore . . . Resolved, That no Man can justly take the Property of another without his Consent: And that upon this original Principle the Right of Representation in the same Body, which exercises the Power of making Laws for levying Taxes, which is one of the main Pillars of the British Constitution, is evidently founded."[45] In returning to the first principles, declarations like this were heavily influenced by the doctrines of Locke, by then common currency in America. In a letter to a friend in 1760, John Adams praised Locke (and the prospects of modernity) in terms reflecting the special affinity between the English philosopher and his American audience:

> In Metaphysicks, Mr. Locke, directed by my Lord Bacon, has steered his Course into the unenlightened Regions of the human Mind, and like Columbus has discovered a new World. A World whose soil is deep and strong producing Rank and unwholesome Weeds as well as wholsome fruits and flowers; a World that is incumbered with unprofitable Brambles, as well as stored with useful Trees; and infested with motly Savages; as well as capable of furnishing civilized Inhabitants; he has shewn us by what Cultivation, these Weeds may be Extirmined and the fruits raised; the Brambles removed as well as the Trees grubbed; the savages destroyed, as well as the civil People increased.[46]

In justifying the Glorious Revolution, and its guarantee to the House of Commons of the taxing power, Locke provided powerful support to the colonial predisposition to force a crisis over the Stamp Act.

As the stamp tax crisis raged, however, and mobs terrorized would-be revenue agents, the colonials began to realize that they would somehow have to translate theory into a new political order. The destruction of the old order had gone furthest in Massachusetts. As the center of resistance to the tea tax, Boston took the brunt of the punishment. Parliament revoked the charter of Massachusetts Bay, suppressed its town meetings, as Andros had earlier, and sent out a military governor. The Second Continental Congress convened in protest, and the Provincial Convention of Massachusetts Bay, meeting in place of the regular government, asked it for "explicit Advice respecting the taking up and exercising the Powers of civil government."[47]

CREATING THE NEW ORDER

As the broad panorama of the Revolution unfolded before the eye of History, the people of Massachusetts settled down to the task of devising a new government. Adams, a delegate to the Continental Congress, urged the Congress to instruct the states, as he now insisted they should be called, to institute governments through constitutional conventions. His speech of June 2, 1775, gives a fascinating insight into the evolution from British colony to American state. Government was necessary to pursue the war, Adams later recalled telling the delegates,

> and as I supposed no Man would think of consolidating this vast Continent under one national Government, We should probably after the example of the Greeks, the Dutch and the Swiss, form a confederacy of States, each of which must have a separate Government. That the Case of Massachusetts was the most urgent, but that it would not be long before every other Colony must follow her Example. That with a view to this Subject I had looked into the Ancient and modern Confederacies for Examples: but they all appeared to me to have been huddled up in a hurry by a few Chiefs. But We had a People of more Intelligence, Curiosity and Enterprize, who must be all consulted, and We must realize the Theories of the Wisest Writers and invite the People, to erect the whole Building with their own hands upon the broadest foundation.[48]

The Congress pondered "these new, strange and terrible Doctrines."[49] It then gave Massachusetts a much more timid answer than Adams had wanted. With a majority still hoping for conciliation, it recommended that the Provincial Convention call elections for a new Assembly, which would elect a Council to replace that appointed by the Crown. This body would then govern until somehow the king would appoint a governor who would uphold the suspended charter. The extralegal Provincial Convention gladly took this advice, and gave way to the reconstituted General Court in July 1775. In spite of protests from the western counties of Berkshire and Hampshire, the temporary government reopened the courts, restoring a semblance of authority.

THE MASSACHUSETTS CONVENTION

The Declaration of Independence destroyed the fiction that the colonies awaited a legal royal governor, so in the fall of 1776 the General Court began steps to frame a new constitution. This process proved unexpectedly difficult. The first Massachusetts constitutional convention convened in June 1777. It consisted of the House of Representatives and the Council, sitting as one body. This procedure, still followed today, was one of the reasons that the towns rejected the constitution of 1778 by a majority of about five to one. Among the host of objections was the theme that the basic law should be formed by a true constitutional convention. "The Compact in this state is not yet formed," argued the Berkshire Constitutionalists, the townspeople in Pittsfield and the Hill Towns, who enforced their position by keeping the executive courts closed.[50] Pamphleteers attacked the Berkshire position, turning the doctrines of "the great Mr. Locke" against them, but this pressure contributed to the calling of a separate constitutional convention in 1779.[51] This convention produced the famous Massachusetts Constitution of 1780, which is still the fundamental law of the commonwealth.

The basic draft of the constitution was written by John Adams, elected to the convention between diplomatic missions. His distinctive influence shows most strongly in the document's exhortations for adherence to the principles "of piety, justice, moderation, temperance, industry, and frugality," all "absolutely necessary to preserve the advantages of liberty and to maintain a free government." Adams sought to preserve this civic virtue by providing for public support "of public protestant teachers of piety, religion and morality." (Although his motives were more civic than religious, this article caused one of the major controversies in the ratification debate.) In a section on "The Encouragement of Literature, etc." he also called on the legislature to cherish public education, "wisdom, and knowledge, as well as virtue, diffused generally among the body of the people," in order to preserve liberty.[52]

These provisions show more than casual understanding that material self-interest is not enough to hold society together. Although in the Continental Congress Adams had insisted on referring to the thirteen former colonies as "states," he reserved the term *commonwealth* for Massachusetts. He was inclined to entrust a greater role to government than were many of his contemporaries. In his republican fervor, he was more willing than most to submit to heavy taxation. In drafting his section on "the encouragement of literature, etc.," he feared that it would founder on the antitax attitudes of his contemporaries. "I expected," he wrote, "it would be attack'd, in the Convention from all quarters, on the score of Affectation, Pedantry, Hypocrisy, and above all Oeconomy. Many ideas in it implied expence: and I knew then as well as I have known since that too large a portion of the People and their Representatives, had rather starve their Souls than draw upon their purses to pay for nourishment of them: and therefore no mercy was to be expected for a Paragraph, that I would not now exchage for a Sceptre, and wish may be engraved on my Tomb Stone."[53] Such was Adams's prestige and the strength of the Puritan regard for learning, however, that the section received general acclaim.

In spite of Adams's Puritan republicanism, the Massachusetts constitution quickly shifts to the rhetoric of John Locke. This influence is especially strong on the system of taxation. Article I of the Declaration of Rights states the Lockean premise familiar from the Declaration of Independence, with the difference that the "pursuit of happiness" is openly identified with "acquiring, possessing, and protecting property." Article X gives more detail on the property-based social contract: "Each individual of the society has a right to be protected by it in the enjoyment of his life, liberty and property, according to standing laws. He is obliged, consequently, to contribute his share to the expense of this protection; to give his personal service, or an equivalent, when necessary: But no part of the property of any individual, can, with justice, be taken from him, or applied to public uses without his own consent, or that of the representative body of the people."[54]

Article XV guarantees jury trials "in all controversies concerning property" except for traditional exceptions; this provision has in mind the British use of admiralty courts to enforce their tax laws. Article XXIII forbids the levying of any "subsidy, charge, tax, impost, or duties" without the consent of the people or their representatives. The section on the General Court carries the principle of the property-based compact into the details of taxation, inserting the crucial word *proportional* in its power to impose and levy taxes. This word has come to imply the doctrine that the cost of the protection of property should be distributed at an equal rate. The constitution turns a cold shoulder to progressive taxation designed to redistribute property. Among other things, this passage has been interpreted to forbid the progressive income tax.

The provisions on taxation appear not to have been controversial. Similar language requiring "proportionable and reasonable assessments, rates and taxes" appeared in the rejected constitution of 1778. In voting on the document, town meetings also made suggestions for improvements; although they protested freely on issues like the establishment of religion and representation, they said relatively little about the language on taxation.[55] To make sure their property received equal treatment, the various classes of property holders had to maintain a presence in the legislature that bore some relation to their wealth or numbers. So the issue of taxation resolved itself into the issue of representation. After launching a revolution to preserve the connection between taxation and representation, the people of Massachusetts found that it remained their most burning domestic issue.

THE DOMESTIC STRUGGLE

The issue of internal taxation arose even before independence. The Coercive Acts had aroused the revolutionary fervor of the "back country." When Massachusetts revived its legislature, inland towns sent many more representatives than they had ever done under the Crown. For a brief moment in October 1775, western and eastern agrarians had the power to shape things their way. Their most controversial act was a tax levy, the "state bill," that sharply raised the burden on capital and merchants' inventories. "The evident intent of this iniquitous bill," complained one newspaper essayist, "is to lay the burden of the encreasing charge of government, on account of the war, on the trading and monied interests." The author of the essay series signed "O.P.Q." anticipated some of the main themes of the supply-side position, including, dare one say, the Laffer Curve. Writing for a western Massachusetts audience, O.P.Q. pleaded with them to return delegates "who will not do every thing in their power to destroy the commercial part of the community, without considering that the value of our lands is enhanced in proportion to the demand, which an extensive commerce, the opulence of the merchant, and the number of mechanics necessarily occasion, and that excessive burdens always operate as prohibitions, and that therefore, the end in view will be frustrated by the very means taken to accomplish it." The "end in view" of this bill was to relieve some of the tax burden on the landed interest. But the measure instead would "drive all trade out of the colony, to such places as have the wisdom and foresight to give it every possible encouragement—and this colony will be proportionally impoverished; having no vent for their surplus produce, either for exportation or consumption."[56] After stating that the trader's commerce was so beneficial to the community "as that they would gain much by not taxing him at all," O.P.Q. warned, "Will not the enormous and now increasing influence of the landed interest at court, ruin the colony—will not the very persons who are intended to be relieved have all his burden charge to pay, when by straining to over burden the merchants and monied men, they generally withdraw, and leave them to the just effects of their iniquitous policy."[57]

The people in the eastern commercial towns did not rest at writing newspaper articles. An Essex County convention in April 1776 complained bitterly about the system of representation that had given the western towns such influence: "It will be found by Examination, that a Majority of Voices in the Assembly may be obtained from the Members of Towns, which pay not more than one fourth Part of the publick Tax."[58]

Its petition to the legislature carried the logic of the Revolution one step further. "The want of a just Weight in Representation is an Evil nearly akin to being totally destitute of it."[59] Within an amazingly short time, Massachusetts' rejection of the doctrine of virtual representation had brought it to the threshold of the doctrine of one man, one vote. When an individual yielded property to the state through taxation, it was not enough to be told that the members of a Parliament 3,000 miles away represented his interests equally with those of every other member of the realm. The men who voted for his taxes had to feel the impact of them in the same way as the Americans did. But why stop there? If each continent deserved its own representation, why not each town, each taxpayer? In the debates surrounding the reconstitution of Massachusetts' government, towns with too few freeholders to merit a representative now demanded one. Taxpayers who fell short of the property requirement asked for the vote anyway. On the other hand, complaints were made against the election of ministers to the legislature, on the ground that they paid no taxes and so should not be representatives.[60] The towns of Essex County broached the ultimate argument that underrepresentation in relation either to numbers or to tax bills failed to give adequate protection to those who had sacrificed some property to join the social compact. Representation by town should give way to some more equal basis. This petition had a dramatic impact on the legislature. It arrived at the end of the session, when many delegates from the west had probably already gone home. Within four days, the General Court had passed an act "for providing for a more equal representation." Larger towns were no longer limited to two representatives. In the next General Court, eastern counties controlled a safe majority of the House.[61]

Western towns could do nothing to regain their brief eminence, but resentment against the eastern coup continued to smolder beneath the surface. In debate on the 1780 constitution, the issue of representation served as surrogate for that of tax burden. A number of petitions from Berkshire and Hampshire, the two westernmost counties, called for a return to town-based representation. The fiscal policy of the Revolution kept the embers glowing. In the first years of independence, the General Court tried to allay the internal tensions of 1775 and 1776 by issuing paper money instead of new taxes. But without any backing the paper bills depreciated rapidly, and a series of wage and price controls were powerless to stop the ensuing inflation. The Massachusetts currency was really a form of debt, eventually to be redeemed by hard money raised through taxation. In 1780, the General Court made an effort in this direction. It ordered an annual tax to be paid in gold or silver to redeem the bills and pay interest on loans. This tax illustrates how misleading the raw numbers of the period can be. It amounted to $240,000 a year for seven years, compared to a total tax levy in 1780 of $38 million. On the face of it, the debt-service tax was less than 1% of the total. But the other taxes could be paid in the nearly worthless paper, and the total collection had an estimated value in hard money of less than $1 million. So the tax for interest payment and note redemption was actually consuming about 25% of the commonwealth's real revenue.[62]

It was bad enough to pay these taxes in a time of deranged currency, but it was worse to see so much of the proceeds go to wealthy speculators. The speculative market was one of the few reasons that the paper currency retained what little value it had, but then, as now, that point had little popular appeal. Furthermore, as one historian put it, "the sanctity of state credit was as yet little understood." Nonpayment of taxes ran to 20% of the total, whether from hardship or evasion. By 1785, the General Court gave up on the debt-service levy and even refused to vote any tax at all.[63]

The tax holiday of 1785 appears to have fed a statewide boom. Merchants sold a flood of newly imported goods on credit terms extending to a year. But when the loans came due, times were worse than ever. Indebtedness was already widespread because of the pressure of tax payments. Now, as credit tightened, it ravaged whole agricultural districts. The newly efficient court system was putting thousands of debtors through legal suits. As in the stamp tax crisis and the period of the Coercive Acts, courts became the target of direct action.[64]

In August 1786, some 1,500 armed insurgents took over the courthouse in Northampton, in the Connecticut River valley, and prevented the sitting of the court. A mob in Worcester followed suit. Within the next month, insurgents closed the courts from Great Barrington, in the Berkshires, to Concord, a night's horse ride from Boston. Towns met in extralegal conventions, demanding redress of grievances and questioning the authority of the constitutional government. Counties began to communicate through committees of correspondence, imitating the bodies that had been so effective in undermining British rule. Shays' Rebellion was under way.

Recent historians have tended to discount the threat of this uprising, possibly because it collapsed with little bloodshed. But at the time it looked extremely dangerous. The upheaval was statewide, not confined simply to the western counties, and it had the active sympathy of much of the population and a faction of the House of Representatives. Daniel Shays, of Pelham, a cashiered Revolutionary War officer, gave the upheaval its name when he emerged at the head of an armed brigade of insurgents that blockaded the Springfield courthouse. Many contemporaries thought he was merely a figurehead for more sinister forces, but the truly dangerous part of the rising was its apparent continuity with the Revolution. Had not the leaders of the struggle for independence also blockaded the law courts, and for long periods too?[65]

As this heresy spread in the western counties, defense of the state government luckily fell to a figure who spoke with the authority of the Revolution. This man was General William Shepard, a farmer from nearby Westfield who had been adjutant on the staff of George Washington himself. Shepard's character came from Washington's mold; he seems to have had a sharp but disciplined temper and a simple, but not simple-minded, devotion to doing the right thing. In September 1786, he marched to Springfield with 600 loyal militia to protect the quarterly sitting of the court. In the town square, he confronted Daniel Shays at the head of 600 insurgents. The groups glared at each other across the square as the judges decided to adjourn their session. Then General Shepard drew his troops aside to let the rebels occupy the courthouse, while he quickly marched to the town's truly important military asset, the Springfield Armory, which housed stores of cannon and munitions. Shepard held this position into the winter, as Boston merchants outfitted a loyal force in the east and Shays' rebels drilled and recruited in the surrounding countryside. On January 25, Shays decided to seize the armory to provision his growing force. He marched on

Springfield with a force of more than 2,000 and met General Shepard's force of 1,200 on the road. After firing warning volleys, Shepard turned his cannon on the advancing column. Four rebels fell. The rest then broke and retreated north. General Benjamin Lincoln's army from Boston arrived on their heels and pursued them up the Connecticut River valley to Pelham. After camping briefly and feigning negotiations for amnesty, Shays tried to retreat farther upcountry. Lincoln pursued him overnight in an icy snowstorm. After a harrowing forced march, he caught Shays at his Sunday breakfast and scattered his forces. Still, isolated guerrilla incidents continued for months in the Berkshires to the west, where rebels stuck feathers in their hats and progovernment men sported scraps of paper. But the armed rebellion had been dissipated.[66]

The issues of taxation and representation remained unsettled, however. Although the western attacks on the representative system focused on the way it reduced the backcountry influence in the General Court, all the old resentments had been rekindled by the rising pressure of taxation. Just before the attacks on the courts, a convention in Hampshire County listed seventeen grievances, more than a third of which dealt with taxation and government spending. One item indicted the entire "present mode of taxation as it operates unequally between the polls and estates, and between landed and mercantile interests." For more than 100 years the General Court had been hearing complaints that the merchant and capital classes were escaping their share of the general property tax. The back country, in its brief moment of legislative dominance in October 1775, had tried to redress this alleged imbalance. Defenders of commerce like O.P.Q. remonstrated that the taxes of that session were self-defeating, that the wealth and general prosperity of the commonwealth would be greater if it *lowered* its taxes on trade.

But many western farmers supporting Shays' Rebellion simply did not care if commerce flourished. In an excellent contemporary account of the rebellion, George Richards Minot traced part of its background to the division in the legislature "upon all questions of taxation." "The men of landed interest soon began to speak plainly against trade, as the source of luxury, and the cause of losing the circulating medium. The vices and indolence of the people were ascribed to its instrumentality. This was urged as a reason that the taxes should be thrown liberally upon commerce, since, if it supported them, the Commonwealth would be eased; and if it failed under the weight, they would be rid of so great a cause of political evil."[67]

Republican virtue was a favorite theme of the Revolutionary generation. Yet there is something contradictory in a tax revolt conducted under this banner. Talk of sacrifice for the public good rings hollow when attempts are made to shift one's tax burden to another, or lower it altogether.[68] The American Revolution was not restricted to this level. The slogan "No Taxation without Representation" implies taxation *with* representation. The independent states ultimately carried a much higher burden under their own legislators than under Parliamentary rule.

Once uncorked, the issue of taxation was hard to get back in the bottle. It developed along two main lines. First, the criteria for representation became more and more refined as unrepresented taxpayers demanded to have more say in government. Second, voters tried to restrict the size of the tax itself. The original colonial position required no great change in the state and local fiscal system. But quickly the institutional question of control of the public purse gave way to the economic question of control of the *level* of taxation.

In spite of the talk about republican virtue, the common answer was that taxes should be low. Massachusetts had fought the battle between commerce and communal virtue well before it launched the Revolution. The memory of classical republicanism gave a dimension of nobility to the struggle for independence and the framing of new governments. But the spirit of commerce was destined to triumph here, too. At the end of the eighteenth century, Mercy Otis Warren, a close friend of those true republicans John and Abigail Adams, wrote this memorable comment on her country's character: "From the general equality of fortune which had formerly reigned among them it may be modestly asserted, that most of the inhabitants of America were too proud for monarchy, yet too poor for nobility, and it is to be feared, too selfish and avaricious for a virtuous republic."[69]

We now leave Massachusetts, birthplace of the not quite virtuous republic, but will return two centuries and many chapters later. Our travels in the meantime will follow the growth of the country and its struggle to preserve and elaborate the ideals of the Revolution, mixed though they may be.

4

Phase Two
Lessons of New York

In 1843, the antislavery lawyer Henry Stanton had to leave his young bride, Elizabeth Cady Stanton, to go to Albany on business. His duties required him to listen to the state legislature wrangle over a bill to enlarge the Erie Canal. He must have fidgeted in his seat, because he complained that for four days the debate "shed darkness rather than light over the subject, and the chamber grew murky." Then one morning a strange figure took the floor, "a tallish man, with iron gray locks drooping on his shoulders, and wearing a mixed suit of plain clothes." Recalled Stanton: "The first sentences arrested my attention. A beam of light shot thru the darkness, and I began to get glimpses of the question at issue. Soon a broad belt of sunshine spread over the chamber. I asked a member, 'Who is that?' 'Michael Hoffman' was the reply."[1]

Almost forgotten now, Hoffman made a contribution to the history of the Tax Revolt that still shapes the politics of New York State. He belongs in the first rank of any fiscal pantheon. Hoffman was both a doctor and a lawyer, from the isolated upstate town of Herkimer, yet he had substantial national experience before entering the state legislature. He had served nearly a decade in the U.S. House of Representatives. A former chairman of the Committee on Naval Affairs, he was still sometimes referred to as "Admiral" Hoffman. His greatest contribution, however, came in Albany, where he ushered in the second phase of fiscal limitation.

In the first phase, Americans demanded representation to control the government's claims on their property. In the second, they began to realize that even a representative assembly could not be trusted with their pocketbooks. The threat of regular elections might still discourage legislators from imposing runaway taxation. Yet there were ways to hide spending from the voters. Foremost was borrowing. By issuing bonds, a government could reap an immediate return and leave repayment to future generations. Public debt, men like Hoffman painfully came to realize, was in reality a form of delayed taxation. It had the same ultimate effect of shriveling the economy, and its burden always came due much sooner than expected. Hoffman and his colleagues had the warning of David Hume to ponder: "The practice of contracting debt will almost infallibly be abused in every government. It would scarcely be more imprudent to give a prodigal son a credit in every banker's shop in London than to empower a statesman to draw bills, in this manner, upon posterity."[2] So Hoffman pioneered the idea of requiring a voter referendum on bond issues. This institution, now almost a commonplace, was a radical innovation at the time, just as Hoffman was considered a radical politican. Those in our time who have noticed his work have been impressed. In the judgment of the eminent New York State scholar Dixon Ryan Fox, "his financial plans and measures for the state, in their wisdom and consistency, should give him with historians something of the character of statesman."[3]

Michael Hoffman is more than the hero of this chapter. He represents a group of political leaders, later known as the "Barnburners," who played a major role in American politics from Andrew Jackson to Abraham Lincoln. This remarkable circle, largely the product of New York's upstate frontier, followed the national lead of the urbane Martin Van Buren, but its rough-hewn numbers included one man of at least equal presidential caliber: U.S. Senator and New York State Governor Silas Wright, who was eulogized in the Senate as a man who "had refused more offices, and higher, than he had ever accepted."[4] In their character and policies, they were Jacksonian Democrats even before Jackson.[5] Their campaign to limit debt offers an insight into the Jacksonian political economy that cuts like lightning through the historians' fog.

New York was an excellent battlefield for these principles. In the 1830s, it went through a period of overbuilding that culminated in a major fiscal crisis surprisingly similar to the debacle of recent memory. Hoffman's counterattack reached its peak in the state constitutional convention of 1846, in a prime example of the attempt to write a constitutional amendment that would control the government's use of money. One can debate at length how well the provisions worked. New York politicians quickly learned how to get around them, but at a cost that confirmed Hoffman's wisdom. Hoffman's shadow ultimately took a memorable revenge. The awesome spectacle of New York's 1975 fiscal crisis may well have generated the momentum of the Tax Revolt of the 1970s.

NEW YORK'S FIRST FISCAL CRISIS

The modern history of New York begins with the digging of the Erie Canal. Visionary leaders had long dreamed of developing the network of rivers and portages that the great Iroquois Confederacy had used for passage from the Hudson to the Great Lakes. Gouverneur Morris, one of the nationalist leaders in the 1787 federal Constitutional Convention, chaired an 1810 state commission to survey the canal route. When the federal government refused to help finance the project, New York, under the prodding of DeWitt Clinton, undertook the unprecedented task on its own. Clinton won election as governor in 1817, and a few months later, on the Fourth of July, ground-breaking for the canal began at Rome, the Great Carrying Place of the Indian canoe voyagers. Even before completion in 1823, the canal began to pay off. As it penetrated new sections of the interior, the price paid for newly accessible farm produce rose fourfold. New York City, which had voted against the project, began its rise to commercial predominance. For sixty years thereafter, much of the state's politics revolved around the benefits and costs of the canal.

For years, canal tolls exceeded projections and swelled the state treasury. "The people had begun to think that taxes need never be imposed again," wrote one canal historian, "for the waterways were looked upon as a veritable treasure trove for supplying funds."[6] But the fatal tendency of government upon any great success is to think it can do the same thing over and over with equal advantage regardless of the circumstances.

The canal-building enthusiasm followed a pattern that has become a recurring theme of New York State government. Because the Erie Canal successfully exploited the most favorable natural route in the East, the state began to commit its credit to every waterway that seemed remotely feasible and to some that were not. The legislature ordered the survey of forty canal routes and chartered some thirty-one canal companies. To satisfy the counties with no access to the canal network, the state chartered a railroad across the Southern Tier, the soon-to-be-notorious New York and Erie Railroad Company. These commitments seriously strained the state government's resources. In the aftermath of the national financial Panic of 1837, the state plunged into a very contemporary problem—a credit crisis.

The credit of the American states was already fragile. During the panic, several had already partially repudiated their debt. At the same time, New York's Canal Commission was taking a second look at a recently approved program of expansion and enlargement. Spending estimates had been far too low. The state was facing cost overruns of 100%, high even by twentieth-century standards, and a possible debt of $30 million. Canal revenues in 1840 were under $2 million. When this report reached the financial markets, New York's "stocks rapidly depreciated, its treasury was practically empty, money could not be borrowed for public uses for long terms, and it was with great difficulty that temporary loans could be procured to meet most pressing emergencies."[7] The financial crisis erupted just as the procanal, prospending Whig Party had won its greatest political triumph. William H. Seward, later a founder of the Republican Party and rival of Lincoln for its presidential nomination, was governor again and his party controlled both chambers of the legislature. He stubbornly defended his aggressive canal borrowing. Long-range toll projections, he argued, were sufficient to cover interest. The principle, he said, could be retired by the state's claim to the proceeds of federal public-land sales. Seward thus became the first New York governor to look for a financial bailout from Washington.

But New York voters wanted immediate controls on state spending. In 1842, Democrats took back the legislature. They quickly passed a rescue plan known as the "Stop and Tax" law. This measure suspended all but essential work on the canals, pledged canal revenue to redemption of its debt, and imposed a direct tax on real and personal property, the first in the state since 1827. The state's credit rose dramatically. Within months, bonds that had been discounted 20% were selling at par.[8]

The Stop and Tax law divided the Democrats into factions called "Barnburners" and "Hunkers." The Barnburners, the radical Democrats like Michael Hoffman who fervently pushed for fiscal controls, were supposedly named after a Dutch farmer who had burned down his barn to get rid of rats. The Hunkers, so called because of their "hunkering" after patronage, supported canal spending. The furious struggle over the canals gave rise to the 1846 constitutional convention, which can be seen as the state's first popular revolt against excessive government spending.

As the crisis passed, the Hunkers joined Whigs in appropriating more canal funds. Radical Democrats took alarm, feeling that the Stop and Tax law was being subverted. They concluded that the only way to protect the state's credit was through a constitutional amendment limiting the legislature's power to issue debt. Assemblyman Arphaxed Loomis, Hoffman's colleague from Herkimer, began to introduce two anti-debt "people's resolutions" in the legislature, but broader social currents were in flux and could be satisfied only by a full-fledged constitutional convention.

THE UPSTATE CAULDRON

New York in the early nineteenth century bubbled with extraordinary ferment. Displaced New Englanders were pouring into the upstate valleys, bringing with them a history of religious fervor but a decaying theology. This rootless Puritanism set loose in the desolate central New York winters produced countless spiritual upheavals. Religious revivals swept the region so frequently it became known as the "burned-over district." Sects and enthusiasms sprang up, some of which later swept the country. The Mormons came from there, as did the Millerites, who in 1843 donned white robes in Rochester and stood on rooftops to await the end of the world. (After several recalculations, their leader, William Miller, went off to found the Seventh-Day Adventists.) An upstate scandal about the murder of a renegade Freemason, and a fear that secret societies were subverting the republic gave birth to a powerful Anti-Mason Party that later melded into the Whigs. Massive immigration to New York City aroused the older stock to form a Native American Party that in 1844 elected a mayor. New York produced or gave a strong push to movements to promote temperance, prohibition, abolition, woman's rights, spiritualism, world peace, and the "Graham" cracker.[9]

This constant tumult, so freighted with ideas of equality and social reform, could not fail to turn against the state's surviving semifeudal institutions. One local but widely noted example was the patroonship. At mid-century, 1.8 million acres in the state were still being farmed under leaseholds. Rensselaerswyck, the largest surviving manor, spread over 436,000 acres around Albany and was occupied by more than 3,000 farms. The "Good Patroon," Stephen Van Rensselaer, had soothed resentments by letting his rent collections lapse, but when he died in January 1839 his tenants were shocked to learn that he had pledged his rent arrearages to cover his outstanding debts.

When his sons tried to collect, they encountered furious resistance. As negotiations failed, tenants organized the Anti-Rent movement, complete with a rural guerrilla auxiliary. Disguised as Indians, wearing sheepskins over their heads and calico dresses to their knees, crudely armed bands assembled on the blowing of tin dinner horns to block the sheriff and his posse from serving eviction papers. Grotesquely costumed groups on horseback terrorized rent-payers and those unwary enough to move onto foreclosed farms.

The protest attracted outside agitators from the National Reform movement, which advocated limited farm holdings and federal land sales only to settlers. The Reformers adopted the marvelously explicit slogan "Vote Yourself a Farm." As the turmoil spread down the Hudson, a mob in Delaware County surrounded a sheriff's posse that was attaching some livestock. In the jostle, shots cracked out, and the sheriff's deputy was cut down. Governor Silas Wright declared a state of insurrection. He moved in militia and largely ended the riding of the "Indians." But more moderate Anti-Renters maintained an organization which exerted considerable influence on state representatives and delegates to the upcoming constitutional convention.[10]

THE 1846 CONVENTION

As these agitations bubbled throughout the state, the convention movement came to a head in the legislature. Conservative Democrats tried to divert it by presenting only the "people's resolutions" for a referendum. But the proconvention coalition of Radical Democrats, Whigs, Native Americans, and Anti-Renters forestalled that device by refusing to give the proposed separate amendments the constitutionally required margin. When a referendum was finally called on whether to convoke a convention, it passed by better than six to one.

The convention assembled in Albany on June 1, 1846, the first in the state "which fully deserved to be styled a people's convention."[11] The 128 delegates (forty-eight of whom were born in New England states) were elected on the basis of manhood suffrage. Judges were made elective and remained so at all levels until very recently. Selection of state officials, such as comptroller, was taken from the legislature and given to the people. Local officials were also put on the ballot. Senate representation was changed entirely to single-member districts. A series of "antirent" provisions was added to the Bill of Rights, culminating in the statement that "all feudal tenures of every description, with all their incidents, are declared to be abolished. . . ."[12]

But the bitterest and lengthiest disputes concerned the state debt. This issue created schisms in the Democratic Party that shaped state politics for the next three decades. The split between the Barnburners and the Hunkers came from specific local interests. Hunkers had a direct stake in the canal, and Barnburners hailed from the counties that lay away from the route of the Erie. Yet the Barnburners had demonstrated earlier that they were willing to stand by their principles even when it hurt their home interests and threatened political disaster.[13]

Writing about later divisions, Michael Hoffman insisted, "Were we not in fact divided about measures, and that too on the most vital principles of public policy, and did not this diversity lead to all the dissensions?"[14] He had made it clear for years before the convention that his paramount concern in that body would be fiscal policy. In 1842, he wrote: "If we were to have further loans and additional debts, I go for a convention and a new constitution. Monopoly may hiss and locality may yell, but a convention of the people must be called to sit in judgement on the past and command the future."[15]

At the convention, Hoffman and his allies controlled most of what would later be considered the Jacksonian agenda. Hoffman's friend and neighbor from Herkimer, Arphaxed Loomis, chaired the Committee on Incorporations Other Than Municipal and Banking. This committee produced the constitutional article restricting special privileges for corporations, the issue at the heart of New York City's Loco-Foco movement. This reform Democratic movement, portrayed by New Deal historians as a protoproletarian party, was actually composed of small-business men devoted to laissez-faire economics. (The name comes from a then popular brand of self-igniting matches.) Support in debate came from State Comptroller Azariah C. Flagg. The convention was the political debut of the young Samuel Tilden, who had first attracted attention in 1837 with a series of articles defending Governor

Van Buren's suicidal but rigorously Smithian currency policy.

Hoffman himself, as chairman of the crucial Committee on Canals and Finance, was easily the dominant member of the convention. His report proposed the most serious innovations and prompted the most fascinating debate. In a series of forcefully stated provisions, he made the state accountable for its money as it had never been before. One section required legislative appropriation for state spending; it was the first time this basic principle had been put into New York State law. Other sections laid out the details of a sinking fund to retire the canal debt. In reaction to the excessive commitments to the railroads, Section 9 forbade the lending of state credit to "any individual, association or corporation." These sections have attracted the lion's share of the attention the legal historians have bestowed on the 1846 convention, yet Hoffman's great work came immediately after, in Sections 10 through 12.[16]

These provisions incorporated the People's Resolutions that Arphaxed Loomis had sponsored in the legislature. They set up an elaborate constitutional framework for popular control of the public debt. Section 10 allowed the state discretion to issue up to $1 million of debt to cover deficits or revenue shortfalls, actually a fairly generous allowance compared to later imitators. In a standard provision for exotic disasters, Section 11 allowed unlimited borrowing to repel invasion, suppress insurrection, or defend the state in war. But contracting any other debt required a law setting up a direct tax to pay interest and retire principal in eighteen years, and each of these laws required the approval of a majority of the people voting at a general election. To emphasize the gravity of the vote, this referendum could not be held when any other law, bill, or constitutional amendment was on the ballot.[17]

The convention debate on the voter referendum rose to a rich theoretical level. Some opponents objected that the direct vote subverted the principle of representative government. Alvah Worden, a lawyer from Saratoga County, objected that taking bond decisions from the legislature and referring them to the voters would "be saying to the world, in so many words, that republican government had proved a failure." He would not admit that the people "were incapable of judging of the acts of their representatives and of correcting their errors," and said that "you will disarm them of that vigilance in regard to the acts of their representatives that is so highly essential to the preservation of public liberty."[18]

Ansel Bascom, a native of the Finger Lakes region, added that the section "did change our representative government into a democracy. . . . It was going back to the old form of personal government as practiced by the Athenians and the Romans."[19]

These arguments have become a standard feature of the debate on the referendum, but Hoffman retorted that, rather than undermine the representative republic, his innovation would cure its most dangerous defect. If a legislator voted a direct tax, he would have to answer for it at the polls. But he could authorize debt with relative impunity. The loophole of borrowing, stated Hoffman, was "the greatest infirmity of republican government," and the bond referendum was the safest cure.

Hoffman left no doubt that debt was dangerous because it was a delayed form of taxation, and he emphatically denied that a state could tax its citizens into prosperity. "It was the accursed power of taxation that made pauperism, produced crime, misery and distress in all countries."[20]

According to the summary by the *Albany Evening Argus*, which served as the convention journal, Hoffman underscored this danger with a somewhat garbled reference to Montesquieu: "He thought it had been demonstrated by the researches of able men, that it was not the Goths and Vandals who overthrew the Empire of Rome, but the taxing officers, that eviscerated the Empire and thus invited the barbarians in. . . . If he was right in this, it behooves those who were desirous of securing free and republican government to find some limitation safe in practice to this most dangerous power." If the legislature makes bad law, said Hoffman, it can be induced to repeal it, but, "it is not so in relation to the subject of debts and compound interest. It is silent, creeps along, gets into the State, and when the act is once passed, the debt incurred, the obligation is as strong as death for its payment. That can only be wrung from the industry of the people, by taxes, direct or indirect." A special remedy is required. "Such a one must be found, or he apprehended representative government would not be successful. Looking into history, it would be found that the worse vice of the worse government is direct taxation, and if representative governments cannot be cured of that, he feared they would not long endure."[21] Hoffman concluded with a burst of Lockean rhetoric that illustrates how the bond referendum, a widespread feature of American state finance, derives from the grand theory of the *Second Treatise*. This peroration, showing as it does the continuity between John Locke and Jacksonian politics, deserves to be rescued from the crumbling fine print of the convention journal. "With all these guards, Mr. Hoffman said a reasonable protection was presented for the rights of property and the sacred rights of labor. The power to labor is the gift of heaven, and the property it produces is just as sacred as the source from which that power comes. The government should never ask for it, unless it can show as good a title for it, as the citizen has who produces it."[22]

Hoffman's rhetoric and the memory of the canal crisis were so powerful that his Whig opponents were reduced to pretending that there was no essential difference between them over principle. They took the parliamentary tack of sponsoring an even more radical alternative, the prohibition of all debt whatsoever. Hoffman and Loomis detected the ruse and argued forcefully that so inflexible a measure would soon be discredited by events. Warned Hoffman, "The legislature would in a few years get back into the debt contracting power, in full force, without any restrictions."[23] This ploy was rejected, and Hoffman's proposals, enshrining the vote of the people, won approval by a vote of 73 to 31.[24] In November, the voters approved the "people's constitution" by better than two to one.

The "people's convention" receives mixed reviews from historians. Critics invariably attack its excessive democracy. Some measures, such as the hectic schedule of legislative elections, did go too far and were subsequently abandoned. Others, such as direct election of judges, survived. But when a locality honors the idea of electoral approval of bond issues, the results must be called "successful." The recourse to the voters does put brakes on the volume of public debt, and when financial, economic, and other factors are equal, those issues that have the backing of public opinion have won a reputation for greater security. This outcome may confound some of the nineteenth-century attacks on democracy. Lord Macaulay's famous warning "Your constitution is all sail and no anchor" predicted specifically that the New York State legislature would despoil the rich to feed the poor.[25] Yet the financial sins of the framers of New York's constitution fall rather on the side of stinginess than prodigality. Pressure for spending came later, from the self-proclaimed elite (and its special constituencies), who chafed under the restrictions imposed by the multitudes.

THE POSTWAR TAX DEBATE

Surprisingly, New York's Jacksonians put such energy into securing constitutional curbs on debt that they remained silent about the best form of taxation. Well into the twentieth century, the state constitution was one of the few to lack the Lockean requirement for uniform and proportional taxation. An attempt to insert this language, in response to the post–Civil War wave of rising tax burdens, ran afoul of the conflict betwen real estate wealth and capital wealth.

The fluid politics of the 1850s and 1860s created a virtually inseparable jumble of party alignments. The radical Barnburners left the Democratic Party en masse over the slavery issue and joined the Republican faction historians then called "Radicals."[26] In supporting a vigorous war effort, they wound up supporting a far higher tax burden than that they had fought against in the canal debates. Tax policy remained a major sore spot in their postwar politics.

This ironic mixture of conflicts fed into the next period of constitutional ferment, when southern state constitutions were rewritten during and after Reconstruction. Radicals in the northern state governments produced a parallel wave of constitutional revisions. One observer sees a similarity and cross-fertilization between the northern constitutional revisions in New York, Illinois, and Pennsylvania and the south-

ern conventions.[27] The renewed attempts at fiscal limitation
came not only from resentment in the South at the excesses
of Radical rule but also from a national reaction to the sharply
rising tax burdens occasioned by the cost of the Civil War and
postwar reforms.

The initial postwar constitutional activity in New York
cut contrary to this trend. The convention of 1867 was a project of the Radical Republican coalition under Governor Reuben Fenton. This coalition had pushed an ambitious program
of institutional reforms (many of which, such as police commissions, gave Republicans a foothold in the large Democratic cities). In calling the convention, Fenton specifically
cited the problem of the state's Civil War debt and the "need
to revise antiquated taxation stipulations." But the major issue became the attempt to remove the property bar to Negro
voting, a liberal-minded effort that brought electoral disaster
on the Radicals.[28]

Clear-cut as the partisan division was on the suffrage issue, it dissolved into a jumble of crosscurrents when the convention took up taxation. Despite a broad consensus that rising
tax burdens were economically unhealthy (or "withering," in
nineteenth-century parlance), a bitter conflict developed over
the various means of shifting this burden. As was true in state
after state, capital escaped a large share of the burden because the tax assessor had no way of determining its value.
The 1867 convention rejected several means of controlling this
evasion.

The first of these efforts came in a minority report from
the Finance Committee proposing the "uniform rule" for taxing all real and personal property. The proposed version would
also have forbidden the deduction of indebtedness from the
assessed value of this property. A common ploy for a man rich
in capital was to claim an inflated level of debt. So this measure predictably was endorsed by the "landed interest" as a
means of shifting more of the tax burden to the commercial
and financial interest.

A delegate from the commercial capital, New York City,
counterattacked by calling for a constitutional provision to
require assessment of real estate at its actual cash value. Such
a measure would have shifted the burden back to the rural

counties, where locally elected assessors habitually made low valuations of their constituents' landholdings. According to Clifton K. Yearley, real estate in some of New York's upstate counties was assessed at 17% of market value, whereas in New York City assessments ran to 50% of market value. In subsequent constitutional conventions, local election of assessors became a furious "home rule" issue.[29]

In the confusing debate, one central point remained clear. Whoever wound up bearing the brunt of the tax burden feared being pushed into economic decline. Delegates representing the rising commercial economy warned about stiff enforcement problems: "A little matter of this kind, though it is in but a single sentence, may drive the commerce from our midst to other States."[30]

On the other hand, asked a bitter upstate Republican, was the tax system to continue to subsidize capital and commerce at the expense of the farmer, "rushing out and grinding down to powder the honest yeomanry of the country who pay the taxes of this State today out of the lands upon which they live, for the purpose of creating an advantage and benefit to the commerce of the State?"[31]

On a last-ditch vote to strike out the entire section, all stripes of Republican and Democrat appear on both sides of the roll call. The most evident line of division is economic and geographic. The minority voting against uniform taxation seems largely to come from commercial New York City; the majority in favor is swollen by upstate, rural delegates of all political persuasions.[32] The taxation section went so far that it alarmed the commercial interests but not far enough that it satisfied the rural voter. Thanks to the suffrage provision, furthermore, any product of the Radicals' convention had a serious problem winning public approval. The taxation section was submitted as a separate question from the proposed constitution, but the voters rejected both.[33]

DEMOCRATS SEIZE THE TAX ISSUE

The turmoil in the 1867 convention had at least one lasting effect. Democratic strategists saw a way to rebuild their shat-

tered party on the intense Republican division over the tax
issue. The Jacksonians who had remained Democrats thought
they had a potential fifth column in the Barnburners who had
turned Republican over the slavery issue. In the turmoil of the
1850s, most younger Free-Soil Democrats had moved into the
new party, giving it a stronghold in upstate counties that had
never gone Whig. More than a quarter of the New York State
Republicans had started out as Jacksonian Democrats, giving
their party one of the highest proportions of ex-Democrats of
the state GOPs.

A common theme underlies Michael Hoffman's attack on
debt and the Free-Soil Democrats' hostility to a slave work
force. The 1846 provisions for bond referendums were intended to prevent the productive class from bearing a stulti-
fying level of future taxation. The "free-soil" campaign was
one more step in preserving a favorable market for this class.
Unlike the abolitionists, who were concerned about the fate
of the Negro slaves, the free-soil partisans tried to keep blacks
altogether out of the western territories to prevent them from
competing with a white work force.

Some older Radicals refused to make this transition,
however. Arphaxed Loomis stated that he could not join the
party of William Seward because, in the past, "he had always
been opposed to Mr. Seward on all points except on the slavery question."[34] The hope of postwar Democrats was to en-
tice the former Barnburners back into their party. The
instrument was a much older Samuel Tilden, Hoffman's junior colleague in the 1846 convention. To complete the historical cycle, Tilden decided to seek the 1874 Democratic
nomination for governor, in part because western Democrats
and Republicans were pushing a bill to subsidize the Erie Canal
by raising taxes. Although some hard-core tax-cutters later
expressed disillusionment, Tilden seemed to restore the
Barnburner tradition. In the words of one recent historian: "At
last, the Democracy had nominated a legitimate Jacksonian,
committed to the continuities in party policy-making . . . who
could reestablish the old political coalition the slavery issue
had shattered."[35]

THE NEW CONSENSUS: PICK ON THE CITY

The Democratic reformers hesitated to plunge once more into the crossfire on state taxation, however. In pushing for fiscal limitation, they turned to an area in which they could build a certain consensus, the control of New York City. Across the nation, the 1870s drive to control government focused on municipalities. The drafters of these constitutional measures may have thought they were in a mopping-up operation. The 1840s limits on debt applied mainly to the state governments. Even if they were meant to apply to localities, the courts ruled otherwise. Complained a Michigan tribunal, "Thus a way was opened by which the whole purpose of the constitutional provisions quoted might be defeated. The State could not aid a private corporation with its credit, but it might require each of its townships, cities and villages to do so."[36]

The focus on the cities also arose from more blatantly ethnic and political concerns. Yearley has painted a richly detailed account of the near hysteria with which the older-stock middle class greeted the rising political power of Irish Catholic immigrants in major cities. This power was especially ominous because it was coupled with a willingness to raise local taxes and debt for welfare programs, or distribution to political retainers. Yearley writes: "Linkage of party, spoils, patronage, and soaring public burdens made indictments of party seem easy. The 'horde of officeholders, retainers, and party scavengers,' or what Cornell's president described as 'a crowd of illiterate peasants, freshly raked in from Irish bogs . . . Bohemian mines, or Italian robbers nests,' were pictured as an endless human chain passing through the public coffers."[37]

Thomas Cooley departs from his judicial tone to deplore bills allowing localities to buy railroad stock: "It cannot be denied that this species of legislation has been exceedingly mischievous in its results, that it has created a great burden of public debt, for which in a large number of cases the anticipated benefit was never received, and that, as is likely to be the case where municipal governments take part in projects foreign to the purposes of their creation, it has furnished unusual facilities for fraud and public plunder, and led almost inevitably, at last, to discontent; sometimes even to disorder and violence." Implicitly offering a remedy, he continues, "In some of the recent revisions of State constitutions, the legislature has been expressly prohibited from permitting the municipalities to levy taxes or incur debts in aid of works of public improvement, or to become stockholders in private corporations." [38]

In New York, ironically, the lead in imposing a fiscal limit, at least in name, came from the most notorious boodler of them all, Boss William Marcy Tweed. In 1871, at the peak of his power, Tweed procured a "Two Per Cent Bill," authorizing the newly established Board of Apportionment to levy an amount for city and county expenses not exceeding 2% of the total assessed value of taxable property. Tax levies previously had been set by the state legislature, so this bill fit naturally into Tweed's program of home rule. It also coincided with his tactic, brilliantly executed in the home-rule Tweed Charter of the year before, of co-opting reform programs and turning them to his own purposes.

Although the Two Per Cent Bill attracted some reform support, it contained a very wide loophole. The definition of total taxable property was so flexible that it could be expanded indefinitely by adding fictitious property. (Of course, tax evasion on personal property was so massive that a fictitious assessment might come closer to the truth than one based on actual returns.) This "limit" in reality expanded Tweed's power to tax. It was repealed two years later, after Tweed's sudden fall. In 1884, it was restored as part of an overall debt limit. By this time, the movement toward state boards of equalization had imposed a measure of discipline on local assessment practices.

The 1884 limit established a constitutional structure that persists to this day. New York City's general obligation indebtedness is limited to 10% of the assessed value of its taxable real estate, using a five-year rolling average. Its real estate tax for operating expenses cannot exceed 2½% of the same base. (Debt service was excluded from this limit and now takes up the bulk of the real estate tax.) [39]

As both the city and the state were subsequently to show, the long-term effect of constitutional fiscal limitations is highly

questionable. Within five years of the 1846 convention, the
state legislature was attempting to evade the bond referendum. By 1915, in spite of the debt limitations, the total net
indebtedness of New York's municipalities made up more than
30% of the entire municipal debt in the country.[40] And the
pattern of evasion had not yet reached its peak. The experience of New York in the third quarter of the twentieth century is a sobering comment on the limits of dictating long-term
fiscal policy through constitutional language.

5

The Fall and Rise of New York

History repeated itself in New York in the mid-1970s. Substitute Nelson Rockefeller for William Seward, housing authorities for the Erie Canal, and the story that unfolds, while not exactly identical to the financial crisis of the 1840s, shares an astonishing similarity in its crucial turning points. Indeed, one may hypothesize a general chronology for fiscal crises. Details and triggering incidents vary, but all of these crises run through five general phases: accumulation, discovery, collapse, austerity, and recovery.

Accumulation refers to the period in which debts, spending commitments, and other postponed costs, such as pension liabilities and deferred maintenance, are allowed to build to unmanageable proportions. In the Erie Canal crisis, this period coincided with Governor Seward's ambitious program of canal enlargement and extension.

Discovery is the point at which the extent of the accumulated costs becomes widely known. Frequently, although not invariably, some series of official disclosures shocks financial circles and the broader public into paying attention. This happened in 1841–42 when the canal commissioners acknowledged their cost overruns and the state Assembly Ways and Means Committee, led by Michael Hoffman, issued a critical report on state finances.

Collapse may be too dramatic a term, but this phase is the most spectacular. The financial markets react to the discovery of unmanageable costs with a prudence not exhibited earlier. The state, faced with operating deficits, depleted cash reserves, and negative cash flow may depend on borrowed money to maintain its current operations. The customary lenders refuse to renew their loans. Political leaders scramble desperately, and perhaps unsuccessfully, to find alternate financing. This phase was not as severe in Governor Seward's case as in the history to follow, but state operations were impaired.

Austerity follows, as the authorities retrench. Their primary goal is to restore positive cash flow, although they must also deal with the accumulated costs. The state legislature introduced this phase vigorously in 1842 with the Stop and Tax law suspending canal work and raising revenue with the first direct state tax in fifteen years.

Recovery ends the crisis, as the government regains its credit standing and resumes a more normal level of activity. Usually, however, it proceeds with more caution and vastly improved fiscal controls. The strong action of the 1842 legislature restored all state bonds to par within eighteen months, but the consummation of the period came with the financial innovations of the 1846 constitution, which required popular control of public debt.

ACCUMULATION: NEW YORK
FORGETS A LESSON

The first attempt to bypass the 1846 provision for bond referendums came scarcely five years later. Canal revenues continued strong, but state officials worried that without a speedier schedule of enlargements the waterway might start losing traffic to railroads and other routes. So Governor Washington Hunt persuaded the 1851 legislature to authorize certificates in effect selling in advance the surplus revenue of the canal for up to twenty-one years. According to the statute, the state was not obligated to make up shortfalls in these revenues or to pay off the certificates from any other revenues. Thus, in order to get around its earlier invention of the bond referendum, New York invented the revenue bond. The state Court of Appeals declared the act unconstitutional, but not before $1.5 million of these certificates had been sold. The legislature then incorporated the revenue bond in a constitutional amendment. This loophole not only allowed the government to circumvent the people, it also evolved into one of the main avenues through which the fiscally irresponsible have accumulated their deficits. The rapid growth of "limited liability" debt in New York, specifically to avoid voter referendums, marked the beginning of the "accumulation" phase of the 1975 fiscal crisis.[1]

During this period, running from the late 1950s to 1975, the state's general obligation debt stayed roughly constant. This is the bond and note debt backed by the total extent of state resources, its "full faith and credit." New York State notes, or short-term debt, must be paid within a year. The long-term bonds require approval in a voter referendum. So, as far as this category is concerned, Michael Hoffman's statecraft remains effective. But state finance in general, and New York's in particular, has been marked by the ballooning of special kinds of debt insulated from this voter control. These limited liability issues carry the backing mainly of the special-district or "public-benefit" authority that produced them. These arrangements, sometimes supplemented by special devices like "lease-purchase" deals, have allowed state and local governments to incur better than $20 billion of debt a year without the approval or even the scrutiny of the taxpayer.[2]

Public-authority borrowing in particular has been designed to evade popular control. According to one recent study, "public officials have increasingly resorted to nonguaranteed debt for corporate projects that are not intended to pay for themselves but are heavily, if indirectly, subsidized by government and its taxpayers. Authority bonds of this type have great appeal because most of them are held to be exempt from all the dollar ceilings, requirements for special elections, interest rate limits, and other constitutional encumbrances on general obligation debt."[3]

For more than half a century, these public authorities have been one of the most distinctive features of New York State government.

THE PUBLIC AUTHORITIES EMPIRE

Originally meant to accomplish temporary tasks, New York's public authorities began their growth as permanent empires with the founding of the Port Authority of New York and New Jersey in 1921. Nominally designed to end a century-old dispute between the two states over Hudson River and New York harbor transportation, the authority issued its first bonds after 1926. It now has its name on nearly $2 billion in outstanding bonds, backed by revenues from its $4.6 billion in assets. (These include the three major New York region airports, the World Trade Center, and a variety of marine terminals, tunnels, and bus stations.)[4]

The first to realize the potential of public authorities for empire building was the phenomenal Robert Moses. During his career, Moses controlled a network of up to ten such entities from his base in the toll-rich Triborough Bridge and Tunnel Authority (TBTA). He brilliantly exploited the nature of the municipal bond market to secure his position. The TBTA was meant to go out of existence after it retired its outstanding bonds, but by constantly refunding its debt and applying the proceeds to new projects, Moses deferred this date indefinitely. Further, he insulated his powers from legislative repeal by writing them into bond covenants. The bonds were a constitutionally protected contract between the issuer and the buyer. If the terms of sale specifically promised that the authority of the chairman would not be altered, then the legislature, or anyone else, was barred from acting for the life of the bond.[5]

The growing power of the authorities became a major issue in the New York constitutional convention of 1938. Over the vigorous objections of delegate Robert Moses, the body adopted an amendment forbidding the legislature from accepting any liability for authority bonds. Sponsors of the measure argued that most authorities "were established simply to evade debt limitations imposed in the Constitution.'' If their bonds were still to be treated as ''full faith and credit'' obligations of the state (as a contemporary Court of Appeals decision had seemed to indicate), the bond underwriters would be getting ''something for nothing.'' The voters subsequently approved this prohibition, and it remains in the state constitution.[6]

THE ROCKEFELLER EVASION

The modern empire builder of the Empire State was not Robert Moses, but Nelson Rockefeller. During his fifteen years as governor, Rockefeller's energetic personality and the judicious application of his personal wealth helped him reshape the state, for better or for worse. He remains one of the state historical figures who, like Huey Long in Louisiana and Hiram Johnson in California, leave an enduring institutional legacy. Rockefeller's distinctive bequest, and a major implement of his power as governor, was a vastly expanded network of public authorities. Their capital spending and borrowing far outstripped that of the state itself, yet it was all done ''off-budget,'' with only remote supervision by the legislature and none at all by the electorate.

When Rockefeller was first elected governor, in 1958, some twenty statewide public-benefit authorities owed less than $3 billion in outstanding bonds and notes. These were mostly traditional revenue bonds. By the time he resigned in 1973 to run for president, the number of these entities had doubled and their outstanding debt had quadrupled. More important, Rockefeller finished the job of insulating them from popular control through the invention of the ''moral obligation'' bond. The evolution of this device is best traced through the history of New York State's housing program, which was to Rockefeller what the canals were to Seward.

In the early 1950s, the two state legislators who ran the Joint Legislative Committee on Housing plumped for a program of state borrowing to aid middle-income housing construction. They were Senator MacNeil Mitchell, a Manhattan Republican, and Assemblyman Alfred J. Lama, a Brooklyn

Democrat; hence the Mitchell-Lama program. For this program multiple-unit middle-income housing companies accept limits on their profits in return for tax breaks and low-interest mortgages financed through tax-exempt bonds. The lower cost of the money obtained through municipal bonds is the key to the public-authority arrangement. By tradition, and some say constitutional prohibition, the federal government does not tax income an investor receives from a "municipal," i.e., state or local, bond. To a person in the higher income tax brackets, a lesser amount of untaxed income can be just as valuable as a higher payment from which the federal government takes its 40% or more. So municipal bonds pay an interest rate up to two percentage points lower than taxable corporate bonds.

At first the borrowing for the housing program was to be through state general obligation bonds, requiring voter approval. But the first Mitchell-Lama issue barely squeaked through the referendum, a second one failed, and a third, in the year of Rockefeller's election, passed by a margin only a shade larger than the first.[7]

This program was stalled because voters remained skeptical about its necessity or wisdom, a skepticism amply justified by subsequent events. But Rockefeller determined to remove the roadblock of voter approval. Instead of financing Mitchell-Lama through general obligation bonds, he set up a Housing Finance Agency (HFA). Under legislation of March 1960, this authority was to borrow under its own name, limited only by a legislative debt ceiling. Thus no referendum would be required. Unlike the Port Authority or the TBTA, however, it could not be counted on to generate the kind of revenue that would bring the bond buyers clamoring to its door. Rockefeller turned to the noted bond lawyer (later U.S. attorney general) John Mitchell to solve this problem. And Mitchell devised what became known as the "moral obligation" instrument.

The constitution writers in 1938 thought they had closed off most routes by which the state could be dragged into paying for an authority's bad debts. But they left one loophole: direct appropriation for operating expenses. Mitchell turned this loophole into a major breach in the constitution. His idea was to have the HFA set up a fund that would cover one year's worth of debt service on its bond issues and to have the legislature undertake to replenish this account if the agency ever had to draw it down. The state thus assumed an obligation only for the intervening fund, not for the bonds themselves. This obligation was binding only as a promise, not as a contract. If the HFA or something like it ever failed to meet a payment to its creditors, it would be a default only of the agency, not of the state. Rockefeller promised that the arrangement would get the HFA off the ground while costing the state "not one penny."[8]

At first the arrangement worked. Thanks to initially conservative management, the HFA confined itself to moneymaking projects. But, as with the Erie Canal, one successful project makes government think it can duplicate the idea ad infinitem. Rockefeller was the politician least able to resist the temptation. When the staff of the HFA planned a bond issue of $50 million, he pushed for an issue of $250 million. Frustrated by the HFA's relatively cautious pace, he planned a more daring successor.

In 1967, Rockefeller unveiled his proposal for an Urban Development Corporation (UDC), with the broadest powers yet given an authority. It would finance industrial and housing projects, but, unlike the HFA, it would also plan them and carry them out. It would have broad power to override local zoning and take shortcuts in state procedures. The UDC bill was working its way through the legislature when, on April 4, 1968, the Reverend Martin Luther King, Jr., was assassinated in Memphis. Rockefeller called for an immediate vote on April 9 and flew to Atlanta for King's funeral. The Assembly balked. Speakers doubted whether the bill would really help the poor. On a first vote, it lost. Rockefeller immediately flew back to Albany and began twisting arms. Late that night, the Assembly reversed its vote, and the UDC was in operation.

Operations of the UDC soon bore out the predictions of its most severe critics. It was based on a fatal contradiction: that it would pay back its bonds and become self-sufficient while rushing ahead with high-risk projects. Yet the agency's leaders never seemed to worry about the first horn of their dilemma. In its first year, the UDC followed what one employee subsequently called a "fail-smash" policy. It repeatedly took on commitments exceeding its debt limit and then pressured the legislature to raise the debt limit.

Yet the UDC bungled its borrowing. In spite of its tax exemption, it wound up paying 8% on bonds it had issued to pay for mortgages it had already made at 7.5%. If you are borrowing money at one interest rate, and want to make a profit in the world of finance, you have to lend it out again at a higher rate. The UDC did the opposite. From 1970 on, according to testimony before an investigating commission, the UDC had to pay more to borrow money than its projects could earn. Even worse, some of its high-risk projects lived up to their description and failed to earn the rent to pay back even these cut-rate mortgages. UDC chief executive Edward J. Logue measured his success in units built, not revenue flows. Successful as he was in his own terms, the UDC became so overextended that any interruption in its ability to borrow would quickly plunge it into default.

Default finally came in February 1975, triggering a chain of discoveries that collapsed the credit of an even more vulnerable New York City, tottered the entire structure of the state's moral obligation authorities, and threatened the state itself.[9] By this time Governor Rockefeller's network of public authorities had evaded the constitutional debt limits on a massive scale scarcely comprehended by the average New Yorker. For every dollar of "full faith and credit" debt authorized by a vote of the taxpayers, the unelected, little-noticed authorities owed four.[10]

Yet another revenue-raising ploy in New York had created still one more category of debt, nearly equal in amount to the voter-approved issues. This device consisted of state lease-purchase agreements, said to be another invention of John Mitchell. In this arrangement, localities issued bonds to put up buildings to be leased to the state; the bonds were backed by the rent the state had already agreed to pay. The state thus managed to pay for the same building twice. The most egregious example of this genre is the Albany Mall. Nearly $1 billion in Albany County bonds (which will cost nearly $2 billion to retire) have been issued to construct the marching marble towers of the Empire State Plaza, the state office-building complex that preserves the memory of Nelson Rockefeller in the heart of the old patroonship of Rensselaerswyck.[11]

The unvoted, off-budget empire of borrowing-and-spending authorities stood at the center of Rockefeller's power. The directors of these agencies were his loyalists, frequently bound even closer to him by outstanding personal loans in the hundreds of thousands of dollars.[12] The constant building they undertook won him the valuable electoral support of the construction unions, and their completed projects were the proudest monuments of his administration.

Yet the problems they created were also uniquely his doing. Instead of costing taxpayers "not one penny," the housing authorities alone have required nearly $1 billion in direct state appropriations to keep afloat. This unexpected turn of events has contributed to a debilitating level of taxation. If voters had been asked to approve these buildings, they might never have been built. Rockefeller would have been deprived of some monuments, but the taxpayers would have been spared some serious problems.

NELSON TAXAFELLER

While debt was accumulating in the invisible empire of the public authorities, another set of burdens was piling up very visibly. New York's budget more than quadrupled from fiscal year 1959 to 1973 (Rockefeller's last in office), and the state tax burden soared. In 1965, nineteen states had higher tax burdens than New York; by 1975, New York was far and away the highest.[13] During this tenure Rockefeller asked the legislature for 18 separate tax votes. According to a "sympathetic yet critical" scholarly study, "No other governor in this century came to his legislature with so many requests for tax increases as did Rockfeller."[14]

New Yorkers have paid the state income tax since 1919, but it was Rockefeller who made it the steeply progressive and destructive levy it ultimately became. He had scarcely arrived in Albany in 1959 when he offered the state's first $2-billion budget and the largest tax increase in its history.

New York

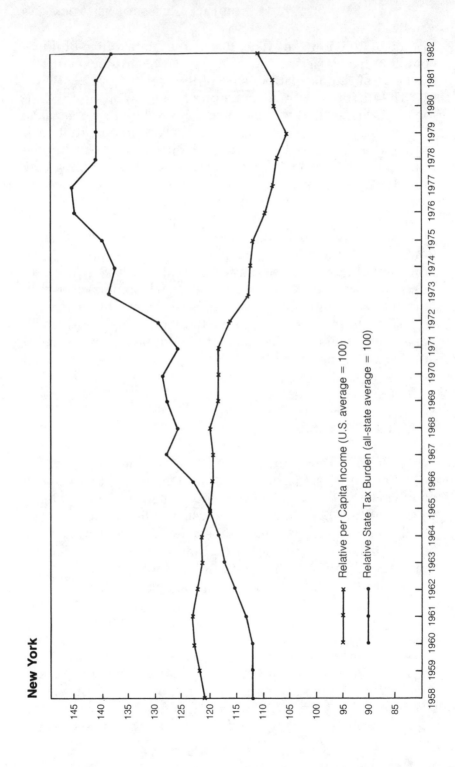

Relative per Capita Income (U.S. average = 100)

Relative State Tax Burden (all-state average = 100)

Blaming his predecessor W. Averell Harriman, for a budget deficit, he asked a very reluctant legislature for a 35% rise in the income tax. He added three new brackets at the top of the schedule and introduced withholding. Several legislators lost their seats the next year for supporting the measure, but Rockefeller wove it into his own reelection rhetoric as an act of political courage. During his first term the tax increase was successful. The automatic withholding captured an estimated half million new taxpayers, and for two years the tax yielded $100 million more than projected.[15]

In the election-year budget of fiscal 1961–62, Rockefeller declared a one-time 10% refund totaling $90 million. During the campaign, stating "I won't let you down," he pledged no new taxes. But redeeming this pledge required increasingly desperate budget shuffles, and in 1965 Rockfeller was back again for a new levy. In a confrontation that ran into the new fiscal year, he bludgeoned and horse-traded the Democratic legislature into accepting a 2% sales tax. In 1969, the rate went up to 3%. Following Rockefeller's political circadian calendar, the main tax action in election-year 1970 was an increase in income tax deductions. But in the 1971 recession, the major crisis arrived. As the preceding year's budget fell $250 million in the red but spending plans continued unabated, Rockefeller asked for $1.1 billion in new taxes. The legislature balked at first, remembering the electoral losses blamed on the 1965 vote, but in a December special session the governor got most of what he asked for. Personal income taxpayers now faced a 2½% surcharge for five years. The top bracket went up again, to 15% on taxable incomes over $25,000. Deductions and credits were pared. And the sales tax went up to 4%.[16]

As Rockefeller piled on the sales and income taxes, he also began to worry publicly about the harm taxation could do to the state's economy. In early 1971, he told a meeting of county executives, "New York State is very close to the limit of what we can raise through additional taxes without very seriously affecting the growth and vitality of our economy and future job opportunities." In his budget fight, Rockefeller pledged to avoid taxes "that affect the present economic structure of the state."[17] Yet he made a fatal mistake in deciding what these taxes might be. He firmly believed that the main influence on the state's business climate was the level of its business taxation. He fought to pass personal taxes instead of business taxes. In 1971 he boasted, "I am proud to say that in the past 11 years there has not been a single new business tax in New York State."[18] This policy produced a substantial shift in the tax burden. In 1959, business directly paid some 20% of the total state-level tax bill, and individuals paid 60%. By 1973, the business share had dropped to 15% whereas that of individuals had risen sharply, to 74%.[19]

Through these programs, observe Rockefeller's academic biographers, "he left New Yorkers the highest taxed people in the nation at the end of his term in office. Though he often expressed a concern for economic growth and sought to act on this concern, when forced to choose, the governor nearly always gave priority to tax increases in order to maintain or improve service levels."[20]

MEANWHILE, BACK IN THE CITY . . .

An even more rapid build-up of the taxpayer's burden was under way in New York City. In 1960, 46.2% of the state's population lived in the 300 square miles south of Westchester and west of Nassau counties. The city's budget slightly exceeded the state's General Fund, at $2.4 billion, and could claim to be second in size to the federal budget. Under the dough-faced regime of the clubhouse Democrats, the traditionally liberal Mayor Robert F. Wagner (1954–65) shunned sharp rises in spending and, even more, in taxes. The city was in a state of "equilibrium." Its population dropped slightly from 1950 to 1960, largely from the suburban migration to the north and east. The beginning of the decline in manufacturing jobs was balanced by the growth of service industries and corporate headquarters.

This equilibrium began to wobble in 1961 when, in a startling conversion, Mayor Wagner decided to run against himself. The county leaders had grown worried about his apparent ineffectiveness and were looking for a new candidate, so the two-term incumbent mayor announced he would seek reelection by campaigning against "boss rule." In the course of his sweeping primary victory, Wagner became, according to one fiscal historian, "possibly the first mayor in the country to organize the bureaucracy as a political force."[21] The potential impact of this new arrangement took several years to materialize, but city employment and labor costs began to rise sharply in his last term.

Discouraged from seeking major new taxes by City Comptroller Abraham Beame, Wagner resorted mainly to budget shuffles to cover mounting deficits. He ran down cash reserves, transferred operating expenses to the capital budget, and dipped into capital funds for operating accounts. The property tax rate rose as steadily as the statutory limit would allow, although about half of the increased revenues actually came from the growth in assessed value of the property tax base. (This technical distinction becomes important later on.) The sales tax went from 1% in 1945 to 4% in 1963. (It dropped back to 3% in 1965 in a political deal in which Wagner supported Rockefeller's state sales tax. The state made up the city's lost revenue by assigning it the proceeds of the state stock transfer tax.) The budget manipulation reached its limit in fiscal 1965–66, the year of John V. Lindsay's election as mayor. The budget year ended with a deficit exceeding $300 million covered by five-year bonds and one-year notes.[22] After his election, Lindsay complained that he would be taking over as "a receiver in bankruptcy."

Lindsay came into office in a burst of fashionable enthusiasm. Standing six foot four, with heroically chiseled features, he was 'preppy" if not patrician and sufficiently if not fabulously rich. He had conducted himself well as a U.S. representative from Manhattan's East Side, the only part of that borough willing to elect a Republican, and he had impressed the public, if not his peers, as the leader of the GOP's liberal wing in Congress. His predominant public mode was moralism trending toward arrogance. Following Rockefeller's model of political courage, Lindsay's first act in office was to seek a major package of new taxes.

Between Lindsay's election and his inauguration, a panel appointed by Mayor Wagner and headed by Bowery Savings Bank Chairman Earl B. Schwulst proposed a "unified plan of fiscal salvation" for the city. It called, most notably, for increased state and federal aid, consolidation of business taxes, and a brand-new personal income tax of 2% on all who earned their income in the city. The report criticized the city's "strongly regressive" tax system. The flat-rate income tax, it said, would introduce mild progressivity and would automatically produce additional revenues as city incomes grew. This package would have minimal impact on the city's economy, argued the report, adding that "steep progressive rates on top of the New York State income tax, already among the most progressive state income taxes in the country, might have more serious economic effects."[23] Although Lindsay called the income tax proposal "the ultimate last resort," he embraced the idea within four months.[24] His own package, however, introduced the progressive rates the Schwulst Commission had warned against.

The mayor asked the state legislature to approve an income tax starting with 1% at $1,000 and rising in $2,000 brackets to 5% for all taxable income over $15,000. "New York City is faced with a choice between financial disaster and financial health," he told his citizens in a "fireside chat." "When a city cannot provide safety and fire prevention and good hospitals and schools, an endless downward spiral begins. Business moves away, jobs are lost, less money comes in, and even fewer services can be provided."[25] The legislature, finding the Schwulst Commission's warning more persuasive than Lindsay's, deadlocked on the income tax for three months and finally trimmed down its progressivity. The version that went into effect on July 1, 1966, started at 0.4% for residents with taxable income under $1,000 and climbed in eight brackets to 2.0% on incomes of $30,000 and up. The "commuter tax" was imposed separately at a much lower flat rate.[26]

With a quarter of a billion dollars in fresh revenue, about half from the income tax, Lindsay had a relatively easy time of the next two budget years. Wall Street was gunslinging through the "go-go" years, real estate was booming, and the city economy seemed vibrant. The city population edged back to its 1950 level, and the work force in 1969 reached its all-time high. Unchecked by any immediately apparent revenue worries, Lindsay let his first three budgets grow at an average rate of 16%. Spending at the end of fiscal year 1969 (June 30, 1969) was more than half again as high as in Wagner's last budget. But the glow on the economy was the flush of a terminal fever. When it peaked in 1969, fiscal collapse followed rapidly.

WHERE THE MONEY WENT

The spending under Lindsay and Rockefeller makes a powerful case for tax limitation. Even though Lindsay emphasized safety and fire prevention in his fireside chat to support the income tax, very little of the new revenue went into traditional services. New types of spending drained off much of the cash. The fastest-growing items were housing, higher education, and welfare. During its heyday, New York City liked to brag that it provided the widest range of services available in any American municipality. During its fiscal crisis, it complained loudly about its welfare burden. To be sure, welfare is now primarily a county or state responsibility. New York City, which pays 25% of the support payments, shoulders a larger share than any other city. From 1965 to 1970, the welfare caseload in the city rose from 531,000 souls to 1,165,000. The budget impact was undeniably devastating, yet the city conveniently forgot to mention that it had originally assumed the welfare responsibility by choice to keep the state from reducing the benefits. Nor did it explore the possibility that the high benefit levels were a major cause for the growth in the rolls.

Furthermore, the growth in subsidized housing and City University costs was entirely voluntary. Lindsay had tried to placate a radical student upheaval on the city-run campuses by promising open admissions; expansion of the system raised costs and lowered standards. The economic perversity of the Mitchell-Lama program was too great a temptation for the city to resist. The city housing authority rivaled the UDC in its tendency to get into money-losing financing arrangements. As a direct result of city policy, housing and higher education doubled their share of the budget.

Yet the most severe spending pressure came not from

specific programs but from the underlying cost of paying city workers. Municipal salaries consume better than 60% of the total budget, and in Lindsay's first six years, labor costs grew by 90%. The main pressure came in fringe benefits and pensions, as union members asked for indirect payment to keep out of higher tax brackets. The full bill for these items, reflected in the high level of unfunded pension liability, remains to be rendered.

State spending accelerated from similar pressures. Due in part to intense pressure from New York City, social programs drained resources away from traditional services. The state had one problem area unique to itself, however. Reflecting Nelson Rockefeller's personal interests, capital construction grew fivefold in the decade after 1959. Start-up costs for his beloved public authorities grew from almost nothing to an outstanding total exceeding $1.5 billion.[27]

Beyond the programs came the debt. The deferred cost of this borrowing came due only after Lindsay and Rockefeller left office. Under Lindsay's successors, debt service consumed 11% of the city budget, an amount that exceeded the appropriations for police, fire, and "municipal services" combined.

Why did these men do it? Why did their spending go haywire? It was not the declining economy. That came later, as the tax burden choked off the state's last flush of prosperity. The spending growth coincided with the economic boom of the late sixties. One answer for Lindsay lies in the fragmentation of New York City's political structure. Since Wagner's 1961 primary, the city bureaucracy and municipal unions had begun to replace the borough machines as the most cohesive force in city elections. Lindsay had to pay heavily, as in the teachers' contract of 1969, to overcome their hostility, even if all he gained was their neutrality. Lindsay furthermore relied heavily on the new brand of municipal social services to build a constituency of his own. His pattern of support shifted dramatically between his first election and his second. In 1965, he received about 37% of the vote in the most heavily black assembly districts. In 1969, denied the Republican nomination and running as a Liberal, he carried those same districts by nearly 80%.[28] Lindsay could say accurately that he had done more for this new constituency than any other mayor in the city's history. An aide later attributed the expansion of New York's black middle class to the growth of the middle-level bureaucracy needed to run Lindsay's social programs.[29]

Rockefeller could draw on a less makeshift political base, derived from the Republican upstate tradition and the swing vote in New York City's suburbs, so one might wonder whether his spending helped or hurt him, especially toward the end. Yet the network of authorities provided a subtle form of patronage, not only in making work for the construction unions but also in providing the financial community with a constant stream of underwriting business.

When the final crisis came, some observers attempted to blame it on the "tax, tax, spend, spend" policies of the New Deal Democrats. Yet the tax, tax, spend, spend formula attributed to Harry Hopkins will still produce a balanced budget. The accumulation of debt that kept feeding the chronic deficits of New York City and the UDC could have been the work only of liberal Republicans. No one else had the inclination toward that kind of policy and the access to the financial community necessary to pull it off.

Even these structural reasons fail to explain, however, why such evidently able men thought they could get away with what they were doing. The most illuminating insight into their frame of mind came when the perceptive journalist Kenneth A. Auletta turned to a book with no apparent connection to New York and its fiscal crisis—Alexander Bickel's *The Morality of Consent*. Writing about other events of the 1960s, Bickel said, "The social fabric is held together by agreement on means. . . . The derogators of procedure and of technicalities, and other anti-institutional forces who rode high, on the bench as well as off, were the armies of conscience and ideology." This spirit led to the creation of the moral obligation bond and the hiding of the city's deficits. The leaders of New York refused to believe that the constitution's limits on spending and bonding were meant to apply to them. As John Mitchell told the special commission investigating the collapse of the UDC, "It became incumbent upon the public official and bond attorneys and so forth to find ways of issuing bonds to avoid these constitutional restrictions, in the public good, of course."[30] The restraints imposed by the constitution were considered to be an unenlightened and illegitimate nuisance for the farsighted and socially aware governing set, especially since these hindrances had been established so long ago. The popular resistance to taxation and debt, thought the "better" element, arose from greed and ignorance.

But the public had more of a case to make than these leaders were willing to admit. The housing bonds of which the voters were so wary were flawed in their very conception. The social spending did little to relieve the problems it poured upon, and in the case of welfare may have made them worse. Taxation, on the other hand, was not the simple transfer of wealth that Lindsay and Rockefeller thought it to be. As the rising tax burdens of state and city went hand in hand with declining population, shrinking work force, and depressed economy, it became a very open question whether the advocates of state spending were ameliorating or intensifying social misery.

THINGS FALL APART

By the time Mayor Lindsay introduced his 1970–71 budget, the national economy was in recession and the bonus from the 1966 tax increase was running out. Personal income tax receipts had begun to fall in constant terms from the year before; with the recession, this economically sensitive tax declined in current dollars as well. Business tax receipts fell even more sharply. But spending was up more than 17% over the year before, in one of its largest increases ever. The year ended with an officially acknowledged deficit of $361 million, covered only by "budget notes." Ominously, a much larger gap remained hidden in the secret world of short-term borrowing.

Lindsay was unable to meet the crisis immediately through tax increases because of the need to go through the state legislature. Perhaps he was unwilling to take this risk as well. So he began to accumulate an invisible burden of note issues. Cities can legitimately borrow to even out their cash flow. Taxes and outside aid come into the treasury in big clumps,

NEW YORK

Taxes and Business Formation

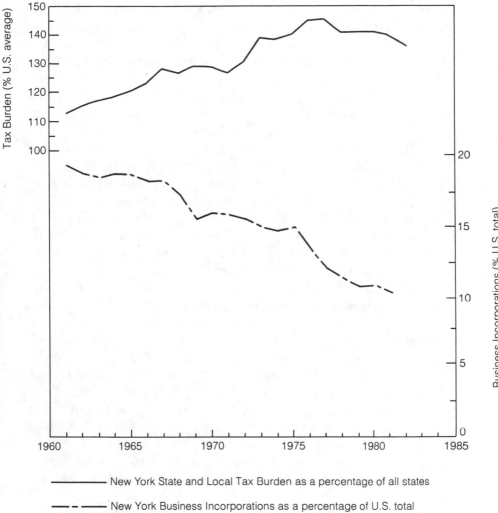

New York State and Local Tax Burden as a percentage of all states

New York Business Incorporations as a percentage of U.S. total

usually once every three months. But payrolls have to be paid at least twice a month. If a city does not have a large bank balance, it will have to borrow to meet these constant expenses. This borrowing can take several forms. Most common are Tax Anticipation Notes (TANs), which are issued with the understanding that they will be repaid when the big tax payments come in. Another large category consists of Revenue Anticipation Notes (RANs), issued against state and federal aid. Bond Anticipation Notes, issued against future bond sales, round out the percussive triad of RAN, TAN and BAN.

RAN-TAN-BAN. It sounded like an Aramaic incantation, and it had the magical property of making a deficit vanish. Wisely used, these notes are relatively routine, but Lindsay, like the Sorcerer's Apprentice, made them multiply beyond control. New York City resorted to selling TANs and RANs to raise money whether or not it would be getting any taxes or grants to pay them off. When the money to back the notes failed to come through, the city sold new notes to pay off the old ones, and also to cover additional hidden deficits. When the 1970–71 budget had run its course, New York City was rolling over more than $1 billion in RANs above and beyond its openly acknowledged deficit borrowing, which was handled by an issue of "budget notes." This sum was the approximate amount of its still-growing subterranean debt. And debt must someday translate into tax burden.[31]

Indeed, this budget pressure quickly led to new tax proposals. Budget crises from this time on came in two painful stages. Headache number one would hit in January, halfway through the fiscal year. The gap in the current year's budget would start growing wider and wider, and City Hall would scramble desperately to close it. Almost simultaneously would come headache number two, the next year's budget. Under the fiscal timetable, it would be announced in April, and officials would be furrowing their brows over a projected deficit three or four times larger than the current gap they presumably would have just finished closing. In early 1971, both headaches were throbbing harder than ever. On top of the official $361-million deficit in the current budget (and an additional unacknowledged deficit about three times as large), Lindsay faced a projected billion-dollar deficit in the rapidly approaching fiscal 1972 budget. Instead of looking for a pain-reliever, he reached for new taxes.

Lindsay's solution meant a major political battle. He called for increased state aid as well as taxes and threatened apocalyptic city layoffs if he did not get it. Governor Rockefeller was in the middle of his own budget and tax crisis, and Lindsay's importuning inflamed the hostility between the two.[32] The legislative battle allowed Lindsay to play the role of urban champion for a national audience, and his maneuvering ultimately got him what he wanted. The legislature boosted the top rate on the city's personal income tax by 75% and raised commuter taxes to keep pace. It also approved new business taxes and a host of minor sales and "nuisance" taxes, a widely detested feature of the city's tax base. The additional revenue made up less than half of the budget gap, and the rest was made to disappear by a dazzling legerdemain of postponed pension-fund contributions, reserve account withdrawals, advanced state aid, and borrowing. Another $700 million was added to the hidden deficit. Lindsay's people did almost everything except cut spending.

In fiscal year 1973, Lindsay again asked for new revenue. He sought added nuisance taxes and water fees, and he reshuffled real estate valuation. The public had had enough. Rank-and-file city councilmen defied their leadership and killed the taxes. But, observes Lindsay chronicler Charles Morris, the upheaval was a tax revolt, not a spending revolt. More loopholes were found to borrow the money, and the accumulated deficit topped $2 billion. At the last hour, the economy granted Lindsay a final reprieve. The national recovery from the 1969–70 recession had finally reached the city; the long-sought federal revenue sharing delivered its pot of gold, and the city managed to reduce its outstanding short-term debt by $350 million. As the first year-to-year reduction in short-term debt since Lindsay's inauguration, it impressed the bond-rating agencies sufficiently for them to raise the city's standing a notch above the minimum investment grade.[33]

This budget marks the end of the accumulation phase. In spite of the economic remission, the double income tax jolt of Rockefeller's surcharge and Lindsay's rate increase was beginning to have its effect. The city tax burden had grown from 7.3% in Wagner's last budget to 8.9%. The bulk of the increase had come in the last two years.

State employment peaked in 1973 below the level of 1969, and the continued growth in the government work force could no longer mask the sharp decline in the private sector. Rockefeller was resigning in Albany. The race to succeed Lindsay in New York City had been won by Comptroller Beame. The new administration was bound to produce disclosures about its predecessor, some of them involuntary. The phase of discovery was about to begin.

During the period of discovery, the public began to learn just what the moral elite had brought about. These revelations set in motion an inexorable chain of fiscal crises. Even more than that, they shook to its roots the public's confidence in the prevailing political and financial leadership.

DISCOVERY: THE NAKED CITY

By 1973, all that sustained the city and state financial structure was the blind faith of the bond market that New York would honor its commitments. In an unconscious act of self-destruction, the New York State legislature now struck directly at this faith. In June 1974, it joined with New Jersey in repudiating the Port Authority bond covenant, a pledge to bondholders that the agency's revenues would not be diverted to money-losing mass transit. The reformers who campaigned to remove the covenant on outstanding bonds thought they were helping to solve the "energy crisis" (and freeing money for transit workers' salaries); they failed to see that they were forcing the financial community to ask a series of fatal questions about the security of New York's bonds.

External forces made these questions more urgent. In late 1974, the Federal Reserve was squeezing down the money supply to fight inflation, but its typically erratic control brought about an exceedingly sharp contraction in December. Banks could no longer pour money into their weakest borrowers, and the shakiest of these in New York State was the Urban Development Corporation. Since the Port Authority uproar, the public market had closed to UDC notes, and New York City's commercial banks were keeping the agency afloat on their own. Despite extensive negotiations, the state and the banks failed to agree on terms of a comprehensive bailout. In the last week of February 1975, the UDC defaulted on both a $100-million issue of short-term notes and a $30-million bank loan. The banks attached the UDC accounts, and it was out of money.

Although the impasse was quickly broken and funding restored, the damage had been done. New York had gone through the largest municipal default since the Depression, and worried investors were beginning to realize they had just scratched the surface.[34]

Abraham Beame, on succeeding Lindsay as mayor, made the predictable pronouncements about the mess he had inherited. Overspending had put the budget in permanent deficit of more than a billion dollars a year. Much of the gap had been closed by bookkeeping shuffles. The money needed to back up the paper balance had really been raised by short-term borrowing, which had constantly to be refunded.

But soon, to the deficit from the transitional 1973–74 budget, which could be blamed on Lindsay, was added the widening gap in the current 1974–75 budget, Beame's own work. Beame filled the headlines with plans for layoffs and spending cuts. But the retrenchment failed to materialize in any serious way. (Beame postponed layoffs scheduled for December because he did not want to discharge city workers just before Christmas.) He adopted the worst of all postures, publicizing the problem but failing to deal with it.[35]

Beame's major financial strategy was to transform some of the accumulating short-term debt into more manageable long-term bonds through the device of a Stabilization Reserve Corporation (SRC), a new moral obligation public authority to be created by the city. This plan was halted by William J. Quirk and Leon E. Wein, who first met as junior bureaucrats in the Lindsay Administration. The pair had previously waged a totally unnoticed academic campaign against the moral obligation evasion of the constitutional bond referendum. "If you want to keep a secret from the world," Wein would exclaim, "write it in a law review article."

To make their point less easily ignored, Quirk and Wein thought of launching lawsuits against the moral obligation bond issues. Under state law they could not get standing in court to sue a statewide authority. But the SRC was the first strictly city-level agency to rely on the moral obligation. It thus lacked the sovereign's protection against suits. Quirk and Wein quickly leaped into the breach. Their suit failed to outlaw the moral obligation, but it forced cancellation of the $520-million SRC bond sale planned for February 1975.[36] The fact that no SRC bonds were ever sold did not prevent the city from counting the nonexistent proceeds as real revenues in its fiscal 1975 budget. In one bold stroke Mayor Beame concealed half a billion dollars of deficit.[37] But the cash still had to be got somehow. Partially to replace the SRC borrowing, the city turned to the now famous mid-February TAN issue.

Two underwriting syndicates agreed to buy these TANs on February 19, thus providing half of the missing SRC money. But on February 26, two days before the closing date on the notes, one syndicate's bond counsel (White and Case, handling their first city note issue) warned that the city seemed to have overrun its legal debt limit for TANs. Suspecting that the city was selling more in notes than it could cover with overdue taxes, they asked for up-to-date figures. The city could not answer, because that was exactly what it was doing. With the UDC debacle fresh in mind, the syndicates canceled their purchase.[38]

In spite of Comptroller Harrison Goldin's attempts at obfuscation, this incident began to pry the lid off the city's underground deficit.[39] Nonetheless, the city urgently needed cash to meet its payroll, and the bankers still hesitated to face the truth peering out of the abyss. A syndicate of major commercial banks (the Clearinghouse banks), floated a "bridge loan" for the city pending a public sale of new bond and revenue notes. (Doubts about the availability of bond funds and state and federal aid were not as pressing as the suspicion that uncollected taxes could never be recovered.) Some bankers began to worry about "possible criminal liability," as in securities fraud, if they participated. But the city managed to float a last-gasp short-term issue of nearly a billion dollars. New York defaulted on these notes within the year.[40]

Historians may render judgment on the banks before the courts do: a massive 1976 class-action suit by noteholders is still pending.[41] But the shelves of depositions crowding the reading room in the federal District Court basement leave little doubt that the bank and brokerage-house underwriters, rating agencies, and bond counsel (in particular, as noted in an extensive SEC report, the law firm of Wood, Dawson, Love & Sabatine) served the public, and New York, very badly.

Mayor Beame and a host of other demagogues attacked the banks for not bailing out the city, when the fact is they had bailed out the city far too long, tolerating its chronic deficits and allowing it to swell its borrowing well past the point of no return. After the newcomers from White and Case started asking questions, figures about the accumulated deficit, un-backed notes, and "bogus receivables" began to bubble up from the city bureaucracy, with each estimate larger than the one before. The city could no longer browbeat the banks. In mid-April, a $600-million note issue came due, and no one would refinance it. The city turned to the state for advances on aid to carry it through the spring. With the money came the state auditors.

For years, commissions and politicians had been expos-ing New York City's budget gimmicks and dangerously high debt level to a largely indifferent public. Reports had regu-larly issued forth from the Scott Commission (appointed by Rockefeller to annoy Lindsay) and the Citizens Budget Com-mission (originally set up after the Jimmy Walker fiscal crisis of the early 1930s). Perhaps 95% of the story had been at least hinted at publicly before 1975. But the 5% uncovered by the state auditors was the most damaging of all. In two dry and technical reports in July and August, the State Comptroller's Office gave the first documented public account of the city's fraudulent borrowing.[42] Nearly 87% of the audited "accounts receivable" (a third of a billion dollars) and 81% of the real estate taxes receivable (or $408 million) were bogus. The city had nothing on hand to back three-quarters of a billion dol-lars of short-term debt. By Labor Day, the officially acknowl-edged deficit accumulation had grown to three and a half times that amount, and the entire nation had discovered the New York City crisis.

New Yorkers faced a shocking series of revelations in that dramatic summer. The seemingly impossible financing crisis was in some ways the least of several simultaneous disasters, which sent shock waves in three concentric rings. The most immediate was the financing scramble, which received most of the attention as the city went to the brink almost weekly. Beyond that lay a budget crisis, which had caused the financ-ing crisis. The city had simply lived beyond its means and showed no sign it could match revenues and spending at any point in the near future. The third and most basic was the economic crisis. The budget was in chronic deficit in part because economic decline had shriveled its revenue base.

New Yorkers had always thought that they lived in the capital of the Western world. Now they made the awful discovery that they lived in a declining city and state. Population was falling statewide, but in the city it was plummeting. There were now fewer than 7.4 million stories in the naked city. The work force was wasting away. By the end of 1975, even though government employment was at an all-time high, the state had lost some 350,000 jobs from the peak year of 1969. The decline was even more dramatic in the city: from the high point of 1970 to rock bottom in 1977, it lost 612,000 jobs. The illusion of economic health had vanished. In 1968, New York City had been recession-proof, with an unemployment rate lower than Houston's. (Among the major cities, only Dallas was better off.) In 1975, its unemployment rate was the third highest in the top twenty metropolitan areas. The flight of corporate headquarters had reached panic levels; even more important, smaller businesses, which provided the bulk of the city's employment, were no longer being generated faster than they died.[43] Although still a high-income state, New York's rate of growth in per-capita income was lowest in the country. In 1968, the average New Yorker statewide earned 18% more than the national average; in 1975, he earned only 8% more and his advantage was dropping. Per-capita income in the New York metropolitan area fell from 129% of the national average in 1969 to 113% in 1976.[44]

New Yorkers could hear any number of partial explanations for their predicament. The nation was decentralizing; manufacturers needed space to spread sideways and were finding it in the Sunbelt; the population was moving to warmer weather; wages and energy costs were too high; and, whispered sub rosa, there were too many blacks and Puerto Ricans. But the answer that the average taxpayer immediately accepted as true and comprehensive was simply that the state and local tax burden had climbed too far and too fast beyond the national rate. In 1965, state and local tax revenue was 11.87% of total state personal income, a tax burden 13.6%

above the U.S. average. In 1975, this burden was 16.65%, a full 35.5% above the nation's. The state's average annual increase for the decade was 3.4%, more than double the U.S. average rate; it was equaled only by Massachusetts and exceeded only by the fiscal freak Alaska.[45]

The statistics fail to convey the gloom and bewilderment of that period. In a display of civic loyalty matched only by its self-delusion, New Yorkers railed bitterly at a host of imaginary villains, from the federal government to Sunbelt demography. The moral depression lasted till the Bicentennial Fourth of July, when the spectacle of the Tall Ships and the facility with which the city handled the celebration gave a wonderful boost to spirits. To the great good fortune of city and state, the fuss and rhetoric did not keep New Yorkers from awakening to the tax connection.

COLLAPSE AND AUSTERITY

New York City's periods of collapse and austerity became an epic with as many close calls as a matinee cliff-hanger. With the market closed and its aid advances exhausted, the state stepped in to create the Municipal Assistance Corporation. This gigantic revival of the SRC faltered and was bolstered by creation of the Emergency Financial Control Board. These state bodies took over control of the city from Mayor Beame and found that even that was not enough. With ultimate collapse facing city, public authorities, and state itself, New Yorkers turned their immense propaganda tools to bludgeoning help from the national government. David Rockefeller traveled through Europe, enlisting Helmut Schmidt to lobby President Gerald Ford for the city (and Chase Manhattan Bank), to the chancellor's later embarrassment. The state imposed the Moratorium Act, a thinly disguised default placing the bulk of the burden on the least organized group of people. Finally, a complaisant Washington responded with a legal fiction and real aid. But all these matters lie outside the thrust of the present narrative.

Likewise, the narrative hastens over the period of austerity, in which city and state budgets grew by less than 6% annually instead of 15%; in which Congressman Edward I. Koch, the candidate most hated by the municipal unions, came from the back of the pack to defeat Mayor Beame; in which crises recurred as the highest state court struck down the unconstitutional moratorium, and federal aid had to be renewed; in which the banks and municipal unions feuded and made up, bound together by their common role as the city's biggest creditors. Of concern now is the way the state, and to a lesser degree the city, developed a tax strategy diametrically opposed to the tax increases that had brought on the disaster.

RECOVERY: THE SUPPLY SIDE
SAVES NEW YORK

In the first response to New York City's mounting deficit, Washington and Albany turned to the old approach of raising taxes. In his first six months, Governor Hugh Carey tried to close his own state budget gap with an emergency one-year gasoline tax, but Republican Senate leaders, insisting that the holdover budget was in good shape, killed the idea. When New York City's deficits burgeoned, U.S. Treasury Secretary William Simon recommended increasing the sales tax and expanding it to food and medicine. At the height of the crisis, Carey sought unsuccessfully to add 16% and 17% brackets to the personal income tax. He did extend Rockefeller's 2½% income tax surcharge through 1977. In a vengeful mood, the legislature also slapped a 20% surcharge on the corporation franchise tax and, with special spite for the closing of the bond market, ran the bank tax up by 30%. The city pegged its real estate tax rate at a record high and added three new brackets on top of the city income tax, to 4.3% on $25,000. Thanks to these measures, New York's state and local tax burden reached its peak in 1977.

State and city recovery began when their leaders stopped scrambling for revenue and began to think about the long-range needs of the economy. The shift in New York City coincided with its 1977 mayoral campaign. One of the year's most significant documents was the final report, in June, of the Temporary Commission on City Finances, called the "McGivern

Commission" after its chairman, Judge Owen McGivern. Although Judge McGivern served as campaign chairman for incumbent Mayor Beame, the report differed firmly from Beame's policy of minimal retrenchment. Drafted by Staff Director Raymond D. Horton, it recommended a "developmental strategy" consisting of fundamental reform of city politics and spending to generate "slack resources"; these resources would then be invested in promoting the competitiveness of the local economy. In spite of the turgid summary, the body of the report made clear that the best investment of slack resources was in tax cuts.[46] About the same time, the city's massive debt to the commercial banks and the municipal unions' pension funds had forced bankers and militant union leaders into a wary alliance in managing the city's fiscal bailout. (Local radicals called it "the junta.") To reduce tensions, bank and union presidents formed a discussion group called, simply, "MUFL" (for Municipal Union/Financial Leaders). The group's second formal statement called for tax reductions.[47]

In the campaign itself, Edward Koch came from fifth to first place as voters saw him as the candidate least friendly to municipal union leaders. But the platform of the most radical Democrat in the race, South Bronx Congressman Herman Badillo (hero of the Puerto Rican community), illustrated how fundamentally the political culture was changing. Citing studies of the McGivern Commission, Badillo called for elimination of three business taxes and the city income tax. After the first two years, he argued, the economy would be spurred so by the tax cuts that it would generate enough new revenue to compensate for them.[48]

At the state level, Governor Carey was also tasting the forbidden brew of supply-side economics. Carey's aides pinpoint his conversion to an Albany committee hearing in which Syracuse University Professor Roy Bahl forecast the continuing economic decline of the state. It is easy to exaggerate the level of economic theory that underlay the evolving state policy. Carey had two additional economic briefings, and, recalls a former adviser, "he was late to one and grumpy at the other." But it took little sophistication to conclude that taxes were killing the state.[49]

In 1978, Carey let the corporation and bank tax surcharges expire and began to phase out the stock transfer tax. The business surcharges had been spectacular failures at raising revenues. The banks had set their accountants to work and actually paid less tax with the surcharge than without it. The stock tax was driving brokers to New Jersey.

Governor Carey's main concern, however, was the personal income tax. It was this tax that put the state at its most severe competitive disadvantage. Although other states had higher top rates or more compressed income brackets, none had the two together. Simply to compensate for the tax burden, businesses had to pay top dollar for middle-level executives, when they could get them.

Not yet a supply-sider, Carey decided to stretch the tax brackets and offer a one-year 5% tax credit; the benefits, he reasoned, would be spread equitably through all income levels. But Republicans in control of the Senate wanted a dramatic gesture for the job-producing taxpayer. They pushed for immediate abolition of the top five brackets. Carey's strategists responded plausibly that too abrupt a tax cut might be reversed quickly; expectations, they said, were the key. People would respond better over time to a tax burden they knew would constantly decline. In a compromise, Carey and the legislature eliminated the three top brackets and announced the phase-out of one more a year until the maximum rate fell to 10% in fiscal year 1982.

Perverse as ever, New York City took its own half-conscious approach to tax cutting. The McGivern Commission recommended sharp cuts in the corporate income tax, but the real reduction came elsewhere. Under pressure from the powerful real estate barons, as well as from the constitutional debt limit, Beame lowered the property tax rate for fiscal year 1978. He promised to freeze it for five years. By itself, the rate cut amounted to only $4.50 per $100 of assessed valuation. But a world of possibilities lies in the phrase "assessed valuation." Thanks to the tax freeze, real estate was one of the first city industries to recover. Property values in Manhattan perked up and then bounced ahead. The city was poorly equipped to capture the boom in its assessments. The real value of taxable real estate in Manhattan increased by 48% from fiscal year 1976 to 1980, but assessments in that period decreased by 2.2%. The combination of frozen tax rates and out-of-date assessments sent the real tax rate plummeting. City and State officials estimate that the effective property tax rate in that period fell by nearly 40%.[50] If anything, the tax rate has continued to fall. In 1981, the state legislature passed a bill to cope with court-ordered reassessments; the bill limited the amount assessments can rise in a single year. Applied to Manhattan, this homeowners' bill gives a tremendous tax break to the one sector of the city's economy that needs it least.

With these measures on the books, the New York tax burden made an impressive turnaround. From 1977 to 1979, the total state and local burden fell at an annual rate of 3.2%. (In the previous two years it had risen at an annual rate of 3.9%, and in the preceding decade, at a rate of 3.4%.) From 1977 to 1979, however, tax burdens nationally were heading down at an only slightly lower annual pace of 3%.[51] Consequently, one would expect a state revival to take the form of a halt in its relative decline rather than exceptional growth. And that is what happened. The economy of New York City and New York State has kept a fairly even keel now through two sharp national recessions. The state unemployment rate remained below the nation's during the harrowing last quarter of 1982. By January 1984, New York City even showed signs of a turnaround in manufacturing employment, which had taken the brunt of the mid-seventies economic collapse. Since its 1977 low point, it had gained back 156,000 jobs.[52]

The foundations of this recovery were far from solid. The first cracks in the policy of tax reduction came during a genuine crisis in New York City subway service in mid-1980. To cope with deferred maintenance and two successive generations of unsatisfactory rolling-stock acquisitions, the state imposed an increase in the general sales tax. (The bulk of the subway tax package was an unrealistic levy on oil companies; it never produced the anticipated revenue.) Mayor Koch, whose taxing tendencies had been restrained by Governor Carey, proposed an increase in the commuter tax with increasing urgency after Carey declined to seek reelection. Running for governor himself, Koch had negotiated generous municipal union contracts.

The tax issue was fought to a draw in the recession year

general election. The irrepressible Mayor Koch, the stand-up comic of American politicians, paid dearly for some *Playboy Interview* wisecracks about upstate New York and was upset in the Democratic primary by the "neighborhood liberal" Lieutenant Governor Mario Cuomo. The Republican nomination went in a landslide to a charter member of the supply-side movement, Lewis Lehrman. But for a referendum on supply-side policies, the election sometimes made it hard to tell which side was which.

In deference to his party's legislative partisans, Lehrman vociferously argued that no good at all had come of Governor Carey's remarkably supply-side oriented fiscal policy. Cuomo wrapped himself in the mantle of the tax limiting middle, pledging no increases in the major state taxes. When Cuomo denounced Lehrman as a dangerous tax radical, Lehrman had foreclosed his chance to reply that Reaganomics was a continuation of Careynomics but on a more timid scale. In the end, Cuomo was the foreordained winner, but no one but Lehrman expected the race to be as close as it turned out to be.

The real difference in policy became much more apparent when Governor Cuomo set to the work of drafting his budgets. In his first year, he faced a projected billion-dollar budget gap swelled by the feckless spending of the state legislature in Carey's lame duck year. Although Cuomo kept his pledge not to raise the broad-based levies, he resorted to a series of minor tax increases to close the deficit. By the end of 1983, however, the alarms about red ink had been dispersed by the economic recovery. New York City, which had renewed the hoary call of an increased commuter tax in January wound up its fiscal year in June with nearly a half billion surplus. Governor Cuomo had the chance to restrain state spending and resume his predecessor's policy of tax reduction. Instead, in January 1984, he chose to let his budget rise by 11%, almost three times faster than inflation.

It remains to be seen after all how fully committed New York's leaders are to nurturing their fragile economy through tax cuts. The lessons of the 1975 fiscal crisis have not even had an institutional embodiment to match the "peoples' amendments" of the 1840s. Yet a constitution alone is unlikely to restrain a political elite determined on "doing good." The history of New York shows that apparently definitive constitutional language can be evaded on a massive scale. The second phase of fiscal limitation failed to save New York from a disastrous debt burden, overspending, and economic collapse.

The state's twentieth-century political history might have been substantially different, however, if its citizens had acquired the power to initiate direct constitutional change. New York's institutions do not include the initiative and the referendum. The state has not been part of the third phase of the Tax Revolt, in which a grass-roots movement uses the tools of direct democracy to impose limits on the actual rate of taxation. That part of the story belongs to California.

6

Phase Three
California the Golden

Myth surrounds the very name California. One scholar, Carey McWilliams, traces it to the Persian *Kari-i-farn*, "the mountain of paradise," a historical hoax. The rest of the nation has never quite been able to believe in the Golden State, a problem that perplexed McWilliams in his classic attempt to explain it. "Those who have written about the state," he warned, "have fallen into two general categories: the skeptics, who in retrospect have been made to look ludicrously gullible; and the liars and boasters who have been confounded by the fulfillment of their dizziest predictions."[1] This warning applies as well to the Tax Revolt as to any other California topic.

The passage of Proposition 13 in 1978 must stand as the high point of the third phase of the Tax Revolt. In later years, the time of this initiative and its immediate successors may well be known as the "Classical Period" of this phenomenon. Even writing so close to the event, one constantly marvels that such a thing could have been done, and that it could have been done with such success. Yet this phenomenon is part and parcel of all the other wonders of California's history.

Strange as Proposition 13 may have seemed to the rest of the country, it arose naturally from the California context. The issue of property taxes had been building for more than a decade; the use of the referendum to attack the special-interest spending web had been debated for about the same length of time. Beyond the local prehistory of the Tax Revolt lie basic features of the state's social and political make-up that explain its exceptional reliance on the initiative and the referendum.

Ever since California came into the United States it has undergone wave after wave of immigration that has obliterated any stable community politics. Without ward politics, Californians have long been accustomed to expressing their will directly at the polling place. In turn, the state's politicians have mastered the techniques of mass communication and mass politics, none better than the Progressive leaders who championed the initiative as the device best suited to their state's unique politics.

The themes as well as the techniques of the Tax Revolt show up throughout the state's history. California has burst with prosperity when government has been nearly absent and has lost some luster when government has made its most extensive claims. The state has produced a rich crop of tax heretics, from Henry George to Arthur Laffer, to proclaim this message. A prime example of harmful taxation came in the governorship of Ronald Reagan, who embraced the high tax policies he later resisted as president. But the most remarkable of the state's object lessons comes, appropriately, at the very beginning of its modern history, in the fantastic episode known as "the Gold Rush."

THE GOLD RUSH AND THE *LEX DIGGERORUM*

In 1848, as far as the civilized world was concerned, California was at the end of the earth. The United States had just acquired the land as part of the booty from the Mexican War, but it was the least sought-after of the new territories. It contained fewer than 10,000 permanent residents other than

American Indians, and only a handful of settlers had begun to trickle in from the outside world. One of these was a German Swiss named John Sutter, a failure in his previous life who by bluff and made-up credentials had secured a Mexican land grant of eleven square leagues in the Great Central Valley. Sutter had established a fort at the confluence of the Sacramento and American rivers and for eight years had been building up the trade and agriculture of his domain of New Helvetia. In late 1847, he sent his employee James W. Marshall forty miles up into the mountains to build a sawmill. On January 23, 1848, Marshall flushed out the millrace, unintentionally duplicating a mining operation. The next morning, he noticed yellow flecks in the stream bed. He had discovered gold, and permanently changed the fate of California.[2]

Word of the gold strike spread like rings on water. Sutter tried half-heartedly to keep the find secret, but his employees could not suppress their excitement. Samuel Brannan, a flamboyant Mormon leader and San Francisco businessman with an interest in the store at Sutter's Fort, heard that workers were starting to pay their bills with gold dust. After a quick trip to investigate, Brannan returned to San Francisco, waving his hat in one hand and a quinine bottle of gold dust in the other, shouting, "Gold! Gold! Gold from the American River!"[3]

As the news sank in, it emptied the California settlements. By the middle of June, three-fourths of the men in San Francisco had gone to the diggings, and both city newspapers ceased publication. In the capital city of Monterey, the military governor, the mayor, and the naval commander joined together to cook their meals; the last of their servants had deserted them for the mines.

Through 1848, gold fever was confined mainly to the West Coast. But in December a courier reached Washington with the military governor's report on the gold fields. He also carried a tea caddy filled with 230 ounces fifteen pennyweights and nine grains of the freshly dug metal. President James K. Polk trumpeted the find in his report to Congress as a justification for his unpopular war on Mexico. The tea caddy went on display in the War Department. With this official confirmation, the gold sensation swept from China to the Baltic.[4]

The argonauts who now flocked to California from all points on the globe gave no thought to the interesting legal question of who really owned the gold. Almost all the finds were made on public land. The mineral was by rights the property of the United States government. But existing federal law made no provision to regulate mining on the public domain. In December 1849, Secretary of the Interior Thomas Ewing complained that "in addition to our own citizens, thousands of persons of all nations and languages, flock in and gather gold, which they carry away to enrich themselves, leaving the lands the less in value, by that which they have abstracted, and they render for it no remuneration, direct or indirect, to the government or the people of the United States."[5] Even if a law had been on the books, it could not have been enforced. The military governor, Richard B. Mason, toured the gold fields in mid-1848 and concluded that the situation was beyond his power to regulate. "It was a matter of serious reflection to me," he wrote Washington, "how I could secure to the government certain rents or fees for the privilege of procuring this gold; but upon considering the large extent of the country, the character of the people engaged and the small scattered force at my command, I am resolved not to interfere but permit all to work freely, unless broils and crimes call for interference."[6]

The noncollection of federal revenues, however, did not stop the heavily prominer state legislature from exempting from property taxation all mining claims on "United States lands." The property tax burden consequently fell disproportionately on the six "Cow Counties" of Southern California, prompting a move there for secession from the northern half of the state. A poll tax applied to miners as to all residents, but nine out of ten of the men in the camps neglected to pay it.[7]

As the argonauts poured in, crowding the mining camps with a turbulence far surpassing that of 1848, they labored at a tax rate of zero. The ensuing burst of prosperity and phenomenal development vindicates Colonel Mason's hands-off policy as one of the wisest economic decisions ever made by an American military officer in the field.

Left to their own devices, the mining camps came as close as at any point in human history to realizing John Locke's state of civil society. The argonauts universally had one purpose: to acquire property by mixing their labor with it. The Mexican mineral law, granting property rights based on discovery, had been abrogated by Colonel Mason almost at the same time Marshall was finding gold in the millrace. The miners filled the vacuum with an improvised law of claims, the *lex diggerorum*. The general principle of this law, adopted by convocations of miners in one camp after another, was that claims rights came from a mixture of discovery and use, with by far the greater emphasis on use. The miners limited the extent of claims to an area workable by one man, allowing a double claim for the finder of new diggings. A man could mark his claim simply by leaving his pick or shovel on it, but if he failed to work it for a certain consecutive number of days he forfeited his rights. Some camp meetings defined exceptions to the rule, such as sickness or visits to sick friends. Camp law left no room for speculative holdings, nor could anyone expect to enforce an absentee title against the will of the assembled miners.[8]

The camp meetings enforced criminal law as well, even when a more duly constituted authority was available. Trials were usually held in the ubiquitous saloons, providing the owners a handsome profit from the sale of drinks and dinners to the spectators. Theft was a serious offense, frequently punished by hanging. This mass justice was always on the verge of becoming mob violence. In 1851, the camp of Downieville went over the line. A drunken Fourth of July reveler broke down the door of a beautiful Mexican woman named Juanita; when he returned the next day (to apologize, he said) he fell into a quarrel with her Mexican consort. In the altercation, Juanita stabbed the miner dead. The camp assembled and demanded her execution. According to legend, Stephen J. Field, later a justice of the U.S. Supreme Court, tried to save her by legal argument. A doctor tried to save her by declaring her pregnant. But the miners refused to listen. On the scaffold, Juanita adjusted the rope with her own hands and stepped calmly to her death. This famous incident has been retold in many versions, and some take it as a turning point in the Gold Rush, as the miners' "loss of innocence." Yet it shocked opinion throughout the fields. Even sobered-up Downieville regretted the deed. Defenders of the *lex diggerorum* argue that camp justice sometimes returned acquittals. In spite of, or perhaps because of, the prevalence of lynch law, visitors to the mines found a surprising degree of order and respect for property.[9]

The mining camps transformed the whole of California society. An argonaut in the diggings could pan an average of $16 in gold dust a day, at that time the highest wage rate in the world. (Of course, the lottery aspect of the enterprise, the chance of a big find, made the hoped-for reward much greater.) With claims open to anyone willing to work them, placer mining set the standard for wages in all occupations throughout the state. Labor in San Francisco could command three to five times the eastern wage scale, and no one could be found for menial work. On arriving in San Francisco in 1849, the German adventurer Friedrich Gerstaecker found dirty shirts lying on the ground every ten feet. With the labor shortage, it cost almost as much to get a shirt washed as to buy a new one. Some merchants too frugal to discard their soiled clothes were shipping them to China for laundering.[10] The pull of the mines drew ranchhands off Mexican estates, hastening the decline of the landowning elite. The digs had opened a shortcut to wealth for anybody, and a spirit of equality spread throughout the social order.

Pressure from the argonauts destroyed the semifeudal society of the rancheros in another way. The sons of New England and New York farmers were unable or unwilling to understand that a broad extent of grazing land was needed to support livestock in a semiarid climate. They looked on the large Mexican land grants as unused land. Applying the *lex diggerorum*, they simply appropriated the vacant acres for themselves. These settlers (or, to the rancheros, squatters) made up a powerful political bloc; they applied intense pressure for redistribution of grant-lands to the newly arrived farmers who thought they had established property rights by their labor. Ironically, most of this territory later wound up in the hands of the notorious land companies.[11]

THE COMING OF GOVERNMENT

When the new settlers turned to organizing the state formally, as they did almost immediately in the 1849 constitutional convention in Monterey, they incorporated some of the most recent innovations of Jacksonian constitution-making. Faced with a shortage of reference material, they worked from copies of the new constitutions of New York and Iowa. (The latter had the advantages of being succinct and recently adopted.) The Jacksonian provisions included a bar on the legislative chartering of currency-issuing banks and on the creation of corporations by special act. The leader in this debate was William M. Gwin, friend and protégé of Old Hickory and later first U.S. senator from the new state. Another article followed New York in prohibiting the issuance of debt exceeding $300,000, unless approved by the people at a general election. Gwin introduced the now standard language on taxation requiring equality, uniformity, and proportionality to the value of property. He compromised with the representatives of the Hispanic Cow Counties, however, on the point of locally elected assessors. The older landed interests wanted control of that office to ensure that they would not be oppressed by the taxing power of the new state.[12]

This provision did not work, however. The settled landowners of the south were much more easily assessed than the transient miners of the north, the property tax bore more heavily on acreage than on mineral finds, and the prominer state legislature, as already noted, exempted the argonauts from most taxation. (One exception was a series of heavy and constitutionally dubious taxes on Chinese miners.) As the Cow Counties came to pay far more than their share of the state revenue, the idea of dividing the state took hold. Even in the constitutional convention, representatives of the south had tried to protect themselves from northern taxation by asking to be split from the new state and left as a territory. Throughout the 1850s, other forms of this proposal appeared in the state legislature. Finally, in 1859, legislators in the new capital, Sacramento, approved a referendum on separation in the southern counties; the reason for secession was given as too much taxation and too little representation. The southern counties approved the measure by nearly three to one. But Washington was in the throes of a much larger secession crisis, and it ignored California. Like eastern opinion of the time, subsequent historians attributed the state division movement to a proslavery plot to bring in another state on the side of the South. But to modern scholars, the Cow County vote for secession looks like an unalloyed tax revolt.[13]

The state's prosperity eroded in the 1870s, partly from decline of the gold fields but also from a sharp change in the government's economic policy. The state had an obvious interest in a transcontinental railroad to end its isolation. But it pursued this interest by excessive subsidies to the Central Pacific Railroad. Even the visionary construction engineer who founded the company, Theodore D. Judah, suspected that his principal backers were more interested in receiving government cash than in completing the line. He was on his way to New York to arrange alternate financing when he died suddenly of yellow fever. His death was an unfortunate turning point in the state's history. The "Big Four" stockholders— Sacramento merchants Mark Hopkins, Collis P. Huntington, Leland Stanford, and Charles Crocker—proceeded to parlay their government backing into a transportation monopoly that dominated the state's economy and politics for more than three decades.[14]

The opening of the Central Pacific coincided with a decade of economic turmoil. As the state became more accessible to new immigrants, the workmen who had already arrived could no longer command such high wages. Nor did pay scales have to compete with the alternative of placer mining. Resentment focused on the competition from "cheap coolie labor." Unrest reached a peak in the Workingmen's movement led by the demagogic Denis Kearney, which played a large role in the state constitutional convention of 1879. The constitution adopted by this body, still the basic law of the state, contained an article of four sections outlawing "Chinese or Mongolian" labor. Playing on racial anxieties, which reemerged recently in a wave of antipathy toward Vietnamese refugees, the constitution ordered the legislature to make provision for "the burdens and evils arising from the presence of aliens who are or may become vagrants, paupers, mendicants, criminals, or invalids afflicted with contagious or infectious disease."[15]

THE PROTEST OF HENRY GEORGE

In 1879, the year of Kearneyism and the constitution, one of the argonauts published his own comprehensive explanation of the state's hard times. He was Henry George, and his ambitious treatise, *Progress and Poverty* (1879), must stand as the supreme intellectual achievement of the Gold Rush. George is famous for his eloquent but monomaniacal championship of the single tax on land. Less well known is the extent to which he drew his analysis and remedy from the experience of the mining camps. George starts from the premise that labor is the producer of value and wealth. Yet labor cannot create something from nothing. "In producing wealth, labor, with the aid of natural forces, but works up into the forms desired, preexisting matter, and, to produce wealth, must, therefore, have access to this matter and to these forces—that is to say, to land. The land is the source of all wealth. . . . It is the substance to which labor gives the form."[16] When labor has access to land, it will give rise to a flourishing economy. "Miners did not go to California and Australia because shoemakers, tailors, machinists and printers were there. But those trades followed the miners."[17] But when the labor is blocked from this free access, "men who are willing to work cannot find opportunity to do so," unemployment spreads, and the society divides into extremes of wealth and poverty. George elaborates this theme at great length, contrasting it with rival economic theories, and, time after time, when he seeks to illustrate a principle in its pristine form, he turns to the Gold Rush.

Thus the California mining camps illustrate the primitive theory of land and its evolution into private property.

The novelty of the case broke through habitual ideas, and threw men back upon first principles, and it was by common consent declared that this gold-bearing land should remain common property, of which no one might take more than he could reasonably use, or hold for a longer time than he continued to use it. This perception of natural justice was acquiesced in by the General Government and the courts, and while placer mining remained of importance, no attempt was made to overrule this reversion to primitive ideas. The title to the land remained in the government, and no individual could acquire more than a possessory claim. . . . Thus no one was allowed to forestall or to lock up natural resources. Labor was acknowledged as the creator of wealth, was given a free field, and secured in its reward.[18]

But this happy state arose only because of the very unusual conditions of the Gold Rush, and it did not last. "With the decadence of placer mining in California, the accustomed idea of private property finally prevailed in the passage of a law permitting the patenting of mineral lands. The only effect is to lock up opportunities—to give the owner of mining ground the power of saying that no one else may use what he does not choose to use himself."[19] One of the prime agents in appropriating the land, and hence in creating California's misery, was the railroad. The advance of the railroad ran up land values, land was snapped up by speculators and held for higher prices than labor or capital could afford. Hence "production was checked, if not absolutely, at least relatively. As the transcontinental railroad approached completion, instead of increased activity, symptoms of depression began to manifest themselves; and, when it was completed, to the season of activity had succeeded a period of depression which has not since been fully recovered from."[20]

George offered an ingenious remedy. Rather than confiscate and redistribute land, the government should merely tax it to the extent that captured the individual owner's economic rent and turned it to the use of the public good. This single tax on land (not to be confused with the ad valorem property tax on buildings) is one of the most famous *idées fixes* of nineteenth-century economics. One would properly be skeptical of an analysis that focused on a single cause and offered a single remedy. Yet the other side of George's thesis still merits attention. He argued not only for a confiscatory tax on the economic rent of land, but also for the abolition of every

tax on production. His argument *against* taxation continues
to be important.

"All taxes," he wrote, "must evidently come from the
produce of land and labor, since there is no other source of
wealth than the union of human exertion with the material
and forces of nature. But the manner in which equal amounts
of taxation may be imposed may very differently affect the
production of wealth. Taxation which lessens the reward of
the producer necessarily lessens the incentive to production;
taxation which is conditioned upon the act of production, or
the use of any of the three factors of production, necessarily
discourages production."[21] These taxes should be avoided
when other sources of revenue are at hand. And these other
sources are the monopolies. They deserve to bear the full brunt
of taxation, "for the profit of monopoly is in itself a tax levied
upon production, and to tax it is simply to divert into the
public coffers what production must in any event pay."[22] But
taxes on production have a life of their own, because the parties which appear to bear them are able to shift the burden
further down the price structure yet draw a special advantage
from the existence of the tax. "Nearly all of these taxes are
ultimately paid by that indefinable being, the consumer; and
he pays them in a way which does not call his attention to
the fact that he is paying a tax. . . ."[23] Yet high tariffs and
license taxes benefit those who nominally pay them because
they act as barriers to entry of new competition.

Because of the opposition of these special interests, "those
taxes which cost the people least . . . [have] been found easier to abolish than those taxes which cost the people most."[24]

In summarizing his argument, George produced one of the
most eloquent passages in the canon of supply-side economics:

> The present method of taxation operates upon exchange like
> artificial deserts and mountains; it costs more to get goods
> through a custom house than it does to carry them around the
> world. It operates upon energy, and industry, and skill, and
> thrift, like a fine upon those qualities. If I have worked harder
> and built myself a good house while you have been contented
> to live in a hovel, the taxgatherer now comes annually to make

me pay a penalty for my energy and industry, by taxing me more than you. If I have saved while you wasted, I am mulct, while you are exempt.

If a man build a ship we make him pay for his temerity, as though he had done an injury to the state; if a railroad be opened, down comes the tax collector upon it, as though it were a public nuisance; if a manufactory be erected we levy upon it an annual sum which would go far toward making a handsome profit. We say we want capital, but if any one accumulate it, or bring it among us, we charge him for it as though we were giving him a privilege. We punish with a tax the man who covers barren fields with ripening grain, we fine him who puts up machinery, and him who drains a swamp. . . .

To abolish these taxes would be to lift the whole enormous weight of taxation from productive industry. The needle of the seamstress and the great manufactory; the cart horse and the locomotive; the fishing boat and the steamship; the farmer's plow and the merchant's stock, would be alike untaxed. All would be free to make or to save, to buy or to sell, unfined by taxes, unannoyed by the taxgatherer. Instead of saying to the producer, as it does now, "The more you add to the general wealth the more shall you be taxed!", the state would say to the producer, "Be as industrious, as thrifty, as enterprising as you choose, you shall have your full reward! You shall not be fined for making two blades of grass grow where one grew before; you shall not be taxed for adding to the aggregate wealth."[25]

CALIFORNIA'S COMMERCIAL EDEN

The utopian vision of Henry George becomes a startling revelation if one considers that he drew his inspiration not from time unknown but from a time remembered in the not too distant past. The unfettered productivity of his untaxed world had its parallel in the hyperactive climate of development that surrounded the Gold Rush. Contemporaries describe the "never-resting spirit" of the San Francisco streets: "You speak to an acquaintance—a merchant perhaps," wrote the journalist and poet Bayard Taylor. "He utters a few hurried words of greeting, while his eyes send keen glances on all sides of you; suddenly he catches sight of somebody in the crowd; he is off, and in the next five minutes has brought up half a cargo, sold a town lot at treble the sum he gave, and taken a share in some new and imposing speculation." Continues another: "In the course of a month, or year, in San Francisco, there was more hard work done, more speculative schemes were conceived and executed, more money was made and lost, there was more buying and selling, more sudden changes of fortune, more eating and drinking, more smoking, swearing, gambling, and tobacco-chewing, more crime and profligacy, and, at the same time, more solid advancement made by the people, as a body, in wealth, prosperity, and the refinements of civilization, than could be shown in an equal space of time by any community of the same size on the face of the earth."[26]

A sufficient number of the argonauts found their fortune to give the new state an extraordinary prosperity. Henry George reports that the high wage scales fell to national levels in the 1870s, yet the disparity in per-capita incomes continued well into the twentieth century. The statistics may be distorted by local inflation (another product of California's isolation) but at the turn of the century per-capita income in the Far West exceeded the national average by more than 60%. The prosperity came from the growth fueled by the Gold Rush rather than from the gold itself; by 1860, the value of both the state's manufactures and its wheat crop surpassed the value of its gold production. All of the gold mined in the state throughout its history, writes the Gold Rush historian John Walton Caughey, is worth no more than twenty orange crops.[27]

Yet the quest for this metal more than a century ago has molded the state's peculiar character to this day. Natural wealth and the surge of human endeavor that followed the government's inability to exact taxation gave the state a head start that exceeded all expectation. From the initial thrust of the gold giveaway, California has hurtled through one boom after another with scarcely the time to look back. As Carey Mc-Williams exclaimed in the flush of the post–World War II immigration: "Elsewhere the tempo of development was slow at first, and gradually accelerated as energy accumulated. But in California the lights went on all at once, in a blaze, and they have never been dimmed."[28]

THE LASTING IMPACT: A CHURNED SOCIETY

The most enduring feature of California's hectic origins has been the rush of people to get there. Waves of immigration have constantly rolled over the state, attracted by a natural bounty advertised as vigorously as Sam Brannan announced Sutter's gold. Any tentative solidifying of community ties has been rolled and smashed in these breakers.

Population growth during the Gold Rush bordered on the unbelievable. The 1850 census counted 93,000 Californians, a tenfold increase over the Mexican days three years before. Men under twenty-four years old made up an absolute majority of the population, and there were only 7,000 women in the state. ("Dame Shirley," one of these women, writes of the "reverence" in which the miners held these "petticoated astonishments.") In a special census in 1852 the population had nearly trebled again, reaching 264,435. By 1860, it had grown to 379,994. More than one Californian in four was now female, and the number of young children, an even greater rarity during the Gold Rush, had increased twentyfold. Even though gold production dropped off sharply by the mid-1860s, the state grew by another 50% in the decade.[29]

When one stimulus to immigration weakened, another picked up the slack. After the bad times of the 1870s came the flush years of the eighties. When the Santa Fe Railroad reached Los Angeles, it started a rate war with the Southern Pacific (a disguised adjunct of the Central Pacific) that launched Southern California on the first and proportionally the greatest of its real estate booms. Prosperity crossed the Tehachapi Mountains from the north and permanently transformed the six Cow Counties.

Immigration through all these years perpetuated some of the features of the Gold Rush. With a much larger base, the percentage increases in population in the twentieth century come nowhere close to those of the hectic first quarter-century of the Gold Rush, but the absolute numbers remain impressive. From 1940 to 1950, net immigration to the state totaled 2.7 million. The male-female ratio did not approach parity until 1950.[30]

Population movements of such magnitude have kept the state's political structure in perpetual flux. Thirty years after the Gold Rush, James Bryce observed: "A great population had gathered before there was any regular government to keep it in order, much less any education or social culture to refine it. The wildness of that time passed into the blood of the people, and has left them more tolerant of violent deeds, more prone to interferences with or supersession of regular law, than are the people of most parts of the Union." The social chaos came not just from the magnitude of the immigration but from the wide variety of sources that fed it. The Midwestern frontier states, Bryce said, were peopled by a steady flow from two or three older states. "But California was filled by a sudden rush of adventurers from all parts of the world. . . . This mixed multitude, bringing with it a variety of manners, customs and ideas, formed a society more mobile and unstable, less governed by fixed beliefs and principles, than one finds in such North-western communities as I have just mentioned." He concludes with a common metaphor about California, in a variation that Californians do not commonly repeat: "That scum which the westward moving wave of emigration carries on its crest is here stopped, because it can go no farther."[31]

The perceptive Carey McWilliams draws out the political consequences of this continued immigration: "The basic unit of most political machines is the ward and the ward, in social terms, means an area of settled residence. . . . Ward politics are face-to-face politics, based on propinquity, family ties, favors, obligations, alliances and patronage.

"Merely to sketch the conditions of machine politics is to explain why party regularity is a negligible factor in California politics. . . . Political Machines simply cannot function with efficiency in areas which are largely made up of newcomers and strangers."[32]

In the absence of ward discipline and party loyalties, the political life of the state has come to rely on mass communication.

Much has been written about the defects and bizarre flourishes of California life; its atomization can be readily guessed at from the jumble of architectural styles encountered in a drive through downtown Los Angeles. In the absence of stable local institutions—neighborhoods, family ties, churches—Southern California produced a series of flamboyant but short-lived religious and political movements, playing the role in the 1920s and thirties that upstate New York had played a century earlier. The obverse of the state's unparalleled development—at least in its most rapidly growing counties—has been a permanent sense of transience in its social arrangements.

ORIGIN OF THE INITIATIVE

A highly mobile, rootless society is bound to evolve political institutions to fit its needs and character. In California, this work was done by Hiram Johnson and the Progressive movement. By the end of the nineteenth century, the corporations that emerged from the Gold Rush economy had come to dominate state politics. The Central Pacific (later Southern Pacific) Railroad had extraordinary control over the state legislature and over a portion of both major parties' nominating machinery. This power may have been on the wane when Hiram Johnson burst on the scene, but it had been exercised so baldly that it was vivid in the public mind.

The portrait of the Progressive Republican Johnson hanging in the state capitol shows a prim little man in high collar, hair parted in the middle; the shrewd glint through his wire-rim glasses and the fullness of his lower cheeks give him the air of a Walt Disney owl. But Johnson may have been first and foremost in understanding how to pitch a media campaign to the California electorate. In his 1910 campaign for governor he toured the state in a crimson Locomobile (in those days the automobile itself would attract a crowd) and harped incessantly on a single theme: "Kick the Southern Pacific out of politics."[33]

Although his campaign was kept simple and direct, the better to reach the public, Johnson as governor offered an ambitious and comprehensive program that set the standard for the Progressive movement. It created state institutions that persist to this day. Among the most important of these were the initiative and the referendum (sometimes together familiarly called the "I and R"). Governor Johnson put the issue bluntly in his inaugural address of January 3, 1911: "The first duty that is mine to perform is to eliminate every private interest from the government, and to make the public service of the State responsive solely to the people."[34] He pledged to root out anyone in government who tried to continue the old ways, no matter how powerful. "If he be the representative of Southern Pacific politics, or if he be one of that class who divides his allegiance to the State with a private interest and thus impairs his efficiency, I shall attack him the more readily because of his power and his influence and the wealth behind him. . . ."[35] And for the day when Johnson was no longer governor, he would "arm the people to protect themselves" with the initiative, referendum, and recall. "If we can give to the people the means by which they may accomplish such other reforms as they desire, the means as well by which they may prevent the misuse of the power temporarily centralized in the Legislature and an admonitory and precautionary measure which will ever be present before weak officials, and the existence of which will prevent the necessity for its use, then all that lies in our power will have been done in the direction of safeguarding the future and for the perpetuation of the theory upon which we ourselves shall conduct this government."[36]

Governor Johnson gave this item high priority in his legislative program. For drafting, he called on Dr. John Randolph Haynes, of Los Angeles, father of the Direct Legislation League. Dr. Haynes had written the initiative, referendum, and recall provisions of the 1903 Los Angeles city charter, the first such provisions to be adopted by any American city. The initiative (our primary concern here) allowed any statute or constitutional amendment to be submitted directly to popular vote provided its sponsors could obtain a set number of signatures; this number was to equal 8% of all votes cast for all candidates for governor in the last preceding general election. With a petition signed by 5% of these voters, "the people" could submit legislation directly to the legislature. If the bill failed there, it would go on the next general election ballot. The referendum, now rarely used, allowed petitioners to call a special election to repeal an act of the legislature.

In the 1909 legislature the Progressives had ventured to seek only the initiative, and that with a petition requirement of 12% of the voters. But Johnson's election sweep had eliminated so many old-line legislators that the full initiative and referendum proposal swept through both houses with only one dissenting vote.[37]

Debate was more lively in the special election on the amendments. Former Assemblyman Grove Johnson, the legislative leader of the Southern Pacific machine and the governor's own father, denounced the proposal as an attempt to substitute an "Athenian democracy for a representative form of government."[38] The con speaker in a debate at the Commonwealth Club of San Francisco called it "the uncorking of all the bottles of crankiness. . . . Any law that ought to be passed, and any law that the people really demand, whether it ought to be passed or not, will be passed by a Legislature; but in the process of legislation it will be licked into some kind of reasonable shape, and can be amended if not right, or repealed when we are tired of it." Dr. Haynes, the pro speaker in that same debate, replied that "the people are conservative and do not enact many, nor ultra radical laws." Direct popular government, he said, was the culmination of a world-wide evolution from despotism to constitutional monarchy to representative republics to pure democracy. His examples are ironic in hindsight; "witness Russia, Turkey, Persia, and even China," he said.[39] But the most prominent voice in this campaign was that of Hiram Johnson himself. Typically focusing on a few issues out of the 800 bills and twenty-three constitutional amendments passed by the 1911 legislature, the governor stumped for two months for the initiative, referendum, and recall. In one famous speech he pursued the logic of direct democracy to its conclusion and wound up denouncing the theory of checks and balances. This heresy fit the popular mood. In the October 10, 1911, special election, voters approved the constitutional amendments by better than three to one.[40]

From these beginnings, the initiative has become the single most distinctive feature of California politics. Initiative campaigns do the work that parties do elsewhere in generating issues. Petition circulators frame the terms of political debate more effectively than do the platforms of Republicans or Democrats. Initiatives have lent themselves well to the state's professional campaign-management industry; one firm even specializes in obtaining the signatures to put measures on the ballot.

Conceived as a general purpose implement, the initiative has acquired a rich history in taxation and finance. In its early years, the followers of Henry George used it six times to push their single tax on land, always unsuccessfully. Their efforts prompted an equally unsuccessful attempt to limit the use of initiatives on tax matters. Among the scrapbooks and memorabilia of the State Library's wood-paneled California Room lies the four-page pamphlet from 1922 reproduced on page 143. Published by the League to Protect the Initiative, the pamphlet explains that these enemies have filed their own initiative petition to raise the required number of signatures from 8% to 15% on petitions involving taxation or assessment. The League, featuring endorsements from a Progressive who's who including Governor Johnson and Dr. Haynes, naturally opposed this ploy to take control of taxation out of the reach of the I and R. Its most arresting argument, in boldface, states: "The power to tax is the essence of government. The control of taxation is the control of government."[41]

PROGRESSIVES AND TAXES

The reformers had nothing against taxation, however. Even before Hiram Johnson's revolution, advocates of good government had launched the state on an overhaul of its fiscal system. Since the 1879 constitution, both state and local governments drew the bulk of their revenues from the general property tax. This tax was paid to the county under the supervision of the State Board of Equalization and then divided among the various jurisdictions. From the 1890s, the state government had increasing difficulty meeting its rapidly growing expenses from its share of this tax.

A succession of governors began to argue for the Progressive tax reform of separating the sources of revenue for state and local governments. A specific proposal emerged to ex-

THE INITIATIVE AND REFERENDUM IN DANGER!

Enemies of Popular Government Renew
Effort to Crush Democracy in California

AND WOULD MONOPOLIZE CONTROL OF TAXATION

Enormous Increase of Signatures Required
for Initiative Petitions

"I insist that if there is anything that is the duty of the whole people never to entrust to any hands but their own, that thing is the perpetuity of their own liberty and institutions."
—ABRAHAM LINCOLN

1922

Published by

League to Protect the Initiative

Los Angeles, 429 Consolidated Realty Building
Telephone 63024
San Francisco, 905 First National Bank Building

empt public-service corporations from the property tax, which would be reserved to the local level, and instead make them subject to a state corporate income tax. Surprisingly, the railroads, utilities, banks, and insurance companies, which fell in this category, supported the idea. Even though it might mean higher rates, corporate executives appreciated the improved predictability in their tax burden and the end of the expense of bribing local tax assessors. After rejecting the idea of revenue separation in 1908, voters approved a constitutional referendum on the measure in late 1910. To the chagrin of these corporations, however, Governor Johnson covered the added expense of his reforms by raising business tax rates twice during his tenure.[42]

A general corporation income tax followed in 1929. In 1933, in the middle of the local finance crisis of the Depression, the legislature passed both a general state sales tax and a state income tax. But the income tax was vetoed, and the sales tax, extending to food, was highly unpopular. In 1935, after Republican Frank Merriam defeated the romantic Socialist Upton Sinclair for governor by aligning himself with President Franklin Roosevelt's New Deal, the state repealed the sales tax on food and substituted a moderate income tax. The major legs of the state's tax system were thus in place by the mid-thirties.

Yet Californians still carried a relatively moderate tax burden. By 1953, the state ranked twenty-second among the states in the percentage of state personal income that went for state and local taxes. The liberal administrations of Earl Warren, Goodwin Knight, and Edmund G. ("Pat") Brown brought California into the top ten. (In 1965, it ranked ninth.) But the most dramatic surge in the state's tax burden, making it third in the nation and second among major states only to New York, came in the administration of the alleged arch-conservative Ronald Wilson Reagan.[43]

REAGAN'S YEARS

When Ronald Reagan took the oath as governor of California a few minutes after midnight on January 2, 1967, he faced the same situation that had confronted Nelson Rockefeller and John Lindsay on coming to power in New York. His Democratic predecessor had been accumulating a hidden budget deficit, and with the change in administrations the bill came due. After some delay Reagan did the same thing Rockefeller and Lindsay had done—he raised taxes. Moreover he adopted a comprehensive tax package exceeding in scope any single measure proposed by the mayor and governor on the other end of the continent and from the other wing of his party. This package was a major step toward the Tax Revolt. The episode turned out to be the most decisive fiscal development in the state until Proposition 13.

During his presidential campaigns Reagan often stated that as governor he had inherited a state government spending $1 million a day more than it took in. This stump one-liner understated the problem. During Reagan's first months in Sacramento, estimates of the gap grew larger by the week. Ultimately he was brought to propose a tax package of nearly $1 billion. But this sum *overstated* the problem. The new tax structure shortly began to generate the kind of surpluses that Governor Jerry Brown later allowed to accumulate to gargantuan, and politically explosive, amounts. How Reagan, who promised in his inaugural to "squeeze and cut and trim" the government, came to give it such an unprecedented flow of money—and how he handled his Frankenstein's monster— merits a closer look.

PAT BROWN'S LEGACY

By Governor Pat Brown's last year in office, spending had been rising more rapidly than revenue for at least three years. According to the Legislative Analyst, a nonpartisan employee of the state legislature, "Temporary solutions alleviated the problem in 1963–64, 1964–65, and 1965–66 with, for the most part, one-time tax adjustments." Basically, these adjustments borrowed revenues from coming years to meet the problem of the moment and made the problems of the coming years even more severe. By fiscal year 1966–67, Brown's last budget, these problems had grown past the point of deferral. Governor Brown

California

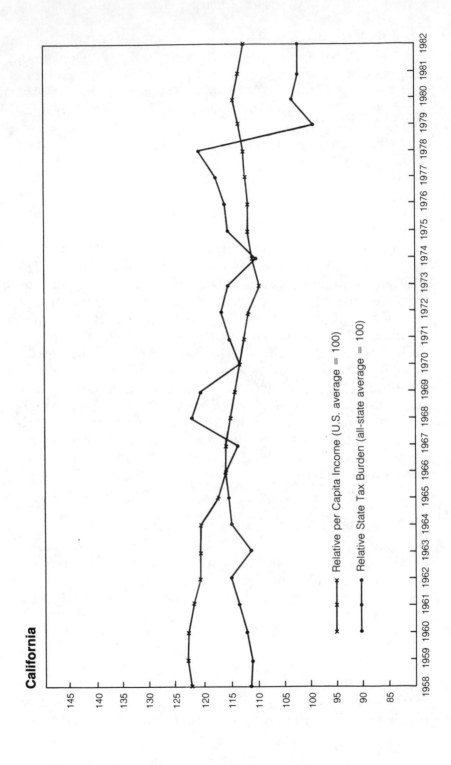

Relative per Capita Income (U.S. average = 100)

Relative State Tax Burden (all-state average = 100)

and Budget Director Hale Champion (Brown's former press secretary) faced a 10% deficit in their General Fund. While planning to close half of the gap by jiggering income tax exemptions, they were still left with a shortfall. So they resorted to the dangerous expedient of changing the accounting rules.[44]

Specifically, Brown and Champion switched revenue accounting from a cash basis, in which the money is counted only when it comes in hand, to an accrual basis. In accrual, revenue is counted as budget income when it comes due on paper. But, as any businessman well knows, bills don't necessarily get paid when they are supposed to be. The budget might be balanced on paper; it might even show a surplus; but the cash the government planned to spend could still be "in the mail."

The change in accounting did not create any additional revenue; it merely masked a deficit. In spite of Brown's hopes that enough of the cash in the mail would materialize to balance his budget in fact as well as in name, the revenue did not arrive. After Reagan took office, he found that the current-year budget that ended on June 30, 1967, was running $180 million in the red, and that another $180 million was being drawn down from reserves. (The second figure later rose to $270 million.)

Borrowing from reserves intensified the budget crisis and added real urgency to the tax increases. The reason lies in California's peculiar fiscal conservatism when it comes to cash flow management. As in many states, California's income is out of phase with its expenses. Two-thirds of the state's revenues come in during the last six months of the fiscal year, which ends June 30. But the monthly expenditures are nearly constant. So during the months of October through February the state has to scrape together some other sources of money to make ends meet. Unlike many states, however, it tries to raise this cash exclusively from its own internal sources. In flush years the prior year's surplus provides enough loose cash to cover this tight period. In lean years the state borrows money from off-budget special funds, such as the Architect's Fund, to get it through, then repays these accounts in the spring as revenues flood in. When times are very lean, the question may arise whether the state will receive enough tax revenue at the end of the year to repay this short-term borrowing. Until 1983, the state refused to issue short-term notes to the municipal bond market. By contrast, New York State floats an annual "spring borrowing" of more than $4 billion in notes.

If the special funds are unable to support this internal borrowing, a judgment made by the state comptroller, and the credit market could not handle it, the state could face a serious crisis. Lacking cash to meet its bills and payrolls, it might be forced to issue scrip, as it had done during the Depression and did again briefly in early 1983. A portion of Reagan's tax increase was earmarked to repay Brown's borrowing from these funds. But the tax increases that improve the cash flow during the lean months will swell the coffers in the fat months. Thus, Reagan is sometimes accused of raising permanent taxes excessively in his overreaction to a temporary cash flow problem.

Reagan then had his own first budget to worry about. The budget for fiscal 1967–68 went to the legislature just a month after his inauguration. His original plan called for a 5% spending cut from the previous budget. The General Fund agencies were asked to reduce their operating expenditures by 10%. This request was too vague to be anything more than a symbolic measure, and the bureaucracy had easy work in sending it to the elephant's graveyard. (Another symbolic request, that state employees work without pay on Washington's and Lincoln's birthdays, provoked passive resistance from senior executives who in the past had used the time to catch up on paperwork.)[45]

As his inexperienced fiscal advisers wrestled haplessly with the budget, Reagan began to move publicly toward tax increases. In a January press conference, he suggested broadening the base of the sales tax but reducing its rate. At the same time he reacted coolly to the idea of increased corporate taxes. "There isn't a corporation tax," he replied, "that isn't passed on in the price of the product to the people." His general attitude toward taxation foreshadowed the supply-side arguments of a decade later. "Now, the thing that has to be considered is, will a tax be regressive, will it dry up its source of revenue, will it make it more difficult for us to have the industries to provide the jobs? But no one has made any decision on that."[46] As decision time drew near, Reagan began to talk more about tax increases and to mention the personal income tax. On February 7, he said: "The sales tax happens to offer the best opportunity for a sizable chunk of money from a wide distribution, but I'm a believer that in our kind of society, a wise tax policy that incorporates both income tax and sales tax in combination is the fairest system of tax we can have."[47] Even so, he refused to abandon completely his previous theme of limiting the government. "I don't want to add a tax on, because I found out, and this is true of any government, including our own, that governments don't tax to get the money they need; governments always need the money they get."[48]

Coming from a man who espoused such sentiments just a month before, the March 8 program was staggering. The 5% budget cut was abandoned. The spending increase ultimately came to 8%, giving Reagan the state's first $5-billion budget. The tax package was more than double earlier estimates. It totaled $865 million and raised the rates of nearly every major state tax by 25% to 100%. Reagan boosted the 3% state sales tax to 4% (but decided after all not to extend it to food, drugs, or utilities). He leaned heavily on the "sin taxes," raising the distilled spirits excise by 50% and more than doubling the cigarette tax. Banks and corporations received proportionally the lowest increase, but the boost of one percentage point— raised by the Senate another half percentage point—put the franchise tax rate on general corporations at 7% and the maximum tax rate on banks at 11%. The most significant change of all, however, came in the personal income tax. Reagan proposed compressing the brackets, adding three new ones to the top, to a maximum rate of 10% at $18,000. This tax thus became highly progressive. When inflation began to soar in ensuing years, the state had windfall revenues to reap from "bracket creep." In announcing the package, Reagan gave a brief nod to the dangers of the personal income tax. "Some view this tax as a damper upon personal initiative," he said. But he quickly explained his reason for raising it anyway:

"Regardless of tax philosophy, the fact remains that few levies generate the volume of revenue needed to meet our financial needs and provide property tax relief."[49]

Reagan-watchers from this period praise the governor's native political skill in escaping popular resentment for such a massive tax increase. He did succeed in diverting most of the blame to the deficit left behind by Pat Brown. The most telling criticism came from his right flank, and it was largely ignored. Some charged that only half of the tax package went for the deficit; the rest covered programs, such as property tax relief and the budget increases, that Reagan undertook of his own free will. Reagan's tax package, one of these critics claimed, would double the personal income tax for every California family earning more than $10,000. "From a governor who campaigned on promises to economize and relieve the tax burden on productive citizens, so that their energies might be released in a 'Creative Society' this kind of tax increase is utterly indefensible."[50]

The package may indeed have been inflated by an entirely separate decision that was Reagan's alone. After acceding to the largest single tax increase proposed to that point by any American governor, Reagan adamantly refused to allow income tax withholding. This feature was one of the few points of difference from the Democratic tax bill supported by Assembly Speaker Jesse Unruh. The dispute delayed passage of the tax bill until a month after the beginning of the new fiscal year. The sound and fury may have diverted public attention from the size of the measure and allowed Reagan miraculously to retain his reputation as an enemy of taxation. Yet on one major point Unruh was right and Reagan was wrong. Withholding would have evened out the cash flow during the budget year, averting a crisis that loomed for that December. The internal cash sources had been so drained by Brown's overspending that, without accelerated revenue, the treasury would have run out of money for current expenses well before the new tax payments started to come in. The final compromise on the tax bill included a prepayment provision for larger-income taxpayers, which gave the administration an extra $115 million to ease the December cash shortage.

Did Reagan seek a tax increase far in excess of his real

need so that he would be in a position to propose tax cuts later in his term? Some cynical political opponents have suggested as much.[51] But to state the record fairly, the administration did not immediately realize just how effectively it had solved its revenue problem.

The fiscal 1968–69 budget, submitted in January 1968, seemed dangerously tight at the time. The Legislative Analyst worried that it underestimated certain expenses. Only as the year wore on did it become plain that it was the revenue from the new taxes that the budget had underestimated. By the end of 1968, personal income tax collections had increased more than 50% over the year before. In January 1969, reviewing the fiscal year 1969–70 budget, the Legislative Analyst noted that the General Fund situation had "brightened a great deal." The current budget was heading for a quarter-of-a-million-dollar surplus at the June 30 end of the fiscal year, and the surplus for fiscal year 1969–70 would be larger still.[52]

The bulk of the surplus came from the extraordinary ability of Reagan's new income tax structure to make money on inflation. If the paycheck of the average Californian merely kept pace with inflation, it would not bring him a higher standard of living. The higher wages would push him into a higher income tax bracket, and he would pay more in taxes just for the privilege of running in place. The tax people express this charming phenomenon in terms of "elasticity." In other words, if personal income grows by 10%, how much more will the tax bill grow? As a result of Reagan's narrowing of the brackets and increasing of the rates, the elasticity factor for the state personal income tax was a whopping 1.55. If a West Covina machinist brought home 10% more in his paycheck, his tax bill on the raise would go up by better than 15%.[53]

This phenomenon produced a sharp jump in the state's relative tax burden. In Reagan's first year, California's taxation jumped from 16% above the national average to 24% above. (The reader may want to consult the chart on p. 146 as a road map to the following discussion.) Among those startled by this surge was Governor Reagan himself. Eight years later, Reagan recalled that his policy in dealing with budget surpluses was to rebate the money to the taxpayer, to whom it belonged. There is dispute as to who originated some of the rebate programs that Reagan later claimed as his own. Yet no one questions that the first of these one-time tax cuts came at the initiative of Reagan and his budget director, Caspar Weinberger. In the spring of 1969, they announced that taxpayers would be able to deduct 10% from their income tax payments in the succeeding year as the means of giving them $100 million from the projected surplus. This tax cut, plus the growth of property tax relief programs, caused the relative tax burden to drop sharply in 1970. This figure fell to a mere 14% above the national average. The relative decline was all the steeper because nationally, state and local taxes had begun their sharp upward jump. Reagan was beginning to control his tax burden as mayors and governors around the country, and especially in New York, were raising theirs.

Without special attention, however, the tax burden began to drift back up. The tax rebate held the growth of income tax collections in fiscal 1970 to under 5%. In fiscal year 1971, a recession year, the growth rate ran at just under 10%. With a sharp decline in aerospace employment, California was more badly hurt than the nation as a whole. The budget was out of balance, but Reagan was running for reelection on a promise of no new taxes. So he signed a deficit budget and finally accepted income tax withholding. He also let the legislature add an 11% top bracket to the income tax. About this time word had gotten out that Reagan, after doubling the income tax, had filed a return with no tax liability, thanks to deductions from his hobby of horse breeding. In a slap at the governor, the legislature passed a "preference tax," requiring upper-income taxpayers to pay at least a set minimum.[54]

In 1972, the legislature passed the first of several major efforts to reform the tax base for public schools. The bill, SB 90, provided more than a billion dollars, primarily in new state aid; the aid helped equalize the tax burden among school districts and increased the homeowner's exemption. To finance the local property tax relief the legislature raised the state sales tax by one percentage point and the corporation tax rate by 1.4 percentage points.

But in the same year, state revenues began to surge. The revised tax structure and the beginnings of economic recovery boosted fiscal 1972 income tax collections by better than 40%. In early 1973, looking at the coming year's budget, Governor Reagan's fiscal planners foresaw a surplus under Pat Brown's accrual accounting of nearly $900 million. The legislature promptly set to the pleasant task of making the surplus vanish. In a bill also numbered SB 90, it granted credits ranging from 20% to 35% on the income tax on 1973 incomes and lowered the sales tax for six months. Reagan finally rolled back some of Brown's accrual accounting. Thanks to these cuts, the state's relative tax burden fell sharply, to 110% of the all-state average. Reagan was able to close his second term with California apparently in its best competitive position in a decade. Yet the excessively productive tax system remained intact, ready to generate a surplus and a rising tax burden whenever Sacramento neglected to return the excess proceeds to the taxpayer.

SERRANO AND OTHER SURPRISES

Reagan's budgets were blindsided by two unpredictable events that to some extent took tax decisions out of his control. The first came in 1971, when the California Supreme Court decision in *Serrano v. Priest* began a prolonged revolution in school finance. Berkeley law professors John Coons and Stephen Sugarman started the suit ostensibly to equalize the school funding base, which varied widely from "poor" district to "rich" district. But Coons later stated that he was less concerned with bringing about equality than with overthrowing what he considered to be an irrational and obsolete financing system. He was much more successful in his second purpose than in his first.

The Serrano case pushed the legislature into drafting the first SB 90, which provided some property tax relief and vastly increased state aid for the schools. To keep some districts from reopening the funding gap by increasing their real estate levies, the bill imposed a limit on school-district property tax rates. Even this attempt to legislate mediocrity failed to satisfy the California Supreme Court, so the case dragged on. The rate limit made little difference ultimately because the real engine of growth in the property tax was not the rate but the underlying assessed valuation.

The gathering property tax crisis hit Reagan's budget from another direction. From his first month as governor, Reagan had been talking about property tax relief. Programs like the "homestead exemption," the "circuit-breaker," and others made up the bulk of the $4 billion he later claimed to have turned back to the taxpayers. But this tax relief was not entirely voluntary. Discontent over soaring property tax bills had already begun to haunt Sacramento; constitutional initiatives to control them were beginning to appear on state ballots.

The property tax, California's largest single source of local revenues, had turned into almost as much of a money machine as the state income tax. Inflation was the root cause for both, but the mechanics were different. Two things determine how much property tax a homeowner pays. The first is the tax rate. The county, city, or school board sets the rate under the public eye, and elected representatives have to answer for it at the next election. The second factor is more hidden, mysterious, and out of control. This is the assessment, the value the government sets on the property it is going to tax. The size of the bill is the rate *times* the assessment, so if the rate remains constant but the assessed value climbs, the bill will go up. Because the rates in California remained roughly constant, the SB 90 limits had little impact. The assessments made the difference.

THE ASSESSMENT TRAUMA

California led the nation in the growth of its housing prices and also in the speed with which this inflation showed up in tax bills. Property taxes are hard to pay, coming due in one or two large bills. These lump sums are even harder to raise for homeowners, such as the elderly, who live in valuable property without earning high incomes. Reassessment to bring property values up to date can be such a political trauma that some jurisdictions shudder to undertake it. (Boston, to cite one extreme example, is just getting around to it for the first time in about a century.) But thanks to a scandal two decades ago, California has one of the most rapid and thorough reassessment schedules in the country.

In 1965, the county assessor of San Francisco went to jail for taking money from businessmen in return for low assessments. Liberal legislators thought that by this corruption, business had been escaping its full share of the tax burden. So they passed the Petris-Knox reform bill requiring full assessment at 25% valuation on a three-year cycle. The bill set up a sophisticated "good government" system for the property tax, aided by computers. But the legislators forgot that homeowners have more votes than businessmen, and anyone who manipulates assessments for personal and political gain is going to give residential property the biggest break of all. The Petris-Knox reforms indeed shifted the tax burden, but against expectations it shifted it away from business and back onto the homeowner. As the bills went out, bumper stickers sprouted around San Francisco pleading, "Bring back the crooked assessor."[55]

THE ASSESSOR'S TAX REVOLT

One other assessor took his own steps to head off the building pressure. In 1968, Los Angeles County's Philip E. Watson introduced a constitutional initiative to cut the property tax. Watson's first ballot effort proposed to restrict the tax to 1% of market value. In response to this drive Reagan and the legislature inaugurated the homeowner's exemption program, forgiving the tax on the first $750 of assessed value. The quick response in Sacramento helped defeat Watson's Proposition 9 by a two-to-one vote.

In 1972, Watson was back again. His new initiative tried to be more "responsible," proposing a 1½% limit on the property tax and making up the lost revenue by raising a variety of state taxes (including sales and corporate income). Reagan upped the ante with the first SB 90, increasing the homeowner's exemption to $1,750 (as well as limiting the tax rates for school levies). Since the bill shifted the property tax burden back to industrial and commercial tracts, business was granted a 50% exemption to the inventory tax, the state's most evidently irrational tax. In a tactic later used in the anti-Proposition 13 campaign, Reagan told the public that none of these good things could be done if the Watson initiative passed. By Reagan's last year in office, the size of these tax relief programs had more than doubled, to well over a billion dollars. Watson's initiatives failed badly at the polls, but they were immediately followed by the sharpest tax burden declines of Governor Reagan's administration. It is a neat question which was more responsible, the governor's policy or the threat of the initiative.

Watson himself resigned in early 1978, applying for a disability pension for a heart condition caused, he said, by the tensions of the assessor's office. In early 1982, he briefly considered running again. Proposition 13, he said, had "taken the pressure off" the job of assessor.[56]

REAGAN'S REACTION: PROPOSITION 1

Reagan's last major effort in office betrayed a deep dissatisfaction with most of what had gone before. In the aftermath of his 1967 tax package, and probably as a result, the state had entered a deeper-than-national recession, the rate of in-migration had hit a modern low point, and total relative personal income had deteriorated throughout his term.

In 1973, Governor Reagan called a special election on his own constitutional initiative. Labeled Proposition 1, it would have limited state revenues to a fixed percentage of state personal income. By today's standards, it was not a very radical measure, yet, to Reagan's embarrassment, it lost by a not-too-narrow margin. In retrospect, however, the Proposition 1 campaign looks like something of a modern turning point. It gave renewed legitimacy to the idea of imposing fiscal restraints by referendum. Several of the figures who helped draft the measure (including Lewis K. Uhler, chairman of the Proposition 1 task force) kept the effort alive by forming the National Tax Limitation Committee; this group exported the referendum idea to other states with increasing success. If one wanted to assign a particular starting point to the decade of the Tax Revolt, the Proposition 1 campaign may be the most logical candidate.

THE TASK FORCE

The planning that led to Proposition 1 began in mid-July 1972. The legislature had just maneuvered Reagan into accepting the final increase in the personal income tax, and work was under way on the first SB 90, with its boosts in the sales tax and the corporation franchise tax. By this time, say Sacramento veterans, Reagan was thoroughly frustrated by his dealings with the representative branch. His Screen Actors Guild experience as a labor negotiator had not kept him from being out-played and out-dealt by his Senate and Assembly rivals. All his rhetoric notwithstanding, state spending had increased by about 12%, the same rate as under Pat Brown.

Reagan decided that only a constitutional initiative could break the stalemate. He set up the Tax Reduction Task Force to design such a measure, yet he left it considerable leeway on the details.

In the world of fiscal initiatives, scholars see Proposition 1 as the product of one of two main intellectual approaches, a comprehensive spending limit rather than a constitutional ceiling on one or several taxes. (Examples of the second approach are the Watson initiatives and Proposition 13 itself.) This distinction was not at all clear, though, as Proposition 1 was being drafted.

A preliminary planning paper for the Tax Reduction Task Force suggested an emphasis on tax cuts. A proto-supply-side agenda item urged the participants to "check the post-war German taxation approach, which placed the burden on consumption and use, not on wealth creation (income) and existing wealth. This appeared to promote profit formation and investment."[57] As the initiative evolved, its main features were a limit on the proportion of total state personal income that could be taken in state taxes and a gradual reduction in the tax burden. In early drafts, the reduction was to be concentrated in the income tax. At least one task force member argued for a limit on state spending instead of state tax revenue, on the grounds that officials would still be able to turn to higher levels of government (in this case, Washington) for aid to keep up their high spending. But after six months of deliberation and four major drafts, the task force retained the idea of a limit on tax collections.

Reagan unveiled the details of the task force's 5,700-word measure in a February 9, 1973, speech to the California Newspaper Publishers Association. Total taxes would be reduced over fifteen years to 7% of total state personal income. The legislature would choose which taxes to cut. "There is no other way to effectively control government spending except to control the amount of revenue that government has to spend," he said, with better sense than grammar. If the legislature refused to approve the measure as a referendum, Reagan threatened to launch his own petition campaign to put it on a special election ballot. And so he did, in an unprecedented drama pitting the governor against the legislature in a direct initiative appeal to the people.[58]

THE PROPOSITION 1 CAMPAIGN

The campaign aroused furious opposition. In an echo of the 1911 position of Grove Johnson, liberal legislators argued that Reagan was undercutting representative government. The California State Employees Association and the California Teachers Association pooled their resources, providing four-fifths of the funding for the "no" campaign and impressing both sides with their potential joint power. The Legislative Analyst's office heckled the measure. State spending, it noted, had fallen within the 7% limit until another of Reagan's task forces had produced the first SB 90: Proposition 1 would force the governor to choose between the new property tax relief programs and more traditional state services.[59]

Although the "Yes on Proposition 1" campaign spent more than any initiative campaign had theretofore, it had a difficult time explaining the unfamiliar measure. On a television talk show two weeks before the special election, Reagan was asked if the average voter really understood the language of the proposition. "He shouldn't try," Reagan replied jocularly.

"I don't, either." This good-humored sally became the watchword of the opposition. On November 6, the measure lost by 54% to 46%, a margin of 340,000 votes.[60]

The defeat seems primarily the result of voter confusion over the complicated amendment, compounded by partisan division. The campaign was so closely tied to Reagan that party lines were strengthened at one of the worst moments in recent Republican history. Then-Secretary of State Jerry Brown called the vote a repudiation of Watergate. Bad feelings and recriminations among the Reagan camp later showed up in the press, with special emphasis on the poor organization of the campaign.

Some voiced suspicions that the campaign had been usurped from its intellectual authors by more political staffers, led by Michael Deaver, who wanted a dry run for the presidential effort. But Reagan's personal commitment to the measure was unquestionably sincere. One can see here his strong predisposition to the themes later codified in supply-side economics. Proposition 1, with its implicit repudiation of the preceding one-and-one-half terms of tax policy, looks like a major event in Reagan's belated conversion to "Reaganomics." From the beginning, traces of supply-side doctrine did show up in Reagan's early press conferences, even as his advisers put together a tax package of vastly different orientation. Yet as late as 1976, he was still isolated from the supply-side political movement. The focus of this movement in the mid-seventies was the Kemp-Roth bill to cut federal income taxes in three annual steps of 10% each. Former *Wall Street Journal* writer Jude Wanniski recounts that at the 1976 Republican convention in Kansas City, Buffalo Congressman Jack Kemp, the bill's co-author, said he would throw his support and his influence in the New York and southern delegations to the presidential contender who endorsed his bill. President Ford was not interested. Some of Reagan's staff were, but they could not get through to their candidate. So neither candidate endorsed the bill, Kemp remained uncommitted, and President Ford won renomination by seventy votes.

Early the next year, the story goes, Reagan and supply-side economist Arthur Laffer were guests at a dinner party thrown by the industrialist Justin Dart. Laffer took the occasion to ask Reagan why he had not endorsed the Kemp-Roth bill. "Why, I was always for that bill," Reagan said.

"If we'd known that last year," Laffer replied, "you'd be president now."[61]

In the meantime, Proposition 1 had started another train of events. Reagan's Tax Reduction Task Force had drawn on an impressive list of academicians and public-finance experts. Its alumni included William A. Niskanen, later chief economist for the Ford Motor Company and member of President Reagan's Council of Economic Advisers; Norman Ture, one of the leading supply-siders in the U.S. Treasury until late 1982; Milton Friedman, the Chicago economist; James Buchanan, the "public choice" theorist; and William Craig Stubblebine, of Claremont Men's College in Claremont, California.[62] Several of these figures joined Lewis Uhler on his National Tax Limitation Committee, providing intellectual leadership to his national network of state politicians and tax protesters. This network sponsored measures modeled on Proposition 1 in other states, hoping to build a national constituency, although after its defeat they may have moved at a slower pace than they had originally planned. And while this was going on, an interested observer from Southern California was noting the advantage of a simple, direct, and nonpartisan approach.

"THE EXALTATION OF CRANKS"

When the initiative and the referendum were first adopted in California, William Howard Taft exclaimed, "Could any system be devised better adapted to the exaltation of cranks . . . ?"[63] Many of California's elite might have echoed that sentiment when Howard Jarvis and Paul Gann joined forces to produce Proposition 13. The earthy "jack Mormon" Jarvis and the Bible-quoting Okie Gann were far removed from the sophisticated world of San Francisco or Beverly Hills. Their panacea, a 57% cut in the property tax, seemed as crude and unworkable as any of the utopian enthusiasms that enliven the history of the California initiative. Yet they produced the first great success of the modern Tax Revolt. They solved the problem the political leadership could not handle. In cutting the Gordian knot of public-sector spending, they took an approach as brutal and direct as Alexander's, and left as many frayed ends. Yet they successfully reversed the state's pattern of rapidly increasing tax burdens. The impact of the Jarvis-Gann landslide turned Sacramento on its ear. In the turmoil, politicians sought in months and weeks to correct the problems they had ignored for years. The authority of political and business leadership lay in ruins. Yet the economy prospered with a rate of relative job creation and decline in unemployment that had not been seen in years. The "cranks" had not only been exalted, they had done their jobs better than the cream of the elite.

THE GROWING CRISIS

In Reagan's last budget, he voluntarily restricted spending to the limit sought by the defeated Proposition 1. But from that point to the passage of Proposition 13, the tax burden had resumed its inexorable rise. This time a strange paralysis seized Sacramento, and it could make no effective response to the grass-roots unrest.

The growth in housing values that had inspired the Watson initiatives paled in comparison to the boom of the mid-seventies. From 1974 to 1978, housing prices increased at an average annual rate in *real terms* of 10.4%, and soared from 1976 to 1977 alone by 20.8%.[64] Assessments lagged behind this surge, even on California's tight schedule, but in fiscal year 1976–77 they, too, were growing at an annual rate in the double digits. In spite of a fourteen-cent decline in the statewide average tax rate (from $11.33 per $100 to $11.19), the property tax levy had increased by over $1 billion (or nearly 13%) from the year before.

The burden this growth imposed, especially on the low-income elderly, was clearly becoming a major issue. Jerry Brown, Reagan's successor, gave property tax relief the featured place in his fiscal 1977–78 budget, proposing a "circuit-breaker" program in which the state paid a large proportion of the "excess" tax. ("Excess" was defined as tax levies beyond a certain proportion of household income.) He called for a constitutional change to a "split roll," taxing business property at a higher rate than residential to reverse the shift of the tax burden. And, foreshadowing future events, he urged stricter statutory limits on property tax growth.

Brown's program responded in some measure to the local ferment. It showed some of the flair which at the time was bringing him an unprecedented level of popular approval. While he appealed to his liberal constituency with rhetoric, he also sought to satisfy the material interests of more conservative lower-middle-class homeowners. But Brown failed to follow through. The tax relief program stalled in the legislature. Liberal Democrats wanted to replace it with an ambitious redistribution of income, financing lower-income property tax relief with even higher brackets on the income taxes. Republicans complained that Brown's package slighted the middle and upper-middle classes. A conference-committee compromise collapsed on the Senate floor, and the legislature adjourned with nothing to show for its work.[65]

THE MONEY MACHINE
GOES OUT OF CONTROL

As if the property tax debacle were not enough, California's revenue system seemed to be going haywire. In 1977, the state surplus began to emerge as a major problem—a novel and refreshing problem perhaps to anyone schooled in the bankruptcy of New York, but a problem nonetheless. The surplus represented an admission by government itself that the tax rates far exceeded the legitimate needs of the state. The government was unable to spend the money but unwilling to return it.

The first major surge in the surplus came from the political failure of the tax relief bill. The bill was expected to consume a fiscal 1977–78 surplus estimated in January 1977 at $1.5 billion. When the program collapsed most of the surplus went into the state treasury. At the same time, inflation was pushing Ronald Reagan's money machine into overdrive, and revenues rolled in beyond the state's expectations.

This unusual fiscal problem was compounded by Jerry Brown's peculiar political personality. Brown in many ways was accurate in claiming to represent a new generation in American politics. Some elements of the New Left in the sixties had been groping toward a basic revision of liberal politics; they hit on some insights that outlasted that movement's descent into self-indulgent fantasy. Unlike the right, they had no distrust of government, but they did despise the way government had been spending its money. They understood the failings of New Deal social programs. They also realized that the automatic growth in these programs would prevent the new political generation from ever having the resources to develop alternatives. Budgets had to be pruned to the trunk before they could grow in new directions. In his early years as governor, Jerry Brown liked to brag that he had averted more than a billion dollars in defensible new spending.[66]

Brown also seemed never to believe that the state revenue growth could maintain its pace. His well-known rhetoric of an "era of limits" was rooted in a western experience particularly pressing at that time. Carey McWilliams has remarked on the paradox that the unparalleled growth of the western states has always seemed on the verge of colliding with their natural limitations. In Brown's first term California faced a genuine shortage of its most indispensable resource—water. A year of severe drought came in 1977. Another year of low rainfall threatened to damage the economy, and it seemed only prudent to maintain the surplus in reserve.[67] No one expected that revenue throughout calendar year 1977 and half of 1978 would surge more than $1.7 billion above projections. Through the first half of 1978, estimates of the surplus fluctuated by $1 to $2 billion at a time, largely depending on one's method of bookkeeping.

JARVIS MEETS GANN

To the average taxpayer it seemed that Sacramento was doing nothing to help him out. Perhaps it was even trying to conceal the extent to which it was hurting him. Legislators reported an eerie tranquillity on the tax issue, which one writer astutely says came about because their constituents had given up on them. But slouching toward Sacramento came two perennial petition circulators, Paul Gann from the north and Howard Jarvis from the south. Their hour come round at last, by late 1977, they had merged their initiative drives for a constitutional limit on the property tax.[68]

Jarvis, a retired factory owner, part-time lobbyist for Los Angeles apartment-building owners, and organizer of grassroots taxpayers' organizations, dates his interest in tax issues to his young manhood in Utah, when he served on a governor's commission on tax reform. Gann, the son of an Arkansas preacher, came to the issue late, on the request of elderly friends he had helped in an anticrime campaign. In 1976, both had circulated property-tax initiatives and both had failed. But their efforts cumulatively had gained 200,000 signatures more than the required half million. After a false start on cooperation involving Assessor Watson, they overcame their mutual distrust in the spring of 1977, and the petition drive on their joint measure began in June.

Their eight-paragraph measure was devastating but succinct, reflecting Jarvis's style. It limited the property tax to 1% of full cash value, 50% lower than Gann's original limit, and made an exception only for servicing debt already approved by the voters. (Gann had allowed a permanent loophole for debt.) Gann's language on tax relief for renters was omitted, as he regrets to this day. Gann did get his provision requiring a two-thirds vote of the legislature for any new state taxes. (Jarvis had earlier been willing, following Watson, to let the legislature substitute other taxes for the property tax.) New language, not in either man's prior version, set the base for "full cash value" assessment at the 1975–76 tax year and limited subsequent increases to 2% a year; it allowed a jump to current full value on the sale of the property. The final limit, also new, required a "two-thirds vote of the qualified electors of such district" to impose special taxes in any city, county, or special district.[69]

Compared to this draconian measure, which cut property taxes by more than $6 billion, Proposition 1 seemed the height of moderation. But the coalition that had embarrassed Reagan could not put a dent in Jarvis and Gann. Unlike the six-year governor, Jarvis was a fresh wrinkled face. His outrageous statements amused the public, says writer Robert Kuttner; he was "like an angry Muppet," and occasionally he landed a bomb squarely on the pomposities of the opposition. "When you see politicians and bankers and union leaders standing together against something you are for," Jarvis once said, "then you know that there is no way in the world that you can be wrong."[70]

Claims of the disasters to follow Proposition 13 became increasingly hysterical and far-fetched. Blackmail tactics like disaster budgets and announcements of potential layoffs backfired badly. Voters made Proposition 13 the focus of their discontent, not only with taxation but also with innumerable government harassments.[71] One nonhomeowner reports that his foremost thought in voting yes was to protest the one-way routing of Berkeley street traffic. Paul Priolo, the Assembly minority leader, caught on to the public mood a bit late. "Whenever I tell an audience that Jarvis will bring local government to a halt," he said, "all I see is smiling faces."

By this time the legislature had finally passed its own property tax relief measure, which appeared on the ballot as Proposition 8. The bill, sponsored by Republican state Senator Peter Behr, cut homeowner taxes by 30% and doubled the tax credit for renters. It also amended the constitution to split the business and residential property rolls and restore the tax burden on business. The increased business property tax would help finance the measure's estimated cost of $1.4 billion. The Behr bill was much more generous to homeowners than any of the previous year's legislative alternatives, following the pattern of the legislative tax relief prompted by the Watson initiatives. But this time the old scenario did not work.

THE EARTHQUAKE

Polls showed that Jarvis-Gann always led among voters who would commit themselves, but that most voters refused to state their opinion until the last month. Then the tax system itself turned the shift to Proposition 13 into a geological upheaval. Jarvis had been predicting that the new assessments would double. According to Robert Kuttner's vivid account, Jarvis calculated that some county assessor would crack under his pressure and release the July reassessments early. One assessor did, and he happened to be in Los Angeles County. Polls were showing the no vote gaining until L.A. County Assessor Alexander Pope revealed new assessments exceeding even Jarvis's predictions. In a panic, county officials dithered over mailing out some of the assessments, all of them, or trying, illegally, to freeze them at the previous rate. Support for Proposition 13 shot ahead. Knowing now the measure would pass anyway, voters shed their residual doubts and gleefully jumped on the bandwagon. According to Kuttner, "the mood turned apocalyptic, even carnival. If it was going to pass anyway, why not really send the bastards a message."[72]

On June 6, 1978, Jarvis-Gann won by 65% to 35%, carrying fifty-five of the state's fifty-eight counties.

The vote swept across a generation of political boundaries. In contrast to the vote on Proposition 1, a healthy majority of Democrats (55%) rallied behind Jarvis-Gann. All income groups supported it, with the peak in the middle-income bracket of $20,000 to $30,000. The yeses were in the 65% range across educational categories until one reached those with college and postgraduate degrees; there, only 51% said yes. The main dissenters were renters (but 47% said yes), government employees, and, most significant, blacks. More than 80% of black voters opposed Jarvis-Gann. Furthermore, this new alignment has held in polls and subsequent initiatives.[73]

The vote for Proposition 13 was to the Tax Revolt what Bastille Day was to the French Revolution. The successful assault on authority completely changed the rules. Governor Brown, a close observer of the public mood, moderated his harsh attacks on the measure in May and began making publicized preparations to implement it. Immediately after the vote he embarked on continuous meetings with the Assembly and Senate leaders and fiscal committee chairmen to figure out how to deal with the massive tax cuts about to descend on the state's local governments. The state surplus was more than enough to cover the immediate revenue loss, but the state government had to reallocate more than $4 billion in an incredibly short time. With three weeks to run before Proposition 13 became Article XIIIA of the state constitution, said one of Brown's staff, "there was just no room to fiddle." The hectic, high-level scramble in Sacramento beat the deadline by a full week, in an impressive display of responsiveness. The bailout bill, SB 154, was far from ideal. Republican insistence on preventing local cutbacks in police and fire departments kept municipal managers from exploiting an almost unique opportunity to trim politically untouchable deadwood. Special taxing districts for irrigation, fire protection, and the like were seriously slighted because of general ignorance about their operations. Some major cities complained of inequities. But in general the bill successfully distributed $4 billion from the surplus, easing local governments through the transition with remarkably little disruption. (An additional $900-million fund for emergency short-term loans was scarcely used.) Brown put on a display of stringency in the state government, freezing state employee salaries and welfare benefits. By midsummer, voters were telling pollsters for the gubernatorial election that Brown had been a supporter of Proposition 13 and his Republican opponent, Evelle Younger, had been against it—an exact reversal of the actual history.

The legislature, also up for reelection, hastened to join the tax derby. It adopted an additional $1-billion tax cut, including increased income tax credits, partial indexing of its brackets, renters relief, and other measures, in twenty-two days, without a single negative vote.[74]

Thanks largely to his success in joining the revolution, Brown won reelection in November by more than a million votes. Other politicians were not as lucky. Seven of ten incumbents opposed by Howard Jarvis lost their seats. About a dozen "Proposition 13 babies" joined the Republican ranks in the legislature, and within two years the pre-Jarvis majority and minority leadership in the Assembly had been deposed.

PARTING OF THE WAYS

By the following year, however, the leadership of the tax revolution had gone through a personal and ideological split. Jarvis and Gann, always somewhat wary allies, parted company over Gann's new initiative for a constitutional state spending limit. The split personified the intellectual divergence in the fiscal-limitation movement. Jarvis, like the early Watson, favored simple, massive cuts in targeted taxes. Gann, like some backers of Proposition 1, preferred overall spending limits.

Gann's "Spirit of 13" initiative, numbered Proposition 4 on the November 1979 ballot, ran to twenty-four complicated paragraphs. Its drafting committee included some veterans of Proposition 1, principally William Craig Stubblebine. According to the measure, state and local appropriations could grow no faster than the change in population or the federal Consumer Price Index (or the California per-capita personal income, if it were lower). Taxes collected byond the spending limit would have to be returned by tax rate cuts over the subsequent two years. Befitting the authors' experience, the technical language made a sophisticated attempt to deal with possible evasions like unfunded mandating of programs.

Jarvis snorted that Proposition 4 was too long and lacked bite. Perhaps sharing that assessment, most of the state's political leadership supported Gann's initiative. After an uncontroversial campaign, a full 74% of the voters said yes to the measure. It carried every county, even San Francisco. Although tax revolt sophisticates noted the divergence between the Jarvis and the Gann approach, voters apparently did not feel it made much difference. One poll analysis found that the main determinant of support for Proposition 4 was the degree to which the respondent favored Proposition 13. And support for Proposition 13 continued as strong as ever.[75]

While Gann savored his triumph, Jarvis was having only limited success in launching a national tax revolt. He decided to return to home soil. On April 16, 1979, he announced a new constitutional initiative to cut state income tax rates in half, permanently index the brackets, and eliminate the amazingly durable business inventory tax. The measure qualified easily but it did so through the expensive services of the Butcher-Forde consulting firm. At the beginning of 1980, polls showed a favorable margin of 54% to 34%. But this time the campaigning roles were reversed. Overscheduled and frequently exhausted, Jarvis began to grate on his public. His wild personal attacks on opponents no longer served as a vicarious satisfaction to a frustrated electorate and seemed merely insulting. "During Proposition 13, he was a character," said one sympathizer. "During Proposition 9, he was a caricature." Although Arthur Laffer made a series of commercials to put the campaign back on a theoretical basis, funds were so depleted that they were never shown.

On the other side, the "No on Nine" committee provided the well-organized, coherent opposition that had been lacking in the Proposition 13 debate. It managed to exploit names previously found on the other side, mainly such adherents of the spending-limit school as Milton Friedman and Craig Stubblebine. Unknown to these lukewarm academic backers, the No on Nine campaign also had the support of the federally funded Legal Services Corporation. In possible violation of federal law, this federal corporation provided $61,665 directly to the Western Center on Law and Poverty in Los Angeles to organize a task force to defeat Proposition 9. Additional funds, possibly totaling $800,000, were released indirectly, and local staff members were delegated to work with unions and their own clientele in building a No on Nine coalition. The chairman of the formal No on Nine committee, Los Angeles lawyer Michael Kantor, was also a director of the Legal Services Corporation.[76]

The main theme of the statewide campaign was that the across-the-board rate cut favored the rich because they would save more money. This argument was statistical nonsense. The higher brackets obviously paid the bulk of the income tax to begin with. Calculations by the Legislative Analyst showed that the combination of rate cuts and untouched tax credits in fact shifted the burden of the levy slightly more to the upper brackets. Leaders of the No on Nine committee later admitted privately that this theme indeed had little influence on the campaign. Their case, they say, was won at the grassroots, which worried that another round of state tax cuts might endanger funding for public education. In a mirror image of Proposition 13, support for Proposition 9 collapsed rapidly in the last month. It lost by a margin of 61% to 39%.

Ironically, Proposition 9 was the most theoretically sound of the entire series of fiscal initiatives. (Running a respectable second was the third draft of Proposition 1, which would have channeled the surplus from the tax burden limitation into reductions of the state income tax rate.) Although Laffer supported Proposition 13's property tax cuts as a "surrogate" for income tax cuts, his supply-siders favored a strategy of concentrating the reductions on the marginal income tax rates that placed the heaviest burden on productive activity.

One major study of the California initiatives concludes that in repudiating Proposition 9 the voters closed the book on the Tax Revolt.[77] Even though California initiative movements have historically had a limited life span, this conclusion is hard to accept. If anything, the Proposition 13 upheaval has shown unusual staying power. Article XIIIA of the state constitution has become a kind of holy writ for California politics. A *Los Angeles Times* poll in November 1981 found a full 70% favorably disposed toward Proposition 13, more than had voted for it.

In November 1980, the California ballot offered what was undeniably the least noticed state tax initiative in the country. (It even failed to make the Associated Press news wrapup.) This Proposition 4 would have amended Article XIII to allow localities to resume issuing general obligation bonds provided that two-thirds of the voters approved. This measure had a good deal to commend it. The two-thirds requirement for the referendum was unusually strigent. (New York's bond referendums require only a majority.) One of Proposition 13's most serious weaknesses was its practical prohibition of general obligation financing, which reduced the funds available for maintaining infrastructure. (Banks especially resented this provision because localities shifted their borrowing into revenue bonds, which financial institutions were not allowed to market.) Proposition 4 of 1980 would have restored local control and headed off expensive state spending; leading conservatives supported it. Yet voters saw it as an attempt to tamper with Proposition 13, and it lost by three to one.

The Tax Revolt remained politically potent even through the adverse conditions of the 1982 recession. Although the combination of national recession and rapid state-spending growth had temporarily exhausted the state surplus, leaving the fiscal 1982–83 budget facing a deficit estimated at one point to be $4 billion, political support for personal tax increases was nonexistent. The Legislative Analyst's office argued that the statutory income tax indexing program was a prime source of the deficit. Yet, in June 1982, voters approved yet another Jarvis-sponsored initiative to expand indexing and give it constitutional status.

THE RESULTS OF PROPOSITION 13

The continuing political support for tax limitation reflects an overriding fact of California life: Proposition 13 worked. Opponents had predicted layoffs of 270,000 public employees, raising the unemployment rate from 7.4% to 10%. Total government employment did decline by 18,000 for one year, but by the end of 1980 it had rebounded to an all-time high, 14,000 above the 1978 level. If one starts from the low point marked by anticipatory layoffs before Jarvis-Gann passed, one can argue that public employment in California grew at a faster rate than the creation of all jobs, public and private, in the national economy. Private job creation in California far surpassed the national rate. For the first time in decades, the state unemployment rate fell consistently below the national average.

Proposition 13 was supposed to create enormous inequities in the tax rolls, accelerating the shift of the tax burden to residential property, which, it was thought, changed hands more often than business tracts did. But this assumption proved false. Business property turned over at a much faster rate than anticipated, and the burden shifted away from the homeowner. Proposition 13 did create a situation in which owners of a newly purchased home could pay a sharply higher property tax than neighbors who had lived a long time in an identical house. Yet the purpose of the measure was to ensure stability of the tax over time, not equality over space. Both Jarvis and Gann speak movingly about the anguish of elderly homeowners forced to sell by rapidly rising tax bills. This is what they sought to eliminate, and they did. But because home sales have continued at a brisk pace, total assessments have been rising at a 17% rate, rather than 2%.

Jarvis-Gann did, however, create serious distortions. By reducing local taxes disproportionately, it eroded local self-government. By the second year under Proposition 13, transfers from the state government to local units had increased by nearly $6 billion (to total aid of nearly $15 billion). Even though the bailout bill of 1979 eliminated some of the worst restrictions of SB 154 (the aid bill immediately after Jarvis-Gann), this 70% increase in dependence means that local government has suffered a substantial loss of autonomy. According to one study, "Sacramento now plays a larger role than formerly in shaping the policies, making the decisions, and influencing the expenditures" of local governments.[78] In a state that could pass for a good-sized nation, this decline in local self-government amounts to a serious weakening of citizen participation.

Another serious problem comes in maintenance. Without some provision for more flexible local bond issues this pattern could translate into costly decay of roads, bridges, and buildings. The constituency for prompt maintenance is one of the weakest of all, since deferring this cost is another way of shifting the tax burden to future generations. Public debt is the Achilles heel of all attempts to limit government spending and taxing. The most gaping loopholes in Proposition 13 have been opened in just this area (specifically by the California Supreme Court decision in *Carman v. Alvord* exempting the costs of pension systems that were approved in a referendum). The framers of Proposition 13 and of all tax initiatives have to choose between clamping down on debt, risking deterioration of infrastructure, or treating it flexibly, risking widespread evasion of their fiscal controls.

The most controversial and regretted impact of Proposition 13, however, has fallen on the schools. This area is particularly vulnerable because it accounts for 50% of all salaries and wages paid by state and local government. By some measures, California's spending on schools fell from among the top ten highest in the country to thirty-fifth. It was 10% lower than the national norm. By contrast, even after Proposition 13, California's state and local spending on public welfare exceeded the national standard by 49%. In the sense that voters hoped to channel government spending away from the "soft" social services and back to traditional duties like education, Proposition 13 failed.

Yet Jarvis-Gann is taking something of a bum rap on education. Outside of California, this measure is commonly blamed for the state's declining Scholastic Aptitude Test scores. Inside the state, educators lay the blame on more than a decade of flaccid curriculums and slipshod enforcement of standards. It does not help to lose funding, but money alone cannot make up for lack of attention to educational basics. California still ranks sixth in its spending for teachers' salaries.

As public concern mounts about the schools, it may produce more intensive work on basic education, a relatively low-cost reform. In 1982, William Honig used this issue to defeat a three-term incumbent for state superintendent of public education. Public concern may also force a shift of state resources to the schools, without necessarily increasing total taxation. In the protracted fight over the fiscal 1984 budget, the education lobby won an $800-million increase, even though Governor George Deukmejian held the line against new taxation. This kind of political pressure may force a correction of spending priorities within the framework of Proposition 13.

It is harder to evaluate the Spirit of 13 state spending limit because it has not yet affected California's budget, and may never do so. Its authors admit that they left too much leeway in defining the spending base. The legislature has opened further loopholes for the benefit of San Francisco. Since the city's population has been declining, a literal application of the spending limit would have forced it to reduce its budget each year. The legislature allowed the city to adjust its spending limit on the basis of statewide growth. In the absence of vigorous court challenges, the spending limit may remain the toothless giant that Jarvis said it would be.

In the broadest terms, however, the Tax Revolt brought about a dramatic change in the state's relative tax burden. From fourth in the country in 1978, California fell immediately to twenty-first and now fluctuates around sixteenth.

Even though the state took a beating in the 1981–82 recession, its economic growth continues to be impressive. In December 1980, 10.76% of Americans with jobs lived in California. By December 1983, in spite of the intervening slowdown, this proportion had grown to 11.08%. Total personal income in the state steadily forged ahead of the national growth, recession or not. In 1979, California accounted for 11.75% of the nation's personal income. By 1982, its share of this pie had risen to 12.07%. The renewed surge in state growth undercuts the argument that the boom after Proposition 13 came simply from the distribution of the accumulated state surplus. This second wind is showing most dramatically in state finances. After several years of doom-crying over deficits and a more or less political crisis over a cash flow crunch in early 1983, the state budget has been balanced with no broad tax increase and may generate a surplus of more than $300 million. The decline that set in under the rising tax burdens of Pat Brown and Ronald Reagan has been reversed.

THE MEANING OF PROPOSITION 13

The Jarvis-Gann landslide was such a shattering event that something of a cottage industry has sprung up to explain it, or explain it away. Robert Kuttner has put his formidable reporting talent at the service of the thesis that the Tax Revolt in reality protested the shifting of the tax burden from business to individuals. Such a shift may have played some role in the California property tax problem, yet the measures designed explicitly to reverse it have invariably been rejected by the voters.

More academic observers have puzzled over the opinion polls to see just what changes the voters wanted to produce in government services. Given the protean nature of the upheaval, this enterprise has the aura of a tourist doing crossword puzzles on the slopes of Mount St. Helens. The poll results are less irrational than some commentators think. Welfare and public housing rank high on the list of cuts because the growth of these expenditures has coincided closely with economic decline. Conversely, the public has been very willing to preserve education spending because it is the best of all investments in "economic infrastructure."

One study found that one of the most explanatory variables in support of the tax cuts was the amount of money the taxpayer personally hoped to save.[79] But this sort of polling fails to capture the intensity of the political phenomenon. The excitement of Proposition 13 did not result simply from a mercenary calculation of costs and benefits. The deeper phenomenon may be that the voters discovered that they were right and their leaders were wrong. The respectable establishment of government, business, the academy, and good-government groups was simply wrong when it tried to defend the existing level of government taxing and spending. The public had an innate sense that the tax burden had damaged the economy because the individual taxpayer was making the sort of decision on whether to work or whether to play, whether to spend or whether to invest, that in the aggregate constituted the economic damage.

Milton Friedman has argued that a special-interest constituency invariably carries the day in any conflict with a public good such as a balanced budget. The constituency, although limited, is highly focused; its concentrated power far outweighs the broader but much more diffuse interest of the general public. In a vote on day-care-center appropriations, for instance, a member of Congress may be lobbied intensively by people who lease buildings to day-care centers, people who run them, and people with an ideological interest, such as feminist groups. Yet the general public, whose interest is to limit federal spending and thus reduce taxes and inflation, may never hear of the vote at all. Time after time, the accumulation of specific items in both state and federal legislatures has broken budgets, widened deficits, and raised taxes. The device of the initiative and referendum together does offer an antidote, however. Friedman supported California's Proposition 13 on the grounds that it reversed the inherent weakness of the general interest in face of special interests. For once, a question of the broader public good was presented in a concentrated, up-or-down fashion. Should government taxes, and hence its special-interest spending, be reduced? Yes or no?

Of course Proposition 13 was not that simple. The broader question could have been put with more elegance (although not with greater effect). Yet the voters discerned the issue, and support for the measure cut across every special constituency in the state except for government workers.

One could object that a device like the I and R, which allows a law to be drafted and passed by direct action of the electorate, clearly contradicts the spirit of the *Federalist* papers and the Constitution. This argument would carry weight were it not for the widespread conviction that the Madisonian system was running out of control. In the current context the dangers of the initiative and the referendum are limited by the fact that they are state devices. To the extent that they are an exercise in direct democracy, they are appropriate for an electorate limited in size. Since state initiatives are the main instrument of the modern Tax Revolt, they give the movement an extra dimension. The Tax Revolt becomes not only an issue of the general interest versus special interests, but it becomes one of states versus the federal government. If the Tax Revolt had been focused on the federal government alone, as in the so far unproductive drive for a constitutional amendment for a federal spending limit, it would have failed.

Phase three of the Tax Revolt has become more than an attempt at fiscal limitation. It has given some states the power to reassert control over their own economic destiny.

III

Applications and Limitations

7

Louisiana and the Sunbelt

In 1977, John Connally led a Houston Chamber of Commerce trade mission to Japan. Even in their most optimistic moments, the delegates were not prepared for their enthusiastic reception. As Japanese bankers and manufacturers lined up to hear about opportunities in Houston, the visitors asked discreetly what had sparked such interest. The surprising answer was that for some reason a New Left polemic against the conservative "Southern Rim" had just been translated into Japanese. The book, *Power Shift*, by Kirkpatrick Sale, heaped scorn and ridicule on the "Rimster Cowboys." His cranky style reeked of contempt for their low-tax, laissez-faire pretentions. Yet the Japanese read it eagerly as a guide to the future growth leader of the American economy. The Houston boosters were besieged by Japanese investors hoping to get in on the ground floor.[1]

Incidents like this give clues as to why the states of the South and Southwest are willing to accept the label "Sunbelt," all the while knowing how poorly it describes their daily reality. The term, invented and popularized by natives of New York, suggests a homogeneous region of growth, prosperity, and pleasant weather. Contrast the image with that the North once held of "the South,"—defeat, indolence, decay, demagogic politicians, lynchings in the sweaty night. The new stereotype is a definite improvement. Yet it lumps together sixteen or more states (no one is quite sure just who is in the Sunbelt), glosses over great differences in their economics, and glazes it all with northern envy.

Some of the weaker states in the South and Southwest might have appreciated the boost in their sales pitch, but more often they must have resented the implicit accusation that they were prospering at the expense of the North. New York's Mayor Koch is fond of saying, "The Sunbelt is getting rich and we are getting poor." The truth is that, even in the most spectacular period of southern growth, the Sunbelt's personal income remained well below the national average. The first South-Southwest state to exceed parity was Texas, and that happened less than five years ago. Per-capita income in the region ranges from the high of Texas, at 103% of the national average, to Mississippi's low, which at 70% of the average ranks fiftieth of the fifty states. Mayor Koch to the contrary, New York is still 11% richer than the nation. It ranks sixth.[2]

If the North exaggerated the wealth of the Sunbelt, it almost totally ignored the battering this region took in the 1980–82 recession. The near depression in the automaking Great Lakes states received national attention, but few seemed to notice that the second most deeply affected region was the East South Central, consisting of Kentucky, Tennessee, Mississippi, and Alabama. From 1979 on, this region has had the second-highest unemployment rate, the second-lowest growth in personal income, and the second-poorest performance in retail sales. In the fourth quarter of 1981, these four states grew in personal income at only 80% of the national rate. This rate was double the growth in the Great Lakes states, but it lagged behind every other region, even the chronically depressed mideastern. Two other southern states, Arkansas and West Virginia, performed as poorly. By March 1982, six of the twenty states with double-digit unemployment were located in the Sunbelt. Alabama, with 14% of its work force out of a job, had the second-highest rate in the country. Only five states in the region lived up to the Sunbelt boast of lower than national unemployment. These five (Florida, Georgia, Virginia, Texas, and Oklahoma) were in different corners of the South and represented very different economies.[3]

This discouraging performance should refute most of the facile explanations for the South's earlier economic renaissance; in its heyday, this revival generated as much myth and nonsense as its alleged counterpart, the decline of the industrial "Frostbelt." People said that southern growth resulted from its warm climate and low energy costs; in almost the next breath, they credited the spread of air conditioning. Conservatives touted the regionwide adoption of "right-to-work" legislation; northern liberals complained about the South's supposedly favorable balance in the flow of federal funds. Frostbelt politicians bewailed southern raids on northern factories. All this may have helped in one way or another. But there is a problem with saying that climate, or labor laws, or energy costs made the South grow, when, even with unchanged weather and legislation, the region began to slump.

THE MISSING PIECE: TAXATION

The vacant space in the Sunbelt jigsaw puzzle, the piece that makes sense of the picture, is taxation. The Sunbelt economy falls into the same pattern as the California Tax Revolt and the fall and recovery of New York: the theme of this mosaic is the centrality of tax policy. Of course, not *only* taxation is important. The southern economy has indeed been shaped by immigration, industrial dispersion, and the oil boom. But as a general theory, changing tax burdens do explain both surge and slump in states from the Southwest to the Northeast. They indicate when growth might subside into stagnation. And they make sense of the *details* of the Sunbelt experience.

The peak period of southern growth followed a steep fall in its tax burden. For two decades following 1953, the South maintained the second-highest rate of tax decline in the country (following New England in the first period and the Mountain states in the second). In the 1950s, the South ranked fourth of the four high-growth regions. In the 1960s, it ranked first. If this thesis holds, there are bad omens for the Sunbelt.

From 1975 to 1979, tax burdens in ten of the twelve south-eastern states rose faster than the national average. Only two other regions had a higher relative rate of increase. From 1978 to 1981, the figures are even more ominous. State tax burdens everywhere were falling. (The national average was −4.0% a year.) But southern tax burdens fell by only −2.8%, and the Southwest ranked last.[4]

This pattern has one major complication, however. Three of these states rely heavily on severance taxes. One used to hear that these "energy states" led a charmed life: the tax on oil and gas production comes as close as a tax can to provid-ing a free lunch. Severance taxes in theory compensate the state for the reduction in the value of its domain as its natural resources are "severed" from the soil. They act more as an economic "rent" than as a tax. New York financier Felix Ro-hatyn once complained that his region could never catch up to the energy states, which could remove the tax burden from individuals and place it instead on their mineral wealth. Dur-ing the seventies, the tax figures for Texas and Louisiana greatly exaggerated the actual burden on personal income.

Yet if a state lets its revenue ride too heavily on the mar-ket for a single commodity, it can be riding for a fall. Since the advent of the "oil glut" in 1981 easterners have had little to envy in Texas or Louisiana. Although personal income in these states has held up, their budgets have been devastated. The Louisiana legislature voted some $163 million in new taxes in December 1983, and this time they fall on personal in-come. Once more the Southwest is riding out the downside of a petroleum boom and bust, a recurring feature of its his-tory.[5]

Even here, however, where the fortunes of petroleum have so dominated the "oil patch," tax policy has shaped the final results. Texas and Louisiana have both been extravagantly endowed with hydrocarbons, yet their economic histories have followed widely different paths. The contrast in their growth is more instructive than their joint interest in the oil patch, especially in the period when, because of federal price con-trols, they were slow to reap the benefits of the world oil price.

The basic question for the Sunbelt remains whether the genuine aspects of the region's success grow from its own special character or from the general economic principles of the tax hypothesis. Certainly specific features, such as available space, sometimes congenial climate, growing population and growing markets, and generally probusiness politics have contributed to the South's growth. Yet discussions of these factors often confuse symptom with cause, and sometimes misdiagnose the symptom. When states in the supposedly moribund Northeast begin to show economic revival at the same time that portions of the Sunbelt fall into supposedly uncharacteristic malaise, it seems high time to look beyond common opinion and search out the uniform theory that explains both northern decline and northern revival, southern boom and southern bust.

THE LOW-TAX SOUTH: JACKSON
TO RECONSTRUCTION

Supply-side economic theory may have found a warmer welcome in the South than elsewhere because of one predominant characteristic. For most of its history, the region has displayed a distinct affinity for low-tax politics. The South has been a stronghold of Jacksonian Democracy, which placed a premium on limited government and popular control of state finances.

One other political experience scarred and shaped the modern South, and, ironically, helped transform it into the Sunbelt. This was Reconstruction. A. J. Liebling once compared the southern regional memory to "an iceberg floating upside down in the sea of history. The iceberg, dear to after-dinner speakers, shows only a fifth of its volume on the surface. The Deep South has gone on for a hundred visible years since the Civil War bemoaning the twenty-five years of its own total history that preceded."[6] Just so, the South lived under Reconstruction for twelve years, as opposed to four years under the Confederacy. The reaction to that experience, which lasted three times longer than the ante-bellum sway of the states' rights heresy of Secession, dominated southern politics for the next century. The period of Reconstruction burned into the southern mind such memories of defeat, humiliation, and racial politics that it seems foolhardy to suggest that other lessons were learned. Yet the fiscal and constitutional issues of this period deserve attention for their own sake. As part of the indispensable routine of government, they have a life of their own. When the Radical Republican Reconstruction governments lauched their social experiment of preparing the freed slaves for citizenship (or, in an alternative view, when they turned to the public purse to consolidate their political constituency), they financed themselves by an extraordinary increase in state tax burdens. According to one anti-Radical historian, E. Merton Coulter, "Though property values in the eleven states which had composed the Confederacy were in 1870 less than one half what they were in 1860, the amount of taxes paid was more than four times the total in 1860."[7] Historians currently argue that some of the vast increase in southern state spending was justified. Any government in power at that time would have faced the enormous expense of rebuilding the South's shattered infrastructure. The demand for state services had vastly increased when the government took over from plantation owners the cost of caring for a still largely dependent black population. The Radicals also made some effort to provide the general population, black and white, with the public-school system that ante-bellum oligarchs had promised but never effectively delivered.

For most of the past century, however, southern opinion has been unwilling to take such a balanced view of Reconstruction finance. The prevailing opinion has been that the Radicals were embarked on the first social-welfare state in the nation's history, redistributing wealth from the prewar elite to the freedmen and themselves through confiscatory taxation. In Coulter's widely shared interpretation:

> With the coming of the Radicals, land was made to bear a greatly increased amount of the tax burden—and not on account of the ease in levying the tax or by simple accident. It was by special design, for those who set the taxes had little land, or, indeed, little property of any sort; but, as they wanted land, they saw that high taxes would depress its value and probably lead to its confiscation by the state for unpaid taxes. . . . The amount of land advertised for taxes increased with the carrying out of this program, until whole sections of some states were for sale.[8]

As tax burdens reached their peak in the early 1870s, a major tax revolt swept the South. In one of the important but unstudied episodes of Reconstruction, taxpayers in a number of states called conventions to protest the high levies. They often urged nonpayment. In Texas the series of "taxpayers conventions" in 1871 helped break the political grip of the Radical Republican E. J. Davis. Tax receipts fell off so drastically that the state's credit nearly collapsed, and northern newspapers raised a chorus of complaint about the alleged corruption of the incumbent governor.[9]

Some of these conventions attracted bipartisan support and shunned racial issues. After a fourteenfold increase in property tax rates, the 1874 Mississippi taxpayers convention delivered what one Republican congressman called the "ablest paper" he had seen in the state in years; its suggestions for spending cuts were ignored by the legislature but endorsed by the Radical Republican governor and the Jackson (Mississippi) Republican Club.[10]

REDEEMERS AND RETRENCHERS

When conservative southern Democrats regained power in the mid-1870s, these fiscal protests became policy. A wave of constitutional conventions swept away the basic law that Radical leaders had written and sometimes written well. In place of the strong-government Reconstruction constitutions so pleasing to modern scholars, the Redeemers (as the reenfranchised southerners called themselves) wrote extensive limitations for their legislatures, their executives, and their fiscal systems.[11] In the name of Retrenchment (another of their capital Rs) they slashed spending, jettisoned services, and brought about spectacular if partly illusory reductions in tax rates. The governor of Florida told his legislature in 1877: "That government will be the most highly esteemed that gives the greatest protection to the tax payer."[12] Some of these tax cuts were directly linked to economic development. In 1882, for example, Mississippi exempted new factories from all state, county, and municipal taxation for ten years after completion.[13]

In such an atmosphere, one can well ask, Why was the long-hoped-for economic growth of the South so slow in coming? One problem may have been that the Redeemers focused much of their Retrenchment on the one service most valuable for economic development—public education. The free public schools were the great achievement of Reconstruction. Yet some of the Redeemers and Retrenchers would state that ignorance was better than public debt.[14] School budgets were so reduced that southern school years did not return to 100-day terms, the highest average under Reconstruction, until after 1900.[15] Illiteracy increased to the end of the century. Yet even before the advent of high technology, industry preferred a work force that could read and write.

Even before Reconstruction tax issues preoccupied southern state politics. The theoretical debates foreshadowed many of the themes that now fall under the supply-side rubric. Each state developed its own fiscal system just as it developed its own political tradition; its economic performance in our generation has been shaped as much by this history as by the demographic and industrial trends so prominent in current literature on the Sunbelt. The two states to which we now turn, Louisiana and Texas, have experienced histories scarcely paralleled among the states in their color and turbulence. Both are rich in oil and gas, yet their economies have followed remarkably different paths. Their highly individual routes to prosperity again illustrate the extent to which a state can rise or fall by its own decisions.

LOUISIANA, LOUISIANA

More color and corruption, more diversity, dishonesty, honor, and earnest endeavor to overcome the burden of the past can be encountered among the 4.2 million inhabitants of Louisiana than in almost any other state of the union. Nominally a part of the Sunbelt, let alone of the United States, it follows its own rules of behavior. Up until the early 1970s, this behavior did not serve the state well. Louisiana lagged behind the rest of the Sunbelt in economic growth, population growth, and general reputation. Then, in the mid-seventies, the state underwent a tremendous economic revival. From the laggard of the Sunbelt Louisiana transformed itself into the growth leader of the Southeast. In its latter stages this take-off owed much to the fabulous wealth generated by the natural gas drilling along the Tuscaloosa Trend. But Louisianans themselves say the turnaround preceded the petroleum bonanza. The economic revival had its roots in a political renaissance in which much of the state tried to shed the worst habits of its past. More or less coincidentally the state also rewrote its constitution, placing such limits on taxation that its relatively high tax burden fell sharply. Yet, old habits die hard. Local corruption continually flares up, sometimes reaching murderous levels. Economic development in the Pelican State has become a struggle, not only for growth but also for regeneration. This morality play is still unfolding.

180 YEARS OF DEMOCRACY

One school of thought in present-day Louisiana attributes its lurid political history to its French colonial origin.[16] In the thirteen British colonies, the settlers jealously guarded the prerogatives of their representative assemblies and drew on a tradition of personal rights they traced back to the Magna Carta. Louisiana, on the other hand, remained the territory of a centralized monarchy until almost the moment before its sale to the young American republic. Unlike Texas, which had been substantially Americanized by immigration under Mexican rule, Louisiana retained, and still retains, the mark of its original population. This substantial portion of the civic body, argue some Louisianans, has had only 180 years of exposure to self-government. Without the imprint of the seventeenth- and eighteenth-century developments in the British political tradition, the background of the Puritan commonwealths, the Revolution and the drafting of republican constitutions, Louisiana has been unusually tolerant of the directed vote, the bought vote, the stolen vote, and the use of public office for personal gain.

Concern about this disparity inspired New England to oppose the Louisiana Purchase. Josiah Quincy of Massachusetts argued that Congress could not successfully transform the politically homogeneous republic into "a *hotch-pot* with the wild men on the Missouri, nor with the mixed, though more respectable race of Anglo-Hispano-Gallic-Americans who bask on the sands at the mouth of the Mississippi."[17] These ethnic characterizations may be just a bit too pat. French Catholic New Orleans has produced distinguished reformers including former mayor Delesseps S. Morrison; Baptist Anglo-Saxon North Louisiana has produced corruption of outstanding viciousness, even by Louisiana standards. The most determined and effective authoritarian in the state's history, the "Kingfish" himself, Huey Long, was a North Louisiana Scotch-Irish Protestant.

From the beginning, Louisiana has been politically and legally unique. Alone among the states, its civil law is based on the Napoleonic Code, a concession granted by the first American governor, William C. C. Claiborne, in his long and successful campaign to conciliate the New Orleans merchants and property owners.[18] Political control remained in the hands of a merchant-planter oligarchy for much of the nineteenth and early-twentieth centuries, thanks to another singular feature. Of all the southern states, only Louisiana has had a big-city machine strong enough to influence statewide elections. Apportionment in the 1812 state constitution gave disproportionate power to slaveholding plantation owners at the expense of small rural farmers. In the constitution of 1852, New Orleans delegates voted to perpetuate this system after making a deal with planters to protect their own interests.[19]

This alliance of city politicians and planters weathered the Populist upheaval of 1896. Its methods were brutal and blatant. When hill-country and Cajun parish Populists swallowed their race prejudice and joined Republicans in a fusion campaign with an antilynching plank, conservative Democrats announced that any means were legitimate to crush the "Populist-negro social equality ticket." The *Shreveport Evening Judge* editorialized: "It is the religious duty of Democrats to rob Populists and Republicans of their votes whenever and wherever the opportunity presents itself and any failure to do so will be a violation of true Louisiana Democrat teaching. The Populists and Republicans are our legitimate political prey. Rob them! You bet! What are we here for?"[20]

When Liebling wrote his classic 1960 articles on Louisiana politics, one of his native guides attributed the bitter intensity of Huey Long's campaigns to the success of the oligarchy in thwarting the 1896 challenge. "They sat on the lid an extra thirty years," he said.[21]

THE RECONSTRUCTION TAX REVOLT

The oligarchic control of Louisiana was intensified by the painful memory of Reconstruction. Defeat of the Confederacy was bitter enough for the South, but in Louisiana it seems to have been exceptionally searing. (A young lady from an old New Orleans family once told the author that her grandfather refused until the age of ninety to divulge the secret that he was related to Union General Benjamin Butler, who occupied the city in 1862.) A substantial minority of the state opposed Secession and even aided the Union, but by the end of Reconstruction this element had become practically invisible. The Reconstruction regime was so disliked that New Orleans leaders attempted briefly to combat it by making their own détente with the Negro vote. Those cosmopolitans who were relatively broad-minded on racial issues were alienated by fiscal misconduct. A major theme in their opposition to Negro suffrage was the threat they thought it posed to their property. Wrote the New Orleans Times, a spokesman for business interests: "If representative institutions are to prevail in this country, the control of taxes must be left to those who pay them, and the protection of property to those who own it."[22] One of the bitterer complaints against Reconstruction officeholders, as tax rates soared, was that very few of them paid taxes.[23] In the aftermath of the war this burden weighed heavily on a devastated tax base. In early 1869, the tax delinquency rate in Louisiana cities for the previous year was 90%. As the tax rates climbed, tax revenues eroded. In 1870, the total value of state taxable property was one-quarter of a billion dollars, yielding tax collections of $6.5 million. In

1871, with the same total valuation, the tax yield had fallen to $4.6 million. Delinquent taxes for that year had accumulated to $5 million. Under this tax burden, real estate values declined 25%. A Democrat complained that if finances continued this way New Orleans would be more devastated than Chicago after its fire. "The reason of it is this: when the city of Chicago was burned to the ground the people had at least the ground left, and northern and eastern capitalists have come there to rebuild it, while with us capital is flying from the state, commerce is decreasing, and everybody who can is trying to get away."[24]

Political chaos intensified the financial confusion. Under the freewheeling administration of Governor Henry C. Warmoth the Republican Party splintered. In the kind of political extravaganza at which Louisiana excels two separate legislatures, two boards of elections, and two chief executives contended for recognition as the sole legitimate state authority. As the turmoil increased, Louisiana natives in May 1872 organized a Tax Resisting Association. The group originally meant to challenge the validity of the Warmoth regime's tax increases by launching a federal-court suit. But as both sides in the 1872 election claimed victory and set up their own governments, the association refused to pay taxes altogether. In mid-February 1873, the Fusionist governor, elected by a coalition of Democrats and Horace Greeley Republicans (ironically, including Warmoth), forbade citizens to pay taxes to the government led by Grant Republicans. Protest meetings reached a peak in April. But the Tax Resisters had become a pawn in the political struggle. The Grant Republicans managed to outlast the Fusionists. Their legislature passed a draconian measure to enforce tax collections, and the Republican governor issued a proclamation attacking the Tax Resisters.

As the Tax Resisters ran into a political cul-de-sac, leading figures in New Orleans cast about for another means of reducing the Reconstruction tax burden. Their solution was a rapprochement with the Negro vote. In the words of the distinguished Louisiana historian T. Harry Williams, "The men who would sponsor the movement were almost without exception conscious of race and racial differences, but under the strain of economic distress they acted to remove race as an issue of politics."[25] In the spring of 1873, a committee of fifty prominent New Orleans white business leaders and fifty of the black elite, many of them "Creole Negroes" who were free and wealthy even in ante-bellum days, met to draft a platform to unify natives of both races to regain control of the state. One of its leaders was the Confederate war hero General P. G. T. Beauregard. In a letter to the press, one of the city's "oldest and best" merchants defended the movement as "our only hope of salvation. The negroes, unless drawn over to us, will constantly elect carpet-baggers. Their election means increased taxation, and this means total and absolute ruin."[26]

The Unification movement issued an amazingly progressive manifesto on race relations, including a call for integration in public transportation and the public schools. But it had little real chance of success. It was sabotaged by black Republican politicians even before it ran up against the racial hostility of the Anglo-Saxon northern parishes. With the collapse of the movement, one paper remarked that blacks had spurned a glorious chance. "The great mass of our people would willingly concede to the colored people the civil and political rights of citizens, which they claim, if they could see the colored people sincerely laboring for a reduction of taxation and for an honest and economical administration."[27]

One can doubt whether the Unification movement offered the freedmen a truly serious political alternative. Since native whites were shortly able to regain control of the government without any racial concessions, one can wonder how long they would have honored the terms of any such agreement. The movement is important as evidence of the economic desperation of the business and planter community. T. Harry Williams, the biographer of Huey Long, sees it as one of the rare moments in which southerners attempted to rise above the false issues of race to address more basic economic questions.

The economic conclusion of the Redeemers, however, was that salvation lay in reduced taxation and limited government. The Redemptionist constitutional convention of 1879 prohibited the legislature from contracting any state debt. The same convention established a rate limit on the state property tax that was a bit less than half of the peak rate under Reconstruction. It applied a somewhat less stringent rate to all parish and municipal taxes.[28]

The oligarchy that returned to power after Reconstruction more or less governed under these principles until its power was overthrown once again, by a native of northeastern Louisiana's Radical Winn Parish named Huey Pierce Long.

OIL AND THE OLD ORDER

Although an oligarchy had controlled Louisiana state politics from the days of its purchase, its composition changed significantly in the twentieth century. The role of the planting interests diminished, ironically, because of the legislative mopping-up after the close call with the Populists in 1896. In the reaction more than 100,000 black voters were disenfranchised; many of these had been sharecroppers who followed the lead of the plantation owner. At the same time, a new industrial mix sprang up as the state began to exploit its fabulous wealth in oil, natural gas, and sulphur. In the late nineteenth century, the most powerful corporation in the state had been the highly liquid Louisiana Lottery; by the early twentieth century, it was Standard Oil. The central theme of a 1912 reform movement was to finance increased state services by taxing this mineral bonanza.

The culmination of this movement came in the 1920 election of conservative reformer John M. Parker, former leader of the New Orleans Good Government League. Parker campaigned for a severance tax on oil and gas. After his election he called a constitutional convention to write the severance tax into basic law.[29] His relations with the oil and gas industry were conciliatory, however. He struck a gentlemen's agreement with Standard Oil by which the new tax was limited to 2%, and the oil companies agreed not to challenge its constitutionality. The 1921 constitutional convention also authorized a state income tax and even considered a subcommittee report advocating that the levy be graduated. But Parker drew the line at progressivity, and after fierce opposition this plan was dropped. The 1921 constitution merely authorized a maximum rate of 3%, with generous credits against existing personal taxation. In spite of this permission, the state government refused to enact such a tax for another thirteen years—after Huey Long had come and gone as governor.[30]

The tax base for reform was economically sound, taking its revenue primarily from the bounty of nature rather than from the enterprise of man. Supply-side theory would make little complaint about a policy of shifting a portion of the tax burden away from the individual and onto natural resources. Initially, at least, this was the policy followed by Huey Long.

THE RISE OF HUEY LONG

Visitors to Louisiana nowadays talk a lot more about Huey Long than the natives do. Louisianans seem to resent this fascination with the state's most famous citizen. It is easy to overread Long into current Louisiana politics. The political division between Long and anti-Long, once the state's equivalent of a two-party system, has been fading for two decades. The ideological cleavages have shifted and new players have emerged, many of whom are irritated by political tourists who harp on the Longite past.

Native demurrers notwithstanding, Huey Long left a deep and highly visible mark on the state. His hand can be seen on driving into downtown Baton Rouge. His thirty-four-story state capitol dominates the horizon. At night, a spotlight from an upper floor illuminates his grave, set alone in the spacious capitol grounds; it is marked by a life-size statue in a double-breasted suit, one foot resting on the inscription "Share Our Wealth." The ensemble is at once grotesque and heroic, a fitting monument to Huey Long's career.

Long's role in Louisiana history, according to his most eminent biographer, was to subordinate southern political myths to more substantive economic issues. More precisely, he repudiated the post-Reconstruction economic policy of low taxation and limited services. His political program may not have seemed impressive compared to the welfare agenda of the rich northern liberal states. His main planks were free school books and increased spending on education, improved and toll-free state roads and bridges, and a charity hospital system. Northern liberals took these services for granted, but for the South of that time they were revolution- ary.[31] To pay for them Long and his successors, including his younger brother Earl, followed another distinctly unsouthern policy: they aggressively sought new tax sources. By 1953, the state's tax burden was third highest in the country.[32]

In his first year in office Long more or less continued the taxing and spending policies of former governor Parker, but he pushed them more vigorously. His main social bill, the provision of free textbooks to all schoolchildren, was a mea- sure especially pleasing to Catholic South Louisiana. To pay for the books, Long changed the base for levying the sever- ance tax. (This shift, from value to quantity, also protected state revenues in a period of falling oil prices.) Furthermore, Long called a special session of the legislature to seek a tax on oil refining. In March 1929, this session erupted in a major coun- terattack on the young governor—an impeachment trial pow- erfully supported by Standard Oil.[33]

Huey Long had already given his enemies ammunition, primarily in a crude attempt to blackmail an editor, and he narrowly won the impeachment trial. He tried to conciliate his business enemies by promising no new business taxes if they would support alternatives. But the postimpeachment regular legislature refused him any more new revenues.

WHO LOOKS AFTER YOU? THE KINGFISH DO!

To break the impasse, Long resolved to renew his public mandate. In 1930, he challenged the incumbent U.S. Senator up for reelection, on purely state issues. Long furthermore let it be known that, because of his hatred of the lieutenant gov- ernor, he would serve the remaining two years of his guber- natorial term before taking the Senate seat. Yet he won in a landslide. Two years later, he brought in a similar margin for his hand-picked successor and surrogate, O. K. Allen. By this time, Senator Long was so much the undisputed master of state politics that his associates habitually addressed him as "gov- ernor," even in Governor Allen's presence. (Earl Long used to say that a leaf once blew on O. K. Allen's desk, and O. K. signed it.)

In 1932, the absentee Kingfish began to push through the new taxes required to pay for his program. Long's levies fell on items like tobacco, soft drinks, electricity, and kerosene. A liberal might call this a highly regressive package. It contrasted sharply with the Share Our Wealth platform Senator Long was beginning to promote on the national level. In launching increasingly savage attacks on President Roosevelt, Long decided, apparently at 3:00 A.M. in his Washington hotel room, that he should lead his own national movement. He named it the Share Our Wealth Society and gave it the slogan "Every Man a King." It grew like wildfire. Its main plank was to tax all huge personal fortunes down to the level of $5 million and use the proceeds to give everyone a minimum "homestead" of $5,000. Observers could not decide whether Long was socialist or fascist, and he did not help them out.

Yet in Louisiana, where Long could have done anything he wanted with the fiscal system, he was loath to tax personal income. In spite of the sanction of the 1921 constitution, he put off passing a state income tax until 1934. Even that belated measure has been criticized for its lack of progressivity.[34] Long's biographer records that the bill was modeled on New York's income tax. "Huey cut a copy of the New York act out of a World Almanac, made a few revisions, and gave the clipping to his legislative lieutenants."[35]

The income tax, furthermore, came as part of a package to finance a series of tax reductions. In essence, it was a mild tax shift designed to shore up Long's lower-income constituency. One of the major elements, which played a significant role much later, was the homestead exemption. This relief measure canceled state, parish, and special-district property taxes on amounts running, at the governor's discretion, up to $2,000 of a homeowner's assessment. This tax shift was meant to bolster Long in a period of political weakness. Counterattacks from Roosevelt had been giving the Kingfish trouble, but he was more seriously damaged by a black eye he received in a fight in a Long Island men's room.

Throughout all quests for more revenue, Long adamantly opposed the general sales tax, calling it a "disaster." In the first campaign after his death, his successors incorporated this attitude in their campaign platform.[36]

Long was most delighted by a tax on Standard Oil. In late December 1934, he finally achieved passage of the five-cents-per-barrel levy on the refining of crude oil that had led to his impeachment in 1929. In an egregious display of what had become his style of governing, he ordered his floor lieutenants to wait until the Standard Oil lobbyist had left the chamber on the last day of the special session. Then they offered this bill as an amendment to an obscure measure up for a final vote. The bill passed both the House and the Senate in ten minutes.[37] In the economic warfare that followed, Long easily put down armed violence by laid-off Standard Oil workers. But he eventually reached a compromise in which the company increased production and refining in Louisiana and the law was amended so that the governor could suspend all or part of the tax. Governor Allen cut the tax by 80%.[38]

Huey Long was not bashful in raising taxes. By the end of his term, some forty-five taxes were in place, and revenues had increased by 75% over 1927.[39] But, to a surprising degree, these levies were "indirect" measures, placing a burden on specific industries or types of goods. In spite of his national rhetoric, he made only a limited effort to redistribute income in Louisiana. The real surge in personal taxation came with his successors. The governor who unsuccessfully attempted to soak the Louisiana rich was the anti-Long reformer Sam Houston Jones.

IN THE WAKE OF THE KINGFISH

Huey Long died at the peak of his power, assassinated in his capitol after a night legislative session on September 7, 1935. Witnesses claim his last words were, "I have so much to do."[40] What his program would have looked like is hard to say, but under the mantle of the martyred leader his successors pushed their version of it much further than Long ever gave sign that he might. Social spending, corruption, and taxation flourished more under governors to come than under the Kingfish.

In the aftermath of assassination, Long's inner circle decided that an Appeals Court judge named Richard W. Leche was Long's chosen successor. Leche ran his campaign on the principles of Longism, including opposition to a state sales tax. Elected with 67% of the vote, he made several important shifts of emphasis. The national Share Our Wealth rhetoric disappeared, and Leche veered to a probusiness posture. This shift was foreshadowed in the very month of Long's assassination by a legislative resolution pledging not to impose new or increased taxes on the oil industry for ten years. Leche took a strong interest in industrial development. He established a state Board of Commerce and Industry and offered a new program of one-year tax exemptions for new or expanded plants. He also compromised further on Huey Long's pet tax, the five-cents-a-barrel levy on the Standard Oil refinery.

At the same time, Leche expanded Long's social programs. He accepted federal funds to set up social security and unemployment compensation systems, provided free school supplies as well as textbooks, and expanded the homestead exemption.[41]

The need to fund such programs collided with the probusiness shift, producing an interesting dilemma. Though he raised severance and corporation taxes, Leche did not want to transfer too much of the tax burden to industry. So he turned to personal taxation. In spite of Long's prior condemnation and opposition from ultra-Longites, Leche pushed a 2% "luxury tax" through the 1936 legislature. Two years later he converted it to a straight 1% sales tax.[42]

As Leche's budget swelled, it soon became apparent that large sums of public wealth were being shared, not with the people, but among the politicians. Federal prosecutions sent Governor Leche and a number of his associates to the federal penitentiary, where Huey Long had predicted they would end up. An electorate finally aroused by the scale of the scandals turned away from the slate headed by interim governor Earl K. Long and elected the reform liberal Sam Houston Jones.

The new governor inherited a state deficit of $10 million, 6% of his proposed biennial budget. But rather than dismantle the Longite welfare program, Jones had promised to extend it. His solution was to propose new taxes and expand some of the older Longite ones. He turned to natural resources first, proposing expansion of the severance tax and a natural gas gathering tax. The gathering tax was the first in a long series of attempts to extract revenue from the natural gas exported from Louisiana; most have been declared in violation of the U.S. Constitution. The legislature attempted to repeal some nuisance taxes and, above all, the general sales tax. At the same time, Jones attempted to increase the income tax rates on middle and upper income brackets, making the levy truly progressive. The income tax attempt failed in the legislature and was rejected by the voters in a November 1940 constitutional referendum.

Complaining that this defeat undermined his finances, Governor Jones returned to the sales tax, which had already been repealed in December 1940. He asked for a 2% permanent levy and eventually settled for 1%.[43] The revised sales tax proved more adequate than Jones had expected. He ended his administration with a $12.5-million surplus, giving Longites the chance to attack him for enacting "excessive taxes."[44]

Passage of the sales tax led one highly competent observer to say that Jones "followed in the steps of Leche's sharp reversal of Huey Long's class-taxing program."[45] This statement is accurate as far as the sales tax is concerned, considering that Long opposed it so strongly and that it is generally, if not necessarily correctly considered to be regressive.[46] Yet the class bias of the fiscal policy of both Long and Jones is less easy to define. Jones's first choice in raising revenue, after all, was to make the state income tax more progressive than Long had contemplated or Longites were willing to support. The issue ultimately does not come down to class division; it is the more technical question of the preferable form of tax, one on business and natural resources or one on individuals. By heaping the burden on oil and gas, Huey Long may have displayed more economic good sense than did his probusiness or good-government successors.

TAXES: WHOSE BURDEN?

The Jones Administration marked something of a watershed in Louisiana history. It instituted civil service, repealed some of Huey Long's most dictatorial laws, and gave the citizen body a not entirely welcome exposure to clean government. To carry on this work Jones, at the end of his term, privately threw his support to the unlikely candidacy of Jimmie Davis, best known as the composer of "You Are My Sunshine." Davis gave the voters cowboy bands instead of vituperation. More important, he promised no further taxation. Although, once in office, he backtracked, Davis never had enough control of the legislature to enact a tax increase. The state fiscal system, aided by the development of tidelands oil fields, generated such consistent surpluses that even a legislative spending spree failed to put serious pressure on revenues.[47]

The halcyon days under Jimmie Davis ended abruptly when Huey's younger brother Earl swept back into office in February 1948. Earl Long revived his brother's spending program with a vengeance but forgot the revenue formula the Kingfish had relied on. To redeem such promises as increased old-age pensions, veterans' bonuses, and hospital construction, Earl Long increased state taxation by 50%. He tripled severance taxes and doubled the gas gathering tax (later found unconstitutional), but he also turned to massive increases in personal taxation. The measure that made the greatest impression on the public (in addition to a fivefold increase in the bottled-beer tax) was the doubling and broadening of the sales tax.[48] By 1952, Louisianans were calling themselves the most highly taxed people in the country. If that complaint was not entirely accurate, Louisiana had at least undergone a very sharp and debilitating increase in its tax burden.[49]

With the election of the anti-Long reform governor Robert McKennon in 1952, the reaction to Earl Long's tax increases reached into the constitution. The new governor introduced a series of "good government" amendments, including a provision requiring the vote of two-thirds of the *members* of each house of the legislature for any new tax, increase of an existing tax, or repeal of an existing tax exemption. The measure was less popular at the polls than one might think, squeaking by with the narrowest of margins. Critics argued that any governor determined to raise taxes could generally control that majority of the legislature, formidable task though it might seem. But this proposal did inaugurate a period of gradually declining tax burden.

By the time the Long/anti-Long split began fading from state politics, Louisiana was left with a tax burden that was extraordinarily high even by national standards. After Earl Long's freewheeling term ended in 1953, state and local taxes were taking 10.43% of the state's personal income, a level nearly 38% higher than the all-state average. Only two other states, North and South Dakota, bore a higher tax burden. By 1965, Louisiana's relative position had improved. Its tax burden had increased to 12.05%, more than 15% above the national average, but seven other states were higher. Curiously, only two of these states, Vermont and Wisconsin, were in the Frostbelt. In both years, Louisiana stood out from the South, but also by decreasing proportions. In 1953, its tax burden was 33% above the southeastern average; by 1965, it was only 20% above.[50]

Louisiana analysts have objected that these statistics are misleading, or at least exaggerated, because the tax burden figure includes the state's extraordinarily high severance tax revenue.[51] This point is important. The tax burden figure does give a distorted picture of the real state of affairs in high severance tax states, particularly for recent years. A correction is needed.

The chart below shows one, admittedly crude, approach. Assuming arbitrarily that only 20% of the severance tax burden falls within the state, subtract the remaining 80% of this tax from the total state and local revenue. The plot compares the tax burden as traditionally calculated with the tax burden without exported severance taxes. The adjusted burden is much lower, of course. In the mid-sixties, it even falls within the average range for the southern states. But the adjusted curve takes some bends not all that evident from the traditional measure. At several periods in Louisiana's recent past, severance tax receipts have flattened out and even declined. The response in Baton Rouge has been to raise other tax rates to make up the lost revenue. Hence, although over the long run the traditional curve overstates the real tax burden, it also masks some points at which the real burden moved up. Significant upturns occurred in the late sixties and again in the

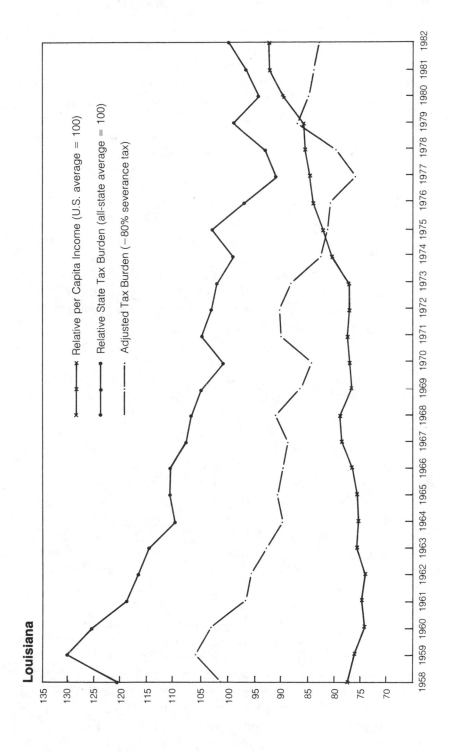

Louisiana

Relative per Capita Income (U.S. average = 100)

Relative State Tax Burden (all-state average = 100)

Adjusted Tax Burden (−80% severance tax)

first three years of the seventies. These points more or less coincide with slowdowns in the state economy.

In the first half of the seventies, the feeling had spread that Louisiana was missing out on the Sunbelt boom. The influential Louisiana Association of Business and Industry (LABI) put out a pamphlet on *The Stalled Economy*.[52] Reporters went to small towns in north Louisiana and described the timeless lassitude so well depicted by Robert Penn Warren. The figures on relative growth in state per capita personal income confirmed this impression. (See chart.) In the last half of the sixties, Louisiana's per-capita income was growing in relation to the U.S. average. But in 1969 it suddenly plunged and remained stagnant until 1974. Population as a percentage of the U.S. total dropped, reaching a twenty-year low point in 1974. Then, just as the press began to harp on the laggard state, the hard times changed for the better.

There is little question that Louisiana began to boom after the mid-seventies. Its personal income and work force grew at the fastest rate in the South. Even more remarkable, given the state's insular character, its population began to grow again, and much of the increase was attributed to immigration. Naturally, there are differing explanations for this turnaround. LABI claims that some of the credit is due to its successful campaign for a right-to-work law. Observers from the North might be somewhat taken aback by the vehement antiunionism of the Louisiana business lobby, but the right-to-work measure does symbolize a political shift toward a probusiness atmosphere. State reformers also argue that Louisiana politics have improved immensely with the rise of a new generation. The state legislature has advanced in decorum and self-respect, and the extraordinarily high level of public corruption has somewhat abated. Members of the new generation maintain that this political rejuvenation was the essential precondition for the economic revival. This is not to say, however, that Louisiana has entirely given up its lurid and even murderous political scandals. Political extortion may not be as pervasive as in previous years, but in certain parishes it still constitutes an extralegal form of tax burden.[53]

The state's general economy has clearly benefited from the boom in oil and natural gas. The greatest growth has come in the parishes most directly involved in the oil industry. Lafayette, the wild Cajun boom town in the heart of the deep-gas drilling belt, led the nation in 1978 in personal income growth. Yet price controls delayed much of this bonanza. In the period of relatively flat prices, Louisiana's production began to drop, so that severance taxes actually declined briefly. In coping with the revenue shortfall, Governor Edwin W. Edwards once more increased the personal tax burden by adjusting personal income tax exemptions. This uptick in the tax burden ran counter to a trend that gave powerful support to all the other forces of regeneration. In the last half of the seventies, Louisiana became the one state in the South to maintain a falling tax burden. It was helped in this effort by a major political event, the adoption of a new state constitution.

CONSOLIDATING TAX CUTS:
THE CHEHARDY CONSTITUTION

The state constitutional convention of 1973 convened just as Governor Ronald Reagan was campaigning for his constitutional spending limit, Proposition 1. The California movement made some ripples in Louisiana. Convention delegate Louis ("Woody") Jenkins introduced a looser version of the California measure. It gained some press attention when Governor Edwards endorsed it two days after the California electorate rejected Proposition 1. But, as Representative Jenkins stated later, he soon discovered that the tradition in Louisiana was not to impose an overall limit but to restrict specific taxes.[54]

The real power on tax issues at the convention, and a true representative of the Louisiana tradition, was Jefferson Parish Tax Assessor Lawrence A. Chehardy. Son of an immigrant tailor from Lebanon, Chehardy commanded enormous girth, wealth, and political influence. Carrying on his father's speculations, he gradually amassed extensive real estate in the parish that became New Orleans's richest and most populous suburb. He based his political career on the proposition that homes should be as lightly taxed as possible.

As the means to this end, Chehardy pushed the home-stead exemption to an extent that Huey Long could hardly have imagined. He wrote a constitutional provision limiting assessment levels to 10% of "fair market value." (One impetus for the convention was a state Supreme Court decision requiring a statewide reassessment of property to 100% of market value.) On top of this assessment limit, Chehardy expanded the homestead exemption from $2,000 of market value to $5,000 of *assessed* value. Thus, a home that sold for $50,000 would be assessed at $5,000, and with the homestead exemption would carry a property tax liability of zero. At one point critics maintained that this mechanism had eliminated the property tax on 97% of the homes in Louisiana.[55]

The convention proceeded to restrict taxation almost across the board. Constitutional language pegged the automobile license fee at $3. It set a ceiling on local sales taxes and prohibited local income taxes. It allowed deduction of federal income tax payments from the state income tax, and continued the constitutional freeze on income tax rates that had been part of the compromise allowing for the 1934 passage of the levy. (The Louisiana tax runs from 2% at $10,000 to 6% at $50,000. With generous exemptions and deductions, it imposes a burden far below the national median.)

The constitution that emerged from this convention was the first to be submitted to popular vote since 1879. It passed with 58% of a low turnout. A major factor for approval, complained the "good government" Public Affairs Research Council, "was the saturation television campaigning by the Jefferson Parish assessor, using misleading scare talk about skyrocketing property taxes if the constitution failed."[56]

The new constitution produced an almost immediate reduction of the tax burden. The property tax per $1,000 of personal income fell from seventh lowest in the country (at 54% of the U.S. average) in 1972 to third lowest (41%) in 1977.[57] The effective income tax rate at the highest bracket fell to the lowest in the nation.[58] From 1975 to 1977, while the state and local tax burden for the country rose at an annual average rate of 2.1%, that of Louisiana *fell* by 3.8%.[59]

The economic impact was equally dramatic. After the stagnation of the early seventies, during which, alone of the southern states, Louisiana showed no relative growth in personal income, its income growth took off. Its growth rate was 127% of the nation's, taking it from a 1975 ranking of forty-fifth in per-capita income to a ranking of thirty-fifth in 1980.

This surge cannot be attributed entirely to oil and natural gas, even though the boom in that industry played a major part. Industrial investment rose from an average of $1 billion per year in the first half of the seventies to a $2.4 billion average for the last four years of the decade.[60] Because the existence of oil and gas has been more or less a constant factor throughout this period (in fact, production has declined through the entire decade), it is fair to ask why the industry chose to change its pattern of infrastructure investment. The traditional attitude had been to channel this money into capital-intensive projects, exporting the raw material from the state with relatively small reliance on the native work force. With the late seventies surge in local investment, state employment took a sharp turn for the better. In the aftermath of the 1973 constitution total state employment appeared to level off as a percentage of the U.S. total, but in 1978 it took a sharp leap upward.

The figures for labor force participation were even more striking. In 1975, an unusually low 53% of the working-age population made up the work force. By 1979, this proportion had risen to 58%, double the increase in the national labor force participation.[61]

THE OIL COLLAPSE

By the end of 1979, Louisiana's potential for reform seemed promising indeed. Belated decontrol promised to swell oil revenues (and partial decontrol of natural gas placed a premium on the state's deep gas fields). In one of its more memorable political dramas, the state had elected David Treen, both a Republican and an honest man, as governor. In his first budget, Governor Treen promised to use the severance tax surplus to phase out the state income tax. The future looked rosy.

Then came the oil glut. As the offshore rigs fell idle, state unemployment soared into the double digits. In spite of the glut and recession, total state personal income continued to grow at slightly above the national average. But severance tax receipts were devastated by the lethal combination of declining production and declining prices. The oil price finally stabilized around $29 a barrel, seven dollars lower than one estimate budget planners had used for their projections. To shore up his shaky finances, Treen proposed a tax on refinery output and suffered an embarrassing defeat in the legislature.

Former Governor Edwards, a charismatic Cajun with an enthusiastic following to equal Huey Long's, had withdrawn to a south Baton Rouge office crowded with good old boys and good-looking women, from which he watched Treen's discomfiture like Charles De Gaulle eyeing the Fourth Republic. In 1983, he emerged to reclaim his position. Under the shadow of the recession, the campaign posed the issue raised by Huey Long. Should the government limit taxes or provide services? Edwards promised more services, and more income taxes, in a style that deserves to be shared with the reader. As reported by The New Republic: "Edwards blasts Treen for his 33 percent tax cut, which he claims has resulted in a reduction of human services across the board, from state schools to the Edwards-created Right to Bite program, which helps senior citizens buy dentures. 'Can you imagine doing that?' Edwards asks the rapt crowds in small towns with names like Bunkie and Ville Platte. 'Let's face it, when you get to 65 there ain't much fun left except eating. Treen's not content to take little bites out of us, he's trying to gum us to death!' "[62] On October 22, 1983, Louisianans returned Edwards to office with 62.3% of the vote.

If Edwards, a highly flexible politician who has delivered both tax cuts and tax increases, keeps his latest promise, the state may once more make the experiment tried by Earl K. Long. A rapid rise in the tax burden could be expected to return Louisiana to the stagnation of the previous decade. One would expect to find even greater clarity in the relation of its tax burden to its economic development. The state's pattern of growth in the seventies helped solve the puzzle of the Sun-

belt. As a maverick with a high tax burden, it failed to participate in the pattern of growth until its tax burden began to
decline. The significance of Louisiana stands out in the contrast with its neighbor and rival, low-tax Texas.

8

Texas: The Jacksonian Nation-State

When George W. Smyth came to Nacogdoches as surveyor in 1830, he entered a brawling, lawless border town where most citizens were fugitives from justice. On the Sabine River, the boundary between the United States and the Texas domain of Mexico, the town was the center of a no man's land, a magnet "not only for bankrupts and debtors, but also for criminals, malcontents, and adventurers of every description." A visiting journalist from Louisiana found that on entering the area, "he was invariably surrounded and accosted sans ceremonie, by numbers of the citizens, enquiring *what he had done* in the United States, that made it necessary for him to seek refuge among them? . . . when a new-comer averred that he had *ran away from his creditors* ONLY, he was regarded as a gentleman of the *first water*, and welcomed on all hands."[1]

With not even that blotch on his record, Smyth, the twenty-seven-year-old son of a German millwright from North Carolina, almost immediately gained the status of leading citizen. Within five years, the Mexican authorities had appointed him land commissioner. In spite of a rising spirit of revolution (with which Smyth sympathized) and an increasing effort in Mexico City to control its turbulent border region, Smyth remained optimistic about his chosen home. Writing in May 1835, he explained: "I am convinced that Texas must prosper. We pay no taxes, work no public roads, get our land at cost, and perform no public duties of any kind."[2]

LOW-TAX NATIONALISM

Smyth's famous statement has practically become the motto for Texas development. The low-tax policies of Texas have roots reaching deeper than its statehood and even its preannexation nationhood. Settlers fleeing the reach of the law remained hostile to the burden of government. Their attitude may have sprung from discontent and frontier anarchy, but with the success of the Texas revolution, it acquired the sanctity of a founding doctrine. Whatever their origins, the adventurers who died in the War of Texas Independence procured for themselves a glorious transformation. Like the brigands who gathered around Romulus and Remus, they are now venerated as the forefathers of a great commonwealth.

The doctrines, or prejudices, of this founding generation are all the more revered in that Texans are the product of a double nationalism. They have their own revolution, their own declaration of independence, their own history as a sovereignty with international recognition.

One can find other states that have been independent nations, and for more extended periods. Vermont can claim to have been a sovereign republic for six years more than Texas, thanks to the personality of Ethan Allen and his interpretation of the state of nature. Hawaii was a constitutional monarchy and briefly a republic until 1898. Every episode of independence leaves its mark. Yet Texas is unique in the degree to which the memory of its national existence continues to shape its character.

The Texas Republic was not only a sovereign nation, it was a nation founded on Jacksonian Democracy. This tradition, still extremely lively, is a tradition of "negative democracy," of limits on the state and on concentrations of economic power. The equality it provides is the equality of pursuit: every man to have a fair chase after his fortune. The government is not meant to nob him or favor his competitor, but to keep the run fair and to prevent the banks and railroads from fixing the race. This climate smiles on the free enterprise of the farmer, the rancher, and the wildcatter, but it can turn sullen and hostile toward the large corporation, especially one from outside.

Ironically, large corporations have flourished in this climate. Aided by the migration of "Yankee" employees and job seekers, they have grown into a formidable counterweight to the native Jacksonian populism.

The economic growth of Texas has compounded irony on irony. From a republic that outlawed banks, it has grown into a center of corporate banking. From its hostility to central government, it has fashioned a constitutional system described as a bureaucrat's paradise. The local Jacksonian tradition produces national politicians devoted to the corporate welfare state. Jacksonian laissez-faire and probusiness laissez-faire coexist uneasily within the legislature, often within the individual officeholder. To resolve the tension, each tradition frequently attempts to turn government against the other.

Both traditions have been largely hostile to taxation, however. Texans agree that the low tax burden is the key to economic prosperity. The tax burden has been lightened further by the state's mineral wealth, which gives it one of the largest oil and natural gas severance tax bonanzas in the country. Until the present crisis of the oil glut, which lowered production *and* reduced prices, increasing revenues from the severance tax had greatly reduced political conflict over the shape of the state's revenue system. As the glut persists, this conflict is reviving and Texans may once again repeat the debate of a not-too-distant past.

Texas faced a similar crisis just a quarter of a century earlier, long before severance tax receipts reached a fabulous level and the state became a beneficiary of OPEC.

The foundations of Texan prosperity were laid down in the financial crisis of 1961, when declining oil prices opened a budget gap and forced the state to adopt a major new revenue source. In choosing a sales tax instead of an income tax, the state compromised between its corporate present and its Jacksonian past. But in many respects it still preserved a fiscal tradition that predates the state and even the republic.

THE FOUNDING OF TEXAS

Not all the immigrants to preindependence Texas were drifters and shady characters. Stephen Austin had carefully selected families of good character for the land grant he inherited from his father, Moses. The Mexican immigration law that applied to Austin's original 400 settlers had been generous: colonists paid no customs duties for seven years and no general taxes for ten. Unlike native Mexicans, they were exempt from military service and mandatory church tithes. On the other hand, they received no military protection or public service at all from the Mexican government. The 20,000 Anglo-American settlers who followed were happy with the bargain. In ten years they did more to develop the land than the Spanish Empire had been able to do in ten decades.[3]

Alarmed by this vigor, the Mexican government responded with the decree of April 6, 1830, suspending Anglo-American colonization and imposing customs for external trade. At the same time, political turmoil in the Mexican capital was subverting the federalist constitution of 1824. As central control spread over formerly semiautonomous provinces, discontent and rebellion flared from Yucatán to Coahuila (the province encompassing Texas). Texans were now being forced to pay customs and taxes; Texas patriotic histories frequently compare the situation to the prelude to the American Revolution.

Even though an uprising of unruly newcomers defeated one Mexican garrison in 1831, the diplomacy of the land impresario Stephen Austin deferred the break. With the emergence of the military hero Antonio López de Santa Anna, Mexican politics seemed to have acquired a federalist champion. But by 1836 Santa Anna had made the transition to "Napoleon of the West," abandoning the principles of decentralization. Austin's peace-keeping mission to Mexico City had ended in a year of imprisonment. In spite of some Mexican concessions to the North American legal traditions of the Texas settlers, Austin returned home ready to support the militants of the War Party.

What followed is the stuff that myths are made of. The devastating siege of the Alamo, the disastrous rout at Goliad, and Sam Houston's final chaotic victory at San Jacinto—these make up the kind of dramatic origin that no other American state can claim as the core of its identity. The political collapse of the new republic, the blunders that made the Alamo a deathtrap and opened Texas to Santa Anna's invasion, even the checkered past of the Alamo's heroes, have been left in the shadows. Attacks on these founding myths anger Texans to this day.

ANOTHER VIEW OF THE FOUNDING: MEXICANS ARE TEXANS, TOO

The other side of the story is still vividly alive to one large group of Texans, however. The Mexican-Americans of southern Texas have their own version of this history, and even had their own brief fling at sovereignty. After independence, neither the Texas Republic nor Mexico had much control over the territory south of San Antonio and north of Monterrey. Federalist landowners in that region set up the Republic of the Rio Grande. It lasted as long as it took a Mexican punitive expedition to chase down the ringleaders, but it gave expression to a separate regional identity that persists today on both sides of the border. The elite of Laredo thinks of itself as a third culture, blending that of the United States with that of Mexico, and the most colorful local fiesta honors the birthday of George Washington.

In the absence of central control, the Mexican population of southern Texas managed to hold on to its land. Expropriations were nearly complete farther north, but around Laredo one can still find Hispanic ranchers who trace their titles to the royal land grants that rewarded the members of Spanish survey expeditions. The rest of the state admires the heroic exploits of the Texas Rangers and their most improbable legend: the rail-thin, consumptive Leander H. McNelly, who faced down both the U.S. and the Mexican armies in a private invasion of Mexico. To the southern Texas Hispanics, however, the Rangers were the hated agents of expropriation; the Spanish corruption of their name, *rinches*, became an epithet for brutal Anglo authority, figuring in hundreds of border corridas and ballads.

The alienation of the Mexican-American began to dissipate only after World War II. Hispanic leaders, from San Antonio small-business men to United Farm Workers president Cesar Chavez, agree that it was the war that inspired the extraordinary Mexican-American political awakening now catching national attention. Military service brought the Mexican-American out of his isolation and gave him the assurance that he had a stake in the United States. All the ambitions of all the government programs conceived in Washington or the states look puny indeed compared to the social change produced by war. This experience, in which Anglo and Mexican Texans fought a common enemy, completed the founding of Texas.

JACKSONIANS GO TO TEXAS

Citizens of the new Texas Republic had come from all corners, but the dominant stream, following George Smyth's own route through Tennessee, was made up of frontiersmen to whom Andrew Jackson was the greatest man in America. Among these was the giant, half-barbarian hero of San Jacinto, Sam Houston, the dominant figure in a republic of striking personalities. Houston had been a protégé and ardent friend of Jackson since 1814, when, at the age of twenty-one, he was commended by Old Hickory for his courage at the Battle of Horseshoe Bend. A leader of the Jackson junta in Tennessee, Houston fought duels for his hero, ran errands for him as a congressman, even toned down the general's angry correspondence. As Jackson's man, he won election as governor of Tennessee in 1828. Then, at the peak of success, his personal life collapsed. After two months of marriage, he sent his young bride back to her family. As scurrilous gossip spread through Nashville and Washington, Houston shut himself in his room, resigned as governor, and packed for the Indian territories.[4]

For the next eight years, Houston wandered on the edge of civilization, living with his old friends the Cherokees, plotting a new republic in the Northwest, and drinking too much. His trips to Texas became more and more frequent. He practised law in Nacogdoches. Mexican authorities complained to President Jackson that Houston was thought to be his agent for sponsoring a revolution in their domain, and Jackson replied that he had assigned a secret agent to watch Houston and thwart any such attempt.[5]

Jackson's watch on Houston, if it indeed existed, was a spectacular failure. In the last act of Old Hickory's presidency, he extended recognition to the Republic of Texas and spent his last night in the White House drinking toasts with its ambassadors.

As the first president under the new Texas constitution, Sam Houston pursued Jacksonian policies as well as he could with a recalcitrant legislature and a financial system based entirely on borrowing. With only $500 in the treasury for most of the first year, frugal government would have been *de rigueur* for anyone. The real test of Houston's principles came in his second term, after the brief but grandiose presidency of Mirabeau Buonaparte Lamar. A poet and historian from Georgia, Lamar had commanded the cavalry at San Jacinto, reciting his own verse to his men before the battle. He had great plans for the independent republic, dreaming of expansion to the Pacific. He launched an ill-fated expedition to capture Santa Fe and rapidly expanded the Texas navy (following authorizations voted by the Texas Congress under Houston's leadership). A revenue system was now in place, drawing most of its receipts from tariffs but also attempting to collect a general property tax and a poll tax. Lamar's spending far outran revenue, however. During his year and a half in office the public debt soared from less than $2 million to some $7 million. Complaints mounted about the tax burden, although Lamar replied that they were exaggerated, since the bill could be paid in the republic's greatly depreciated "redback" currency.[6]

When Houston reentered the president's office, his first concern was to cut spending. He eliminated offices and suspended interest on the debt; he even attempted to sell off the navy. To make this stringency possible, he insisted on a pacifist policy. He restored friendly relations with the Indians and faced down public pressure to declare war on Mexico. When the Texas Congress laid claim to Alta and Baja California, he vetoed the resolution. (But Congress overrode the veto.) Finally, Houston cut taxes. But Congress wiped out the effect by refusing to let tax bills be paid as heretofore in government notes at face value. It required tax collectors to discount the notes to their market value. As the market value plunged, the cash-starved settlers held protest meetings; many refused to pay the property tax at all. Under Houston, revenues from internal taxes fell to half of what they had been under Lamar.[7]

But any attempt at direct taxation, wrote one contemporary observer, was probably doomed. The republic was constantly changing its schemes of internal revenue but "they all produced nothing, or next to nothing." And no wonder. "The most experienced financier would have found it difficult to collect a revenue of any amount from a community so small as the Texans, scattered over a large territory of one to every three or four miles, and whose industry was liable to frequent interruptions from alarms of incursions by the Mexicans and the Indians. Even to assess taxes, in such a community, was an undertaking of no small difficulty."[8]

The Jacksonian immigration brought one further financial prejudice, still a distinctive feature of Texas politics. Many of the settlers were refugees from the depression following the 1837 Panic; they commonly chalked "G.T.T." on their abandoned homesteads—"Gone to Texas," out of the reach of banks and creditors. When commercial agents in Austin obtained a Texas charter to found a bank and issue bank notes, popular reaction was so intensely negative that the Texas Congress in 1844 passed "an Act to Suppress Private Banks."

To Jacksonians, the effort to fund a National Bank of Texas jeopardized the soul of the republic. President Lamar was planning to capitalize the bank with a $5-million loan to be guaranteed by the French government. In the middle of negotiations, a herd of swine in Austin belonging to a Mr. Bullock ran loose in the stable of M. de Saligney, French minister to Texas. Saligney's servant killed one of the pigs. Bullock thrashed the man. The minister made a formal complaint and had Bullock arrested. Amid general furor, the Texas government requested Saligney's recall. But Saligney was a brother-in-law of the French minister of finance, and on his return to Paris, the envoy scuttled the loan. William Gouge, the same Jacksonian financial writer who had led the propaganda attack on the Bank of the United States, chronicled the incident on a visit to Austin, observing that "as Rome was saved by the cackling of geese, so Texas was saved by the squeaking of pigs. . . . All honor, then, to Mr. Bullock and his pigs; and this heretofore much despised animal must be regarded hereafter as possessed of classic interest. If his figure, carved in marble, should be placed over the entrance of the treasury of Texas, it would serve as a memento to future ages of his having been the salvation of the Republic."[9]

The antibank sentiment carried over as Texas entered the Union. The first state constitutional convention had just convened on July 4, 1845, when it heard of the death of Andrew Jackson. Sam Houston returned from his mentor's deathbed bearing a letter that Jackson had written some months earlier urging Texans to repudiate private banking in their new constitution. After donning crepe armbands, the delegates granted his request.

The current Texas state constitution still contains a prohibition on branch banking. But just as a loophole in the republic's statute allowed a mercantile firm in Galveston to circulate notes that were twice as sound as the republic's redbacks, modern financiers have circumvented the branch-banking ban. The single-office banks that sprang up under the constitution have generally been too small to be profitable and are largely being absorbed by the giant bank holding companies that now dominate Texas finance.

THE NEW STATE GETS A FREE RIDE

The Texas Republic was perpetually under threat of bankruptcy, staying afloat by means of loans and paper money. Ironically, the salvation of the new state's finances came not from Houston's economizing but from Lamar's imperial pretensions.

When the United States finally became eager to annex Texas, the Lone Star republic had diplomatic relations with four European powers and could play a strong hand. It gained highly favorable terms. The United States paid some of the republic's debts, and the state of Texas retained title to all its public lands to pay the rest. Federal negotiators promised to honor the Texan claim to the headwaters of the Rio Grande.

This boundary would have given Texas half of New Mexico and part of Colorado. Antislavery forces furiously opposed the claim, even staging something of a coup to organize New Mexico separately. Ultimately, in the kind of finely balanced deal between free and slave states that preceded the admission of every state during the period from the Missouri Compromise to the Civil War, the federal government compensated Texas with a series of cash grants.

Texas finally had funds for real public spending. The legislature started a school fund, splurged on public buildings, and turned back nine-tenths of locally raised revenues to the counties, which went on their own spree. Through the decade of the 1850s, Texas was able to improve its infrastructure vastly without levying a dollar in direct state taxes. Modern historians generally deplore this period. Writes Rupert Richardson, "The people learned to look to outside sources rather than to taxation as the means of supporting their government and were not prepared for the day when windfalls would cease." But the decade produced some of the most rapid growth in the state's history. In 1850, the value of aggregate taxable property totaled a bit over $50 million. In 1860, it totaled nearly $300 million. The 1860 census counted just over 600,000 residents, a tripling of the population.[10]

TAXES AND TYRANNY

Texas had a relatively easy time of the Civil War. Fighting was rare and fortunes were made on the cotton export route through Mexico, the Confederacy's only secure outlet. As refugees from the rest of the Confederacy shipped in their slaves for safekeeping, the state's taxable property base hit an all-time high in 1864.

Reconstruction was a far different story. Although the stereotypes of this period do little justice to the fascinating reality, one can argue that this was the school in which Texas, and most of the South, learned to abhor an energetic, aggressively taxing government.

Some of the expanded state spending was inevitable, and more was justifiable. Even the most hated of the "scalawag" governors, Edmund J. Davis (1870–74), was given credit for his efforts to improve the Texas public-school system. For the first time in its history the state was funding its schools, and half the eligible children in the state were enrolled.

But other programs, not nearly as benign, were swelling state spending. For example, Governor Davis established a state police that defended the frontier against Indian raids but also played a detested part in maintaining his political control. For a variety of reasons, the Texas budget in his first two years increased by 250%. Tax rates rose even faster. In 1866, the ad valorem property tax rate had been fifteen cents per $100 valuation. In 1871, it had risen to a possible maximum of $2.175 per $100. The soaring rate cut short a gradual recovery of the Texas economy. In 1871, the total aggregate taxable property base had reached a postwar high, growing 30% over the year before. In 1872, however, the property base fell by 7%. Over the next four years it stagnated at the quarter-of-a-million mark, below the level of 1861. Growth did not resume in earnest until 1877.[11]

As the harshness of the military-backed government alienated moderate Republicans and unionists, the state's high tax burden became the common ground for attack. At the peak of Radical Reconstruction a coalition of disaffected Republicans and newly reenfranchised Democrats staged a major tax revolt.

Partly in preparation for the crucial congressional elections later that year, anti-Radical politicians in 1871 called a series of taxpayers conventions to protest the high spending and taxation of the Davis administration. At a preliminary mass meeting in Galveston the chairman complained: "The aggregate of all the various taxes now imposed to support the standing armies and various State and local troops and which have been deemed necessary to deprive us of our liberties, and keep us in subjection, amounts to fully fifteen and *sometimes twenty and even more than twenty times* any tax the people of Texas were ever before called upon to pay in the times of our greatest prosperity."[12]

The main taxpayers convention was held in Austin in September; its leadership included all three of the Reconstruction governors who had preceded Davis.[13] Prominent Republicans acted as spokesmen for the convention in a committee of seven delegated to present its grievances. A subcommittee on taxes and statistics reported that spending had surged under Davis, that the tax rate had increased fifteenfold, and that the state would have ample funds for its business at one-third of the revenue. The convention furthermore declared that one portion of the levy earmarked for building schoolhouses was "illegal and void" and urged taxpayers to seek court injunctions against any sheriff attempting to collect it. The convention asserted that its concern was fiscal, not racial. In an indirect reference to the Ku Klux Klan, it condemned all violations of law and order and resolved: "That we recognize the right of every person in the State, without regard to race or previous condition, to equal civil and political rights under the law, and to have protection for his life, liberty and property. That we are in favor of paying all lawful and reasonable taxes for the establishment of public free schools and to carry on the government; but, at the same time, we recommend to the people that they do not pay such portions of the tax now demanded as we here show to be illegal."[14]

The taxpayers movement played a major role in realigning the Reconstruction factions. It produced some remarkable reconciliations. Andrew Jackson Hamilton, the former Republican governor who was one of the Austin convention's committee of seven, told an audience in Galveston why his brother Morgan, formerly a political rival, had joined his cause: "My brother sided with the authorities, but on his return (to Texas from Washington) he found an argument *ad pocketum*, for though my brother, he has now to pay about $3,000 in taxes. He does not like to be robbed in a day." Morgan Hamilton was then a U.S. senator, elected at the same time as Davis. He had served as chief theoretician of the Radical faction. His conversion shows the extent of concern over fiscal policy.[15]

One could dismiss this tax protest as another manifestation of racism and Bourbonism. From the specific mention of the schoolhouse levy, one could conclude that the tax protesters were really objecting to the use of their money to educate the children of ex-slaves and the "lower orders." Yet something more was going on at the Austin convention. A substantial constituency existed for a public-school system, which had been promised in the first state constitution. Even after the abuses of Reconstruction, Texas voters approved a referendum for a special education levy. Subsequent events showed that the tax protesters really were concerned about taxes.

The distinguished leadership of the Austin convention did not prevent a pro-Davis newspaper from attacking the delegates as "tax-howlers . . . [who] can't pay their taxes but have money enough to travel hundreds of miles and pay heavy bar-room bills in order to add a little fuel to the Ku Klux Klan disaffection and hostility that disfigures and disgraces the state."

But the tax protest did overwhelming damage to the incumbent. Anti-Davis Democrats swept the congressional seats, and the state legislature promptly started to dismantle the governor's program. Taxpayers, "sensing the inevitable victory of the Democrats and tax relief," refused to pay their levies. The cash shortfall was so severe that Governor Davis tried to sell bonds to cover operating expenses. But Democrats threatened to repudiate the issue, and it was practically unsellable. Even northern Republican newspapers joined the hue and cry. Horace Greeley's *New York Tribune* warned Texas Republicans "to squelch their embryo Tweeds."[16]

At the next gubernatorial election, in December 1873, Davis was soundly defeated. Yet his partisans found a technical defect in the conduct of the voting and launched a court challenge of the results, hoping that President Ulysses S. Grant would intervene to keep him in power.

When the new legislature met in January 1874, Davis refused to yield his office. He ensconced himself on the second floor of the capitol, guarded by armed members of his hated state police. The new legislature posted its own armed forces on the first floor and convened to swear in his successor, Richard Coke. When Grant finally declined to intercede, Davis quietly left his office, locking it and pocketing the key. Coke's men had to break down the door to get in. Davis was the last Republican to govern in Texas until the 1978 election of William P. Clements, Jr., who held a very different attitude toward taxation.[17]

DISMANTLING THE EXECUTIVE

In Texas the excitement over "tax and tyranny" had lasting consequences. When the Democratic ex-Confederates (the so-called Redeemers) regained power, they summoned a constitutional convention to replace the basic law written by the Reconstruction Radicals. Historians are nearly unanimous in reading the constitution of 1876 as a reaction against the excesses of Governor Davis. It stripped the executive of much of his power. Important departments were split off, and their heads made elective. A series of subsequent amendments put even more departments under the control of independent boards and commissions. Since these commissions consist of part-time citizens' representatives, much of the state bureaucracy is free of effective executive control.

In an even more dramatic attack on executive control, the 1876 constitution made no provision for an executive budget. The legislature was left free to disregard the governor's budget and write its own, and that is exactly what it does. The important spending decisions are made by the professional staff in the Legislative Budget Office. This twist means that the lieutenant governor, as presiding officer of the Senate and chairman of the Legislative Budget Bureau, has potentially more say in state government than the governor.[18]

The 1876 convention also attempted to impose strict fiscal limits on both the governor and the legislature. It set a maximum rate of fifty cents per $100 on the general property tax, less than a quarter of Governor Davis's peak rate. This limit was significant at the time, since the property tax was the main source of state and local revenue. But the drafters allowed most other levies, including an income tax. They worked hard at other types of limits, but at least one modern scholar is not impressed by the result. In a pamphlet distributed in the early 1970s to aid the cause of a new constitution, George D. Braden called their handiwork "a monstrous fiscal mess." It set up a "cumbersome" structure of special funds and compounded the inflexibility by earmarking tax receipts. It prohibited state debt entirely, but the currently outstanding state debt totals more than $1 billion. (Voters in Texas authorize a specific bond issue by passing a constitutional amendment.) The drafters tried to limit spending by prohibiting the wrong sort of people from receiving the money. Overall, Braden found this "clutter" to be "fiscal madness," "confused and confusing," "just plain silly," and even "weird." But this constitution, all 60,000 words and 242 amendments, is still the fundamental law of Texas. When the legislature tried to write a new one in 1975, voters rejected it by a margin of 73 to 27%.[19]

The 1876 convention reacted not only against Reconstruction but also against high government spending in general. Delegates, for all their distrust of the executive, did not hesitate to give him the substantial power of a line-item veto to check the spending power of the legislature. (This provision was introduced to America by the constitution of the Confederacy and was incorporated into Texas's 1866 constitution.) According to the research of John Walker Mauer, delegates paid attention to the recent conventions in Illinois and Pennsylvania as well as to the abuses of Davis. They were alarmed by the continued high spending of Davis's successor, Richard Coke. The budget figures bear this statement out. In 1874, which would have been Davis's last budget but the first year of Coke's administration, the state spent $2.5 million. In 1875, spending fell to $1.9 million. After adoption of the 1876 constitution, spending tumbled to $1.7 million and stayed under the $2 million level for another year. For the first six years of Reconstruction, by contrast, state budgets had averaged half a million dollars a year.[20]

This fiscal record may be the most grievously neglected aspect of the largely neglected history of Reconstruction, yet it has left an extremely important imprint on the financial and political behavior of southern states.

THE OLD ALCALDE

In spite of the stringency of the 1876 constitution, state finances did not come under control until the administration of Oran M. Roberts, who later, as an elder statesman, was known as "the Old Alcalde" (Spanish for mayor). Roberts had been the president of the secession convention in 1861 and chief justice in the first post-Reconstruction government. He emerged as a compromise Democratic candidate for governor in 1878 after the main contenders had exhausted themselves.

As governor, Roberts tried all available means to end the state's persistent deficit. He sold public lands and improved tax collection and assessment. Since taxes had already reached their limit under Reconstruction, Roberts turned his hand to reducing services. When the legislature ignored his recommendation to reduce public-school spending, he created a furor by vetoing the entire appropriation. Governor Roberts emerged from the uproar with public support. He was re-elected easily to his second term but refused requests to break tradition and run for a third. At the end of his administration the public debt had been reduced, the budget was running a surplus, and the state property tax rate had been cut by 40%.[21]

As a distinguished jurist and educator—he presided over the opening of the University of Texas and taught law there for the rest of his career—Roberts also left a theoretical argument for the state's tax policy. In 1889, he wrote an article, "The History and Burden of Taxation," that restated southern agrarian grievances against the federal government, particularly the high-tariff policy that Roberts traced from the middle of James Monroe's second term.[22] Federal tax policy, he charged, was making the rich richer and the poor poorer because it was manipulated by a multitude of special interests. The only way to prevent such abuses was to impose "specific directions, restrictions, and limitations upon the power of taxation. . . . Texas has in the main carried out the just principle by making the burdens of taxation upon the people correspond with the protection of their rights of person and property."[23] Because the purpose of the government is to provide this protection, the bulk of its revenue has come from its ad valorem tax on general property, supplemented by a poll tax on individuals. The state constitution severely limits the state's ability to use the tax code for other social purposes. "The effort to produce moral results or material benefits to the community indirectly by imposing high taxes upon particular pursuits is seldom effective and is wrong in principle."[24]

Roberts urged an even greater state reliance on the property tax and criticized the "occupation tax," a primitive form of income tax by which everyone except farmers and workmen could be assessed a set fee each year depending on their profession. His administration, however, had actually shifted the burden away from the property tax. The occupation tax, he said, might be paid "in the first instance by those persons who are taxed, but is eventually paid by those persons who deal with them, and is therefore a tax upon the labor and industry of the persons who deal with them." After thus acknowledging the problem of incidence, which modern tax policy is struggling to rediscover, he launched into a discussion of general principles that the supply-side school would find thoroughly congenial. "Permanent property is human labor materialized into shape, producing values in the way of profits. A very small portion of those profits taken as taxes will support the government without taxing the labor of those who are in the struggle to acquire it. In a republic it surely is the interest of the political organization to facilitate the acquisition of property by the greatest number practicable in the association by honest labor, without placing any drawback upon their laudable efforts."[25]

This passage harks back to the principles that Henry George, theorist of the single tax, stated with such passionate eloquence. In more involuted style, Roberts says that the burden of taxation should fall on the *product* of labor rather than on the act of labor. His argument is interesting in that it reverts explicitly to the political tradition of Jefferson and Jackson, which Roberts, the unreconstructed secessionist, traces to the Virginia Resolutions of 1798 and 1799. The purposes of government must be limited so that its need for tax revenues can be kept low. The lower the tax burden, the less the chance it can be manipulated to give a minority of special interests an unfair advantage over the majority which is striving to acquire property through the exercise of its labor. With fewer government hindrances, a greater number of citizens will be able to convert their labor into property. "Certainly the greater the number of permanent property holders in a State the greater will be the means of progress in civilization. The object of good government should be to shape its taxes so as to promote that result." Roberts endorsed the gist of Henry George's approach without embracing all the details of his monomania. The best policy, he said, lay in "making the property already acquired bear mainly the burden of supporting the government."[26]

Texas should adhere to this policy, furthermore, to avoid compounding the damage already done by federal tax policy. "The State has an inducement to rely mainly on taxation on property in view of the fact that the government of the United States levies and collects its revenues directly and indirectly upon the labor and industry of the people to a degree that excludes the State from resorting to that source for the support of its government."[27] This statement, which anticipates the federal income tax by several decades, also applies to the protectionist tariff, argues Roberts. That burden falls heaviest, he says, on the farming class, which receives no tariff protection but pays an artificially high price for imported implements of production. Roberts leaves no doubt that he is an agrarian. "Should the day ever come that this country shall come to be classed as a manufacturing country, as England is today, and the independent agriculturist no longer holds the balance of power in the government, it will be a day of mourning for the lost freedom and equality of the people. Republicanism will be dead, for dependent operatives, and farm renters, and trades people can not maintain it."[28]

DEVELOPING TEXAS

Oran Roberts claimed that his tax theory had its roots in the agrarian tradition. Yet his prescription for a sound tax system differed significantly from the political program of the state's agrarian movements. Spurning Grange requests to restore the income tax, Roberts balanced his budget by cutting spending and selling land. This policy, furthermore, coincided with the state's first sustained prosperity since the 1850s. Cotton production, the main cash crop, more than doubled between 1876 and 1886. Rail mileage quadrupled. Population by 1890 had increased 270% over 1870, and stood at 2.2 million. Taxable property increased 240% in the decade after the adoption of the 1876 constitution.

Gradually, despite Roberts's warning, the political climate in Texas began to foster the transition to an industrial economy.[29] In 1870, 95% of the Texas population lived and worked on farms, ranches, and in rural settlements. With the exception of cotton and the cattle drives, the bulk of the produce was consumed at home or used for barter. In the last thirty years of the century, however, farming became commercial. Wheat, rice, and sugar cane became major cash crops, subjecting farmers to the risks of a market economy. In 1870, flour and grist mills ranked high on the list of the negligible Texas industries; their output served mainly local communities. By 1900, the custom mills had given way to commercial processing. Even so, food processing had been surpassed by the manufacture of timber and cottonseed oil and cake. Some 17% of the population now lived in cities, and urban growth was accelerating at almost three times the rate of rural growth. With a population density of eleven persons per square mile, Texas no longer qualified for the Census Bureau's list of frontier states.[30]

SPINDLETOP

As Texas grew, it produced boosters and visionaries with schemes to make it grow even faster. One of these was Paltillo Higgins, a native of Beaumont, in East Texas. Higgins was convinced there was oil to be found under Big Hill, a local mound seeping sulphuric gas. He persuaded town leaders to invest in a company to purchase the hill and begin drilling. After the primitive wells collapsed in loose formations, an

Austrian engineer named Anthony Lucas answered an adver-
tisement to take over the project. As Lucas worked, inventing
the basic techniques of modern oil drilling, a succession of
geologists passed through town and announced there was no
chance of finding oil. But no one told the well. At 10:30 on
the morning of January 10, 1901, the drilling crew was lowering a new bit into the hole when it spewed mud with such
force that four tons of pipe went sailing through the air. As
the thoroughly shaken crew turned to the drilling platform to
survey the damage, the well erupted again with deafening
thunder, belching a geyser of sand, rock, gas, and oil. The roar
stampeded cattle ten miles away.[31]

The gusher that was to change Texas immediately caught
the public imagination. The world's first find of a "giant" oil
field, it spewed plumes 175 feet high, at a rate of 100,000 bar-
rels a day. Newsmen rechristened the hill "Spindletop."

Railroads put on special excursion trains, and 15,000
sightseers a day took the trip. They were witnessing the birth
of an industry, of a petroleum-based economy, and of modern
Texas. Beaumont went through a boom unparalleled since the
California Gold Rush. Four major oil companies emerged from
the Spindletop chaos to challenge the monopoly of John D.
Rockefeller's Standard Oil. (Standard Oil's geologist was one
of those who thought the place would never show petroleum.) Within a year of the gusher, the companies in the field
were capitalized at $200 million.[32]

Corporations suddenly emerged as a major element of the
state's economy. During the previous three decades, they had
been the whipping boys of Greenback and populist rhetoric,
but now they were home-grown powers. As a part of the true
Texas tradition, and not the least exciting part at that, oil
companies and business in general felt they had a legitimate
role to play in the state's politics. Collisions with the older
Jacksonian tradition were bound to follow. One of these fights
concerned a state income tax and helped set the shape of
Texas's modern tax system.

TEXAS RULES OUT THE INCOME TAX

One of the strengths of the Texas economy is its complete avoidance of a state income tax. Yet the nineteenth-century state constitutions expressly authorized the legislature to impose one. In the first state constitution, 1845, language allowing a tax on incomes was introduced by George Smyth, the same Nacogdoches land commissioner who even before independence had praised the no-tax climate of Texas. But Smyth had not been converted into a big spender. He and his colleagues were drafting a general property tax requiring "equal and uniform" application. To make it work, they wanted a way to reach the intangible property that evaded the tax assessor. As a farmer and former land commissioner, Smyth had the landed interest at heart. In theory, the income tax (as well as the somewhat similar occupation tax) was the means of preventing the shift of a disproportionate tax burden onto real estate and personal property. But the legislature exercised this option only for brief periods during the Civil War and again during Reconstruction. From 1867 to 1870, taxpayers struggled with a graduated levy of 1% on the first $1,000 of net taxable income, rising by brackets to 3% on incomes above $5,000. The 1866 law listed specific deductions, and granted a $600 family exemption. The similarity to the modern federal income tax is striking.[33]

This tax was repealed in the waning days of Reconstruction, prompting protest from the growing agrarian movement of the seventies. The state platform of the Greenback Party called for restoration of the income tax. The issue was joined squarely between land and capital. The Greenbackers saw the income tax as a means of shifting the state tax burden away from their highly visible and immobile property and onto the invisible streams of capital. This agitation was defused by Governor Roberts' retrenchments, which also shifted some of the burden to the occupation taxes. According to Alwyn Barr, "the real key to Roberts' success lay in his efforts to lighten the taxes that landowning farmers paid by reducing state expenditures and by finding revenues elsewhere, especially through the sale of public land. Although in some ways shortsighted, his measures had an irresistable and immediate financial appeal exceeding even that of greenbacks."[34]

The issue emerged again in the reform administrations of Dan Moody (1927–31). An advocate of a rationalized state government and a civil service bill, Governor Moody also broached the idea of replacing the "antiquated" ad valorem tax with a state income tax on the federal model. His arguments contained equal measures of agrarianism and administrative reform. The shift would give relief to the farmer and would replace an outgrown, cumbersome-to-administer tax with a simple, conveniently collected levy based on the federal income tax form. This progressive argument has a thoroughly modern ring; it has become familiar through the debates that have led forty-one states to adopt a broad-based individual income tax and forty-five to adopt a corporate income tax.

But in 1929 Texas business struck back vehemently at the tax, wielding the growing power of the state's new urban and industrial interests. Although the legislature seemed no more friendly to this proposal than to most of Governor Moody's unsuccessful reforms, the mere mention of the idea drew a sharp retort from one of the state's leading business journalists. The main source of economic and social reporting on Texas from 1928 to 1940 was the succession of magazines edited by Peter Molyneaux. In 1929, his organ was *The Texas Monthly*, a far different publication from the glossy, ad-swollen regional magazine of today. A staunch advocate of capital, urbanization, and industrialization, Molyneaux made an impressive case for the benefits that all three brought to the farmer. They provided a growing home market for his produce. They paid such a large proportion of taxes that rural areas often received more in services than they contributed in their levy. The states' rights tradition in Texas had inspired much talk of diversifying its economy, but it was only in the last years of the twenties that this goal had come within reach. The proposal for a state income tax, wrote Molyneaux, jeopardized this development. It would unfairly shift the tax burden to corporations, to some 10% of the population, and to the urban areas in which they were concentrated. But the chief objection, he argued, was that "it would place a discriminatory handicap on industry and place unnecessary obstacles in the way of economic progress. This matter of taxation is of fundamental importance in relation to development. One of the chief influences which had been driving the textile industry out of New England into the South has been excessive taxation."[35]

TEXAS DEBATES THE SALES TAX

Peter Molyneaux, like his constituency, did not oppose all taxation. During the Depression fiscal crisis of 1933 he supported the proposal for a state sales tax offered by the impeached former governor James Ferguson. Ferguson, the Pa of the Ma and Pa Ferguson team, had just been returned to effective power through the election of his wife as the state's first woman governor. Wrote Molyneaux in his magazine, then *The Texas Weekly,* "The State Government must be supported and . . . the people ought to share the responsibility of supporting it."[36]

The bulk of political opinion seemed unwilling to go even this far, however. During this crisis, state legislators on the Legislative Committee on Organization and Economy issued a "Plea for Reduction of Taxes and Bonds in Texas." Complained the authors, "the simple, inexpensive government on which, less than a century ago De Tocqueville congratulated this country, has as its successor today a vast complicated mechanism of which the running expenses absorb almost one-fifth of the income, from all sources, of the American people." Quoting Montesquieu, Adam Smith, and Dr. Milbank Johnson of the California Taxpayers' Association, the authors concluded: "There is but one sound method of dealing with the double problem presented by the need of the people for tax relief and the condition of the state's finances. We must eliminate unnecessary State agencies, functions and employees, consolidate agencies now existing and cease to create new ones. As has been said by Dr. Milbank Johnson of the California Taxpayers' Association 'The juggling of tax burdens, reassessments and the shifting of tax bases, will never bring tax relief.' "[37] This advice carried the day. The legislature re-

jected the proposed sales tax of 3% and reduced general appropriations by 21%. To provide unemployment relief the
legislature authorized a constitutional amendment to issue
more than $40 million in "bread bonds."[38]

Given the severity of the economic and fiscal crisis, the
political resistance to increased general taxation was indeed
impressive. But it was by no means to be confused with probusiness politics. In spite of the opposition of the petroleum
industry, the same crisis gave rise to the state's modern structure of severance taxation.

TEXAS FINDS SEVERANCE TAXES
A MIXED BLESSING

Spindletop had barely stopped spouting when the state legislature began to tax the new resource. The tax on crude-oil
production was passed in 1905 and raised twice by the thirties. During the fiscal crisis of 1931, the legislature added a
special tax on natural gas production. As the Depression wore
on, the state raised both taxes again, as well as taxes on other
natural resources. These taxes are commonly used to explain
away the economic and fiscal strength of Texas.

Because of the relative tightness of the oil market through
much of the 1970s, the general public grew to consider petroleum an unmixed blessing. Texas has had a far different experience, however. The thirty years after Spindletop were filled
with painful trials and errors (both practical and legal) as the
state learned how to handle this resource. The Spindletop field
itself was substantially ruined by its promoters' delight in
showing off their gushers. In the twenties, an eccentric wildcatter hit black gold in West Texas, and find after find glutted
the market. The price of oil plummeted to ten cents a barrel.
Efforts to boost the price by controling production ran into a
legal thicket. Another giant strike back in East Texas threatened to devastate the market; wells were running flat out, and
in desperation Governor Ross Sterling placed the new field
under martial law.

The break in the oil price also wreaked devastation on
severance tax revenues, which were levied on the market value

of production. In 1933, the legislature protected the treasury by splitting the tax into two parts. Whenever the market price fell below $1.00 a barrel, the tax would be two cents a barrel; when the price rose over $1.00 the tax would be 2% of market value.[39]

The history of oil production has been a succession of tightness and glut. In the fifties, Texas again felt the pinch of a falling world market. Waggoner Carr, speaker of the Texas House of Representatives, warned one audience in 1957: "The entire revenue situation . . . could change drastically almost overnight. We are more or less at the mercy of foreign dictators. Their whims can easily determine how much tax revenue the State of Texas will collect during the next two years."[40] Carr's warning was almost immediately borne out. Even though the Eisenhower Administration had begun to yield to pressure for oil import controls, so much cheap foreign oil was undercutting the artificially maintained domestic price that Texas severance tax receipts plummeted by 15% from 1957 to 1958. By 1961, the state General Fund had accumulated a deficit of $100 million. The legislature was forced to confront the rest of Carr's warning. Texas, he said, must "broaden our tax base in order to at least reduce the effects which foreign powers can exercise over the finances of our state. For years, we have sidestepped the unpleasant chore of completely overhauling our tax structure."[41]

Established opinion nowadays attributes the prosperity of Texas to its extraordinary fossil fuel wealth or, in a more sophisticated version, to the fiscal bonanza of the severance tax. But, as Carr's warnings indicate, this bonanza has been erratic. Although severance tax receipts rebounded slightly in fiscal year 1959, they fell again during the next two years. These revenues stagnated throughout the sixties. By 1973, the tax on both oil and natural gas production provided only 7.5% of the state budget, the contribution it made in 1960. World oil prices by that time had been rising sharply, as OPEC was finally able to exploit a seller's market. (Texas had many interests in common with OPEC, which had been founded about the time of Texas's 1959 fiscal crisis, because its members were going through the same experience.) But the Lone Star State failed to reap the immediate benefits of the 1969–73 "energy crisis" because of President Richard Nixon's price controls on oil. The severance tax made relatively little contribution during the crucial years 1965–73, when the Texas tax burden fell sharply and the state began to improve its share of national income.[42]

After 1973, the pattern changed. With gradual decontrol, oil prices and severance tax receipts boomed. In 1973, oil and natural gas production taxes yielded $335 million. For 1983, they were projected to yield $2.7 billion. From 7.5% of the budget, they ballooned to nearly 30%.[43] After 1973, the state's personal income has risen hand in hand with petroleum prices.

In 1982, however, history finally caught up with the oil cycle. A world glut broke oil prices (at least moderately and at least for a time), state drilling declined from its historic high, and revenue officials began a sharp-eyed watch over their severance tax projections. It remains to be seen whether this glut can force a fiscal crisis, let alone another fiscal overhaul, on the order of 1961. Important as the severance taxes are, the state still has a cushion in the state sales tax. Although oil revenues had imparted an explosive and dangerous impulsion to the Texas economy, the state's fiscal system rests on a broader base.

THE SALES TAX

During every major fiscal crisis of the past fifty years, Texas governors have strongly urged a sales tax, but they generally had little more luck than Ma Ferguson in 1933. In 1939, Governor W. Lee ("Pappy") O'Daniel started a major fight to obtain a sales tax constitutional amendment. But a core of House members held out against his pressure and earned themselves the sobriquet the "Immortal Fifty-six."[44]

One of these Immortal Fifty-six, Price Daniel, happened to be governor when the 1962 fiscal crisis hit. The demand for increased services, and increased public-employee salaries, largely limited the state government's interest in cutting spending, but public opposition to general taxation still ran very strong. The state had reached a dead end, however, in meeting its periodic fiscal crises with omnibus bills of selective taxes.[45] The debate on general taxation then took an unusual turn. The Texas Commission on State and Local Tax Policy issued several reports debunking the conventional belief that the sales tax was always regressive and that the best income tax was progressive. The states in which the income tax yielded the highest revenue, reported the commission, were those which placed the burden most heavily on the lower and middle incomes. At the same time, the commission ran its own survey, using a *Ladies' Home Journal* series on family budgets as the model, to determine the impact of the sales tax. When the tax contained broad exemptions on necessities such as food, shelter, and utility bills, its burden fell in proportion to declining family income. It did not overtax the poor.[46] The state legislature apparently listened. Its final compromise imposed a 2% sales tax with a lengthy list of exemptions. (They now total forty-six.) The income tax was once again rejected.

During the fiscal pressure of 1968 to 1971, the sales tax rate was raised three times, to today's level of 4%. From 1971 to 1978, however, there were no major changes in the state tax structure.[47]

As the chart on page 235 shows, a fiscal system based on the limited sales tax behaves very differently from one based on a progressive income tax. The progressive tax structure in California extracted revenue at a rate well beyond inflation. The sales tax, however, tracks the fluctuations of the economy without providing the state with an inflation bonus. As a result, the tax burden lags behind real economic performance; it does not outrun it or shut it off. Thanks to Texas's venerable tradition of limited taxation, it adopted a "modern" fiscal system, which minimized the damage to the economy.

THE POPULIST AND THE CORPORATION
MUST BE FRIENDS

In spite of a two-year pause following the tax burden increase from 1969 to 1971, economic growth since the mid-sixties has been impressive. In 1968, the state's unemployment rate was only three-quarters of the national average; and by 1982 it had

Texas

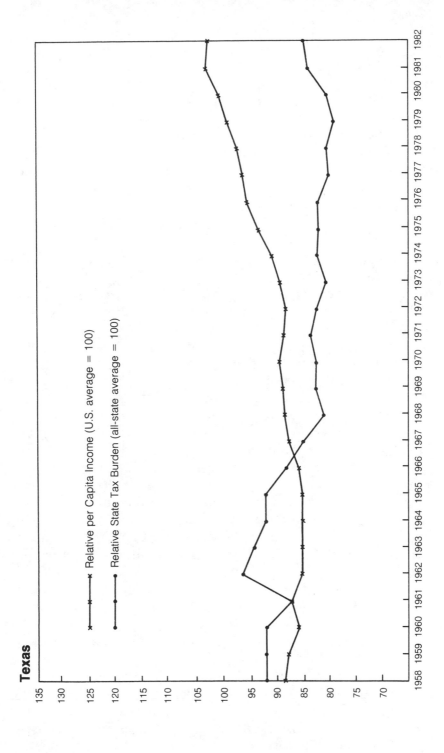

dropped to two-thirds. Its population growth was nearly four times the nation's. The main engine of growth since 1968 had been immigration. Before that turning point, up to 50,000 more people were leaving the state in a year than settling in it. In the decade after 1968, some 100,000 a year poured in. The immigration has swelled urban centers, such as Houston, dramatically shifting the nature of the state's population. From 95% rural in 1870, Texas is now 80% urban. It boasts three of the nation's ten largest cities.[48]

Texans show remarkable unanimity in attributing this success to their low taxes and limited government. Although state spending has been lavish by historical standards, it is concentrated in á few areas which return the greatest payoff to the economy. The two largest items in the budget two decades ago were education and roads. Although transportation has been eclipsed in recent years, education continues to command up to 47% of state spending. By contrast, Texas has been extraordinarily stingy in making transfer payments. It ranks second from the bottom in the proportion of its own funds devoted to welfare payments.[49]

The consensus on taxing and spending, however, masks a persistent division between the state's original Jacksonian agrarianism and its twentieth-century corporate politics. Since both political traditions favor lower taxes, they may appear to act in concert. Yet whenever revenues cease to expand, these two tendencies break apart in bitter quarreling over where to locate the tax burden. In the nineteenth century, the issue polarized around the income tax, favored by farmers to reduce the load of the state property tax. In the middle third of the twentieth century, the issue focused on the attempt to replace the state's grab bag of indirect business taxes with a general sales tax. (Pappy O'Daniel's sales tax constitutional amendment would also have imposed a limit on oil and gas severance tax rates.) The two forces of immigration and urbanization would seem to have tipped the scales in favor of corporate politics. Yet the agrarian tradition smoldered beneath the surface, bursting into the open in the electoral surprises of 1982.

The career of Jim Hightower illustrates the latent populist strength. Rail-thin, with a doleful countenance, Hightower had made his mark as the talented editor of the defiantly liberal *Texas Observer*. In 1980, he conceived the idea of running for a seat on the powerful Texas Railroad Commission. (In spite of its name, this commission regulates the state's oil and gas production.) The author remembers "setting" with Hightower on the balcony of the aging frame house that served as the *Observer* office, enjoying a breeze in the Austin afternoon as he revealed his plans. A daydream, it seemed, at best a symbolic candidacy. Not so. An authentic Texas type to begin with, Hightower gambled on a revival of fiery old-time Populist rhetoric in an era supposedly dominated by the "cool" electronic media. He captivated the press with a whistle-stop railroad campaign. On Primary Day he came within an ace of defeating the incumbent commissioner. But the most remarkable aspect of his vote was that it stood the traditional liberal-conservative pattern on its head. His weakest vote came in the Mexican-American Rio Grande valley, but he swept right-wing Dallas. Two years later, Hightower had his vindication. Running for state commissioner of agriculture, he upset the incumbent in the primary and triumphed in the general election with better than 60% of the vote. His victory margin far exceeded that of the Democratic gubernatorial candidate, Attorney General Mark White, a populist figure in his own right, who upset the incumbent Republican William P. Clements, Jr.

This political division also played a role in the 1978 debate over a constitutional limit on taxes and spending. It may seem strange that a state with the low-tax tradition of Texas should feel the need to join the Proposition 13 Tax Revolt. Yet, in the summer of 1978, the state legislature adopted a multipart constitutional amendment increasing a variety of property tax exemptions and adopting a mild state spending limit. One feature combined both a corporate and an agrarian appeal. This section directed the legislature to value farm and ranch land on the basis of the income it generated rather than on its speculative value for real estate development. On its face this measure would lessen the tax load on farmers and ranchers, making it easier for them to stay on their land. But corporate lobbyists slipped in a provision allowing the legislature to treat timberland the same way. As a result, because of a merger with the timber interests of Arthur Temple, the largest single beneficiary of the Texas "Tax Relief Amendment" was Time Inc.[50]

The same vote began the phasing out of the state property tax, mainstay of state finance since admission to the Union. The next year, the legislature accelerated the process, adopting a token rate of .0001%. Revenues from this historic source dropped to 1.6% of the total in 1981. A growing movement among farmers and ranchers, the Proposition Zero campaign would also eliminate local property taxes. In this respect, at least, the populist goal of shifting the tax burden away from farms and ranches is nearing its ultimate conclusion.

The spending limit was modeled after a Tennessee measure adopted in 1977. It is the culmination of efforts that began in the Texas constitutional convention of 1974 in the aftermath of Reagan's Proposition 1. Compared to the later generation of spending limits, however, the Tennessee-Texas model is relatively weak. Since the limitation can be overridden by a set percentage of the legislature, it merely shifts the burden of proof for spending increases from the opponents to the proponents. At this writing, state spending, even at its growth rate of 18.5% over the preceding biennium, has not yet encountered the constitutional ceiling. The Legislative Budget Board is watching for such a conflict in the 1984–85 biennium.[51]

These measures raised no serious conflict between the state's latent populism and its business interests, and so the Tax Relief Amendment received the full support of the state's fiscal consensus. It passed with 80% of the vote. But the consensus began to break down almost immediately, when younger Republican legislators tried to push the limitations further. Business lobbyists averted an attempt to write a constitutional ban on an income tax. They argued that if that revenue source were ruled out, the state would inevitably turn to higher business taxes on the day its severance bonanza ran out. By the same token, organized business, and especially the major oil companies, opposed Governor Clements's agitation to introduce a state initiative and referendum. They feared that the instruments would immediately be used to propose a "refinery tax," a levy on the value of all crude oil passing through Texas refineries.[52]

The conflict between the two dominant Texas traditions, Jacksonian agrarianism and industrial capitalism, has only recently been reignited and fanned by the impact of the national recession and the international oil glut. It remains to be seen whether the interruption in the state's economic success will last long enough to cause a change in its basic fiscal policies. (Even though Texas unemployment turned sharply upward in the fall of 1982, it remained more than three points below the national rate and started dropping again immediately after the election.)

But no one can say at the moment what would happen in the event of continued decline in oil prices, in oil production, or, of most political relevance, in severance tax receipts. In particular, it remains to be seen which tradition will prove more attractive to the more than 1 million immigrants who have entered the state from both north and south in the past fifteen years. The potential irony is that this population, attracted by the success of Texas, might forge a new departure in its politics, less rooted in its rich and brawling history.

9

Ohio: The Middle-aged "Middle Region"

At the age of twenty-one, Alfred Kelley decided to seek his fortune in the West. His family had already joined the great migration from the original colonies, taking Alfred from his birthplace in Middletown, Connecticut, to settle in upstate New York. In 1810, he set out with a group of fellow townsmen for a promising wilderness called "New Connecticut," surveyed two decades earlier by a party of Hartford businessmen led by Moses Cleaveland. Kelley's group followed the route being prepared for the boldest construction project yet conceived in the young republic, the Erie Canal. His companions on the weeks-long journey recalled later how at every stop he talked for hours with the local farmers about the benefits the new canal would bring in opening the vast interior.[1]

The prospects that so fired the mind of the young Kelley were those of the frontier, which later fascinated a generation of American historians. According to Walter Prescott Webb, the most impressive of the Texas historians, free access to open land allowed wealth to be accumulated at a much more rapid rate at the edge of western civilization than at its center. Webb stretches the point to say that discovery of the Western Hemisphere, the greatest of all frontiers, provided the surplus of land and capital that generated Europe's 400-year "Boom Era."[2]

Webb offers the following citation from Adam Smith:

> The colony of a civilized nation which takes possession either of a waste country, or of one so thinly inhabited, that the natives easily give place to the new settlers, advances more rapidly to wealth and greatness than any other human society. . . . Among savage and barbarous nations, the natural progress of law and government is still slower than the natural progress of arts, after law and government have been so far established, as is necessary for their protection. Every colonist gets more land than he can possibly cultivate. He has no rent and scarce any taxes to pay. No landlord shares with him in its produce, and the share of the sovereign is commonly but a trifle. He has every motive to render as great as possible a produce, which is thus to be almost entirely his own.[3]

Can one also invoke the frontier to account for the rapid growth this narrative has ascribed to tax policy? The two dramatic examples of California and Texas fit Webb's model of states whose natural resources are only now reaching their peak of exploitation. These gifts of providence are not to be despised; yet human wisdom or folly determines how they will be used. The range of motives in Adam Smith's view of the newly opened territories extends farther than those recognized by the frontier school. In moving now from the West and Southwest to the center of the nation's traditional population and economy, we see the contrast between natural resources and human policy become more pronounced. The laboratory of the older states will help analyze the ingredients that produce economic success, and tax policy will not be lacking.

The Ohio that Alfred Kelley helped to shape is one of the most exacting experiments. The boom of freshly opened land has long since passed; the more elaborate economies that followed also appear to have run their course. Kelley's frontier is well into middle age. Does tax policy have any further relevance to its fate?

The question bears not only on economics but also on the ability of human institutions to shape events. Ohio offers an essay in the rational creation of a political unit. Hewn out of the Old Northwest by one of the most fundamental of the constitutional compromises, its growth to statehood reveals the genius of the American federal union. The circumstances that forged it into a single political unit also gave it a low-tax policy.

The Buckeye State has held each of its array of taxes below the national average, giving it one of the lowest tax burdens in the United States, and for much of its history its economy has flourished. In the past decade, however, its population has trekked south, its high incomes have failed to keep pace, and its heavy industry has dwindled. The 1980–82 recession brought devastation to an already weak economic base. Political upheaval followed. Some in state government seemed bitterly disillusioned with the fruits of tax limitation. After years of conservative Republican domination, Democrats, headed by their liberal gubernatorial candidate, Richard F. Celeste, swept all the state constitutional offices and took control of both houses of the legislature. The new regime promptly doubled the income tax increases of the past two deficit years.

This increase, rammed through the legislature with a minimum of debate, provoked an intense reaction that at first had all the earmarks of a classic tax revolt. A referendum movement ranging from Libertarians to United Automobile Workers locals placed a tax repeal measure on the ballot with a record number of signatures. Early polls showed that it had 70% support. But on November 8, 1983, Ohio voters rejected the Tax Revolt by a three-to-two margin.

Was this the last gasp of low-tax politics in Ohio? Had the Tax Revolt sputtered to a stall? The details of the campaign suggest that the story is not so clear-cut. The Celeste Administration staged an all-out last-minute media blitz that definitely contributed to the margin of defeat. But a majority of the voters did acquiesce in the demise of the state's low-tax tradition. It remains to be seen whether the mature economy of an exhausted frontier can be taxed back to health.

THE MIDWESTERN FRONTIER

When the original colonies proclaimed their independence, they could easily have fought as violently over the rest of the continent as the European powers had done. Thanks to the seventeenth century's uncertain grasp of American geography, six colonial charters set east-west boundaries stretching "from sea to sea." Virginia and Connecticut, as well as Massachusetts, the Carolinas, and Georgia, channeled their ambitions westward in narrow bands that still influence American politics. The hemmed-in remaining states shuddered at the potential power of the internal colonizers. The first American map of the United States, printed by Connecticut's Abel Buell, shows a truly colossal Virginia straddling the central third of the nation. Connecticut's claims, not slighted by Buell, leapfrogged New York and nearly led to bloody fighting between Connecticut and Pennsylvania settlers in Pennsylvania's Wyoming valley.

But the most eagerly contested area was the Ohio country. Its glacier-pulverized landscape of deep rich soil and game-stocked forest was among the best the American settlers had yet reached. New York, acting as suzerain of the Iroquois Confederacy and its vassal tribes, extended a tenuous claim. Connecticut projected its charter boundaries along the southern shore of Lake Erie and across to the Mississippi. But Virginia held the strongest hand. During the Revolution, its state militia under state orders had physically conquered the region.

Behind the state claims stood the land companies. Even before the Revolution was won, they were poised to make speculative fortunes. Confronting this pressure, the Indian tribes—the Shawnee, the Miami, and Wyandot—made desperate stands to preserve their lands. One reads with a tragic thrill how the great leaders Pontiac and Tecumseh rose above their tribal limits and attempted to rally all the natives against the encroaching Anglo-Americans, just as Mithridates once tried to unite the barbarian peoples against the rising Roman Empire.[4]

The expanding United States was consciously working to avoid the fate of Rome. For all its flaws, the Congress under the Articles of Confederation seriously tried to create a successful federation. But the potential power of the states with western domains seemed to threaten the future security of the smaller states until Maryland, with no western claims, showed the way out. As early as 1777, it proposed that the federal Congress take control of the western lands until their growing population allowed them to be organized into states. And it refused to ratify the Articles of Confederation until the giant states agreed to limit their domains.[5]

With the western lands in federal hands, the post-Revolutionary Congress set out to draw boundaries more fit for a republican confederation. The original thirteen states adopted a principle almost unprecedented in human affairs. Although the federation was solely their creation, it received the authority to create new states which would become fully equal partners. In an earlier time, the first thirteen would have claimed special status as the founding partners, but they waived the privilege. All the states could claim to be constituent elements of the confederation, even those that, in a constitutional irony, had actually been organized by the central government. Such an innovation was by no means the least achievement of a generation devoted to proving the viability of republican government. The experiment naturally attracted the attention of Thomas Jefferson, who tried his hand at state-making in the Ordinance of 1784; he proposed a division into ten states, with names like Chersonesus, Assenisipia, and Polypotamia.[6]

Jefferson's ordinance was too ambitious for the Congress, but the next year the Land Ordinance of 1785 produced the famous rectangular survey of the Old Northwest, with its grid arrangement of streets and townships. Jefferson's ideas reemerged in the even more famous Northwest Ordinance of 1787. One of the most impressive acts of legislation in American history, this ordinance set forth the common denominators for a federation of republics. The future states were to provide unqualified freedom of worship, prohibit slavery, legislate equal inheritance laws, establish public schools, grant broad if not universal suffrage, and agree never to pass measures impairing the obligation of contracts. Montesquieu had observed that confederate republics ought to be composed of states of the same nature. The coming tragedy of the "house divided" showed the wisdom of the preconditions established by the Ordinance of 1787.[7]

These measures became law when the United States was still organized under the Articles of Confederation. They can be seen as the culmination of the millennia-long history of republican federations. The fragmentary records of the Lycian League may have offered some precedent, but there is certainly no parallel to the willingness of the original thirteen states to sacrifice their political preeminence in the federation and arrange for the creation of fully equal additional partners. This decision, observes Frederick Jackson Turner, "insured the peaceful and free development of the great West and gave it political organization not as the outcome of wars of hostile States, nor by arbitrary government by distant powers, but by territorial government combined with large local autonomy. . . . By this peaceful process of colonization a whole continent has been filled with free and orderly commonwealths so quietly, so naturally, that we can only appreciate the profound significance of the process by contrasting it with the spread of European nations through conquest and oppression."[8]

THE MIDDLE REGION FINDS ITSELF

Although Virginia, New York, and Connecticut gave up their western ambitions, some land claims persisted. Virginia retained its Military Tract between the Scioto and Ohio rivers to pay land bounties to its Revolutionary veterans. Connecticut held on to the Western Reserve along Lake Erie; Moses Cleaveland went there in 1796 to establish the colony that still bears his name.

These two land tracts became the focus for distinct streams of immigration. Ohio still has a southern, Appalachian flavor south of Columbus, its centrally located, preplanned capital. North of Columbus and the old National Road (now Route 70), traces of New England politics and folk life, such as the township and maple sugaring, are evident to this day. As the meeting place of these population movements, along with a less-well-defined influx from the middle states, Ohio took on the character of moderator and mediator of the older sectional rivalries. Turner called it a new "Middle Region," whose politically central position produced six presidents.[9]

As a middle region with a divided population, Ohio was slow to develop its own distinctive identity. The early settlers seemed to consider it an empty terrain on which to impose the culture they brought with them. "They had fought for the independence of the United States, but they had not fought for Ohio," wrote one constitutional historian. "Ohio was to them a place, not a state."[10]

A state identity finally began to emerge with the Battle of Fort Meigs and Commodore Perry's stirring naval victory on Lake Erie. By 1835, state pride had been sufficiently aroused to fuel a brief comic-opera border war with Michigan over possession of Toledo. But Ohio's identity truly began to crystallize when native son William Henry Harrison, hero of the War of 1812, ran his log-cabin campaign for president in 1840. The ultimate gamble of a war may provide the most vivid of the experiences that create a sense of political unity, but the political rhetoric that preserves and embroiders the memory of war runs a close second. General Harrison's campaign wove together his military exploits and frontier self-consciousness; after the opposition sneered that he was better fit to sit in a log cabin and drink hard cider than sit in the White House, log cabins made from buckeye trees became the standard feature of his tumultuous rallies. And Ohio became the Buckeye State.[11]

A CONSTITUTION FOR THE STATE DIVIDED

Frederick Jackson Turner offered a useful antidote to his contemporaries' "germ" theory that American institutions had budded and flowered from the seeds of Teutonic folkways, unaffected by the neutral soil of the new continent. But one can acknowledge the extraordinary native influence on American institutions without forgetting that some institutions are more important than others. The most basic of them all is the constitution. Turner maintained that the population movements and economic relations of the great frontier prov-inces make up the hidden structure of America. Yet as each "province" becomes differentiated into territories and states, political decisions take on increasing importance. Constitu-tions define the political unit. States follow their genius within this framework.[12]

And so the growing self-awareness of Ohio came to full flower in its 1851 state constitution. Its main feature was to limit state government. But this approach was the state's own way of handling an excess of tension, not a lack of it. The in-flux of two or three distinct cultural and demographic streams into neutral ground seems to have moderated the ambition of its government. By limiting the role of the state, Ohioans sought to avoid arousing the passions behind the Civil War, passions that also left a bitter mark on their politics. From the time of the Northwest Ordinance, the territory adamantly refused re-quests to admit slaves; some of the strongest opponents of this institution were immigrants from the Virginia and Kentucky frontiers who also tried to exclude free blacks. But from 1815 on, an antislavery and problack Abolition movement steadily gained strength. Quakers and New England sects formed the core of an underground railroad, spiriting escaped slaves into Canada. On the other hand, the Copperhead politician Clem-ent Laird Vallandigham opposed the war against the South. Arrested, tried for treason, and expelled to Canada by the Union army, he ran for governor from exile. After the most excited campaign in Ohio's history, Vallandigham lost by 100,000 votes. An immensely relieved Lincoln exclaimed in a telegram, "Glory to God in the highest, Ohio has saved the nation."[13]

Political scientists find a strong continuity between the vote for Vallandigham and the current strongholds of rural Democratic support. With growing ethnic Democratic voting in the state's evenly distributed industrial metropolitan cen-ters, Ohio became a closely balanced swing state. In the cen-tury since the Civil War, the governorship changed party hands some twenty times. With such partisan parity and emotional history, each party has seemed content, for the most part, to neutralize the state government rather than turn it into an in-strument for carrying out a platform. There seems almost to have been a tacit understanding to minimize the role of issues in state politics. One contemporary observer writes of the Midwestern states along the Ohio River (Indiana and Illinois have a similar make-up): "These states saw politics in terms of jobs and spoils, not issues; they saw government as something to protect the people from, as they strove to keep taxes and the services they might provide to an absolute minimum."[14]

THE FISCAL FRONTIER

Limiting state government may have seemed the most practical means of dealing with Ohio's internal political tensions. But it also grew out of the state's fiscal history. Ohio was one of the pioneers of constitutional limitation on state finances. As the recent history of New York State has amply shown, paper limits provide little real protection in the absence of a will to enforce them. Ohio has displayed such a will. Its fiscal practice has been even more stringent than its constitution requires.

The windfall from the Ohio frontier was slow in coming. The value of the Western Reserve development was limited by its distance from large markets. Its produce glutted the local outlets and sold at low prices. During the first quarter of the nineteenth century, settlers in New Connecticut lived on the brink of foreclosure by the ultimate mortgage holder, the Connecticut School Fund.

Rescue from these hard times came in 1825, when the state began construction of the Ohio-Erie Canal. Ohio plunged heavily into debt in undertaking the project; its total real estate in 1826 was valued at less than $16 million and the total cost of the canal was estimated at more than $3 million. But as the waterway gave the Ohio interior access to both Lake Erie and the natural network of tributaries feeding the Ohio River, the farming economy began to reap immediate benefits.

Like all good things in government, the spate of canal building in Ohio was overdone. The canal went through a serious financing crisis in 1842 in which its most distinguished director, Alfred Kelley, was able to meet interest and princi-ple payments only by borrowing funds in New York on his own personal credit. He carried the debt for several months before the state legislature approved the refinancing.

Chastened by the drama, Ohio followed New York in drafting strict fiscal limits in its 1851 state constitution. The 1850–51 convention had to deal with an existing form of gov-ernment heavily weighted toward the legislature. According to a Progressive Era commentator, this body "had become the pliant tool of individual greed," mainly in granting loans and charters. The 1851 constitution strictly limited both powers. Its provision on debt went even further than the New York Barnburners had gone in 1846. It allowed only $750,000 in borrowing for "casual deficits" and an unspecified amount for war, insurrection, and invasion. Beyond that, it forbade all state debt.

The practical effect of such stringent constitutional con-straints is to require voters to approve debt by voting on a constitutional amendment rather than a bond referendum. Since 1921, Ohio voters have approved ten constitutional amendments authorizing more than $3 billion in specific is-sues. The constitution has been successful, however, in keep-ing the state debt burden—and hence the tax burden on future generations—at a moderate level.[15] According to the state Of-fice of Management and Budget, per-capita state debt (includ-ing revenue bonds) ranks twenty-ninth among the states.[16]

Ohio's political atmosphere has frequently been even more restrictive than its constitution. The main tax limitation in the 1851 constitution merely required a "uniform rule," applied both to investments and to "all real and personal property, according to its true value in money." This provision was the work of Alfred Kelley, whose fortune and reputation had grown apace with the territory for which he foretold such a bright future. In the years since his trek across New York State, he had become easily the most important figure in Ohio public finance. He not only supervised the building of the canal and the first successful railroad in the Western Reserve, but also designed the state's banking law.

His "crowning work" was the General Property Tax Law of 1846, the "first successful attempt at uniform taxation in

Ohio." The reform, explained Kelley in an 1845 legislative report, met the need for new taxes to pay the canal debt. But it also followed the principle of limiting the load. "Whenever the public burdens are necessarily heavy, justice, as well as good policy, requires that these burdens should be made to bear as equally as possible, in order that they may bear as lightly as possible, on those who are compelled to sustain the weight."[17] Kelley's proposal successfully broadened the tax base, reducing the rate dramatically. It tripled the state's taxable property and allowed the 1847 tax rate to be cut to one-third of its 1846 level. The uniform rule was later incorporated in the 1851 constitution. Yet it aroused a furious controversy. Opponents called it the "Plunder Law" and thundered against it in a campaign newspaper called The Tax Killer.[18] Kelley acknowledged that his new fiscal age abolished a cherished frontier institution—that undeveloped land should be taxed as heavily as the farms brought into being by the settlers' sweat. This major subsidy for the frontiersmen, said Kelley, was no longer necessary. "Most of the tracts or parcels of arable land sufficiently large for a farm are now more or less improved, and it is no longer necessary to abstain from taking improvements into view in determining the value of land for taxation, from a fear of preventing or discouraging the making of these improvements."[19]

1912: PROGRESSIVES OUTRUN THE PEOPLE

The uniform rule continued to be a major issue through the next successful revision of Ohio's constitution, in 1912. Constitutional amendments to allow classification of the subjects of taxation were submitted to the voters seven times between 1889 and the 1912 convention. Each time but one the amendment received a plurality of the people voting on it but failed to make the constitutional threshold of a majority of all people voting in the election. Along with the separate agitation to adopt a state initiative and referendum, the tax agitation helped promote the 1912 constitutional convention. Opponents of uniform property tax levies nowadays generally favor split rolls so that business can be made to assume a higher share of the burden. The alignment in 1912 was almost the opposite. According to the historian Charles B. Galbreath, who also served as secretary to the 1912 convention, "for the most part, those favoring the classification of property belonged to the conservative class and included manufacturers, bankers and merchants, with interests assumed to run counter to the welfare of those advocating the Initiative and Referendum." They wanted a split roll so their intangible property could be taxed at a *lower* rate than real estate.

The argument for the uniform rule had run full circle. Before Kelley's reform, real estate had received the tax break. Now it bore the brunt of the burden, while more easily concealed personal property such as stocks and bonds escaped the scrutiny of the assessor. Said one delegate, supporting classification: "The strictest of inquisitorial policies have been applied, grave penalties, threats of prosecution for perjury and the tax inquisitor's system, with its money inducements for the recovery of property, all of these have but demonstrated the futility of further attempts to correct a weak system which is universally regarded as unjust and unequal in its results, and which the people refuse to respect, and entirely inadequate to bring out for taxation personal property such as stocks, bonds and money in banks." Lower rates on personal property, it was argued, would reduce the incentive for concealment and bring this wealth back on the tax rolls.[20]

The convention was dominated by the Progressive movement, however. It adopted the initiative and the referendum by better than four to one and refused to change the uniform rule. (The "conservative class" had to try four more times to obtain this reform through constitutional referendum, finally succeeding in 1929.) The convention took a different approach to broadening the tax base. It allowed the legislature to adopt an inheritance tax, excise and franchise taxes, severance taxes on coal, oil, and gas, and, most significant, an income tax. On this, as on some other issues, the convention was well ahead of the state's political climate.[21]

In spite of the permissive constitution, Ohio refused to consider new forms of taxation until absolutely forced to by the fiscal crisis of the Great Depression. In January 1931, Governor George White told the General Assembly that burgeon-

ing pressures on local government required the state to seek
new revenue to provide local relief. Yet, at the time, he opposed a sales or income tax. Times worsened. Jobs dried up.
Homeowners could not pay their taxes. In two years a majority of the state's school districts were in the red and local
governments were running out of cash. In desperation, Governor White, in May 1933, proposed both a sales tax and a
graduated income tax.

Public reaction was furious. "Crowds Storm Capitol In
Protest," records the yellowed headline in *The Cleveland Plain
Dealer*. The legislature grappled with the program through the
turbulent spring while some voters suggested it try to tax pet
dogs instead. By the end of June, Governor White's program
was dead, except for a tax on movie tickets, and Ohio was
primed for a Tax Revolt.[22]

OHIO'S FIRST TAX REVOLT

While the legislature dithered, homeowners and realtors began to draft a constitutional initiative to cut the existing fifteen-
mill limit on the local real estate tax. (The fifteen-mill or 1.5%
limit had been adopted in the 1929 referendum that ended
the uniform rule. It had previously been a statute.) The proposal to set the limit at ten mills reached State Attorney General John Bricker for certification in early July. It ultimately
received more than 325,000 signatures. Its advocates, headed
by P. A. Howell of Sidney, Ohio, argued:

> Real estate's unequal tax burden has crushed its value and in-
> come, dispossessed many home owners, discouraged home
> ownership, destroyed the morale and proper viewpoint toward
> government of its owners, advanced the insolvency of many fi-
> nancial institutions and investors, and is now bankrupting our
> cities and counties. . . .
>
> This burden of taxation MUST BE REDUCED and we have
> found that the Government will not demobilize itself; it will
> not economize; it will not discontinue its useless functions so
> long as it can collect the money to maintain the present bu-
> reaucracy.
>
> The chief weakness of our present day government is that

there is too much of it. We are governed almost to bank-ruptcy.[23]

This heartfelt eloquence overwhelmed the opponents of the limit. They argued in vain that it would wipe out $49 million in existing revenues, setting Ohio on a "dangerous and un-tried road most certainly leading to governmental catastro-phe."[24] On November 7, 1933, voters approved the limit by a three-to-two margin.

The cut in local revenue intensified the pressure on the legislature for fiscal aid, and in 1934, Governor White resub-mitted his sales and income tax program. By the end of the year, the General Assembly finally accepted the general sales tax, even though a throng of 1,500 protested in Cleveland. But the income tax never made it past the House. The issue was postponed for another thirty-five years.[25]

AFTER THE WAR: THE LOW-TAX HEYDAY

Ohio's low-tax ethic prevailed through most of the postwar period. Democrats held the state house from 1944 to 1956, but Governor Frank J. Lausche preferred to draw down the state's wartime surplus rather than impose new taxes. Son of a Slo-venian-born steelworker and former mayor of Cleveland, Lausche was able, through his fiscal policy, to combine urban ethnic Democratic support with conservative Republican votes. Services did expand, however, financed by a state treasury swollen during World War II by the combination of inflation-driven revenues and wartime restrictions on spending. Cur-rent spending outran current revenues for eight of the ten fis-cal years from 1947 to 1958. Lausche's Republican successor tried to deal with the built-in deficit by two years of austerity.

In 1958, another Democrat, Michael V. DiSalle, gained the governor's seat. Working from a base far different from Lausche's, the labor movement, he offered broader services and expanded taxes instead of austerity. The legislature rejected his main revenue proposal, to broaden the base and remove probusiness loopholes from the sales tax, and DiSalle lost his office after one term.[26]

The man who beat DiSalle was Republican James A. Rhodes, a native of the southeastern hill country. A shrewd, earthy, and homespun man who kept his distance from the press but showed up at every ribbon-cutting, Rhodes proved himself to be one of the most successful and practical politicians Ohio has produced. A story from the 1980 presidential primaries shows the secret of his style. In a meeting with George Bush, Rhodes threw his wallet on the table and slapped it three times. "That's what the people are worried about," he told the startled candidate. In his first gubernatorial campaign, Rhodes made the fiscal issue the centerpiece. He threw the label "High-Tax Mike" at the incumbent and promised "no new or increased taxes." For most of his four terms, he was successful enough to earn himself the label "No-Tax Jim."

It is not that Ohio offers the dramatic absence of taxation to be found in Texas or New Hampshire. In absolute terms, Ohio's per-capita state and local taxes ranked only a bit below the national median, at thirty-fourth in 1980, and its per-capita local taxes alone actually were above the midpoint, at twentieth. But because *all* of its state taxes fell below the national average, the cumulative total was low indeed. State per-capita taxation in 1980 stood at forty-sixth in the nation. Since the other side of the ratio, state income, came in at a far higher level than in most low-tax states, Ohio's tax burden was practically the lowest in the nation.[27]

With this record, Ohio should have been at least as healthy as New Hampshire and Massachusetts, if not Texas. Yet its economic performance has been exceedingly dismal.

THE MYSTERIOUS STAGNATION OF OHIO

During two decades dominated largely by No-Tax Jim, Ohio fell further in recessions and climbed back more slowly in recoveries than the rest of the nation. From 1960 to 1980, the Ohio work force fell from 6.5% of the U.S. total to 5.3%. In 1955, Buckeyes earned 6.1% of total U.S. personal income. In 1980, they earned only 4.7% of the total. The state's per-capita personal income had hovered about 10% above the

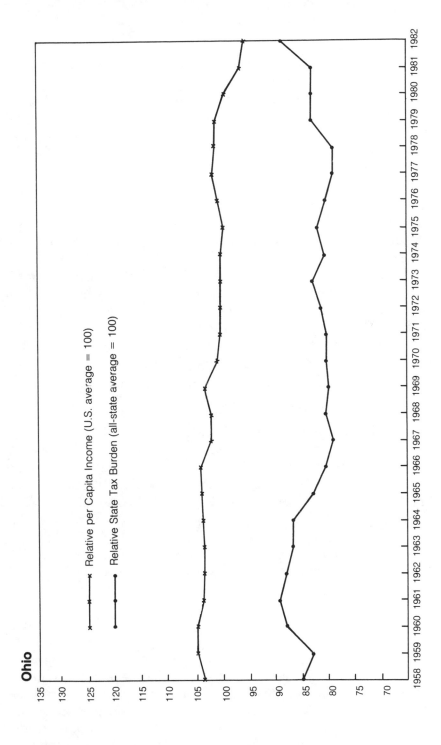

Ohio

Relative per Capita Income (U.S. average = 100)

Relative State Tax Burden (all-state average = 100)

national average from 1930 to 1954. In the 1960s, it seemed to stabilize at a level about 3% above the average. But by 1980, Ohio had slipped into the lower half of the chart.[28]

Even the population was in relative decline; from 1970 to 1980, the number of Buckeyes grew by only 1.3%, a minuscule increase of 140,000 in a total state population of 10,797,630. From the 1960 to the 1970 census, some 130,000 people had left the state. But the outflow was concentrated in the last half of the decade, and the flight accelerated in the seventies. From 1970 to 1980, the number of emigrants totaled 560,000. The population flow cost Ohio two congressional seats.[29]

Ohio, in short, is the model of Frostbelt decline. It pays the federal government more in taxes than it gets back in benefits. Its people feel the lure of warmer climates and swell the demographic tide to Florida and the Southwest. Its industries labor in outmoded plants while new development goes to the wide-open Sunbelt, less cramped by congestion and labor unions. This, at any rate, is the conventional version.

THE MUSCLEBOUND GIANT

Before too readily accepting the standard account of Midwestern decline, however, one should look more closely at its economic structure and some alternative theories about its reluctance to change. To some extent Ohio has been a victim of its early success.

The Western Reserve was enjoying its prosperity in the early 1840s when reports began to circulate about gigantic copper and iron deposits on the rim of Lake Superior. Cleveland men sent expeditions to explore these iron mountains. With high-quality coal deposits to the east, in the Mahoning valley, and a water route to the mineral trove to the northwest, Cleveland shortly became the center of a thriving iron and steel industry.[30] In Akron, farther south along the Ohio and Erie Canal, a New York doctor named Benjamin Franklin Goodrich found local businessmen willing to invest in a factory to make a new product called "rubber." The location made little sense in terms of access to the raw material, and the factory was in operation a decade before the bicycle craze of the 1880s gave it a mass market. But Dr. Goodrich's success led to imitation by local entrepreneurs. By the 1920s five major rubber companies had sprung up. The Western Reserve was becoming a leading colony of the automobile industry.[31]

Traditional heavy industry reached its postwar peak around 1953. Manufacturing employed some 45% of Ohio's work force, paying wages about one-third higher than other industries. According to critics of the state's economic policy, the state government became obsessed with smokestacks. In cultivating its traditional steel and automobile-supply industries, it ignored new technologies. In the late sixties, one observer warned that Ohio and the other Great Lakes states were failing to win their share of federal research-and-development funds and consequently were losing their best scientific and engineering talent to R & D centers like California. This warning went unheeded even as traditional industry entered a long decline.

Nationally, manufacturing employment reached its high point in absolute numbers in 1969, but as a percentage of the total work force, this sector has been declining for two decades. Ohio's slump outran the nation's. In 1970, 7.3% of the national manufacturing work force was located in Ohio. By the end of the decade, the state's proportion had fallen to 6.7%; jobs in heavy industry were not only disappearing, but also being shifted elsewhere in the country. Even so, the structure of the state's economy remained heavily weighted toward durable manufacturing. Nearly 40% of the people at work in manufacturing drew their paychecks from rapidly declining industries such as steel and nonelectrical machinery. The state was vulnerable to recession in the first place, since downturns hit durable goods first and hardest. When a variety of forces concentrated the recession on steel and automobiles, the impact on Ohio was devastating.[32]

GILLIGAN'S ISLAND

Faced with slow but steady economic decline, Ohio's politicians split into sharply opposing camps. Those who were disillusioned with the low-tax policy and those who had never believed in it joined in arguing that the state needed more spending. The stagnation, they said, came from decades of malnourished services. Education in particular had to contend with the ten-mill limit; spending over that point required budget referendums, which became annual events. Anyone pushing for increased state revenue invariably claimed the money was needed to aid local schools.

The more traditional camp blamed the decline on deviations from the tax policy. The state fell from grace, in this view, when No-Tax Jim Rhodes ended his second term in 1970. The constitution prohibited a third consecutive term, and the statehouse fell to the aristocratic liberal Democrat John J. Gilligan. The new governor had campaigned on the need for fresh revenue. His first major act was to propose a 185% increase in the biennial General Fund budget and to advocate a state personal income tax. Governor Gilligan asked for a steeply progressive rate structure, moving in nine brackets to a maximum 8% on adjusted gross incomes of $50,000 and over. He attempted to make some of the new levy a tax shift rather than a tax increase by dedicating some revenue to property tax relief. To round out the program, he also asked for a new franchise tax on corporate net income. The new corporate tax was a political concession to labor. The stiffest resistance to the personal income tax came surprisingly from union leaders, who insisted that part of the new tax burden be imposed on business.[33]

Gilligan's package plunged the legislature into a memorable battle. Tax and budget deadlines came and went as the Republican-controlled House and Senate whittled down the governor's spending plans. The income tax package ran into a stalemate prolonged by splintering of the Republican position and opposition from prolabor legislators. A compromise emerged only in late November. Gilligan signed it into law on December 20, nearly six months into the fiscal year. The new version of the tax package changed the nature of property tax relief and instituted a state severance tax on oil, natural gas, coal, sand, and gravel. (These mineral taxes were the state's first, even though they had been expressly authorized by the 1912 constitutional amendments.) The main alteration, however, came in the personal income tax. The legislators had toned down much of its progressivity. It now ran in six brackets to a top rate of 3½% on income above $40,000. In later years, tax reformers complained that they got only half an income tax.[34]

Half a tax or not, the new levy became a *bête noire* for those who wanted no additional tax at all. In analyzing its impact, supply-side arguments mingled with traditional attitudes. Richard Vedder, then a staff economist on the U.S. Congress's Joint Economic Committee, ran a study showing that the rising level of Ohio's tax burden had a depressing effect on the state's personal income. Even more important, in Vedder's view, was the shift toward reliance on the income tax. "The higher the proportion of Ohio tax revenues derived from income taxes, the lower the level of real per capita income relative to other states. The relationship is highly significant statistically."[35]

Coincidentally or not, Gilligan's term marked an acceleration in Ohio's economic decline. For the two decades up to 1970, Ohio consistently ranked first or second in manufacturers' investments in new plant and equipment. After the tax package took effect, Ohio ranked fourth in 1974, fifth in 1975, and sixth in 1976. The rate of out-migration spiked dramatically in 1976 at more than 100,000.[36]

The new tax by itself might seem a slender reed to bear such drastic consequences. Yet as significant as its size was the political shift it seemed to portend. To liberal national observers, the Gilligan administration was "exemplary," a breakthrough of social activism in Ohio's tradition of limited government. Local businessmen, however, still speak of it with a curled lip. They blame the liberal Irishman for eroding the probusiness climate on a variety of issues from the environment to workers' compensation. Gilligan did for a time seem to have weaned the public from its low-tax tradition. A referendum attempt to repeal the state income tax in 1972 failed by better than two to one. Apparently voters considered the new revenue a solution to the chronic financial problems of the local school districts. Yet advocates of repeal were able to spend only $17,000 for the entire campaign. The delayed political reaction to the taxes, and Gilligan's own abrasive personality, ended his career after one term. In 1974, former governor Rhodes rode the issue to a comeback.[37]

BREAKING THE TAX TABOO

Passage of the income tax so many years after the 1912 constitution shattered a political taboo, which Governor Rhodes was neither able nor willing to restore during his next two terms. The barriers had been lowered, even though the voters continued to show their distaste for this levy. In 1980, a coalition of municipal unions and community groups led by the Ohio Public Interest Campaign (OPIC) placed a "Fair Tax Initiative" on the ballot. The measure was designed to generate an extra billion dollars of state revenue per biennium by increasing income tax rates on the rich. It also offered some tax relief to property owners and lower-income groups. The campaign was in some respects a left-wing effort to exploit the political energy of the Tax Revolt. OPIC, one of the more successful political action groups founded by the community activist wing of the New Left, thought that Proposition 13 was a protest against shifting tax burdens, rather than their increase. This interpretation of Jarvis-Gann held, with some justification, that California's property tax had been transferred by inflation away from business and onto the homeowner. Accordingly, the Ohio Fair Tax Initiative Committee claimed that business had been escaping its share of the 1971 tax increases. Its releases protested against loopholes opened by legislated tax exemptions.

The Fair Tax referendum proposed to freeze some of the probusiness exemptions. It would also have raised the top rate on the personal income tax to 6% on incomes over $50,000, thus restoring some of Gilligan's original program. On November 4, 1980, the voters did approve a more moderate version of a tax shift, a constitutional amendment authorizing split property tax rolls. But they rejected the Fair Tax proposal by a resounding margin of more than 2 million votes.

This expression of the popular will seemed to make little impression on a political elite about to endure the most severe fiscal trial of its generation. Within two years, Columbus

responded to the 1981–82 recession and fiscal crisis by raising income taxes sharply and often.[38]

THE 1982 RECESSION

When Ronald Reagan misspoke during the 1980 campaign and
called the recession a "depression," he may have been wrong
about the national downturn, but he was close to the truth in
describing the Great Lakes states. A regional pattern emerged
in the 1980 slump that has persisted through the even more
severe second dip of 1981–82. The most widely cited causes
of the first dip were energy costs and high interest rates. During the second dip, the oil market was glutted but interest rates
remained high. The result was devastating to a state whose
main products were bought on consumer loans. Ohio's con-
sumer-goods industries were oriented toward automobile
supplies and large home appliances, and unemployment
soared.

By the spring of 1982, Chrysler had abandoned its
trouble-plagued Lordstown assembly line, steel production in
the aging Mahoning valley plants plummeted, and the last
automobile-tire factory in Akron chained its gate. On top of
the industrial slump, Ohio's important agricultural sector was
being hit on both sides. Severe winter weather destroyed much
of its harvest, and bumper crops elsewhere depressed market
prices. In the fourth quarter of 1981, personal income growth
in the Great Lakes region was by far the lowest in the country; and Ohio's, growing at 39% of the national rate, ranked
forty-eighth among the states. In April 1982, it had the
second-highest unemployment rate in the country.[39] Workers
who a year earlier were denouncing welfare cheats over their
beer now lined up for general relief as their unemployment
insurance ran out. Bad times reversed the flow from rural areas
to the city as out-of-work natives of the Appalachian counties
returned home to eke out a living on their family farms.

This economic sinkhole swallowed up the state's hopes
for a balanced budget. Tax revenues fell and spending for
welfare bounced upward. In 1981, the second year of the
biennial budget was heading for a major deficit. State Budget

Director Howard Collier, a civil servant with as much longevity as Governor Rhodes, exercised his formidable statutory power to impound state spending, and the legislature started to raise revenue. By the end of the fiscal year, the sales tax rate had temporarily been raised from 4% to 5% and a 15% surtax had been imposed on the corporate franchise tax. The state General Revenue Fund, which had run a surplus of $246 million at the end of the previous biennium, now had a balance of $200,000.

But Ohio's fiscal troubles were just beginning. Uncertain about federal revenues and worried about the impact of the federal tax changes on its own tax collection, the governor and legislature relied on interim appropriations for the first four months of the new biennium. The reason for their hesitation soon became clear enough. The formal appropriation act adopted in November 1981 required another substantial tax package. The 5% sales tax rate was made permanent; the corporate franchise tax was increased and expanded; and another temporary corporate surtax was enacted.

The sharp increase in these taxes began to take an additional toll on the state's economy. Partly in reaction to the rate increase and partly from the unpredicted depth of the recession, sales tax receipts fell well below projections. After a series of other bad breaks, the budget faced a final-year deficit of better than a billion dollars. The legislature had to tackle yet another round of tax increases.[40]

This time, in spite of public reluctance, legislative leaders turned to the income tax. The two sales tax increases of the preceeding nine months notwithstanding, at least one poll showed that a further sales tax increase had more public support than any added burden on income. The legislature was more impressed, however, by the notion that the state income tax had not been substantially changed since its inception in 1972. In mid-May 1982, in a surprisingly bipartisan atmosphere, legislators voted a 25% surcharge on the personal income tax, and added a new top bracket of 4% on incomes of more than $80,000.[41]

REVOLUTION AND REACTION

Ohio's financial crisis polarized the parties on the tax issue. There had been a temporary bipartisan vote for the spring tax increase. Governor Rhodes himself, abandoning twenty years of policy, had even fleetingly proposed a higher income tax surcharge than the one adopted. Yet as the recession deepened, the approaching gubernatorial election became a referendum on "Reaganomics" and supply-side ideas. In spite of the worsening conditions, the Republican primary voters gave a surprisingly strong margin to the most orthodox supply-sider, U.S. Representative Clarence L. Brown. The Democrats lined up behind an unabashed liberal, former Peace Corps director Richard F. Celeste. The general election took place in the trough of the national recession. In Ohio it was a Republican debacle. Celeste defeated Brown by a three-to-two margin, pulling in a strong Democratic majority in the House and a one-vote edge in the formerly Republican Senate. Supply-side tax policy seemed to have been driven from Ohio's halls of power. Yet there were crosscurrents. Voters defeated thirty-two of thirty-four local income tax increases earmarked for school-district budgets. Facing an immediate deficit of more than half a billion dollars in his fiscal year 1983 budget and a projected deficit of $2.5 billion over the 1984–85 biennium, Celeste proposed what amounted to a 90% permanent increase in the income tax. (The previous year's temporary surcharge was ready to expire, so Governor Celeste made it permanent and rolled it into his package.) Ramming it through the legislature on party-line votes, he signed his taxes into law by the end of February 1983.

It is hard to tell which enraged the public most—the appearance of railroading the tax increase, the permanence of the surcharge, or simply its size. Celeste's popularity plunged. A group of libertarians, tax protesters, and right-wing Republican politicians began meeting to plan strategy. The result was a new group, with the self-explanatory name "Ohioans to Stop Excessive Taxation" (S.E.T.), and the draft of two voter initiatives.

THE FAILED TAX REVOLT

The Stop Excessive Taxation coalition went to the streets with the two measures. The first, a reaction to the partisan rail-roading of the tax increase, would have required a three-fifths majority in the legislature for future tax increases. The second would have repealed the February tax increase. S.E.T. executive director Ron Braucher argued that the two measures together would, basically, instruct the legislature to start over on a tax package but impose a higher threshold for its decision. The problem with the existing increases, he said, was that they exceeded the state's real financial need. The surplus revenue, he said, would be swallowed up in overly generous labor contracts for Celeste's public-employee-union constituency.

In the hectic drive to qualify the measures for the ballot, S.E.T. seemed to be riding high. Celeste stumped the state to denounce the measures, but insisted on portraying his tax increase as a tax cut (because it granted some additional property tax relief). The more he made this argument, the greater was the ground swell for the referendums. Two weeks before the September deadline, signatures poured into S.E.T.'s sparsely furnished walk-up headquarters in an aging downtown Columbus office building. More than half a million voters signed the double petitions, the largest number to sponsor a referendum in Ohio's history. S.E.T. field workers would count on one hand the number of people who turned them down. Polls indicated support ranging from 60% to 70%.

But the measure lost decisively. What happened? For one thing, the tax supporters vastly improved their rhetoric. Celeste summoned former budget director Collier from his state job as medical-school financial officer to head the committee against the repeal. Instead of whitewashing the tax increase, the administration party emphasized the alleged disasters that would follow a 17% cut in revenue. Celeste did not stop there. He mobilized all the resources of the state government to fight the referendums. Every department received a worst-case account of the cuts it would suffer in the case of repeal, and the bureaucrats were urged, none too subtly, to communicate the threat to their clientele. The welfare office in rural Pike County, for instance, sent out a letter informing recipients that "a no vote would defeat the issues, and your benefits would be increased in January 1984." Confused voters received a barrage of letters, from medical centers, nursing homes, schools, urging a no vote. The antirepeal campaign outspent S.E.T. by three to one. No other state government in the tax revolts here examined had deployed such a massive counterattack with such little regard for the bounds of propriety.

Yet even this effort fails to explain the Tax Revolt's defeat. Even allowing a substantial margin for scare and confusion tactics, one has to admit that the voters lacked the resolution they had displayed in other states. As in 1972, Ohioans hesitated to overturn a new tax, pointed as it might be. One can also speculate that voters were reacting in part to the unimpressive results of Ohio's low-tax tradition. There were no dramatic surges in tax burden to blame for the decades of stagnation, as in Massachusetts and New York, nor was there any exceptional economic reward for tax restraint.

If Ohio's problems are rooted in its economic structure, however, its salvation depends on the transition from smokestacks to computers. At least one other example suggests that this transition will not be aided by a rapidly rising tax burden. The example is Massachusetts, the oldest frontier of all, where the Tax Revolt is a high-tech operation. But Ohio has to look no farther than its neighbor Michigan for evidence that the tax factor is not entirely impotent, even in the middle-aged Midwest.

10

Michigan: Tax Revolts and Hard Times

Michigan bore the brunt of the recession of 1980–82. Its unemployment rate was highest and lasted the longest. Crime, family violence, and all the afflictions of the out-of-work hit hard. A listless depression hung in the air, coupled with bitter resentment of any of the imagined villains of the malaise. Almost as soon as one drove across the state line toward Detroit, one began to meet the bumper stickers: "Buy a foreign car and put ten Americans out of work," "Remember Pearl Harbor, Buy American."

The prime scapegoat was supposed to be Reaganomics. Had the extravagant tax cuts for the rich not swelled the federal deficit that drove up interest rates that destroyed the market for new cars? Such was the argument put forth by union leaders and liberal Democrats, hoping to discredit forever the threat of supply-side economics. But something went wrong. As the state government tried to cope with its fiscal crisis by raising taxes, voters reacted with a resounding no. A grassroots Tax Revolt had been gathering for the better part of a decade. In the summer of 1983, it erupted in a series of protests ranging from a constitutional initiative to an attempt to recall the governor.

Behind the political turmoil was an agonizing economic transition. As the center of the nation's automobile industry, Michigan felt the pain of every dislocation in America's dominant technology. Gasoline-price-induced economy, government-induced retooling, the collision of high interest rates with a rigid and unrealistic congressional timetable requiring huge auto-industry capital spending—all these and more were traumatizing carmakers. At the same time, the entire Midwest watched its durable-goods market shrivel under the high cost of consumer financing. It came as a shock to Michigan that newer technologies were bringing prosperity to states less committed to heavy industry.

In responding to this crisis with a tax revolt, Michiganders were repeating a reaction that had occurred throughout their history. Since their suffering came from state policy as well as a broad regional decline, this reflex may well have been the right thing to do. The combination of hard times and tax revolts can be political dynamite, but it can also be salutary. In either case, it has deep roots in Michigan history.

THE ORIGINS OF MICHIGAN

Michigan today is the quintessential American heartland, but at its first western settlement it formed part of a hostile encirclement of the English colonial seaboard. French outposts at Michilimackinac and Detroit controlled the Great Lakes access to the Indian fur trade. Forays down the Mississippi established a link with Louis XIV's dominion in Louisiana. A reminder of this link remains today in the name shared by one of Detroit's most elegant hotels and by the large fresh-water lake north of New Orleans: both are called Pontchartrain, after Jérôme Phelypeaux, Comte de Pontchartrain, the Sun King's colonial minister.

France's enthusiasm for converting the American Indians and monopolizing their trade helped win this domain, but its mercantile policy proved inadequate to hold it. According to

Thomas McIntyre Cooley, the nineteenth-century laissez-faire jurist and historian of Michigan, while English colonies flourished under the "indulgence" and "neglect" of the British government, the French bore the chains of their monarch's zealous regulation. Successive grants of trade monopolies "had the effect to prevent immigration and settlement, [and] also tended to paralyze trade of every sort, to check enterprise, and to incline the lower classes to prefer a life of slothful ease and independence in the woods to one of unprofitable service for the monopolists."[1]

This restraint of commerce and individual enterprise frustrated the growth of a self-supporting economy and destined the thinly populated French domain to fall ultimately into Anglo-American hands.

Barriers to settlement remained even after the British conquered Canada. English policy in effect maintained the encirclement of the American colonists, declaring the Old Northwest off-limits to immigration and private land purchases. The home country thus attempted to protect the interests of the Indians and also the habitat that produced its lucrative fur trade. Observed Cooley, "It might be thought, perhaps, that there was something unnatural and inhuman in preserving for wild animals the territory by the settlement of which the poorer classes of Britain might greatly better their own condition; but the preservation of forests for game was in the line of British traditions and practice, and so long as the nation permitted a considerable portion of the home country to be kept from cultivation, to gratify a passion for the chase, it was not likely to let sentimental considerations interfere with the preservation for profitable hunting of this distant wilderness."[2] It was not just wilderness preservation that led the British to garrison their northwestern forts after recognizing American independence. Watching the weakness of the Articles of Confederation and perhaps waiting for the American experiment to collapse from what many considered the inherent instability of republican government, the Redcoats sat in Oswego, Niagara, and Detroit more than a decade after the peace treaty required these points to be rendered. Not until after General "Mad Anthony" Wayne's campaign against the Indians and the signing of Jay's Treaty was the American flag raised above Detroit. The date was July 11, 1796.

Michigan remained such an isolated outpost that it was easily recaptured by the British in the War of 1812. Substantial immigration began only in the late 1820s, after completion of the Erie Canal. By 1835, the territory was home to more than 60,000 free inhabitants. This was the threshold at which the Northwest Ordinance promised a territory the right "to form a permanent constitution and State government" and to be admitted into the Congress "on an equal footing with the original States, in all respects whatever."

A Detroit convention in 1835 drew up a constitution. But before Congress would finally accept the new state, one matter had to be cleared up—the mock-heroic border war with Ohio.

The same article in the Northwest Ordinance that promised statehood also seemed to grant Michigan a southern boundary including the settlement of Toledo. (Michigan historians still maintain the justice of this claim.) The territory rallied behind the rousing cause. Michiganders burned Ohio flags, and militias of the two states threatened each other from a safe distance. The nickname "Wolverine," Michiganders like to say, was thrown at them by the Buckeyes because of their ferocity in the dispute. Yet the only casualty came in a barroom brawl.

Congress offered a compromise, swapping Toledo for the western part of the Upper Peninsula. Manipulation by the Jacksonian party obtained a showing of popular opinion that seemed to accept the deal. President Jackson accepted Michigan as the twenty-sixth state on January 26, 1837. Before this formal admission, however, Michigan had been carrying on a state government for more than a year.

Even before entering the Union, the new state government adopted an ambitious program of internal improvements. New arrivals from New England and upstate New York had been deeply impressed by the Erie Canal that helped them get there. So a section of the 1835 constitution ordered the state legislature to start work "as soon as may be" on surveying new roads, canals, and navigable waters. In the period before joining the Union, the newly formed state legislature frenetically laid out townships and state roads and chartered railroads and banks.[3]

BOOM AND BUST

The contagion of internal improvements spread all the more rapidly in the feverish western economy produced by Andrew Jackson's famous campaign against the Bank of the United States. When he removed federal reserves from the central bank and spread them to state banks, the money supply in the interior expanded rapidly. This produced an artificial boom in business, credit, land prices, and speculation. This "money plethora" was swelling just as Michigan prematurely assumed the powers of self-government. One of the first measures of the new state legislature greatly aggravated the problem.

Less than two months after finally gaining statehood, Michigan abolished the practice of granting individual bank charters and opened the field to any group of ten persons who could meet certain minimum requirements. The state's reasoning, as Thomas Cooley reconstructs it, was that special charters amounted to government-endorsed monopolies; free competition should be allowed as in other businesses; the supply of banks should be regulated by the demand for them; if a bank was not needed, it would go out of existence; and, if the general law provided sufficient protection for depositors, no one would be hurt.[4] But this free-market experiment overlooked the crucial public function the Bank of the United States had served in issuing adequately backed notes that circulated as legal tender. In effect, Jacksonians had launched an attempt to "privatize" money, disciplined only by the laws of competition. The result was disastrous.

The sine qua non for a successful free market in money is instant communication, so that the people giving and taking the notes will know which are sound and which are the work of "paper-hangers." Early-nineteenth-century merchants, who had to deal with a multitude of state bank issuers, understood this very well.

Bills with doubtful reputations were discounted against

those of sound banks. According to Cooley, tradesmen "kept couriers by whom they hurried off to the banks of issue the bills they were compelled to take, that they might if possible exchange them for something in which they had more confidence."[5] Workers and farmers, less well informed about the comparative value of their money, were the ones who got stuck.

Fraud was possible everywhere, but Michigan's banking laws extended it an engraved invitation. The farther away a bank could be from people who might present its notes for payment, the more profit it could turn; and Michigan was one of the most remote corners of the Union. Banks were organized "by scheming men in New York" for the sole purpose of printing notes to be shipped abroad—the more inaccessible the bank's location the better. Harried state bank examiners found themselves slogging through the backwoods to inspect one institution, and discovering several new ones on the way.[6] During 1838, funny money flew around the state, and business was flush. But the speculative fever was already breaking. By the end of 1839, nearly 90% of the new state banks were in receivership. Michiganders were left holding several million dollars in worthless banknotes.[7]

Even with this loss and the subsequent recession, Michigan's troubles were not over. In the euphoria of the first year of statehood, the legislature had rushed to carry out the mandate for internal improvements contained in the new constitution. Just a week after passing the 1837 general banking law, it authorized a $5-million bond issue to pay for three rail lines and several uphill canals. At the time, the state's total assessed property value was only $43 million. Even with an optimistic allowance for the state's rapid growth, the bond issue was clearly too much for it to handle.[8] Things started to go wrong right away.

The first problem was the national economy. The previous summer, Jackson had begun to notice the inflationary impact of his anti-Bank policy. A hard-money man at heart, he slammed on the brakes, requiring specie payment for federal business. Rapid inflation gave way to sharp deflation. By the time Michigan's governor came to New York to peddle the bonds, the money market had shut down, and no one was interested.

In desperation the state's agents grabbed at an offer from a private company headed by E. R. Biddle, a cousin of Nicholas Biddle of Bank of the United States notoriety. This company, the Morris Canal and Banking Company, brought in Nicholas Biddle's bank, by then the Pennsylvania Bank of the United States, to handle the bulk of the issue. Like a fading actor, the Bank of the United States had obtained a Pennsylvania state charter to replace its lost federal status and was eking out a living on the provincial stage.

Michigan's dealings with this combination ranged from naive to incompetent. Governor Steven Mason made the fatal mistake of handing over the state bonds to the Biddles before they put up collateral. The Biddles' companies were deeply troubled, and the bonds were too great a temptation to be passed up. The bank sent the bulk of the Michigan paper to Europe as collateral for its own borrowing. The bonds were sold to private investors, but Michigan never received the money. In 1841, both Biddle companies were in default to Michigan, and the state was unable to meet the interest payments on its own debt.[9]

The state was plunged into a roaring fiscal crisis. It had meant to back its bonds with the proceeds from its internal improvements, but these had run way over budget and were earning little. The state budget was in the red, and state officials were borrowing to close the gap.

REPUDIATION AND THE TAX BURDEN

In these circumstances, Michigan took the course that fiscal conservatives considered the "meanest thing in creation" and English investors scorned for years afterward. Michigan repudiated the bonds. To be sure, it could plead a more ambiguous situation than the other states that defaulted in this period. Michigan continued to pay the portion of the bonds from which it had obtained the proceeds, but it denied any obligation for those that had never paid it a penny. The state finally reached a settlement with its bondholders, in part through selling them its most profitable railroads. Historians still argue about the justice of Michigan's conduct. But the interesting point here is what it showed about the state's attitude toward taxation.[10]

An alternative to repudiation could have been a tax increase pledged to working off the debt. The ultimate pledge for any state debt, and in fact for the intangible quality known as "public credit," is the willingness of the people to tax themselves to redeem an obligation. The new federal government had demonstrated this will to the entire satisfaction of its foreign creditors, but by the end of the 1830s the crucial English market was having well-justified doubts about the states. A member of the London Stock Exchange named Alexander Trotter explored these concerns in 1839 in a fiscal travelogue of the states. Heavily influenced by Tocqueville, he warned that "the probable disposition of the inhabitants to submit to taxation" was being weakened by the "prevalence of democratic principles." With some prescience, he wrote that "should the states be obliged hereafter to have recourse to taxation to defray the interest on their loans, it will not, probably, be till the different undertaking for which the loans were raised will have been rendered unpopular by want of success; and although it does not follow that the people, under these circumstances, will refuse to submit to the necessary sacrifice, their adhering to their engagements cannot be so confidently depended upon as it might be if the legislative bodies were returned by classes more directly interested in the maintenance of the financial integrity of the states."[11] Political conduct in such a pinch, however, depended on the character of the people, and the factor that Trotter singled out was "the prevalence of religious principles." This shrewd financial observer admitted that purely economic analysis was not enough; "no views of expediency, however farsighted, or even principles of national honour, can, under the supposed circumstances, be relied upon."[12] By this standard the spiritual state of Michigan was sadly wanting. Its public opinion was nearly unanimous against levying taxes to redeem its $5-million debt. "No one dreamed of increasing the taxes at that time and the executive was convinced the state of public pinion would not warrant suggesting it," wrote one historian.[13] Careful lobbying by a bondholders' representative ultimately won passage of a bill to fund interest payments, but Governor

John Barry balked at a clause providing taxation as a last resort. He claimed that "he and the Democratic party would be ruined politically if the measure became a law."[14] Governor Barry did sign after all, but a settlement was so long delayed that he did not get to test his prophecy. Nonetheless, Michigan unmistakably showed its aversion to increased taxation in times of adversity, setting a precedent for later hard times.

ANOTHER BITTER LESSON

Along with many other states, Michigan also learned a bitter lesson about its financial limitations. Its next constitutional convention, in 1850, completely reversed the overoptimistic mandate of 1835. Instead of ordering the legislature to survey roads, canals, and navigable rivers, the new basic law forbade the state from engaging directly or indirectly in works of internal improvement. With the memory of the $5-million loan in mind—in fact, with most of it still outstanding—the convention limited the state's routine debt to $50,000.[15] This constitution stayed in force until 1908.

Michigan's disasters in wildcat banking and internal improvements also left a deep impression on the next generation of political leaders. Radical Republicans dominated the state after the Civil War, but they were not the governmental activists who imposed Reconstruction on the South. Even the leading advocate of a strong state government warned that economic development depended on private endeavor. The Reconstruction Era Governor John Bagley stated in a legislative address: "History has failed to demonstrate that either legislative enactments or executive policies can provide the means of general prosperity or ensure the revival of industries over an extended country, but it has taught the practical lesson that a people, relying upon their own industry and economy for advancement, will most surely succeed, while those who await the aid of government, will find even the most direct and liberal legislative enactments inadequate."[16]

THE PURITAN EXCEPTION: EDUCATION

Badly burned as they were by their experiment in government-stimulated development, Michiganders retained faith in one area of state intervention: as part of the western swath of New England migration, they believed in public education. Even in the crude days of territorial government, the eccentric Jeffersonian chief justice Augustus Woodward drafted an act to establish "the Catholepistemiad or University of Michigania."[17] This measure contemplated a comprehensive school system, from elementary school to the state university. Even though most residents of the territory could not pronounce Justice Woodward's pretentious title, they went forward with the idea of tax-supported public education. Along with the limits on fiscal policy, the constitution of 1850 required free instruction in every school district. The tradition of fiscal limitation had strong roots in Michigan's history, but the Puritan tradition led straight to at least one tax-supported state activity.

THE GREAT DEPRESSION
AND THE TAX REVOLT

By 1908, Michigan had begun to take its place in the front rank of the states. Its population was nearing 2.8 million. Exploitation of lumber, copper, and iron in the Upper Peninsula wilderness had generated a significant pool of capital in Detroit, and investors had been putting their money behind the growing number of inventors working on the internal-combustion vehicle. Ransom E. Olds, of Lansing, had already popularized lightweight, low-price cars, which had the practical status of upscale bicycles. General Motors had just been incorporated. And the first of Henry Ford's thoroughly practical Model Ts had just gone on the market.[18]

The state, however, had still not forgotten its lesson in fiscal self-control. The growing Progressive movement had won a call for a constitutional convention, but the body that convened in 1907 continued the state's political traditions. (Only eight of the ninety-six delegates were Democrats.) It produced a constitution in 1908 that only modestly updated the 1850 fiscal limits.

Tax issues drew slight comment compared to the heated debate over the Progressive panacea of initiative and referendum. One delegate opposed the I and R on the ground, ironic in terms of later history, that the exercise of "direct democracy" was connected with "rapidly increasing taxation and debt" and with "broken credit."[19] The 1908 constitution provided only a watered-down version of the constitutional initiative. Voters secured the full panoply of the initiative and the referendum through constitutional amendment five years later, at the peak of the state's Progressive movement.[20]

These devices did not really come into their own until the 1930s. During the Depression, Michigan voters were offered their greatest number of referendums and constitutional initiatives, and with good reason.[21] The economic collapse provoked a tax revolt. It is not much remembered today, but it did what the tax protesters wanted it to do.

The Depression created a local fiscal crisis of awesome proportions. Value evaporated from all kinds of property as well as from the stock market. The assessed valuation of Michigan's real and personal property had reached a high point of some $8.5 billion in 1930. But as the economy plummeted, the tax base for the general property tax contracted by up to $1 billion a year for the next three years. By 1933, the total assessed valuation of Michigan property had declined by more than 30%. Total property tax levies also declined somewhat in the first two years of the Depression, but the tax base was falling so much more rapidly that tax rates continued to climb. In 1932, the average rate reached an all-time high of $32.80 per thousand dollars, 13% above the average rate during the prosperous twenties. The tax burden increase was enough to boost the delinquency rate in the best of times, but for homeowners thrown out of work and scrabbling for survival, it was the final crushing blow.[22] In fiscal year 1932–33 the delinquency rate for Detroit was 35%. For the rest of the state it was 40.5%. This record of nonpayment was twice that of the nation. In the Detroit suburbs of Macomb County it reached an unimaginable 92.5%.[23]

As the state legislature dithered, taxpayers decided to defend themselves with the constitutional initiative. Following the example of Ohio, they adopted a "fifteen mill limitation amendment" in the November 1932 general election.[24] The vote was 52% to 48%. This narrow margin put into effect a precursor of Proposition 13 that radically reshaped Michigan's tax structure. The total amount of property taxes was limited to no more than 1.5% of the assessed valuation. As in California's Proposition 13 later on, an exception to this limit was made for outstanding debt, but not for new bond sales. (The problem of controlling debt is the Achilles heel of fiscal limitation in general; and it became the downfall of the fifteen-mill limit.) In an attempt to allow some flexibility in the rigid controls on taxing and borrowing, the amendment allowed an increase in the tax limit to 5% on a vote of two-thirds of a district's electors. It also left a confusing loophole allowing localities with charters to observe their own tax limits.[25]

The impact of the vote was immediate. To relieve the pressure on localities, the state turned its portion of the general property tax over to them. And to substitute for the abandoned portion of state revenues, it installed a retail sales tax. Michigan thus turned its back on the venerable attempts to tax property according to the Lockean social contract.[26]

The fifteen-mill limit seemed to bring a sharp reduction in overall property tax rates. By 1936, the state's average rate had fallen to a low point of 25.6%, a reduction of 22%. But other forces, such as increased state and federal aid and the new revenue from the sales tax, also pushed property tax rates down. A recent sympathizer argues that cities that chose the fifteen-mill limit, such as Flint, had sharply reduced their per-capita levy by 1938, while taxes in non-fifteen-mill cities had begun to edge up again. Disastrous cuts in services were averted as back tax payments began to trickle in and the relief programs of the New Deal took effect. (Federal aid to Michigan increased tenfold between 1932 and 1935.) Contemporaries pointed to Flint, site of the famous General Motors sit-down strikes, as a victim of "extravagant economies." Yet by one important indicator, the city's health was actually improving. Thanks to federal programs, maternal mortality rates in that city fell sharply just as the tax limits took effect.[27]

THE "YENSING" OF THE TAX LIMIT

As Michigan recovered from the Depression, assessed valuation inched upward. In the decade after the 1935 low point, the tax base grew by a third—not a spectacular increase, but enough to allow growth in local revenues without much increase in tax rates. In addition, a series of court decisions expanded the loopholes in the tax limit. In 1948, another constitutional initiative allowed a much lower threshold for override votes. Rapidly increasing property values in the fifties further eased the pressure. Yet the doom of the tax limit was sealed in 1963 when, as one of the aftershocks of the 1958 recession, the state convened its first constitutional convention since 1908.

The convention's "good government" agenda featured elimination of the tax limit. But the delegates compromised on that point, apparently deciding to retain the fifteen-mill language. They may have thought they merely made technical corrections in a provision that retained popular support. When the revised limitation became the subject of court tests, however, the public received a rude surprise.

The sting lay in a loophole designed to allow new debt issues. Article IX, Section 6 of the 1963 constitution contained an exemption for "taxes imposed for the payment of principal and interest on bonds or other evidences of indebtedness." In a glaring oversight, it said nothing about voter control of these local bond issues. When a taxpayer's suit on this section finally reached the state Supreme Court in 1972, the justices split in a bewildering variety of opinions.[28] Could a locality turn its operating expenses or past deficits into a bond issue, and thus sneak them past the limit? Or did the new language apply only to genuine capital spending? Did the logic of the constitution require a vote of the people to authorize bonds, even though the new section said nothing about it? Or, as one justice reluctantly concluded, had the 1963 convention perpetrated an artful fraud on the voters? Had it nullified the fifteen-mill limit altogether? About Section 6, Justice Eugene F. Black wrote: "Bluntly stated truth . . . exposing fairly the actual purpose of 6, probably would have defeated the narrowly surviving Constitution of 1963. Yes, the

property taxpayers of Michigan were yensed in 1963, by 6."
"Yensed," Justice Black explained, was an "upper Peninsula colloquialism meaning deluded and duped, or conned and cozened, or beguiled and bilked; sometimes in a ribald or suggestive sense."[29]

The courts and the legislature subsequently backed away from this extreme conclusion, but the status of the fifteen-mill limit remained, at the least, uncertain by the time the shock waves of Proposition 13 passed through Michigan.

THE MODERN TAX REVOLT: PRELIMINARIES

Half a century after the introduction of the Model T and the 1908 constitution, Michigan was the world-famous center of America's most important industry. Detroit's gamble on internal combustion had paid off handsomely. State planners measured their economic health by the automobile production rate.

Henry Ford's breakthrough in high wages attracted a large pool of factory workers. The unions had followed, winning respectability and political power in a sometimes violent struggle. The two-party system in the state seemed to be divided between automobile worker and automobile executive. (When Arthur Summerfield, a General Motors marketer, was state Republican chairman, GM dealers formed a large part of the GOP party structure.)[30]

The dominance of automobile making brought high personal incomes, but it also held the state hostage to cyclical swings in the national economy. The sharp recession of 1958 plunged Michigan into a severe political and fiscal crisis. Automobile output nationally fell by more than 30%, but because of decentralization the decline in Michigan was more than 40%.

Tax receipts shrank, but the state budget kept growing. Governor G. Mennen Williams asked for a state income tax to close the gap. Opposition was furious. In the protracted political stalemate, the state kept up its cash flow by delaying payments to its suppliers and liquidating its Veterans Trust Fund. The legislature ultimately enacted a 1% "use tax," a

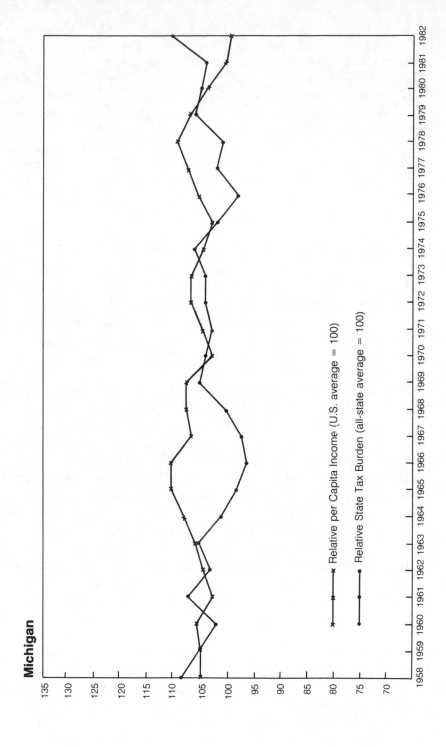

Michigan

Relative per Capita Income (U.S. average = 100)

Relative State Tax Burden (all-state average = 100)

blatant circumvention of a constitutional limit of 3% on the sales tax. When the courts struck down this device, the legislature submitted a constitutional amendment raising the rate to 4%. This measure was presented to the voters on the 1960 ballot headed by John F. Kennedy. It narrowly passed.

In the same canvass, voters also approved an easier method of calling a constitutional convention. Many Democrats hoped that a new constitutional revision would ease the tax limits and fiscal restraints.[31]

At first liberal Democrats sought the constitutional convention as the means of making it easier to raise state revenue. By the same token, conservative Republicans opposed it. But when Republicans swept the election for delegates for the "out-state" (non-Detroit) seats, positions changed. Fiscal conservatives by no means controlled the body. A majority of the Republican delegates were moderates, led by American Motors Chairman George Romney, who was using the convention to break into public life. Yet Romney's personal ambitions helped preserve the tradition of fiscal limitations.

Several months into the constitutional convention, in February 1962, Romney announced himself a candidate for governor. To preserve a façade of party unity, he negotiated a compromise on the new constitution. Sitting down in a hotel room with former state treasurer D. Hale Brake, leader of the convention's GOP conservatives, he endorsed the "Brake-Romney" agreement. It retained most of the tax restraints of the 1908 constitution (with the exception of the fifteen-mill limit) and added some new ones.[32] The 1963 constitution required balanced budgets and voter referendums on state (as opposed to local) borrowing. Above all, it declared "no income tax graduated as to rate or base shall be imposed by the state or any of its subdivisions."[33]

This provision became especially important in ensuing years when Governor Romney made a major effort to obtain a state income tax. In 1967, he finally succeeded in passing a flat-rate personal income tax of 2.6%[34] As a concession to liberal Democratic legislators, the package included a referendum on an amendment to make the tax progressive. In November 1968, voters rejected this measure by better than three to one, with a margin of nearly 1.5 million votes.[35]

THE MODERN TAX REVOLT IN BLOOM

Michigan advocates of a progressive income tax tried twice more to carry an initiative, each time losing by more than a million votes. In its last appearance on the ballot, in 1976, this measure crossed paths with the emerging tax revolt of the late seventies. The voters who rejected the graduated income tax also had the choice of supporting Proposal C, a spending limitation closely modeled on Governor Reagan's Proposition 1.

The Michigan measure was an offshoot of the California campaign. Advocates of Proposal C, primarily an organization called "Taxpayers United," led by Dow Chemical engineer William Shaker, began their work in 1974 under the tutelage of Proposition 1 veterans. They were in touch with Californians Lewis K. Uhler and William Craig Stubblebine. But they held even closer counsel with William Niskanen, the former Berkeley professor and Proposition 1 task-force member who had taken the position of chief economist with the Ford Motor Company.

Proposal C would have limited all state revenues other than federal aid to 8.3% of state personal income. Any excess would be returned as an income tax refund. Local governments and other subdivisions would have to obtain a majority referendum vote to levy new kinds of taxes. On the other hand, the state government would be forbidden to mandate expensive programs without paying for them. And the state's local aid as a whole was not to be reduced below its then current proportion of the budget.

The details of this measure tracked Proposition 1 closely, down to the formula used to maintain the spending limit. And for a time it seemed likely to suffer the same fate. In 1974, when it was first proposed, it fell far short of the signatures needed to get on the ballot. In 1976, it made the ballot but ran against heavy odds. Public-employee groups led by the Michigan Education Association outspent its advocates by five to one. The moderate Republican governor, William Milliken, opposed it. According to Proposal C advocates, state agencies such as the Office of Services to the Aging and Michigan State University circulated broadsides against it. Inadequately publicized or explained, and lacking the galvanizing example of

Proposition 13, Proposal C lost by four to three—a margin of 460,000 votes.

But its backers took heart from the 1.4 million yes votes and vowed a better organization for 1978. One of Shaker's most important steps was to approach Richard Headlee, a successful insurance executive and former chairman of the state Chamber of Commerce, to serve as front man for the campaign. With minor modifications, Proposal C became the Headlee amendment.

While academics and business leaders pushed for the spending limit, an authentic populist was preparing an even more drastic remedy. In rural Shiawasee County, a short drive from the state capital, Robert Tisch was brooding about the injustice of the property tax. A lean, gangling man with the natural eloquence of an Alfred P. Doolittle, Tisch had been serving his townsmen as a jack-of-all-trades of local government, holding posts from school board president to drains commissioner. As town assessor, he had gone through the ordeal of a countywide reassessment. When a state-ordered reassessment came a few years later, he agreed to help some older friends protest the increased burden and decided the best tactic was to change the law. In early 1978, he drafted a complicated constitutional initiative to reduce the property tax. But he held back on his campaign while the Proposition 13 phenomenon unrolled in California, fully prepared to abandon the effort if Jarvis and Gann failed to carry the day. The Californians not only won their ballot, but also generated a national tax-cutting enthusiasm that swept Michigan. Howard Jarvis toured the state in behalf of the Tisch initiative. In eleven weeks the Tisch measure qualified for the ballot with more than a quarter of a million signatures.

The head-to-head conflict between the Headlee and Tisch amendments brought the two strands of the Tax Revolt into clear relief. (The referendum ballot was further complicated by a school-voucher measure potentially imposing a heavy fiscal burden on the state.) Headlee, the country-club executive, conducted rallies in suburban Detroit's wood-paneled Huron River Hunting and Fishing Club. The self-taught Tisch ran a shoestring campaign from the basement of a rambling, fantastical tin-roofed, wood-beamed chalet and workshop that he had built for himself across from the Laingsburg firehouse. Tisch breathed the populist fire of Howard Jarvis. But Headlee had the resources for a statewide campaign. In November 1978, Headlee's moderate spending limit won by 52% to 48%. Tisch lost by 37% to 63%.

THE HEADLEE AMENDMENT

When Michigan voters awoke the day after passing the Headlee amendment, the new revolutionary age looked very like the *status quo ante*. The measure made no cuts in existing taxes, so there was none of the crisis atmosphere Californians faced on the day after Jarvis-Gann. The spending limit applied to the growth in *future* state revenues; these were not allowed to swell beyond their current percentage of state personal income, roughly 9.5%. Spending in the previous budget year would have been a problem, but the growth in the years after Headlee stayed well below the limit. In fiscal year 1980–81, state revenues fell about $1.4 billion below the limit of $8.6 billion. Local property tax revenues were geared to the U.S. consumer price index, but the rapid rate of inflation at the time nullified this limit. Ironically, the main impact of Headlee came in a sleeper provision. To keep state government from making up any losses by pulling funds from local aid, the amendment prohibited any reduction in the proportion of state spending going to local government. So perverse is the legislative animal that the main deterrent to spending in Lansing became the thought that each additional state dollar would have to be matched by seventy-two cents for the local governments.[36]

The performance of the spending limit, then, was mixed. Real estate taxation continued to swell. Yet it seems unfair to call it completely useless, as many in Michigan were willing to do. The sheer fact that a majority of the voters approved the measure may have changed the atmosphere in Lansing at least enough to hold future spending below the limit.

TAX REVOLT: DISARRAY

From one viewpoint, the three-way contest in 1978 seems to have exhausted the Tax Revolt constituency. Robert Tisch qualified another property tax rollback for the November 1980 ballot. It was six times longer than Tisch I and much more stringent.[37] The campaign, as usual, had almost no money and was further hobbled by Tisch's eccentricities, endearing as they were. (As a commendable point of honor, he insisted on personally signing each copy of all his press releases.) As usual, the measure lost. Yet the margin had narrowed. This time around, the Tisch amendment received 44% of the vote.

If anything, the left-wing Tax Revolt was faring worse. The legislature called a special election on May 19, 1981, to vote on the establishment's answer to Tisch. The only measure, Proposal A, claimed to be a reduction in property and city income taxes, but it also provided a sales tax increase that would more than make up the difference. Skeptical voters demolished the measure by a negative margin of 72%. Liberal Republican Governor Milliken supported Proposal A, and the debacle may have persuaded him not to seek reelection in 1982.

Both Tisch and Headlee put aside their referendums and ran for the open governor's seat. For all the controversy over the toothless spending limit, Headlee proved to be a formidable campaigner. He routed Governor Milliken's annointed successor in a four-way Republican primary, making a staunch defense of President Reagan's economics. In spite of depression conditions and a few supposedly antifeminist gaffes, he closed an imposing gap in the final weeks and finished with 45% to Democrat James Blanchard's 51%. Tisch pursued a typically individual course, forming his own Bob Tisch Party. None of the candidates could match his native genius for invective, much of it directed against Headlee.[38] But very little of it reached the voters, and Tisch received only 80,000 votes out of 3 million, a mere .02%.

Populist tax rebels seem to have a hard time transferring their success with referendums to a personal political campaign. In California, Paul Gann suffered a diastrous defeat against U.S. Senator Alan Cranston and bounced back with a string of initiative victories. But Tisch announced that his campaign would be his final request for public support. True to his word, he subsequently withdrew from the world of tax initiatives.

This diversion of energy was not the reason for 1982's respite from referendums, however. Before launching his campaign for governor, Tisch had tried and failed to place a third version of his amendment on the ballot. The problem may have been too much interest rather than too little. During the summer of 1982, no fewer than four groups were gathering signatures for four separate petitions. Tisch may have come close to the legally required number but had no cushion against invalid signatures. A barber in the Detroit exurbs named Jim DeMar collected 170,000 on behalf of his organization, Silent Majority Speaks. If these efforts had been pooled they might easily have qualified an initiative, but there was no coordination. And the state was preoccupied with more urgent worries.

MICHIGAN ON THE BRINK

As the nation headed into the trough of the 1982 recession, Michigan stood on the brink of a far deeper abyss. The state had been hard hit in 1979–80, but resumed its old-time spending in the false recovery of 1980–81. The renewed recession pushed its unemployment rate to 15.5% and the total number out of work to 664,000. It was the worst year since the Depression, and unemployment had already been in double digits for the two years preceding it. The unemployment insurance fund was deeply in debt. Welfare costs were soaring. Yet tax collections were falling below projections and in some cases below the actual dollar amounts of the years before. Governor Milliken had asked for some temporary tax increases, including an income tax surcharge, but, like his Yale College classmate John V. Lindsay, he had also attempted to paper over his accumulating deficits. Not a single American financier would touch a major seasonal borrowing coming up in September, and the notes were ultimately picked up by a consortium of Japanese banks as a good-will gesture. Insiders in Lansing were saying, with only slight exaggeration, that the state government was weeks away from financial collapse when Milliken left office.

To be sure, Governor Milliken had tried to rebuild some state reserves in his last year. But the incoming Democrat, James Blanchard, inherited a looming deficit and a seriously depleted treasury. His answer, like Ohio Governor Celeste's, was a quick and massive tax increase. He boosted the income tax rate by 1.75 percentage points to 6.35%, a 38% increase. Unlike Celeste, Blanchard put some effort into laying the political groundwork. An independent blue-ribbon commission certified that the crisis was real. The legislature gave his tax proposal a thorough debate. The Republican minority was allowed to impose some conditions, notably a trigger to phase out the income tax surcharge and hypothetically even reduce the permanent rate. But the public reaction was no more understanding than it had been initially in Ohio.

THE TAX REVOLT RESURGENT

The widespread reaction against the 38% tax increase seems to have tapped the frustration of three years of hard times. The most spontaneous movement attacked Governor Blanchard and state senators who had voted for the tax, using the quixotic means of the recall. The state constitution allowed citizens to petition for a new election, but the legislature set the conditions. Its requirements would have been a challenge to Hercules. Petitioners had to collect signatures of 20% of the number that originally voted on the target of the recall, and they had only ninety days to do it. The recall drive against Blanchard had to obtain more than 785,000 valid names. The wonder is that anyone would attempt such a task! But when the deadline passed and the petition drive inevitably had fallen short, it had still gathered half a million signatures. The local recalls were more of a threat, and as they continued to pop up, people started talking about "recall fever." With more than a dozen under way, the Democratic Party tried to slow them down with "clarity hearings." The legislature had recently allowed challenges to the recall drives on the grounds that the petitions could be misleading. Even the courts found this ploy exasperating. To the loosely knit recall committees, it was fuel on the fire. By December 1983, two state senators who had voted for the tax had been removed from office by humiliating margins. In subsequent special elections, Republicans captured these blue-collar swing districts by equally wide margins, taking the Senate out of Democratic control.

An even more basic challenge came from the revitalized tax initiative committees. After the splintering of 1982, two of the local leaders agreed to cooperate in a grand coalition. By January, representatives from eight grass-roots groups had met and begun drafting a new proposal. Jim DeMar, the barber from Romeo, recalls, "We wrote it concise enough so the legislature could not circumvent it but simple enough so they could understand it." The "Voter's Choice" amendment would roll back all tax increases after 1981 unless they were approved by a majority in a popular referendum. Changes in fees and permits would require an 80% vote of the legislative body or a majority of a referendum. In a nod to Detroit suburbanites, local taxes on nonresident incomes would be limited to one-half of 1%.

The Voter's Choice drive had until June 1984 to collect 304,000 signatures. By the fall of 1983, it already had gathered 300,000, on an outlay of $5,000. Between clips of a customer's hair in his one-chair barbershop, Jim DeMar talked of generating several more tax initiatives by the June deadline. In November 1984, Michigan voters may well join ranks in the Tax Revolt with the citizens of California and Massachusetts.[39]

IV

Vindication

11

New Hampshire: The Oldest Frontier Revives

A strange experience frequently befalls hikers in western and northern New England. Tramping through the backwoods, snagging their jeans on blackberry brambles and pushing aside the woody mountain laurel, they may suddenly emerge into an unexpected clearing marked off by a tumble-down stone wall. At one end of the field they will find, drifted over with decaying leaves, the cellar hole of some long-forgotten farmhouse, abandoned perhaps a century earlier. On an autumn afternoon, when the peculiar backlighting of the declining sun sets off the reddish yellow glow of the foliage, it can be a ghostly sight.

These haunted cellar holes perforate the crescent of mountains that swings around the heartland of New England. They bear witness to the flight of the hardscrabble farmers from the region stretching from the Maine coast through New Hampshire and Vermont and down along the Berkshires and the Valley (as the westering Puritans called the course of the Connecticut River). The region is aptly called "the Old Frontier."[1]

In the early nineteenth century, the region's steep riverbeds provided the hydropower for the nation's earliest industry. The abandoned hulks of textile mills and light manufactories now disfigure small towns throughout the mountain valleys. As the nation discovered one natural resource after another in its expanding western territories, the Old Frontier fell into eclipse. For decades its most valuable export was people—settlers filling the belt of territory stretching 2,000 miles due west.

At the turn of the century, it was fashionable to bemoan the degeneration of the New England stock, supposedly deprived of its most vigorous members by migration to the West.[2] But not until the 1960s and early 1970s did New England come to be a prime example of regional decline. Its mountain settlements rivaled those in the central Appalachians as examples of hard and insular life.

Followers of the historian Walter Prescott Webb could explain the decline in terms of the exhaustion of the windfall from the opening of the Old Frontier. Partisans of the Sunbelt-Frostbelt conflict could blame the weather, the raiding by southern industrial commissions, and all their other scapegoats. The technological school of Francis Kelly and Jerry Brown could argue that New England was trapped on the inevitable downward slope of an industrial life cycle: textiles, leather, and wood pulp, having had their day of growth and peak performance, had topped out and were now dragging the region down with them.

But in the mid–1970s, just as the talk about New England's stagnation was hitting full stride, a few corners of the new Appalachia refused to be tucked into the stereotype. Instead of displaying the somnolence and drift expected of northern New England, New Hampshire began to bustle. For two decades, its rate of population growth led not only New England but also the entire corner of the country north of the Mason-Dixon line and east of the Rockies. In the seventies New Hampshire outstripped every state east of the Mississippi except Florida. The example was contagious. In the 1970s, only two other states in the country's northeastern quadrant attained a double-digit rate of population growth. These were New Hampshire's neighbors Maine and Vermont. By 1980, even Massachusetts, the ailing giant of New England, began to display a renewed vigor. Not many of the popular theories of decline could explain why.

FEUDING NEW ENGLAND

To understand New England is to recognize how little each of its states likes the others. Maine spent 150 years as a colony of Massachusetts after the Boston Puritans bought out its royal patent. Emancipation in 1820 was such a relief that citizens of Maine, called "Maineiacs" by some, still insist on referring to their home as "the *State* of Maine, b'gosh."[3]

New Hampshire narrowly escaped a similar fate, thanks to the intercession of Charles II. Its earliest settlements were sponsored by royalists and Anglicans, perhaps encouraged by the king's party as a check on the aggressive Puritans to the south. Native New Hampshire historians sometimes show more sympathy to Stuarts than to Bostonians. One, as late as 1904, refers to the province's "early emancipation from the bigotry and barbarity of pharisaical Puritanism in the near neighborhood."[4]

Vermont has felt the same way about New Hampshire. During the Revolution, the Green Mountain Boys asserted their independence not only from Great Britain but also from New Hampshire and New York, rival claimants for their territory. When the Continental Congress rebuffed the Vermonters' claims, they concluded that since everybody was in a "State of Nature" anyway, they had as much right as any other to become an independent republic. Ethan Allen, the most flamboyant personality in Vermont's history, tried to conduct his own foreign policy and found himself facing a charge of treason by the Continental Congress. After the Revolution, Vermont was in no hurry to sign the Articles of Confederation, not wanting to share the war debt of the Continental Congress. Independent, it became a tax haven for its neighbors. A contemporary described its reward: "Encouraged by the mildness of the government, the smallness of the taxes, the fertility and cheapness of the lands, large additions were annually made to their numbers and property, by the accession of inhabitants from other states. . . . The body of the people felt that they were in a better situation, than the people in the neighboring states: And it was the general inclination and desire not to be connected with the union, if it could be decently avoided."[5] Vermonters claimed their republic lasted from 1776 to 1791, when it became the fourteenth state under the Constitution; it had twice as long a run as the Republic of Texas.

VERMONT VERSUS NEW HAMPSHIRE

Vermont and New Hampshire lie side by side, but when it comes to attitudes about government, all they have in common is the border. Vermont emphasizes state government; New Hampshire emphasizes the township. In Vermont, the state collects 57% of the total state and local tax revenue; in New Hampshire, the state sees only 41% of the total. (A decade ago, the disparity was even greater.) Vermont also seeks federal aid more aggressively. Both states get an above-average share, but Vermont's, 32% of its general revenue, is relatively the highest in the country. It is tempting to say that the memory of winning independence has led Vermont to maintain a tradition of centralized state services. But one could equally say that New Hampshire defiantly maintains the tradition of the township; no other state in the union places greater reliance on local property taxes and local government.

The most important difference, however, comes in taxation. Vermont collects both a sales and a general income tax: New Hampshire is the only state in the Union with neither. Vermont's tax burden was highest in New England until the late sixties; in 1974, it was third highest in the nation. New Hampshire's tax burden has been lowest in the region for nearly three decades. It is now the lowest in the country.[6]

Why such a contrast? Beyond historical memories, there are some more immediate theories. New Hampshire conservatives blame Vermont's more elaborate government on the number of New Yorkers who have settled there. New Hampshire liberals blame their own state's limited government on the conservative influence of French-Canadian and Irish Catholic Democrats. Jack Menges, a Dartmouth College eco-

New Hampshire

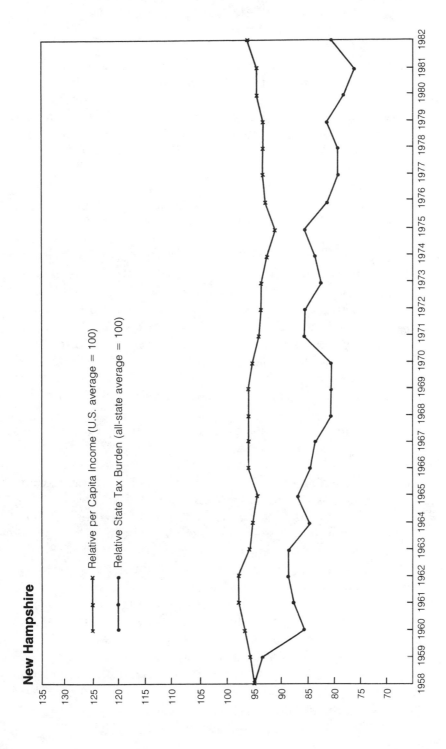

Relative per Capita Income (U.S. average = 100)

Relative State Tax Burden (all-state average = 100)

nomics professor and former Democratic state representative, argues that because of its geography New Hampshire developed a different economic and ethnic make-up from that of Vermont. The alluvial river valleys of Vermont were richer than New Hampshire's rocky hillsides, and so it remained far more agricultural and rural. Even today, Vermont is the least urbanized state in the Union.

Furthermore, according to Menges, New Hampshire's richest territory, along the Merrimac and Piscataqua rivers flowing to the Atlantic, had early been taken over by manufacturing. The mill towns attracted a largely Catholic French-Canadian, and Irish work force, who supported the Democratic Party because it supported their unions against the Yankee bosses. Because so much of their education and welfare were provided by the church, they had little need for a program of state social services. A Catholic family paying tuition to a parochial school and contributing to a church benefit society was understandably reluctant to support government spending for the same services. New Hampshire thus contained a powerful bipartisan constituency for limited taxation, which was lacking in Vermont.[7]

The trouble with this thesis is that census figures fail to show a significant difference between the ethnic distribution in Vermont and New Hampshire. In 1970, for instance, 13.1% of New Hampshire's residents were Canadian-born or had one or more Canadian parents. In Vermont this figure was 10.4%.

A more crucial factor may be political. In Vermont the "old Yankee" elite has maintained itself far better than in New Hampshire. New Hampshire politics has elbowed aside the "Concord gang" of pedigreed families and their law partners, despite their commercial and legal leadership in the state's capital. The reasons for the real difference in tax policy may lie less on the Vermont side than in New Hampshire. Over the past thirty years, populist candidates in both parties have exploited the historic tension between the yeomanry and the elite. Class divisions among a decidedly nonhomogeneous WASP Republican electorate have played a political role that Ronald Reagan's managers skillfully exploited to defeat patrician George Bush in the 1980 presidential primary.

NEW HAMPSHIRE'S TAX FIGHTS

The issue of taxation is deeply rooted in New Hampshire's history. The draft of a charter for the royalist first settlers states, in the name of Charles I, "we do covenant, that we, our heirs and successors will not impose at any time hereafter any impositions or customs or other taxations, how small soever, upon the dwellers or inhabitants of New Hampshire."[8] The early New Hampshire settlers may never have seen this document, however, and for nearly a century much of their energies went into fighting the land-title claims of the descendants of Thomas Mason, who probably prepared the draft charter. When in 1683 an agent of Mason and the Crown tried to levy taxes against the will of the General Assembly, the people "uniformly refused to pay: and threatened the would-be revenue agent with beating or worse." The intimidated collector complained, "The wife of Moses Gilman did say that she had provided a kettle of scalding water for him, if he came to her house, which had been over the fire two days."[9]

In this fight, New Hampshire settlers often adopted the tactic of claiming to want union with Massachusetts. But when the Boston colony eagerly took the initiative and started arresting colonists in New Hampshire for not paying *its* taxes their interest rapidly waned. The final boundary line was drawn only in 1741; George II's Privy Council sided with New Hampshire. Unlike those in Massachusetts, at the beginning of the Revolution, New Hampshire's merchants and educated men favored loyalty to the Crown. Their loyalty may have been cemented by a low tax burden. In a closing address to the General Assembly on April 16, 1770, Governor John Wentworth observed: "It is with the greatest pleasure that I congratulated you that no man can justly say the taxes are heavy, for the whole does not exceed 3s. 8d. proclamation money to each rateable in the province. Perhaps if exactly known and taken, not 3s. 6d.; an instance, I believe, heretofore unexampled in any province or country whatever."[10] The less affluent subjects differed strongly with this estimate, complaining of upper-class tax evasion. A 1769 petition from citizens of Portsmouth charged "that the trade and business is signally decayed, that the inhabitants are filled with the most gloomy apprehensions, especially the middling and poorer sort, who looked upon themselves to be greatly distressed and aggrieved by the weight of public taxes, which by the present method of assessment fall exceedingly heavy on them."[11]

Whatever the merits of this claim, the coastal supporters of Royal Governor Wentworth were no match for the more aggrieved "middling sort," or for the rural, upcountry poor, to whom the tax issue was paramount. Resentment against the tea tax was overpowering even in Portsmouth, center of the seaboard elite. A mass meeting there in 1773 was one of the first to denounce Lord Townshend's legislation. With the collapse of the royal government two years later, the burden of running New Hampshire fell primarily on its local institutions.[12]

One historian notes that fervor for the Revolution increased in proportion to the distance from the coast, and this pattern continued in the struggle to organize the new state. Angry over seaboard dominance in the provisional 1776 state constitutional convention, sixteen towns along the upper Connecticut valley, egged on by Dartmouth College, threatened to join independent Vermont.[13] Under this pressure a prolonged series of constitutional conventions offered draft after draft, gradually whittling down the dominant legislature and strengthening the governor. After continual rejection, the constitution drafters settled on a House of Representatives weighted to represent townships and a governor checked by a Governor's Council. (This body of five, a colonial survival, still has veto power over all the governor's appointments.) The constitution finally ratified in 1784 and revised in 1792 remains the basic law of New Hampshire.[14]

Thus originated the state's basic political themes. The authority of the executive was limited. The Governor's Council retained significant power. Townships gained an important degree of autonomy and influence. In a direct corollary, democratic control has been thoroughly enforced. Governors must stand for election every two years; the legislature still sits part-time with low pay; and to accommodate the towns, the House of Representatives has 400 members. As the third-largest representative body in the free world (after Great Britain's House of Commons and the U.S. House), New Hampshire's House must have the lowest ratio of members to population to be found anywhere. With rows of folding seats (no room for desks), its chamber looks like a medium-sized cinema.

Time and again New Hampshire has been swept by a populism discomfiting to its more restrained neighbors. From 1829 to 1855, it was the North's strongest bastion of support for Jacksonian Democracy. The dominant New Hampshire Democrats drew their strength from the resentment of newer Baptist and Methodist sects against the privileged Congregationalists. The party also exploited the popular resentment against native-son Daniel Webster for defending Dartmouth College and for moving to Massachusetts.[15] This dynasty ended with the sorry prosouthern presidency of Franklin Pierce, another native son. (Wrote Robert Frost of New Hampshire's only president, "Pronounce him Purse, / And make the most of it for better or worse.") Remnants of the faction opposed the war against the Confederacy. At their peak, however, the Jacksonians had given New Hampshire a government "of Republican frugality and prosperity." Over the generation from 1823 to 1857, the school tax increased 260%. Population grew only 130%, but bank capital quadrupled. By contrast, in the ten years following the start of the Civil War, taxes tripled and the population fell by 2.4%.[16]

THE ENDURING TAX STRUCTURE

In spite of the turmoil, the nineteenth-century tax structure survived remarkably unchanged into the twentieth. Its basic feature was the general property tax. After 1843, the state also added a series of special taxes on corporations and business interests. In 1878, a special tax commission reaffirmed the principle of the property tax. All the suggested improvements, it wrote, appealing to Adam Smith "are a departure from the first principle of taxation laid down by the pioneer of English political economists and generally reasserted by his followers." As Maurice Robinson, the historian of New Hampshire taxes, summarizes their conclusion: "The commissioners believed with M. Say that 'The best tax is always the lightest,' and adopted as a corollary the proposition that the 'lightest tax must be the one that is the most widely and equally diffused.' "[17] Another commission two years earlier had disagreed sharply. The tax on personal property was so easily evaded, it argued, that it would fall disproportionately on the people without the means to escape it or else would require draconian measures to enforce uniformly. In Robinson's paraphrase of the 1876 report: "If the taxation of any classes of property drives such property from the state or necessitates inquisitional or despotic laws, such taxation is at least questionable."[18] Robinson concludes, with some clucking of the tongue: "The fact that the state so tenaciously clung to the old system, even after its defects had been made so clear and the remedy had been so plainly disclosed, shows how firmly the theory that is based upon the taxation of all property was imbedded in the minds of the citizens of the state."[19] The remnant of this attempt to tax all property equally degenerated in the twentieth century into the business inventory tax. But inventories can be just as movable as personal property. A major impact of this tax in New Hampshire, and California as well, was the development of a booming warehouse industry just across the borders, in Vermont and Nevada. New Hampshire abolished its stock-in-trade tax in 1971 (along with other remnants of the general property tax, such as its tax on cattle), replacing it with a modern business profits tax. In California the inventory tax lingered on until the peak of the Tax Revolt.

But other nineteenth-century tax principles still remain firmly rooted in New Hampshire. The constitution requires "Proportional and reasonable assessments, rates and taxes."[20] The state Supreme Court interprets this language as forbidding graduated tax rates, including the progressive income tax. New Hampshire residents wryly observe that they have held on to their "archaic" flat-rate tax principles so long that they are beginning to come back in fashion.

The property tax system received its greatest shock during the fiscal crisis of the Depression. But New Hampshire refused to follow Vermont in supplementing its finances with a broad-based tax. (Vermont inaugurated its personal income tax in 1931.) Instead, the frugal folk dwelling in the White Mountains decided to augment their revenues by preying on the vices of their neighbors. The state imposed a cigarette tax, justified constitutionally as a health measure, and established a monopoly on liquor sales, and then sold both tobacco and alcohol at low prices in a chain of state stores concentrated along the border. In the 1960s, these "sin taxes" brought in up to two-thirds of the total state revenue.

POPULISM AND "THE PLEDGE"

In spite of this tax tradition, by the beginning of the fifties New Hampshire seemed to be increasing its spending roughly in line with the other states. For most of the decade from 1942 to 1952, its direct general expenditure actually took a bigger bite from state personal income than did Vermont's. In 1953, this pattern began to reverse. New Hampshire never thereafter exceeded Vermont, and in 1971 the ratio of spending to personal income in Vermont (16.4%) exactly doubled New Hampshire's (8.2%).[21]

New Hampshire politicians trace this turnabout to the last administration of Governor Sherman Adams. Faced with growing spending, Adams warned that bankruptcy was imminent unless the state passed a sales tax. The legislature refused, Adams left to be chief of staff in President Dwight D. Eisenhower's White House, and the state stayed solvent. Adams's successors, from the Republican populist Wesley Powell to the Kennedy Democrat John King, all ran on a program of limited government spending. In 1968, Professor Walter Peterson ran on the same antitax platform. But he quickly accepted the need for more revenue and appointed a Citizens Task Force, which recommended a business profits tax. It was adopted in a 1970 special session of the legislature. This levy replaced the stock-in-trade taxes, which had been criticized for 100 years. But it also developed into the state's largest single source of revenue. Nonetheless, reformers felt more levies were needed. Professor Menges introduced an income tax bill linked with property tax relief. (He was told later by a conservative Democratic colleague, "That was the best broad-based tax bill I ever voted against.") Governor Peterson proposed his own 3% state income tax in a 1972 special session, and never got to a third term.

The tax issue split the 1972 election wide open and brought Meldrim Thomson to the fore. A Pennsylvania native who had been brought up and educated in the South, Thomson had settled in his wife's hometown of Orford, a pleasant farming center north of Dartmouth and historically one of the centers of protest against the 1776 constitution. As a member of the Orford School Board he fought against accepting federal school aid and attracted the vociferous support of the state's most influential (and controversial) newspaper, *The Manchester Union Leader*. Riding the tax issue into the Republican primary, Thomson eliminated Governor Peterson from the running. Infuriated, the "Concord Gang" sponsored the independent candidacy of Concord Mayor Malcolm McLane. The general election pitted Thomson against McLane and an antitax Democratic nominee. Thompson won with a plurality in the three-way split.

In his three terms, Thomson elevated the consensus against broad-based taxation into a rhetorical institution. Labeled "The Pledge" by the press, it amounted to a ritual declaration by candidates for governor that if the legislature were somehow to pass a broad-based sales or income tax, they would veto it. Since Nebraska had passed both taxes in 1966, New Hampshire became the last state in the Union to have neither. (It has, however, imposed an income tax on interest and dividends since 1923.) The most familiar criticism of The Pledge is that it left the state without an "adequate" revenue base. Yet under Thomson the state budget increased by 194% and state government employment jumped by more than one-third.

At the same time, most New Hampshire citizens seem happy with their level of public services. In 1975, Dartmouth College Economics Professor Colin D. Campbell undertook a project for the Wheelabrator-Frye Corporation to compare the fiscal systems of New Hampshire and Vermont. In this celebrated study, Campbell concluded that despite the great divergence in their tax burdens "there is little evidence that public services are better in Vermont than in New Hampshire."

Teachers' salaries were actually higher in New Hampshire than in Vermont, although class size was slightly larger (17.0 pupils per teacher as opposed to 16.1), and New Hampshire provided less for handicapped education. The median level of schooling in both states was exactly the same. Scholastic Aptitude Tests scores were slightly higher for New Hampshire males, and roughly similar percentages of draftees flunked their Selective Service mental tests. Both states did significantly better than the national average. (In recent years, in fact, New Hampshire's SAT scores have been highest in the nation.) On more specifically state-level services, welfare payments were similar, though total spending was a higher percentage of state income in Vermont than in New Hampshire because of tighter eligibility control in New Hampshire. But Vermont spent 20% more per road-land mile for highway maintenance.[22]

This study has been a thorn in the side of Vermonters, who argue that the states are too dissimilar to be fairly compared. For instance, Vermont is far more rural and has a greater number of school districts. Yet when such contrasts are compared to the much greater disparities found throughout the nation, the similarities between the two states remain impressive. The real difference, as Campbell concludes, is a matter of public policy: New Hampshire relies far more heavily on its local government to provide services. Property taxes in New Hampshire are not low. In 1978, measured per $1,000 of state personal income, they were sixth highest in the country. (Vermont's were eighth highest.) But local government is under such public scrutiny that it provides the most efficient return for the dollar. Economies of scale and consolidation do not appear to work for government. Studies elsewhere have shown that some service costs are lower where a variety of local units provides for some competition. On the other hand, says Campbell, government costs rise to meet the revenues available. As a corollary, a higher level of federal grants increases the state and local tax burden. The main reason that Vermont spends more than New Hampshire is that it has both a sales and a general income tax, whereas New Hampshire does not.[23]

THE NEW HAMPSHIRE BOOM

The benefits of the New Hampshire tax system extend far be-yond enforced frugality in government. By the middle 1970s, the state came to realize that it had entered its greatest boom in eighteen decades. The 1970 census showed that its popu-lation had grown 22% since 1960, a rate more than two-thirds higher than the nation's and nearly three-quarters higher than New England's. The surprises continued in the 1980 census. New Hampshire's growth rate had risen to 35%, more than double the national rate and nearly six times New England's. State statistics attributed 50% of the 1960s growth to in-migration, but by the end of the 1970s, the stream of new ar-rivals was adding more than 70% of the increase.

Some of the newcomers were retirees, attracted by the state's recreational possibilities and its natural beauty. Many more were commuters to jobs in Massachusetts, who crowded into Hillsboro and Rockingham counties, just north of the Bay State's tax jurisdiction. But New Hampshire's revival had taken on an economic life of its own. An especially bright sign for the future is that the state has been able to attract high-growth, high-salary, high-technology industry. With this boom, the state's total personal income has grown from a .33% share of the nation's in 1960 to a .39% share in 1980, at a time when the rest of New England's was sharply declining.

This success was too striking for the neighbors to miss. In the late seventies, while New Hampshire grew complacent and allowed its tax burden to creep up, Vermont began to squeeze spending down. New Hampshire was the only state in New England whose tax burden declined consistently from 1953 to 1977. But from 1975 to 1980, its rate of decline was more than matched by its rival across the Connecticut River. In those five years, Vermont lowered its level of taxation from more than 25% above the nation's to 10% above. By this time New Hampshire's burden had fallen to 79.5% of the U.S. av-erage, displacing Ohio as the lowest in the nation. But, to re-peat the old refrain, the crucial question is the rate of decline, not the absolute level. And Vermont had begun to share in the benefits. Vermont's employment in that period grew even faster than New Hampshire's.[24] Its population growth between the 1970 and the 1980 census was 15%, well behind New Hampshire's but still second best in the quadrant of the country bounded by the Mason-Dixon Line and the Mississippi River.

NEW HAMPSHIRE'S FUTURE

The growth in competition caught New Hampshire at a time when the debate over its own policy had reached a new turning point. After three terms of conservative rhetoric and populist showmanship, Meldrim Thomson fell victim to Democratic challenger Hugh Gallen on another pocketbook issue. Thomson had allowed a state utility to pass on construction costs for the Seabrook nuclear power plant to the consumers' utility bill in a period when energy costs were rising anyway.

In Governor Gallen's first term, New Hampshire took a beating from the 1980 recession. One side effect of its growth had been its increased vulnerability to national downturns. From one of the least cyclical economies in New England, it had grown into one of the most cyclical. And the downturn took a large bite out of the business profit tax receipts, by this time the largest single component of state revenues.

To meet two declining years of revenue, New Hampshire's legislature enacted a minimum business profits tax, which was widely resisted, then repealed, and then declared unconstitutional by the state Supreme Court because it had a graduated impact. In an agonizing special session, the part-time legislators imposed a surcharge on the business tax. In one voice vote, quickly overturned on a roll call, the House even approved a bill for a state income tax. As several candidates in the 1982 gubernatorial election, including Governor Gallen, refused to take The Pledge, observers feared (or hoped) that the state might soon plunge into the treacherous waters of broad-based taxation. But New Hampshire's tradition held firm. In a bad year for Republicans, GOP candidate John Sununu upset incumbent Gallen. Sununu, a Tufts professor, had not only taken The Pledge but had made opposition to new taxation the centerpiece of his campaign. Ironically, the debate unrolled just as New Hampshire was recording one of its most impressive achievements: national employment figures released in May 1982 showed that in spite of the recession the state's work force had grown at 103% of the national rate, better than all of New England and most of the states of the Sunbelt.[25]

12

Massachusetts: The Tax Revolt Continues

In 1980, most of the nation debated the merits of Ronald Reagan, Jimmy Carter, and John Anderson. Massachusetts debated the Tax Revolt. For the Bay State, the parade of presidential candidates was an alien distraction from the serious business at hand, the proposal to cut property taxes to 2½% of full cash value. The issue roiled local meetings and even pushed the candidates off automobile bumpers. In the end, the one state that had voted for George McGovern in 1972, a self-proclaimed last holdout of liberalism, supported the attack on government spending by a sixty-to-forty margin.

The Proposition 2½ upheaval in Massachusetts was the East Coast equivalent of the Proposition 13 earthquake in California. It proved that the Tax Revolt "had geography," that the phenomenon spanned the continent. But it also showed that the Tax Revolt had ancient roots. Where California often seemed to lack history, the Bay State reveled in it. Even the terms of debate in 1980 echoed the protests of the eighteenth century.

In 1980 as in 1780, tax rebels complained that the General Court failed to represent the people. The legislature, the

present-day tax rebels charged, was more concerned with securing wealth for its members and places for their friends.
Using the procedure that had discredited the proposed constitution of 1778, the legislature kept a stranglehold on popular attempts to amend the constitution. The state government
had even displayed more than a trace of Puritan self-righteousness in expanding its spending. The greatest surge in the
budget came not under the Irish Catholic Democrats but under the patrician Republican Yankee Francis Sargent. Frustration with the commonwealth's high tax burden spread from
property owners to aggressive new members of the business
community. The rhetoric of the modern Tax Revolt took
chapter and verse from the supply-side economic movement
and applied them with great competence. But the basic argument had been addressed to the voters of western Massachusetts in 1776: commerce (read industry) generated the
wealth that lightened the burden of all commonwealth taxpayers, and the less it was taxed the more wealth it would
produce.

The protest of the twentieth century was shaped by a tradition stretching back to the eighteenth. Proposition 2½ dealt
primarily with the real estate tax, which, as the remnant of
the general property tax, was almost the sole source of revenue for Massachusetts cities and towns. Yet local government
in the commonwealth shouldered an unusually high proportion of the public duties (a memory of the Revolution, when
the state government collapsed and public order was maintained by town meetings). The need to provide for high and
increasing local government services from the single revenue
source of the real estate tax was bound to push the levy to
painful extremes.

BEGINNINGS OF AN "ARCHAIC" SYSTEM

At the state level, the ideology of the general property tax had
finally collapsed in 1915 after repeated assaults. A constitutional amendment authorized the substitution of a flat-rate tax
on income for the unenforceable tax on "intangible" personal
property. (In light of the later history of income taxes, it is

worth noting that some support for this amendment came from Boston's State Street financiers.) The amendment provided a nominal tax cut. Its supporters argued that the lower rate of an income tax would produce more revenue than the high but unenforceable "intangible" property tax, and so it did.[1]

The income tax amendment did not delete the crucial word *proportional*, however. In spite of the progressive orientation of the 1917–18 constitutional convention, a concerted effort to strike out this powerful adjective failed. Advocates of the change maintained they were seeking favorable tax breaks for industry, but other delegates saw the graduated income tax coming close behind. Removing the word *proportional*, warned Charles Francis Adams, would "give notice that we are to welcome every sort of change in our tax system known to the world."[2]

The language of 1780 survived the Progressive challenge, and the Massachusetts constitution maintained its commitment to "proportional and equal taxation." A tradition of strict court interpretations ruled out levies such as the graduated income tax that might have generated windfall revenues from inflation. The lack of an automatic money machine kept the state government under political pressure whenever it became necessary to vote new taxes to close deficits. Yet this "archaic" and "inflexible" system may have allowed the Massachusetts economy to rebound as quickly as it did when the political decision was made to reduce the commonwealth's tax burden.

PROLOGUE TO REVOLT: "ACCUMULATION"

Yankee dominance in Massachusetts politics ended with the New Deal. The state government went through a succession of Irish (and pseudo-Irish) Democratic administrators with less-than-Puritan standards of public service. Yet, in spite of an occasional spectacular financial misdeed, it was not the ethnic Democracy that won the title "Taxachusetts" for the commonwealth. By 1965—after the Curleys, the Hurleys, the Devers, and the Furcolos—the tax burden in Massachusetts was only three percentage points above the national average.[3]

Massachusetts

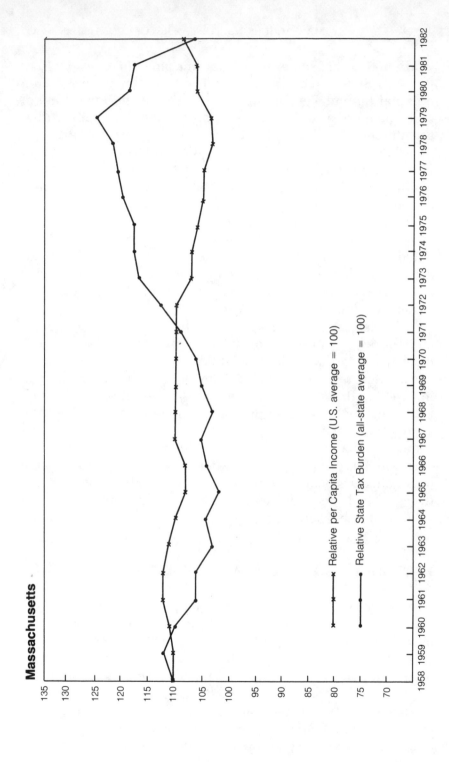

x Relative per Capita Income (U.S. average = 100)

• Relative State Tax Burden (all-state average = 100)

Chapter 5 presented a five-phase morphology of fiscal crises. In Massachusetts, the first phase, accumulation, in which the problems develop, began in 1966. Moderate Republican John A. Volpe returned to office after a hiatus for a second term marked by a sharp increase in state spending. This surge cannot be blamed entirely on Volpe, a short, dignified Italian contractor who in 1968 was runner-up to Spiro Agnew in what *The Washington Post* that summer described as Richard Nixon's search for a "political neuter" as vice president. During this term, the shrewd manipulation of the secretary of the commonwealth and the personal ambition of the speaker of the House caused the state government to assume a very expensive responsibility. The secretary was Kevin H. White, who in 1967 was elected to what became nearly a generation of tenure as mayor of Boston. The House speaker was John F. X. Davoren, who coveted White's state office.

In the summer of 1967, the state government had decided to take over the administration of welfare, but to let the cities continue to pay for it. As Mayor White recalled the scene in an interview with *Barron's*, "I get elected in November. Somebody walked in and said, let me tell you a little fact of life that's going to make your head spin. They're running it and you're paying for it. And that I know enough about!" The mayor's threats and blandishments had no effect on the legislature, until an idea dawned on him. "And that was simply, I announced that I would not resign as Secretary of State. . . . The Speaker of the House wanted my job. The vacancy was filled by the legislature. That meant that everybody in the legislature could move up one notch. And I said, I will not resign until the legislature reverses the bill and picks up the entire bill, which was a staggering cost." Headlines the next morning denounced the mayor's "cheap politics." And the next day, the legislature changed the bill. John F. X. Davoren became secretary of the commonwealth. Kevin White "became a more contented mayor." And the state government, with no advance preparation, began its sorry experience with direct administration of the welfare system.[4]

In 1968, after the welfare takeover, Massachusetts' state spending on the major aid programs increased better than tenfold. The increase was substantial enough to boost overall state spending by 50%. If the state were simply substituting its employees for local welfare workers, total state and local government employment would have stayed the same and not much damage would have been done. But things did not work out that way. By 1970, some 1,700 welfare workers had left local payrolls—but 4,600 had been added to the state's.[5] The state had already shown a free hand in setting benefit levels. By 1973, its "aid to families with dependent children" (the AFDC program, largest and most notorious of the welfare categories) provided the largest monthly check in the nation.[6] State administration of the program had so collapsed that the perennial problem of welfare fraud became an epidemic. When network television crews went to Boston to cover the latest scandal, they drove right past the gilded dome of the statehouse and headed for the Roxbury welfare office.

Welfare was not the sum of the commonwealth's spending trouble. In 1968, Governor Volpe left for Washington, not as vice president, but as secretary of Transportation. Lieutenant-Governor Francis W. Sargent moved upstairs to the governor's office. In 1970, Sargent won election to a full four-year term.

A Yankee patrician and darling of the liberal Democratic *Boston Globe,* Frank Sargent played the role in Massachusetts that John Lindsay played in New York City. During his administration, the state's direct general spending increased from 6.8% of state personal income to 9.6%.[7] This 40% surge in proportion of spending to income came *after* the initial impact of welfare assumption. Welfare costs continued to soar, but so did general state spending. Sargent preferred building to minding the budget. The state junior college system expanded greatly during his term, opening new vistas of education for the Bay State's students and new patterns of enrichment for its legislators. (The sophisticated advances in corruption that accompanied this construction, such as fee-splitting via politically connected architectural firms and dummy consulting contracts, were fully documented in 1981 in a famous investigation by the Special Commission on State Building Construction. Copies of the commission's final report are nearly unobtainable, however, because the legislature refused to appropriate money to print it.)

All this spending required more revenue. The tax burden mounted even more dramatically during this period than did the government outlays. From 103% of the national average in 1968, it sheered upward to 118% of the average in 1973. The commonwealth turned heavily to the broad-based income and sales taxes. In 1966, Volpe had introduced a "temporary" 3% sales tax, which was made permanent within two years. But the constant spending pressure had its greatest impact on the income tax. Nearly every year from 1967 to 1971, an emergency act increased the scope or rate of the income tax. By 1971, it had grown to a 5% levy on wages and salaries and 9% on so-called unearned income from interest dividends and capital gains.[8] The one saving grace was the importance the courts attached to that powerful constitutional adjective *proportional*. The tax remained at a flat rate. It could grow no faster than the growth in personal income, unless the legislature openly changed the rates. That way, at least taxpayers received notice that their burden was going up.

With legislated tax increases constantly before their eyes, taxpayers quickly discounted claims that the local burden would be reduced. In 1965, Volpe coupled his new sales tax proposal with controls supposedly designed to reduce local property tax rates. In 1967, he claimed that the tax increase for the welfare takeover would shift that burden from the property tax to the income tax. Yet by 1973 property taxes had increased from 5.8% of state personal income to 7.5%.[9] From the beginning of Volpe's second term to the end of the Sargent administration, the Massachusetts tax burden swelled from twenty-eighth among the states to fifth.

DISCOVERY AND COLLAPSE

The rapid increase of taxes under Bay State liberal Republicans bore a strong resemblance to the New York experience under Lindsay and Rockefeller; and like New York, Massachusetts ended in a crash. In 1974, the voters turned Governor Sargent out of office by a ten-point margin. The successful challenger was the articulate young attorney Michael Dukakis, well known as the moderator of the public-television

debate program "The Advocates." Dukakis was shy and in-
telligent, two qualities which may have combined to give the
impression of arrogance; a liberal reformer in many areas, he
preached a tight hand on the budget. National pundits began
to see him as an antipolitical "austerity Democrat," cut from
the same cloth as Jerry Brown, who was then beginning his
spectacular career in California. During the campaign, Dukakis had said that it was a "lead-pipe cinch" there would be
no new taxes in *his* administration. This statement later came
to haunt him.

Dukakis took office in the middle of the most severe
postwar recession to date, just as Sargent's fiscal sins were
demanding retribution. The new governor inherited a budget
deficit that mounted as the spring wore on to $450 million
out of $3.8 billion of total spending. Income tax collections
plummeted, and, for all of the tax increases of the preceding
four years, total tax revenue fell 1% *below* the previous year's.[10]

To cover the fiscal year 1975 deficit Dukakis floated a
$450-million bond issue, largest in the commonwealth's his-
tory and at the time the second largest ever presented to the
municipal bond market. Some minor tax increases were earmarked for the new debt, but Dukakis refused to present a
major tax program. A levy sufficient to replace the bond issue, he said, "would be a devastating blow to our efforts to
rebuild the Massachusetts economy and provide jobs and income for our people."[11]

But even before the bonds were sold, Dukakis plunged
head-on into a budget crisis of his own. His first full budget
fell deeper and deeper into red ink as tax receipts declined,
he and the legislature wrangled, and the new administration
kept finding unpaid bills literally tucked away in the backs
of desk drawers. The change in administration had triggered
the discovery phase of the fiscal crisis; more and more of the
true deficit emerged, until it finally totaled $700 million.

At the same time, Dukakis's "antipolitical" posturing offended powerful legislative leaders. As the governor and the
legislature squabbled, the General Court reserved its deepest
budget cut for the Massachusetts Arts Council, a pet project
of the governor's wife. The budget stalemate stretched four
months past the July 1 fiscal new year. Most of the delay,

claimed legislators, came from the governor's resistance to new taxes.[12]

As November came with no state spending plan, Boston bankers took a step that still inspires controversy. Richard D. Hill, chairman of the First National Bank of Boston, made a dramatic journey to the statehouse. He warned the governor and legislative leaders that without a signed budget, his bank could not market an upcoming rollover of Housing Authority notes. The statehouse listened to State Street, and a $3-billion budget was signed on November 8, 1975. Boston left-wingers still call this incident a political coup by bankers; municipal market observers, including *The Wall Street Journal,* praised it as the call to reason that the business community in New York had conspicuously failed to issue.[13] Intervention by the banks tempered the phase of collapse; the credit markets remained open (at a price) to Massachusetts, whereas they slammed shut on New York. Yet the tax package that resolved the crisis was the largest in the commonwealth's history. (The sales tax jumped by 40%, a 7½% surcharge was added to the personal income tax, and the corporate income tax went up 10%.)[14]

THE COST OF GOOD INTENTIONS

In explaining his fiscal solution to New York bankers in mid-November, Governor Dukakis lamented, "Unfortunately our good intentions didn't keep up with our revenues."[15] Too awful to contemplate was the possibility that years of good intentions had helped to undermine the commonwealth's revenue base. The cost of liberal Republican rule was starting to show in the state's economy as well as in the taxpayer's wallet. Massachusetts had been in a slow decline during the decade from 1957 to 1967, but in the early seventies, the bottom fell out. In the first ten-year period, Massachusetts ranked thirty-sixth in growth of real personal income; from 1967 to 1977, it ranked forty-fourth. In 1967, the commonwealth's per-capita personal income stood at 109% of the national average; by 1975, it had fallen to 104% of the average. During the late sixties, the Massachusetts work force held roughly constant at 3% of the national total; by 1976, it had deteriorated to a low point of 2.72%. The manufacturing work force fell even more, declining from 3.6% of the nation's in 1966 to 3.1% in 1976.[16] When political leaders took note of these figures, they explained them away as signs of the decay of the textile, leather, and defense industries, of the "maturing" of the state's economy, and perhaps of the unfair competition from the Southeast. Massachusetts, they said, had fallen victim to the energy crisis or the overall decline of the Frostbelt.

The undeniable fact, however, was that a pall of lethargy and demoralization had settled over the commonwealth. In a role the Bay Staters had played before and felt they might play for the foreseeable future, unemployed men waited at home for jobs, snapped at their families, and made plans to relocate to more abundant economies. By 1977, Massachusetts was losing population from the decade high point of 1973. At the end of the census decade, it had gained only eight-tenths of 1%, compared with a national population growth of 11.4%. Only three states and the District of Columbia had done worse.[17]

Because Rhode Island, Pennsylvania, and New York all lay in the Mid-Atlantic or New England region, the common notion arose that the entire Frostbelt was suffering a general decline from common and uncontrollable causes. This idea inspired the formation of coalitions of northeastern governors and members of Congress, whose paid staffs perpetuate the Sunbelt myth. There were exceptions, however. New Hampshire's population grew by 11% during the five intercensal years in which Massachusetts lost 1%. Economic developments at the regional level can negate much of a state's economic policy, but the example of New Hampshire (which greatly annoyed Massachusetts politicians) suggested strongly that the "Northeast decline" was not simply a regional phenomenon. Closer to home lay the supply-side explanation that the tax burden had risen at a debilitating rate. Even after the phase of discovery and near collapse, the momentum of the fiscal crisis caused tax burdens to continue to rise. By fiscal year 1979, Dukakis's last budget, the state was staggering under a tax burden 24% above the national average. Again, the rate of change, more than the absolute level, was the crucial factor. A diagnosis and a remedy were right at hand, for those who chose to take them.

THE SUPPLY-SIDE ALTERNATIVE

As Governor Dukakis imposed the phase of austerity required by the Massachusetts fiscal crisis, some in the commonwealth began to look for an alternative to the bipartisan liberalism of the past. Nothing teaches the importance of the tax factor better than passage through the ordeal of a tax-induced fiscal crisis. So it may not be surprising that Massachusetts, like those other liberal strongholds California and New York, suddenly became receptive to supply-side policies.

Further, Massachusetts had become one of the intellectual centers of the new doctrine. Many leaders of the supply-side movement had settled in and around Boston. Arthur Laffer had been associated with the local consulting firm of H. C. Wainwright Economics before a dispute with the other partners led him to establish his own company in California. Furthermore, in 1976, *The Boston Herald American* began publishing carefully reasoned statistics-buttressed columns by reclusive former businessman Warren Brookes. Like Nero Wolfe, Brookes seemed never to leave his house, but he became the main public voice of the Massachusetts supply-siders. Governors, legislators, and business leaders have known him only as a voice on the phone, yet his advice has frequently shaped their policies.[18]

Two extraordinary business lobbyists helped translate the intellectual ferment into public policy. They were Howard Foley and K. Heinz Muehlmann, friends and associates on a mid-seventies public-service organization called "Jobs for Massachusetts, Inc." The two became sophisticated and effective advocates of the supply-side solution. Foley, an engaging silver-haired Irishman, went on to help organize the Massachusetts High Technology Council, the very visible lobby for the state's aggressive electronics, computer, and semiconductor industries. Muehlmann, an athletic Austrian, went on to become chief economist for the Associated Industries of Massachusetts (AIM), representing the high-tech companies and more traditional manufacturers. In a previous incarnation at the Massachusetts Department of Commerce, Muehlmann had written a report on the decline of the state's manufacturing sector, mentioning in passing the "poor industrial climate predicated on high taxes." [19]

Two unexpected developments gave Foley and Muehlmann a golden opportunity to advance supply-side policies. One was the rapid emergence of a high-tech business constituency. The other was a political upset.

A devotion to learning derived from the Puritans and embedded in John Adams's 1780 constitution had long been paying handsome dividends for Massachusetts. Its educated, highly skilled citizenry had several times led the nation in developing new technologies. The Boston area, attracting graduates from Harvard and the Massachusetts Institute of Technology among others, has been a nursery of new companies. Route 128, the peripheral highway around its outer suburbs, has become synonymous with entrepreneurial new companies seeking commercial profit by applying the scientific and technological advances of the universities. The declining defense spending of the 1970s had momentarily depressed these industries, but by the end of the decade a revolution was under way in microcomputers. Massachusetts was poised to ride the boom, except for one problem—taxes.

High-tech companies were proliferating, drawing their names from seemingly endless permutations on *data, graphics,* and *computer.* They required relatively little capital for heavy equipment, since their main assets were skilled scientists and engineers. These technicians were highly paid, and intense national competition was driving their salaries even higher. Employers in a high-tax state like Massachusetts found themselves in an uncomfortable situation. Many upper-bracket recruits refused to settle in a state where the tax burden would eat up much of their income. Or, if recruits were willing to relocate to Boston, they demanded a salary premium that escalated business expenses and placed employers at a competitive disadvantage. High-tech companies had the choice of leaving the commonwealth to expand or lobbying for lower personal taxes.

This pressing business interest set the high-technology

companies apart from the less mobile downtown business establishment. The Boston financial community had a venture-capital stake in high technology, but the highly regulated banks and insurance companies also wanted to preserve their accommodation with state and city political leaders. Through their traditional "good government" group, the Massachusetts Taxpayers Foundation, downtown interests maintained a distinctly ambivalent attitude toward the High Tech Council lobbying. Their wariness was intensified by the clash between the personal style of the Brahmin Boston executives and that of the brash, aggressive entrepreneurs along Route 128.

The political upset came in the Democratic primary of 1978. In spite of the disastrous first ten months of the Dukakis administration, when people were calling the governor a "four-year lame duck," the incumbent seemed to have recovered politically. His budgets had stabilized, he was doing a creditable job of controlling state spending, and he seemed strong enough to face down his many enemies. One of these was Edward J. King, former executive director of Massport, the agency responsible for Boston's Logan Airport. King had been cashiered by the Massport board. He blamed Dukakis and took his revenge by running against him for governor. Some voters may have confused him with Tax Revolt leader Edward F. King, who ran unsuccessfully in the Republican primary. Others may have turned against Dukakis for his sneering remarks about Proposition 13, then at the crest of its national popularity; for his self-righteousness; or for the rising tax burden of the past four years. Whatever the cause, Dukakis held an eighteen-point lead in the polls on the morning of the September Primary Day, and found himself the loser by ten percentage points in the evening. It was one of the greatest of the many surprises in that Tax Revolt summer.

A conservative Irish Catholic, King was emphatically probusiness. During the campaign he promised to lower Bay State taxes by half a billion dollars. In the general election he demolished a liberal Republican whose main pitch was a crusade against alleged property tax evaders. The High Tech Council found King enthusiastically receptive when it approached him with a proposition. The council offered a "Social Contract" packaged by Howard Foley: its eighty-nine members would generate 60,000 new high-technology jobs in Massachusetts over the next four years if the state government reduced the overall tax burden by 13%. Quoting consultants' reports and statistical tables (including Chicago's Harris Bank's Genetski-Chin study on state growth and taxes), the proposal concluded: "If tax rates are reduced, jobs and hence tax revenues in Massachusetts will over time actually increase so that the Commonwealth will have greater financial resources to address its social problems and public responsibilities."[20] The Social Contract was an unalloyed version of the Laffer Curve. It was also a polite way of saying that without a change in the Massachusetts tax situation high-tech companies would be directing their expansion out of the state.

With this stimulation, the state government began a sincere if spotty effort to cut taxes. One of Governor King's first acts in 1979 was to impose a 4% two-year cap on local government spending increases, a legislative compromise of his original "zero-cap" proposal. The cap reduced local property taxes by $36 million (before assessment growth), a far cry from the governor's $500-million goal. Still, it was the first property tax reduction in memory. The General Court chipped in with another small but symbolic tax cut. The Senate wanted to cut personal income taxes, eighth-highest per capita in the nation, and the House wanted to cut property taxes, the nation's second-highest. To break the stalemate, both houses in June voted nearly unanimously to cut the capital gains tax by 60% over three years. This cut was suggested in a column by Warren Brookes, but, significantly, it was carried by the chairman of the Senate Ways and Means Committee, the young "austerity liberal" Chester G. Atkins.[21]

These two measures gave testimony to a striking change in the commonwealth's political atmosphere, but there were still doubts about its permanence. Even before the 4% cap expired in December 1980, property taxes surged once more as town meetings overrode the limits. With the capital gains cut, legislative leaders seemed disposed to wait and see how the budget worked out. Governor King himself ran afoul of the liberal opinion led by *The Boston Globe*. The paper's reporters destroyed a succession of bad appointments (one of whom had falsely claimed degrees from Oxford and Heidelberg). But the *Globe*'s most devastating blow came in an investigation of the governor's personal expense account. Its reporters discovered a $3,000 entry for lobster-crabmeat-salad lunches. The paper ran the story on the top of page one under a large picture of a lobster, and for the rest of the governor's term in all corners of the commonwealth, he was known primarily for his expensive dining.[22] By mid-1980, just as the economic benefits of tax reduction had begun to be visible, the political leadership seemed to lack the strength or inclination to push the tax-cut policy forward.

THE SUPPLY-SIDE RECOVERY

It is difficult to know what might have happened to the Massachusetts economy if matters had remained in the hands of the political leaders. The frugality of Governor Dukakis did manage to control the surge in the state's tax burden, so in absolute numbers it declined in his last year. Yet tax burdens around the country were dropping even more rapidly, so the *relative* tax burden continued to climb until 1979, when it peaked at a rate 124% higher than the national average. King's administration was the first to produce a substantial *relative* decline. In 1980, thanks to the property tax cap and general stringency, Massachusetts' relative tax burden had dropped to 119% of the national average.

The recovery from the fiscal crisis began under Dukakis, who is fond of citing the surge in the work force in the last two years of his first term. In raw number Massachusetts did gain an impressive 200,000 jobs from 1976 to 1978. But the rate of this growth was only slightly ahead of the national recovery, which was beginning to boom. Governor King's first two years added another 125,000 jobs. These are lower numbers than Dukakis could boast, to be sure, but the real story lies in the comparison with the national performance. The job growth tracked the national rate in King's first year, but in his second year, in which the commonwealth recorded its first substantial drop in *relative* tax burden, Massachusetts kicked ahead of the exhausted national economy. From 1979 to 1980, it gained nearly 50,000 jobs, nearly four times the national growth rate.

By 1980, the commonwealth was beginning to show some payoff from its attempt to control its tax burden. But this attempt soon faltered, and the gains were on the verge of dissipating. Voters were about to conclude that economic growth was too important to be left to the politicians. A tax revolt on the California model was about to break out. But no state is just like any other. The upheaval in Massachusetts came out of its unique context and had to work with its peculiar brand of initiative. A flashback to their origins is necessary to understand the involuted sequence that was about to unfold.

TOOLS OF THE TAX REVOLT

Popular movements can change Massachusetts law if they are really determined, but the tools at their disposal can be tricky to work with. Early protests had given the commonwealth the precedent of the popularly elected constitutional convention, and four had been convened in state history. More commonly, changes in the constitution follow provisions of the 1820 convention: the General Court adjourns and then reconvenes as a convention to consider proposed amendments and submit them to the electorate.

In 1917, leaders of the state's progressive movement forced the calling of a popular constitutional convention; high on their agenda was adoption of an initiative and a referendum. The measure gave the electorate two sets of tools, one to change the constitution, the other to write specific legislation. But the 1917–18 convention divided almost evenly between progressives and conservatives. By the time the I and R reached its final form it had undergone considerable metamorphosis. After long debate, the conservative head of a strike-plagued factory proposed a compromise restoring the central role of the General Court; progressives, frustrated by the nip-and-tuck, increasingly bitter parliamentary maneuvering, accepted it in hopes of getting something done.[23]

Under the peculiar Massachusetts system, constitutional

initiatives originate in petition drives and then go to the legislature for a cooling-off period. Both houses of the General Court sit in joint session as a constitutional convention. If the initiative receives at least one-fourth of the vote, it is held over for the next legislative session. If it again receives at least one-fourth of the vote, it goes on the general election ballot for a final decision. Amendments originated by the legislature require a majority vote of the joint session to appear on the ballot. Statutory initiatives (changing laws but not the constitution) do not have to run so long a gauntlet. If a proposal receives the required number of signatures, but the legislature rejects it, the petitioners can obtain more signatures, this time one-sixth of the original requirement. If they succeed, their proposal goes on the general ballot. In an unusual and, it turns out, very important provision, the legislature retains the power to revise petitions for constitutional amendments. This twist answers one objection against earlier forms of the initiative and referendum—that they could not be changed if defects were discovered—but it also can put constitutional petition drives at the mercy of the legislature.[24]

The Tax Revolt thus had the choice of a short route to write a statute or a long route to insert an amendment in the constitution. Each route had its pitfalls. The leaders of the revenue-and-spending-limit movement ultimately chose to take both.

THE CONTEXT OF THE TAX REVOLT

Massachusetts was now primed for a full-scale Tax Revolt. Public anger over state tax levels had been festering since at least the end of World War II. Property taxes were the chronic problem, as they grew from eighth highest in the nation in 1957 to second highest in 1978. Proposals for reform had been circulating for the past century. An initiative petition in 1936 proposed a constitutional amendment limiting real estate taxes to no more "than two and one-half per cent of the fair cash value." This early version of Proposition 2½ actually received enough signatures to qualify for the ballot, but the Supreme Judicial Court ruled it off on a technicality. Between

1932 and 1980, the legislature received another 125 local tax or spending-limit proposals—and passed none.[25]

Frustration with the property tax may have been mitigated by recognition that it was almost the sole source of revenue for local government. Voters could see a close connection between their payments and the services they received. Yet this connection began to erode in the sixties, when Beacon Hill presented new state taxes as a means to reduce the property tax. Instead, both property taxes and the new state taxes continued to grow. Angry taxpayers may also have been assuaged by the widespread but unconstitutional practice of underassessing homes and overassessing businesses. This practice violated the constitutional language requiring proportional and equal assessments. In 1974, the Supreme Judicial Court ordered the practice stopped. For the next six years, taxpayers watched anxiously as localities struggled to postpone the judgment day of full-value reasssessment. Cynical about legislative "tax relief" and worried by the threat of reassessment, taxpayers in the mid-seventies were also staggering under a rapid tax burden increase.

While this kindling was being laid, a handful of conservative friends organized a group in 1973 that hoped to light the match. Called "Citizens for Limited Taxation" (CLT), it entered its first major fight in 1976 when a liberal group put a measure on the ballot to allow a graduated income tax. The measure received overwhelming approval from the House and the Senate, but public opinion in the commonwealth rallied against it. Voters buried the graduated tax measure by a margin of nearly three to one, practically eliminating it as a political issue.

This triumph gave CLT ideas of bigger things. Under the leadership of businessman Edward F. King (no relation to the later governor) and executive secretary Donald Feder, the group began to circulate petitions for a constitutional state taxing limit. This proposal, the "King amendment," came to the legislature just as Proposition 13 hit California. With shock waves rumbling across the commonwealth, the legislators did not dare vote against the proposal. Instead, they altered it in committee, inserting such a gaping loophole that CLT disavowed the product.[26] At the same time, CLT joined several Republican legislators in preparing a statutory version of the 2½% property tax limit. But State Attorney General Francis X. Bellotti refused to certify the petitions, on what appeared to be a minor point.[27]

Public opinion was too aroused to let the issue die. An encouraging column by Warren Brookes drew 14,000 replies, more than half supporting a 2½% limit. CLT began again in 1979, drafting both a constitutional tax limit and a statutory 2½% lid on the property tax. About this time, Heinz Muehlmann and Howard Foley decided that the initiative and the referendum would best hold the state government to their Social Contract. Their lobbying groups, Associated Industries of Massachusetts and the Massachusetts High Technology Council, prepared their own versions of a statute and a constitutional limit.

With two overlapping measures in each category about to circulate in the field, the two lobbies worked out a coalition. AIM–High Tech offered funding and respectability; CLT offered manpower. Rather than dilute their energies on both measures, the business leaders dropped their statute and CLT gave up its constitutional amendment. They then took their joint package into the streets for an arduous campaign of collecting signatures. It proved more difficult to get signatures for two measures at once than for one, and the petitions barely made the deadline. Once in the legislature, their paths again diverged. Neither route was safe.[28]

CLT spent most of the winter defending its petition signatures from harassing challenges by the Massachusetts Teachers Association. When the statutory initiative now known as Proposition 2½ came up for the required vote in the legislature in early 1980, it received only five yeas. CLT returned to the streets again, to get the proposition on the ballot.

By this time, CLT had gone through several changes in leadership. Edward F. King had resigned in 1978 to run for governor, and was later appointed by Governor Edward J. King to the Boston Finance Commission in a rare public display of the governor's sense of humor. Donald Feder had moved out of state. The groundwork of Proposition 2½ was laid by Gregory Hyatt, who was forced by CLT's lack of funds to leave for a paying job. Although he retained a role as a consultant,

his secretary, Barbara Anderson, a former volunteer, was elevated in July 1980 to the post of executive director. Anderson, a tall, sun-burned redhead who had worked as a
swimming instructor, turned out to be the right person at the
right time. Her ability to dispense accurate detail in rapid-fire
delivery won her valuable credibility with the press. For many
weeks that rapport was CLT's main asset. With almost no
money, the group struggled along in two tiny offices, crammed
with files and clippings, located three floors above a pizza
parlor.

The measure that Anderson spelled out to visitors amid
the rising aroma of mozzarella cheese had expanded into a
budget-cutter's omnibus. It featured the property tax rate limit
of 2½% of "full and fair cash value," which had given the
measure its name. Those cities taxed above that limit were required to cut their levy 15% a year until they reached it. Once
at that limit, real estate revenues could grow by only 2½% a
year. This second limit was actually the more stringent. By
inflating assessed valuations in the base year, localities could
reduce the amount they had to cut, but the restriction on levy
growth thereafter allowed little manipulation, especially since
it made no allowance for population increase. Anderson explained that the second mechanism was the means by which
CLT ultimately hoped to reduce the property tax burden to
the national average of 1.9% of full value. The proposition also
cut the automobile excise tax by more than 60%, to $25 per
thousand, a measure the CLT had picked up from the state
automobile dealers' association.

The nonfinancial provisions of 2½ were almost as important. Designed to give officials the tools to cope with
reductions, Proposition 2½ allowed localities to ignore state-
mandated programs that carried insufficient funding. It abolished the fiscal autonomy of local school boards. It outlawed
binding arbitration for labor disputes with police and fire
fighters. And it prohibited counties, authorities, and special
districts from increasing their assessments on localities by more
than 4% a year.[29]

In the meantime, AIM–High Tech was taking the longer
road, trying to get its constitutional amendment into a convention session. This succinct nine-section measure was de-

signed, basically, to limit the Massachusetts tax burden to the average tax burden of all fifty states. It also established a constitutional property tax limit of 2½%.

CLT had entrusted that side of the struggle entirely to its business allies. After all, it was their amendment, and Foley and Muehlmann were the inside men on Beacon Hill. Relying on customary channels, AIM–High Tech had reached an understanding with the legislative leaders. If an acceptable alternative emerged from the General Court, AIM–High Tech would not fund CLT's Proposition 2½ campaign.

Foley and Muehlmann were sure they had the fifty votes to move the amendment along. But the legislature backed off. It convened in convention session and passed only minor measures. Nothing happened on the taxing limit. The convention went through postponement after postponement, and finally prorogued on July 3 without even debating the AIM–High Tech measure. The public outcry was furious, and nowhere more so than among the High Tech Council.[30] A barrage of angry editorials, letters, and visits from business lobbyists persuaded Governor King to reconvene the convention in September. Even while he issued his proclamation, the High Tech Council was having serious second thoughts about its hands-off policy toward Proposition 2½.

Over the summer, while CLT floundered, public-employee unions had been organizing a coalition to fight Proposition 2½. The anti-2½ effort was weakened by internal bickering but, at the time, it looked formidable. Two years earlier, during the general concern about reassessment, a similar coalition had passed a constitutional amendment for real estate tax classification. (This measure allowed the assessment of business property at a rate higher than that for homes.) The public-employee coalition had money. Anti-2½ media spots were already running. High Tech strategies worried that Proposition 2½ could lose. On September 2, High Tech Council President Alexander V. d'Arbeloff wrote to his board of directors: "a defeat for '2½' in November would surely convince most legislators that tax limitation is dead as a political issue and that it is safe to resume 'spending as usual.' A defeat, coupled with defeat of our constitutional amendment, would also stop the High Tech Council's tax-limitation program dead in its tracks. . . ." On

September 8, the board voted to "commence planning" for support of 2½. Foley took the vote as a mandate to hire campaign consultants and start polling. By the end of September, while AIM stayed neutral, the High Tech Council was publicly supporting CLT.[31]

This move put the High Tech Council at serious risk of losing its statehouse clout just when its other main priority, the constitutional total tax limit, had suddenly come to life. Legislative leaders unexpectedly produced a compromise version of the amendment and then accused the High Tech Council of breaking faith with its original agreement not to back 2½. The timing of this compromise was suspect, but there it was. AIM rushed to embrace it, while High Tech accepted the compromise without enthusiasm.

The new measure came from State Representative Gerald M. Cohen, chairman of the House Taxation Committee. It replaced the nine sections of the original amendment with an involuted twenty-two-section text more than twice as long. High Tech and AIM were pleased that it seemed to maintain the original purpose of lowering the Massachusetts tax burden to the level of its main competitors. In mid-September, the Cohen amendment passed the reconvened constitutional convention (the joint legislative session) by a vote of 172 to 9.

But the compromise was clearly a ploy to distract the two groups from support for 2½. AIM took the bait, avoiding any involvement in the 2½ campaign and even, through its chairman, Walter Muther, expressing mild disapproval. High Tech, however, was not deflected. Its leaders felt their original understanding with the legislature had been abrogated by the fast shuffle in the June session, and with a clear conscience they poured money into the 2½ campaign.

CLT leaders credit the sudden infusion of High Tech money with saving their measure. The High Tech polls showed that just two weeks before the November election Proposition 2½ had lost its early lead and was trailing 39% to 50%. As soon as favorable ads appeared on radio and TV, it bounced back into the lead.

On November 4, 1980, the rest of the nation returned a landslide vote for Ronald Reagan. In Massachusetts, the issue was Proposition 2½, and it passed, 59% to 41%. The consultants to CLT and High Tech claim that in spite of the fluctuations in the polls, voters never wavered in their fundamental desire to cut property taxes and "send the politicians a message." The opponents had tried to warn about service cuts without sounding as hysterical as the anti-Proposition-13 campaign in California. They apparently misjudged their tone, since, according to CLT consultants, "they actually did worse among people who have seen their ads than among those who did not." The great advantage of the CLT campaign, summed up one consultant, was that "we were selling the joy of sex and our opponent was selling the fear of pregnancy. Once the average voter learned about birth control, the election was never in doubt."[32]

THE DISAPPEARING INITIATIVE

As the euphoria over Proposition 2½ wore off, and the time for the second vote on the Cohen amendment drew near, in 1982, the grass-roots people began to wonder what their business allies had done. With some caretaking revision of Proposition 2½ successfully completed over the Christmas holiday of 1981, CLT Executive Director Barbara Anderson began to study the Cohen amendment, and found she could not understand it. Her suspicion grew that the fine print of Cohen might actually repeal Proposition 2½. As a constitutional amendment, it unquestionably would take precedence over her statutory initiative.

In April 1982, CLT broke openly with its business allies and urged a no vote on the amendment. Business leaders turned on Anderson with raised hackles. The plot thickened when Senate President William Bulger requested a Supreme Judicial Court advisory opinion on the Cohen amendment. Bulger asked if the measure was still a version of the initiative petition, which would require only fifty votes to go on the ballot, or whether it should be considered an amendment originated by the legislature, which would require 101 votes. The court said it was the latter. In the summer's constitutional session the Cohen amendment received only seventy-eight votes and died unlamented. The episode, Anderson observed, merely confirmed the lesson she drew from the King amendment fiasco in 1978: "You never turn your back on the legislative leadership. Never, never trust them."[33]

The High Tech Council and AIM, who had rejoined ranks on the constitutional front, took the issue back to court, trying to save the Cohen amendment. When they failed, CLT raised this interesting question: What had happened to the original initiative submitted by the voters? If the Cohen amendment was a legislative substitute, what had happened to the nine-section taxpayers' amendment for which it had been substituted? The mystery lingered until December 6, 1983, when the Massachusetts Supreme Judicial Court dismissed the CLT suit. In a decision that left CLT puzzled, the court said that a yes vote on the substitute Cohen amendment was the same thing as a no vote on the original initiative.

Rather than get bogged down in mystical legalisms, both the business and grass-roots leaderships seemed inclined to extricate themselves from the morass and start over again. Even though the Proposition 2½ statute seemed secure, the political climate was changing. In the September 1982 Democratic primary former governor Dukakis took his revenge on Governor King. The voters, it seemed, were less impressed by King's efforts on tax cuts than by vague and never-substantiated charges of lower-level corruption and, of course, by all those expense-account seafood lunches. Dukakis rode a lobster back to office, winning the primary against the incumbent by the same margin with which King had ushered him out in 1978. The Tax Revolt had lost an erratic but well-meaning and occasionally very helpful ally. The most urgent task for the Anderson-Foley-Muehlmann axis was to restore the high tech–business–grass-roots coalition that had produced such a revolution in the political culture of Massachusetts Bay.

THE MEANING OF PROPOSITION 2½

That Proposition 2½ shattered the old ways of the commonwealth seemed undeniable. The 59%-to-41% vote was a fact of life too massive to be ignored. Furthermore, like Proposition 13, this vote defied traditional analysis. It cut across ethnic and political lines. The most immediately obvious pattern was geographical. Opposition was centered in Cape Cod, western Massachusetts, and college towns. The common denominator for the first two regions seemed to be that their property taxes were already below the 2½% limit and their population was growing. Hence they felt they already had control over their spending but wanted to preserve flexibility to cope with expanding demands of their infrastructure. The hostility of the college towns may reflect the influence of the liberal academic atmosphere, or, in the case of the Northampton-Amherst area, the popularity of a state senator who had vehemently opposed the measure.

But Boston and those of its suburbs that expected the most serious disruption from Proposition 2½ supported it the most strongly. The voters there simply wanted their property taxes cut. This sentiment was not so irrational as to prevent local officials from sharing it. Mayor Kevin White of Boston remained neutral in the campaign, and Mayor Joel Pressman of Chelsea, the most impacted city of all, became one of 2½'s most articulate supporters.

Pollsters, as usual the prisoners of their technique, have thus far failed to elucidate the mystery of the measure's support. Their studies have concentrated on debunking the conclusion that the 2½ supporters wanted lower levels of services and more limited government. The surveys seem to say that supporters of the measure supported it because they thought it would work, and opponents opposed it because they thought it would not. That is, opponents expected cuts in their favorite services; supporters did not. Financing for the tax cuts, said the supporters, would come from reduced waste and corruption in local *and* state government.[34]

The emphasis on cutting state government is not as irrational as some analysts have maintained, given that Proposition 2½ affected only local taxes. The majority of the first-year tax losses, it turned out, were covered by increased state aid, squeezed out of the state budget by a politically cowed General Court. One of the most interesting poll results, however, is the overwhelming agreement with the statement that Proposition 2½ would attract more business and industry to Massachusetts. Almost three-quarters of all respondents and 87.5% of supporters said it would. This response, one of the highest recorded in this particular survey, indicated public support for the principle of the High Tech Council's Social Contract.

By the third anniversary of Proposition 2½, this measure had been amply vindicated. Only a few localities were in danger of serious fiscal disruption, and in the most publicized of these cases, Boston, Proposition 2½ was responsible for only about a third of the problem.[35] A hostile academic study group, the Impact: 2½ Project, concluded that "neither its costs nor its benefits have been as great as predicted."[36] Localities had adapted, as CLT's Barbara Anderson predicted they would, by inflating the full-value property assessments for the base year. They turned to new user fees, deferred maintenance (as in California), and even found more room for budget discipline than they had imagined. Opponents of the measure, such as the Massachusetts Tax Foundation, now happily admitted that it seemed to be working out after all.

But the most spectacular success, still ignored by the academic critics, came in the measure's supply-side economic impact. Massachusetts, which less than a decade ago had been one of the sickest state economies, was now the healthiest. The commonwealth had reversed its long-run decline in relative personal income, employment, and even population. It was one of the few states in which the manufacturing work force had grown in the past decade (Texas was first). The most forceful statement of this turnaround came from Warren Brookes in a November 1983 symposium on the question "Is supply-side economics dead?"

> For nearly 26 months, once impoverished Massachusetts has been enjoying the lowest unemployment of any major state. In July, when the national unemployment rate dropped from 10.0 percent to 9.5 percent, Massachusetts dropped from 6.9 percent to 5.9 percent, nearly 40 percent below the nation. In August, that rate dipped again to 5.9 percent. The nearest major state is Texas with 7.8 percent unemployment.
>
> In fact, Massachusetts is now employing almost 64 percent of its adult (over 16) population. Not only is this an all-time record for the state, it is a record for the nation. The highest

figure ever reached by the U.S. was 59.8 percent, and the best Japan has ever done is something like 55 percent.

To put it bluntly, Massachusetts may well be the best performing state economy in the world.[37]

THE TAX REVOLT CONTINUES

Vindicated by the economy, the Massachusetts tax rebels have broadened their activity. They fired a warning shot at Governor Dukakis in the spring of 1983 when he sponsored a measure to weaken Proposition 2½. The bill, introduced primarily to help out Boston, would have made it easier for eleven of the most hard-pressed communities (left unnamed) to override the 2½ limits. CLT and the High Tech Council escalated the eleven-community bill into a referendum on Proposition 2½. Shaken by an outpouring of public abuse, rank-and-file legislators rebelled against leadership discipline. The chastened administration and the previously omnipotent House and Senate leaders quietly abandoned the bill.[38]

Citizens for Limited Taxation split in two directions. A group of its grass-roots activists decided to push on with another tax-limit initiative, this time to repeal the 7½% income tax surcharge imposed at the peak of the 1975 fiscal crisis. But CLT Executive Director Anderson was still fuming at the General Court's fast shuffle on the Cohen amendment. Further constitutional initiatives would be futile, she argued, until the legislature was brought in line. So she brought the CLT into an unlikely "good-government" coalition including Common Cause, reform Democrats, and the Republican Party to draft an initiative to curb the power of the legislative leaders.

The initiative proposed to rewrite the legislature's rules of procedure, which gave the Senate president and House speaker such dictatorial powers.[39] It might seem a far stretch for a tax movement, but across the country Tax Revolt veterans, including California's Paul Gann and Michigan's Richard Headlee, were turning their attention to the workings of their representative bodies. The Tax Revolt itself would have been unnecessary, they reasoned, if a gap had not somehow opened up between the voting taxpayer and the government they elected. In focusing on that gap, these initiatives raised anew the question asked by John Locke: What happens if a legislature begins to act on behalf of its own interests and not those of its electors? From California to Massachusetts, the tax protest had come full circle to the issue of representation. The Tax Revolt and its intellectual counterpart, the supply-side movement, had given fresh life to the political and economic theories of the eighteenth century. Its proponents had joined ranks with their ancestors who toppled a government on the slogan "No Taxation without Representation."

V

Implications

13

Revealing the Secrets of the Tax Revolt

From Massachusetts to Michigan, from Texas to California, each excursion to the states has been like a geologic field trip. The face of an upthrust escarpment and a deeply cut canyon wall show their history in the strata, here a layer of shell-studded clay that was once a sea bed, there an obliterating flow of lava, the eroding hand of wind or a river, perhaps the grinding of a glacier. Some of these cuts may show strata from the original cooling of the earth. The states also show layer on layer of history. Fiscal and legal theories are embedded in their constitutions, successive strata of institutions laid down by changing political climates. In some states the layers from the earliest levels lie broad and close to the surface. In others, they are buried under dozens of yards of overburden.

Descriptions of these individual patterns have so far avoided the grand picture. But with eight samples, the landscape begins to make sense. In tracing each stratum from one state to another, a picture emerges of the world of each period. The primordial landscapes begin to yield their secrets.

1. THE ECONOMIC SECRETS

Much of this prehistory was purged from the public mind by the economic catastrophe of the 1930s. The successful supply-side policy of Andrew Mellon, Warren Harding, and Calvin Coolidge became inextricably entangled with the memory of the Great Depression. Historical apologists for the New Deal obscured the laissez-faire roots of the Jefferson-Jackson tradition. These origins could not be recovered until the free market economists had cleared themselves of the charge that they had somehow caused the Depression.

This achievement was the triumph of Milton Friedman, who showed convincingly that it was the disastrous contraction of the money supply in 1929–30, not the hangover of the probusiness 1920s, that transformed a conventional downturn in the business cycle into something close to the collapse of capitalism. The public seemed inclined to hear this appeal because of the poor performance of the alternatives. Keynesian self-confidence had collapsed, almost to the day that Richard Nixon publicly embraced the doctrine. New Deal economics was mired in stagflation, the demoralizing combination of slow growth and high inflation. The Carter Administration offered no way out but constantly increasing taxation.

In this context, people were willing to heed the economic experience of the states, ranging from fiscal crisis to vigorous growth. The common elements of this experience decipher to a magic formula for economic growth. It can be stated in six words: *falling tax burdens and rising technologies.*

Massachusetts begins and ends the cycle of state histories because it exemplifies this formula so well. The entrepreneurial spirit is encouraged by the prospect of keeping more of its reward for itself, and it has a natural affinity for new technology. An advance in the application of science promises high profit as well as risk; development of a new product has the best potential for creating vast new markets overnight. We are living through a revolution in microcomputers and telecommunications that must parallel in scale the original Industrial Revolution. In Massachusetts, this revolution has gone hand in hand with the supply-side revival. The scientific centers around Boston have spawned hundreds of new high-technology enterprises; high-tech businessmen, not coincidentally, provide intellectual and financial leadership for what may be the most sophisticated of the state tax revolts.

There are states with low (but not necessarily falling) tax burdens that have been declining because they ignored the new technologies. The industrial Midwest put such faith in its traditional manufactures that it devoted relatively little of its resources to research and development. Small suppliers lived at the sufferance of the major corporations, and scientific talent left for other regions. With the recession, high technology became the focus of the region's hopes. There are sufficient opportunities to apply microcomputers and robotics to the traditional industries to allow the states of the Midwest to make the transition to a new level of sophistication. Yet the transition will probably be hampered by the rising tax burdens forced on them by their regional depression. Their temptation will undoubtedly be to support high technology through targeted business tax breaks. This corporate-welfare policy is more likely than ever now that supply-side-oriented candidates for governor in Ohio and Michigan have been defeated by progrowth Democrats heavily backed by traditional unions. (Let no one be surprised by the notion that labor might support the corporate-welfare state. Both corporate executive and labor leader have a stake in the established big-industry economy, and both are unnerved by the fluid, high-risk, and largely nonunionized world of the entrepreneur.)

Such a strategy would ignore another major lesson of the Tax Revolt. *Forget the special breaks for business. Lower the personal tax burden.* This sounds like a paradoxical prescription for economic growth, but it works. It is also a major source of confusion in discussing the tax factor. All those studies that found tax policy to be irrelevant to economic growth invariably focused on business taxation. The conclusion that industrial inducement packages are a waste of money was most likely accurate. They are, basically, another form of special-interest payoff, subject to all the abuses of that solution. But even the surveys of plant relocation cannot disregard personal taxation. Business has proved adept at passing its tax burden on to the consumer, but employees have learned the same game. Business taxes wind up in the product price, but personal taxes wind up in wage demands. Nelson Rockefeller thought he was helping the New York economy when he loaded his tax increases on the individual and bragged that he had not raised business taxes during his term as governor. The results speak for themselves.

In reducing personal taxation, do you concentrate the cuts in the top brackets or lower the rates across the board? It may not matter which. The first approach favors high incomes, in the belief that entrepreneurs in that bracket are the ones who will create new jobs. The second approach should benefit all wage earners, reduce pressure for higher payrolls, and lower business costs all around. Similarly, one cannot say whether the reductions should come in one swoop, as in Proposition 13 and Proposition 2½, or be phased in over several years, as in the New York compromise between Governor Carey and his legislature. Tax cuts are so difficult to obtain, no one is inclined to quibble about the timing.

What is crucial, however, is the *rate of change*. The burden should continue to decline, or at least not rise again, in the foreseeable future. The wary taxpayer watches distrustfully to see which way things are going before he commits himself. Roller-coaster tax burdens, as in Reagan's years as California governor, do less good than a slow, steady, and predictable decline.

A final conclusion, perhaps the most important, is: *tax cuts are not everything*. In the current bloated state of government, to be sure, they have certainly been better than the alternatives. Almost every dollar taken from a state bent on income redistribution can probably be spent more beneficially in the private sector. But some government services do advance the well-being of the civic body. The most indispensable of these is not police or fire protection, but education. The magic formula does have two parts. A well-educated work force is indispensable to growing technologies. The heirs of the Puritans have received enormous benefit from their insistence on public education, just as the South suffered grievously from reacting against it. Along the 2,000-mile belt of New England emigration, descendants of the Puritans were willing to tax themselves to provide free public education. The same spirit that drafted the "Old Deluder Satan Law" in 1647 brought ambitious plans for school systems to the wilderness of Ohio and Michigan. This spirit moved south during Reconstruction to give that region its first massive experience with tax-supported schools. The worst mistake the Bourbon South made in its reaction against the high cost of "carpetbag" government was to destroy this budding educational system. Ignorance crippled the work force and retarded the technological development of the region. In spite of its low-tax policy, the South did not recover from this blunder for more than half a century.

2. THE THEORETICAL SECRETS

Beyond the economic advice, the study of the tax revolts uncovered a rich vein of political theory. Current historians have rejected the claim made gravely in the 1920s and 1930s that the Founders had no real interest in political ideas. The drafters of the Declaration of Independence and the U.S. Constitution obviously knew their theory well. It just happened to be a theory that Progressive historians did not like. Still, it is surprising to see how fundamental John Locke has been to American fiscal policy. State tax laws of the nineteenth century came almost directly from his version of the social contract, with an occasional detour through Adam Smith and Jean Baptiste Say.

This background to the "uniform rule" and the general property tax is so esoteric that it counts as a major secret of the Tax Revolt. Yet the issue comes down to the eternal question of man and state. Is the citizen obliged to the state for his upbringing, or is the state obliged to the citizen for its existence? Locke came down squarely on the latter, modern, side of the question when he argued that the state is an instrument for preserving individual gain. If the purpose of the state is to protect the property accumulated by individual labor, then the conclusion follows rapidly that taxation ought to be limited. The principal means adopted by the nineteenth century was the uniform rule, requiring taxation to apply at a single rate in proportion to a person's holding of the total property protected by the state. The basic result, as Lockean philosophy evolved into American ideology, was to rule out a fiscal system designed to redistribute wealth from the rich to the poor. Courts interpreted the "uniform" and "proportional" requirements as prohibitions on a progressive tax system.

This ban on redistribution delves into the deeper questions of Locke's philosophy. Of the thinkers who helped the seeds of Locke's psychology sprout into the economics of Adam Smith, the one who spoke most favorably of a progressive tax was Montesquieu, the writer who, above all of Rousseau's predecessors, showed the most understanding and sympathy for the ancients. Significantly, Montesquieu referred to a tax levied by ancient Athens. Those with the highest income paid proportionately the most; those with the lowest income paid nothing. "It was judged that each had an equal physical necessity, that that physical necessity ought not to be taxed; that the useful came next, and that it ought to be taxed, but less than the superfluous; and that the great size of the tax on the superfluous impeded superfluity."[1] This tax, in short, was based on the natural demands of the human body, as defined presumably by some objective measure. It was not proportional to men's goods, but it was proportional to their needs. The sharpest break from the Lockean tradition was not, however, that this tax protected the essentials of life, but that it condemned the "superfluities." This type of standard vanishes by the time one reaches Adam Smith. The standard of justice is no longer nature, but a natural right based on a contract. Each person should pay taxes in proportion to the extent of the protection he receives from the state. His relative position should be neither enhanced nor diminished. A state based on the social contract has much less authority to regulate human appetites than one that takes its references from an external standard of nature.

Although Locke became the dominant American tradition, he was not the only one. At the very beginning his influence was resisted by the Puritan commonwealth. The Puritan opposition lost the struggle, but the tension between Lockean greed and religious communalism continues to give the American soul a hidden depth. It emerges in the issue of education, a constant counterpoint to the theme of limited taxation. The descendants of the Puritans who stood ready to tax themselves for a school system have been saying that there should be more to life than the pursuit of property. This tradition almost self-consciously tries to correct the inadequacies of Locke as the foundation of a political order. A striking example comes in John Adams's schizophrenic Massachusetts constitution of 1780. Its fiscal provisions quoted the Lockean tradition, but other provisions originated by the great republican Adams recognized the need for something more. His favorite paragraph, which he wrote "from the heart . . . rather than the head," laughing to himself "at the Oddity of it" and later saying, "I would not now exchange for a Sceptre, and wish may be engraved on my Tomb Stone," was the somewhat eccentrically titled "The Encouragement of Literature, etc."[2] As it still stands in Part the Second, Chapter V, Section II of the Massachusetts constitution, it reads:

> Wisdom and knowledge, as well as virtue, diffused generally among the body of the people, being necessary for the preservation of their rights and liberties; and as these depend on spreading the opportunities and advantages of education in the various parts of the country, and among the different orders of the people, it shall be the duty of legislatures and magistrates in all future periods of this Commonwealth, to cherish the interests of literature and the sciences, and all seminaries of them; especially the university at Cambridge, public schools and grammar schools in the towns; to encourage private societies and public institutions, rewards and immunities, for the promotion of agriculture, arts, sciences, commerce, trades, manufacture and a natural history of the country; to countenance and inculcate the principles of humanity and general benevolence, public and private charity, industry and frugality, honesty and punctuality in their dealings; sincerity, good humor, and all social affections, and generous sentiments among the people.[3]

Adams appealed to government to humanize and soften the overly harsh and self-centered disposition of his people. "General benevolence," "good humor, and all social affections" are traits sorely lacking in the Lockean scheme of things, yet they are essential to a successful political community. Even today the promotion of "generous sentiments" seems beyond the scope of American government.

The strangeness of Adams's concerns to the modern ear illustrates the nineteenth-century triumph of the laissez-faire spirit. Through the 1830s, one could even trace a parallel development of post-Locke and post-Smith economics and American political platforms. As the tradition that was nurtured from Locke to Smith flowered in the classical economists, the American Jacksonians grasped at the new ideas to further their fight against government-supported monopolies. Writers like Jean Baptiste Say completed the implications of Locke's basic principles, just as Jacksonian laissez-faire advocates completed what they were convinced was the program of the American Revolution. The threat to the republic came from the moneyed interest and its ability to entrench itself behind government intervention. The solution was more reliance on free enterprise and the free market.

3. THE HISTORICAL SECRETS

The three waves of the Tax Revolt have already been described. Left unsaid was the extent to which each grappled with a central problem and failed to solve it. The failures of each wave gave rise to the new solutions of the next one, solutions that produced yet another problem.

The first wave revolved around the new invention of representation. The state needs to levy taxation to carry out its job of protecting property. But this demand must be controlled by the principle of consent of the majority, "giving it either by themselves or their representatives chosen by them."[4] But what constituted representation? The English Parliament told the colonists that they had their say through the doctrine of "virtual representation," in which the members of Parliament in London defended the interests of the entire empire. The colonials retorted that they wanted representatives who shared their own burdens and knew their situation at first hand. After launching a revolution on the slogan "No Taxation without Representation," the colonials struggled to define what constituted fair representation. The French historian Elie Halévy sees a straight progression from the rejection of "virtual representation" to the principle of one man, one vote.[5] The first chapter on Massachusetts, in which Locke came to America, illustrates the evolution of this logic.

Yet Locke himself warned of a flaw in representation. He admitted that a legislature could come to have interests separate from the citizen body. He left little guide for dealing with this possibility, except to say that a senate which started to confiscate property would be illegitimate. Future generations had to cope with intermediate cases, in which legislatures imposed tax levels that the citizen body thought to be too high.

The second wave met this problem head on, in the form of public debt. Public borrowing had become a dangerous loophole in representative government. By issuing debt, a legislature could amass a heavy financial burden for future generations without triggering the electoral reaction that would inevitably have followed an equally large tax increase. The principle of consent through representation had proven inadequate; so the Jacksonian Democrats in New York returned to the idea of direct majority consent, expressed in the referendum requirement for bond issues. The subsequent history of the state showed both the wisdom and the futility of this approach.

The debt backed by the "full faith and credit" of the people remained sound and was issued at moderate levels. But the governing elite turned to loophole after loophole, generating a huge volume of off-budget debt, unaccounted for and scarcely understood by the public. The tools of government credit have become so flexible that they can be controlled only by a very rigid fiscal structure, and such a structure becomes almost too brittle to endure. This dilemma threatens to frustrate all of the major constitutional fiscal limits yet divised.

The ultimate futility of static constitutional controls has given rise to the third and most powerful wave of the Tax Revolt, the turn to direct democracy. The initiative and the referendum have allowed the voter to bypass representative consent altogether. In voting directly on initiative proposals, the citizen body can directly express its consent to taxation or withdraw it from a level it deems excessive. Unresponsive legislatures have aroused a reaction threatening to repudiate representation altogether. But direct democracy has had a checkered past. Tocqueville gives ample warning of the despotic tendency of unrestrained popular passion. Historically, the first victim of this tyranny has been private property. Ominously, the same passions in California that produced Proposition 13 subsequently unleashed a spate of rent-control ordinances.

This warning notwithstanding, the dangers of direct democracy are not yet overwhelming and may never be. In the circumstances of constantly rising taxation and special-interest domination of the representatives, the Tax Revolt has done much more good than harm. Its contribution has gone well beyond fiscal policy.

Someone once warned that the United States in the 1940s and 1950s was being subverted by the philosophy of the countries it had conquered, that its Lockean origins were being submerged by the overbearing ideologies of nineteenth-century Europe. Supply-side theory and the Tax Revolt have joined to melt away this frigid weight. As the thaw progresses, the outlines of an earlier America have emerged with renewed freshness. This country was a great experiment, unique in world history, based upon a political economy that, for all its oversights, created one of the most humane and tolerant political orders known to man. The supply-side movement will repeat this experiment.

Like any product of man, the supply-side approach will have its blind spots. Perhaps it will submerge the Puritan alternative too decisively, weakening the tension that gives the American character its resilience. In time, this movement could congeal into another *idéologie froide,* freezing American politics in its brittle grasp. Then some other set of ideas will melt the new glacier, revealing yet another set of possibilities in an alternative landscape. This geologic succession may be inevitable in time, but it is not likely in our generation. The climate is young. The landscape is fresh. The new world buds with infinite possibility.

NOTES

1. The Supply Side and the States

1. U.S. Office of Management and Budget, *The Budget of The United States Government* (Washington: GPO, various years), Table 19, "Federal Finances and the Gross National Product."
2. U.S. Department of Commerce, Bureau of the Census, *Statistical Abstract of the United States, 1982–83* (Washington: GPO, 1983), p. 432, Table 714.
3. Arthur B. Laffer and David Ranson, *Inflation, Taxes and Equity Values: An Economic Study* (Boston: H. C. Wainwright & Co. Economics, 20 September 1979), p. 13.
4. Advisory Commission on Intergovernmental Relations (ACIR), *Significant Features of Fiscal Federalism*, 1980–81 edition (Washington, D.C., December 1981), Report M-132, p. 37, Table 24. The federal tax burden figures in this table are not compatible with the budget series cited above because the ACIR omits Social Security taxes.
5. *Stat. Abs.*, p. 250, Table 421.
6. *Stat. Abs.*, p. 282, Table 475.
7. Jean Baptiste Say, *Le Traité d'économie politique*, II:175, quoted in *History of Economic Doctrines*, by Charles Gide and Charles Rist, trans. R. Richards (Boston: D. C. Heath and Company, n.d.), pp. 115–16. The major modern restatement of Say's outlook appears in W. H. Hutt, *A Rehabilitation of Say's Law* (Athens, OH: Ohio University Press, 1974). Academic interest in Say seems to have revived about a decade ago, just as the supply-side movement began to coalesce. See the ubiquitous Thomas Sowell's *Say's Law: An Historical Analysis* (Princeton: Princeton University Press, 1972).
8. Charles W. Kadlec and Arthur B. Laffer, *An Analysis of Fiscal Policy and Economic Growth in Massachusetts* (Rolling Hills Estates, CA: A. B. Laffer Associates, 16 April 1981), pp. 11–29. It is unfair to many lesser-known supply-siders to single out Professor Laffer as the main proponent of this approach, yet he has paid for the attention by also taking the brunt of the abuse.
9. Charles W. Kadlec and Arthur B. Laffer, *The Jarvis-Gann Tax Cut Proposal: An Application of the Laffer Curve* (Boston: H. C. Wainwright & Co., 27 June 1978).
10. Joseph J. Minarik, "A Wrinkle in the Laffer Curve," *Tax Notes* (Arlington, VA: Tax Analysts and Advocates, 9 October 1978), p. 421.
11. Robert J. Genetski and Young D. Chin, *The Impact of State and Local Taxes on Economic Growth* (Chicago: Harris Economic Research Office Service, Harris Trust and Savings Bank, 3 November 1978). Genetski encountered a problem with "outriders," states that fell so far off the line that they distorted statistical analysis. The reason for these was

clear enough. Some state economies depended so much on a single commodity, such as oil in Alaska, copper in Arizona, coal in West Virginia, that their income was largely determined by world markets. Additionally, all state tax burdens were not equally burdensome. States with a high severance tax would show on the high side of the chart, even though the economic damage was limited compared to an equally high burden composed of a personal income tax. Because the identity of the outriders changed with changing external conditions, Genetski now says that his original attempt to draw a regression line giving a hard-and-fast ratio for this relationship was the wrong approach. But the basic relationship between tax burden and growth remained extremely valid, as he found in his updated and expanded version, *The Impact of State and Local Taxes on Economic Growth: 1963–1980*, by Robert J. Genetski and Lynn Ludlow (Chicago: Harris Economic Research Office Service, Harris Trust and Savings Bank, 17 December 1982).

12. Genetski and Chin, p. 2.
13. Victor A. Canto and Robert I. Webb, "Persistent Growth Rate Differentials Among States in a National Economy with Factor Mobility" (Los Angeles: February 1981, mimeographed). A version of this paper was delivered at the Conference on Taxation of Income from Capital held at the University of Southern California's Center for the Study of Private Enterprise in Los Angeles on January 22, 1981.
14. See charts on pp. 349–354.

State and Local Tax Revenue in Relation to State Personal Income, Selected Years, 1953–1981

1. Tax Revenue as a Percentage of Personal Income.

State and region[a]	1981	1980	1978	1975	1965	1953	Annual Average Percent Increase or Decrease (−) 1978–81	1965–78	1953–65
United States[a]	11.29	11.57	12.75	12.29	10.45	7.58	−4.0	1.5	2.7
New England	11.82	12.35	13.49	12.79	9.97	7.90	−4.3	2.4	2.0
Connecticut	10.20	10.55	11.64	10.82	9.08	6.06	−4.3	1.9	3.4
Maine	11.89	12.50	13.29	12.59	10.98	8.95	−3.6	1.5	1.7
Massachusetts	13.28	13.90	15.11	14.20	10.21	8.77	−4.2	3.1	1.3
New Hampshire	8.68	9.20	10.51	10.75	9.51	8.28	−6.2	0.8	1.2
Rhode Island	11.53	11.89	12.52	11.94	10.19	7.02	−2.7	1.6	3.2
Vermont	12.58	12.73	14.48	15.46	12.72	9.62	−4.6	1.0	2.4
Mideast	13.11	13.68	14.50	13.94	10.54	7.46	−3.3	2.5	2.9
Delaware	10.84	11.60	12.28	11.66	8.98	4.21	−4.1	2.4	6.5
Dist. of Col.	14.69	13.57	13.63	10.67	8.09	5.90	2.5	4.1	2.7
Maryland	11.24	12.03	13.02	12.26	9.34	6.33	−4.8	2.6	3.3
New Jersey	11.21	11.72	12.42	11.59	9.07	6.59	−3.4	2.4	2.7
New York	15.84	16.34	17.19	16.65	11.87	8.79	−2.7	2.9	2.5
Pennsylvania	10.92	11.56	12.25	11.68	9.47	6.17	−3.8	2.0	3.6
Great Lakes	10.59	10.66	11.60	11.35	9.73	6.78	−3.0	1.4	3.1
Illinois	11.05	11.25	11.80	11.73	8.89	6.37	−2.2	2.2	2.8
Indiana	9.23	8.82	10.29	11.15	10.24	7.08	−3.6	0.0	3.1
Michigan	11.57	11.50	12.67	11.66	10.67	7.31	−3.0	1.3	3.2
Ohio	9.20	9.35	9.93	9.69	8.64	5.87	−2.5	1.1	3.3
Wisconsin	12.24	12.47	14.16	13.83	12.55	8.91	−4.7	0.9	2.9

State and Local Tax Revenue in Relation to State Personal Income, Selected Years, 1953–1981
1. Tax Revenue as a Percentage of Personal Income. (Continued)

State and region	1981	1980	1978	1975	1965	1953	Annual Average Percent Increase or Decrease (−)		
							1978–81	1965–78	1953–65
Plains	10.45	10.80	11.77	11.73	10.83	8.25	−3.9	0.6	2.3
Iowa	11.08	11.07	11.62	12.14	11.63	9.22	−1.6	0.0	2.0
Kansas	10.03	10.00	11.29	10.86	11.70	8.71	−3.9	−0.3	2.5
Minnesota	12.00	12.74	14.16	13.94	12.72	9.38	−5.4	0.8	2.6
Missouri	8.77	9.30	9.94	10.35	8.74	6.14	−4.1	1.0	3.0
Nebraska	10.37	11.06	12.15	10.96	9.34	7.69	−5.1	2.0	1.6
North Dakota	11.24	10.22	11.63	10.95	11.77	11.27	−1.1	−0.1	0.4
South Dakota	10.85	10.59	11.48	11.60	12.60	10.79	−1.9	−0.7	1.3
Southeast	10.12	10.31	11.01	10.70	10.04	7.86	−2.8	0.7	2.1
Alabama	9.85	9.64	10.21	9.94	9.74	7.00	−1.2	0.4	2.8
Arkansas	9.32	9.87	10.18	9.90	9.77	7.92	−2.9	0.3	1.8
Florida	9.34	9.75	10.64	9.94	10.53	9.20	−4.3	0.1	1.1
Georgia	10.55	10.78	11.26	10.79	9.96	7.67	−2.1	0.9	2.2
Kentucky	10.32	10.39	11.26	11.32	9.62	6.47	−2.9	1.2	3.4
Louisiana	11.54	11.60	12.25	12.99	12.05	10.43	−2.0	0.1	1.2
Mississippi	10.78	10.86	11.77	11.84	11.85	9.37	−2.9	−0.1	2.0
North Carolina	10.29	10.62	10.93	10.58	9.97	8.25	−2.0	0.7	1.6
South Carolina	10.66	10.68	11.09	10.46	9.67	8.61	−1.3	1.1	1.0
Tennessee	9.56	9.37	10.74	10.04	9.71	7.32	−3.8	0.8	2.4
Virginia	10.05	10.25	11.05	10.67	8.55	6.09	−3.1	2.0	2.9
West Virginia	10.71	11.21	11.29	12.27	9.85	6.81	−1.7	1.1	3.1

State and region	1981	1980	1978	1975	1965	1953	Annual Average Percent Increase or Decrease (−)		
							1978–81	1965–78	1953–65
Southwest	10.56	10.36	11.15	11.06	10.16	7.34	−1.8	0.7	2.7
Arizona	11.49	13.27	14.28	13.26	12.15	8.50	−7.0	1.3	3.0
New Mexico	14.02	12.18	13.26	13.54	12.16	8.66	1.9	0.7	2.9
Oklahoma	11.05	10.16	10.66	10.53	10.44	9.07	1.2	0.2	1.2
Texas	10.04	9.75	10.55	10.56	9.60	6.68	−1.6	0.7	3.1
Rocky Mountain	11.25	11.90	12.91	11.78	11.61	8.60	−4.5	0.8	2.5
Colorado	10.20	11.31	12.55	11.61	11.40	8.93	−6.7	0.7	2.1
Idaho	10.01	10.39	12.00	11.02	12.14	9.00	−5.9	−0.1	2.5
Montana	12.87	13.03	13.76	12.57	11.78	7.62	−2.2	1.2	3.7
Utah	11.89	12.47	12.66	11.63	11.78	8.44	−2.1	0.6	2.8
Wyoming	15.53	14.76	15.95	13.43	11.28	8.73	−0.9	2.7	2.2
Far West[b]	11.30	11.91	15.13	14.07	11.79	8.34	−9.3	1.9	2.9
California	11.49	12.17	15.80	14.59	11.98	8.41	−10.1	2.2	3.0
Nevada	10.26	10.52	13.10	13.23	10.69	7.93	−7.8	1.6	2.5
Oregon	11.85	11.41	12.80	12.13	10.94	8.24	−2.5	1.2	2.4
Washington	10.04	10.88	12.73	12.06	11.18	8.07	−7.6	1.0	2.8
Alaska[c]	50.02	36.78	17.49	21.45	8.11	5.03[d]	42.0	6.1	4.1
Hawaii	13.75	14.75	14.02	14.44	11.72	8.23[d]	−0.7	1.4	3.0

Sources: ACIR staff computations from data tape for FY 1981 supplied by U.S. Bureau of the Census. U.S. Bureau of the Census, *Governmental Finances in 1982*. See also *Significant Features of Fiscal Federalism* (prior years).

[a] Excluding the District of Columbia.

[b] Excluding Alaska and Hawaii.

[c] Because most of Alaska's revenue is derived from the taxation of oil production and the income of oil companies, the recent figures for the state of Alaska greatly overstate the actual tax burden borne by the residents of Alaska.

[d] Estimated, based on the U.S. average change between 1953 and 1957 (the earliest year readily available).

State and Local Tax Revenue in Relation to State Personal Income, Selected Years, 1953–1981

2. State Percentage Related to U.S. Average (U.S. = 100.0)

State and region	1981	1980	1979	1978	1975	1965	1953
United States[a]	100.0	100.0	100.0	100.0	100.0	100.0	100.0
New England	104.7	106.7	110.0	105.8	104.1	95.4	104.2
Connecticut	90.3	91.2	94.9	91.3	88.0	86.9	79.9
Maine	105.3	108.0	106.0	104.2	102.4	105.1	118.1
Massachusetts	117.6	120.1	123.3	118.5	115.5	97.7	115.7
New Hampshire	76.9	79.5	83.1	82.4	87.5	91.0	109.2
Rhode Island	102.1	102.8	107.8	98.2	97.2	97.5	92.6
Vermont	111.5	110.0	115.7	113.6	125.8	121.7	126.9
Mideast	116.1	118.2	116.5	113.7	113.4	100.9	98.4
Delaware	96.0	100.3	100.8	96.3	94.9	85.9	55.5
Dist. of Col.	130.1	117.3	109.0	106.9	86.8	77.4	77.8
Maryland	99.6	104.0	104.9	102.1	99.8	89.4	83.5
New Jersey	99.3	101.3	100.6	97.4	94.3	86.8	86.9
New York	140.4	141.2	137.6	134.8	135.5	113.6	116.0
Pennsylvania	96.8	99.9	98.8	96.1	95.0	90.6	81.4
Great Lakes	93.8	92.1	93.3	91.0	92.4	93.1	89.4
Illinois	97.9	97.2	93.6	92.5	95.4	85.1	84.0
Indiana	81.8	76.2	81.2	80.7	90.7	98.0	93.4
Michigan	102.5	99.4	103.1	99.4	94.9	102.1	96.4
Ohio	81.5	80.8	81.2	77.9	78.8	82.7	77.4
Wisconsin	108.5	107.8	113.5	111.1	112.5	120.1	117.5

State and region	1981	1980	1979	1978	1975	1965	1953
Plains	92.6	93.3	96.1	92.3	95.4	103.6	108.8
Iowa	98.2	95.7	92.3	91.1	98.8	111.3	121.6
Kansas	88.9	86.4	93.4	88.5	88.4	112.0	114.9
Minnesota	106.3	110.1	116.7	111.1	113.4	121.7	123.7
Missouri	77.7	80.4	82.6	78.0	84.2	83.6	81.0
Nebraska	91.9	95.6	98.8	95.3	89.2	89.4	101.5
North Dakota	99.6	88.3	88.5	91.2	89.1	112.6	148.7
South Dakota	96.2	91.5	89.6	90.0	94.4	120.6	142.3
Southeast	89.7	89.1	90.3	86.4	87.1	96.1	103.7
Alabama	87.3	83.3	83.0	80.1	80.9	93.2	92.3
Arkansas	82.5	85.3	82.5	79.8	80.6	93.5	104.5
Florida	82.8	84.3	87.3	83.5	80.9	100.8	121.4
Georgia	93.5	93.2	93.7	88.3	87.8	95.3	101.2
Kentucky	91.5	89.8	93.6	88.3	92.1	92.1	85.4
Louisiana	102.3	100.3	101.2	96.1	105.7	115.3	137.6
Mississippi	95.5	93.9	96.7	92.3	96.3	113.4	123.6
North Carolina	91.2	91.8	90.4	85.7	86.1	95.4	108.8
South Carolina	94.5	92.3	90.3	87.0	85.1	92.5	113.6
Tennessee	84.7	81.0	84.6	84.2	81.7	92.9	96.6
Virginia	89.0	88.6	89.1	86.7	86.8	81.8	80.3
West Virginia	94.9	96.9	98.0	88.5	99.8	94.3	89.8
Southwest	93.6	89.5	89.1	87.5	90.0	97.2	96.8
Arizona	101.8	114.7	117.8	112.0	107.9	116.3	112.1
New Mexico	124.2	105.3	107.4	104.0	110.2	116.4	114.2
Oklahoma	97.9	87.8	88.1	83.6	85.7	99.9	119.7
Texas	89.0	84.3	82.9	82.7	85.9	91.9	88.1

State and Local Tax Revenue in Relation to State Personal Income, Selected Years, 1953–1981
2. State Percentage Related to U.S. Average (U.S. = 100.0) (Continued)

State and region	1981	1980	1979	1978	1975	1965	1953
Rocky Mountain	99.7	102.9	105.9	101.3	95.9	111.1	113.5
Colorado	90.3	97.8	103.5	98.4	94.5	109.1	117.8
Idaho	88.7	89.8	93.8	94.1	89.7	116.2	118.7
Montana	114.0	112.6	111.0	107.9	102.3	112.7	100.5
Utah	105.3	107.8	106.6	99.3	94.6	112.7	111.3
Wyoming	137.6	127.6	132.1	125.1	109.3	107.9	115.2
Far West [b]	100.1	102.9	100.6	118.7	114.5	112.8	110.0
California	101.8	105.2	100.3	123.9	118.7	114.6	110.9
Nevada	90.9	90.9	105.5	102.7	107.6	102.3	104.6
Oregon	105.0	98.6	101.5	100.4	98.7	104.7	108.7
Washington	89.0	94.0	100.9	99.8	98.1	107.0	106.5
Alaska [c]	443.1	317.9	194.6	137.2	101.3	77.6	66.4
Hawaii	121.8	127.5	121.7	110.0	117.5	112.2	108.6

Sources: ACIR staff computations; see previous table. Data tape for FY 1981 supplied by U.S. Bureau of the Census. For prior years see U.S. Bureau of the Census, Governmental Finances in 1982. See also Significant Features of Fiscal Federalism (prior years).

[a] Excluding the District of Columbia.

[b] Excluding Alaska and Hawaii.

[c] Because most of Alaska's revenue is derived from the taxation of oil production and the income of oil companies, the recent figures for the state of Alaska greatly overstate the actual tax burden borne by the residents of Alaska.

15. John Ross and John Shannon, *Measuring the Fiscal "Blood Pressure" of the States—1964–1975* (Washington, D.C.: ACIR, February 1977), Report M-111.

16. Will S. Myers, *Regional Growth: Interstate Tax Competition* (Washington, D.C.: ACIR, March 1981), Report A-76, p. 55. This report otherwise had the meritorious purpose of discouraging federal intervention to counteract state tax differences.

17. David S. Dahl and Samuel H. Gane, "Impact of State and Local Taxes on Economic Growth," Working Paper No. 129 (Minneapolis: Research Department, Federal Reserve Bank of Minneapolis, 19 May 1979, mimeographed).

18. See especially the often-quoted article "Studies of State-Local Influences on Location of Industry," by John F. Due, *National Tax Journal* 14 (1961) 2:163–73. Professor Due downplayed surveys that did show that the tax factor had weight because, he wrote, "the anti-tax attitude of many business men conditions them to stress the tax factor." This "somewhat irrational reaction," he complained, presented "a major obstacle to reform of tax structures" (pp. 165, 169, 171).

19. David Hume, *Essays Moral, Political and Literary*, vol. 3 of *The Philosophical Works*, ed. Thomas Hill Green and Thomas Hodge Grose (Aalen: Scientia Verlag, 1964), p. 359.

20. ACIR, *Significant Features*, p. 7.

2. The New-Old Landscape of the Tax Revolt

1. Thucydides, *The Peloponnesian War* 1.76, trans. Thomas Hobbes (Ann Arbor: University of Michigan Press, 1959), p. 44.

2. Ibn Khaldun, *The Muqaddimah*, 3 vols., trans. and ed. Franz Rosenthal, The Bollingen Series (Princeton: Princeton University Press, 1967), 2:89. See also Muhsin Mahdi, *Ibn Khaldun's Philosophy of History* (Chicago: University of Chicago Press, 1964), pp. 17–62; Suphan Andic, "A Fourteenth Century Sociology of Public Finance," *Public Finance/Finances Publiques* 20 (1965): 22–44. This quotation was first introduced into the supply-side debate by a letter-writer to *The Wall Street Journal* (Stanley Ungar, of Valley Stream, N.Y.) in the July 31, 1978, issue. It was reprinted in that paper's editorial page "Notable & Quotable" feature (29 September 1978) while the first Kemp-Roth debate was raging in Congress. Participants say it helped win some support for the bill. It subsequently appeared in most of the popularized supply-side books. But the moment of glory for this well-traveled quote came when President Reagan trotted it out for an astonished press conference on October 1, 1981. No other statement of medieval Arabic philosophy has had quite the same impact on American politics.

3. John Locke, *The Second Treatise on Government* (Indianapolis: Bobbs-Merrill, 1952), p. 17.

4. Ibid., pp. 25–26.

5. Ibid., p. 79.
6. Ibid., p. 80.
7. Ibid., p. 81.
8. Charles Louis de Secondat, Baron de Montesquieu, *The Spirit of the Laws*, trans. Thomas Nugent (New York: Hafner Publishing Co., 1949), p. 208. I have occasionally modified Nugent's archaic language.
9. Ibid., p. 207.
10. Ibid., p. 210.
11. Ibid., pp. 216–17. Montesquieu drew on this characteristic of tax structure to explain a phenomenon attributed by a large portion of mankind to divine intervention. "It was this excess of taxes[d] that occasioned the prodigious facility with which the Mahommedans carried on their conquests. Instead of a continual series of extortions devised by the subtle avarice of the Greek emperors, the people were subjected to a simple tribute which was paid and collected with ease. Thus they were far happier in obeying a barbarous nation than a corrupt government, in which they suffered every inconvenience of lost liberty, with all the horror of present slavery. . . . [Footnote] d. See in history the greatness, the oddity, and even the folly of those taxes. Anastasius invented a tax for breathing. 'Ut quisque pro haustu aeris penderet.'"
12. David Hume, *Essays Moral, Political and Literary*, vol. 3 of *The Philosophical Works*, ed. Thomas Hill Green and Thomas Hodge Grose, (Aalen: Scientia Verlag, 1964), p. 358. Long after completing the following discussion, I became aware of an excellent paper covering much of the same ground, beginning with the mid-eighteenth-century Physiocrats and ending with the post-Depression turn to Keynes. For further illustration of the venerable roots of the supply-side movement, see Robert E. Keleher and William P. Orzechowski, "Supply Side Effects of Fiscal Policy: Some Historical Perspectives," Working Paper Series (Atlanta: Federal Reserve Bank of Atlanta, August 1980, mimeographed). A shortened version of this paper appeared under the title "Supply-Side Fiscal Policy: An Historical Analysis of a Rejuvenated Idea" in Robert H. Fink, ed., *Supply-Side Economics: A Critical Appraisal* (Frederick, MD: University Publishers of America, 1982), pp. 121–59.
13. Hume, *A Treatise of Human Nature* (Oxford: Clarendon Press, 1978), p. 493.
14. Ibid., p. 492.
15. Ibid., p. xvi.
16. Elie Halévy, *The Growth of Philosophic Radicalism*, trans. Mary Morris (Boston: Beacon Press, 1955), p. 9.
17. Adam Smith, *The Wealth of Nations* (New York: The Modern Library, Random House, 1937), p. 816.
18. Ibid., p. 817.
19. Commonwealth of Massachusetts, Constitution of 1780, Part the First, Article I.
20. State of New Hampshire, Constitution of 1783, Part First, Article XII.

21. "Publius," *The Federalist*, ed. Jacob E. Cooke (Middletown, CT: Wesleyan University Press, 1961), pp. 221–22.

22. Quoted in Dumas Malone, *Jefferson the President: First Term, 1801–1805* (Boston: Little, Brown and Company, 1970), p. 100.

23. Thomas Jefferson, "First Annual Message," December 8, 1801, in *A Compilation of the Messages and Papers of the Presidents, 1789–1897*, vol. 1, ed. James D. Richardson (Washington, D.C.: GPO, 1896), pp. 328–29.

24. Malone, *Jefferson*, p. 106.

25. Jefferson, "Second Annual Message," December 15, 1802, in *Compilation*, p. 344.

26. Jefferson thought *The Spirit of the Laws* to be a dangerous book because it lent its great prestige in America to Federalist positions. He sponsored the American publication of several critiques, possibly translating one himself, to undercut Montesquieu's authority. See Gilbert Chinard, *Jefferson et les Idéologues*, The Johns Hopkins Studies in Romance Literatures and Languages, Extra Volume I (Baltimore, MD: The Johns Hopkins Press, 1925), pp. 31–96.

27. Joseph L. Blau, ed., *Social Theories of Jacksonian Democracy*, The American Heritage Series (New York: Liberal Arts Press, 1954), p. 9.

28. B. U. Ratchford, *American State Debts* (New York: AMS Press, 1966), pp. 77–86; Reginald C. McGrane, *Foreign Bondholders and American State Debts* (New York: Macmillan Co., 1935), pp. 1–21.

29. Ratchford, *Debts*, pp. 121–22.

30. James Bryce, *The American Commonwealth*, 2 vols. (New York: Macmillan and Co., 1891), 1:491–96.

31. Thomas M. Cooley, *A Treatise on the Constitutional Limitations Which Rest Upon the Legislative Power of the States of the American Union* (Boston: Little, Brown & Company, 1868; reprint, New York: Da Capo Press, 1972), p. 495.

32. Bryce, *Commonwealth*, 1:493.

33. Ibid.

34. Roscoe Martin, *The People's Party in Texas* (Austin: University of Texas Press, 1970), p. 52.

35. Cooley, *Limitations*, p. 479.

36. *Providence Bank v. Billings*, 4 Peters 514 (1830). Quoted in Cooley, *Limitations*, p. 480.

37. Clyde E. Jacobs, *Law Writers and the Courts* (Berkeley and Los Angeles: University of California Press, 1954), pp. 98–159. Jacobs assumes that this prohibition comes out of a probusiness ideology, even though business would have the most to lose from being denied access to this easy source of financing.

3. Phase One. Massachusetts: Where It All Began

1. Edmund S. Morgan, *The Puritan Dilemma: The Story of John Winthrop* (Boston: Little, Brown and Company, 1958), pp. 107–10.

2. George F. Willison, *Saints and Strangers* (New York: Time, 1964), pp. 135–36, 347.
3. Morgan, *Puritan Dilemma*, p. 67.
4. Bernard Bailyn, *The New England Merchants in the Seventeenth Century* (Cambridge: Harvard University Press, 1982), pp. 41–44.
5. Ibid., p. 44.
6. Morgan, *Puritan Dilemma*, pp. 93–95.
7. Henry Steele Commager, ed., *Documents of American History* (New York: Appleton-Century-Crofts, 1949), pp. 15–16.
8. Morgan, *Puritan Dilemma*, pp. 84–92.
9. Ibid., pp. 108–10.
10. Quoted in Nathan Matthews, *The Proposed Amendment to the State Constitution; Shall the word "proportional" be eliminated from the Clause which restricts the Power of the Legislature in the Matter of Taxation to the Imposition of "proportional and reasonable Assessments, Rates, and Taxes"? Argument for the Remonstrants* (Boston, November 1909), p. 25.
11. Ibid., pp. 25–26.
12. Ibid., p. 20, footnote.
13. Ibid., p. 27.
14. T. H. Breen, *Puritans and Adventurers: Change and Persistence in Early America* (New York: Oxford University Press, 1980), p. 88.
15. Matthews, *Proposed Amendment*, pp. 29–30.
16. Ibid., p. 29.
17. Alexis de Tocqueville, *Democracy in America*, 2 vols. (Garden City, NY: Anchor Books, 1969), 1:44–45.
18. Wayne M. Holmes, "A Study of the Legal Aspects of Fiscal Independence of School Committees in Massachusetts" (Ph.D. dissertation, University of Connecticut, 1960), p. 14.
19. Albert Bushnell Hart, ed., *Commonwealth History of Massachusetts* (New York: State History Company, 1927), vol. 1, chap. 19, "Expansion and King Philip's War," by John Gould Curtis, pp. 552–53. See also Alden T. Vaughan, *New England Frontier: Puritans and Indians, 1620–75* (New York: W. W. Norton and Co., 1979). pp. 309–22.
20. Breen, *Puritans*, p. 88.
21. Ibid., p. 89.
22. Matthews, *Proposed Amendment*, p. 39.
23. Hart, *Commonwealth*, 1:583–94.
24. Perry Miller, *The New England Mind: From Colony to Province* (Boston: Beacon Press, 1961), pp. 155–57, 292–301.
25. Breen, *Puritans*, pp. 102–04; Miller, *New England Mind*, pp. 160–62.
26. Miller, *New England Mind*, p. 170.
27. Ibid.
28. David Hume, *Essays Moral, Political and Literary* (London: Oxford University Press, 1963), pp. 452–75. Cf. Elie Halévy, *The Growth of Philosophic Radicalism*, trans. Mary Morris (Boston: Beacon Press, 1955), pp. 9–11, 43–47.

29. Perry Miller, *Jonathan Edwards* (Cleveland: Meridien Books, 1959), pp. 52–65; idem, *New England Mind*, p. 432.

30. Political theory gets short shrift in so many areas these days that one should be grateful, perhaps, for the revival of interest in the ideas and pamphlets of the period before independence.

   The best-known example of this interest is the writing of Bernard Bailyn. See *The Ideological Origins of the American Revolution* (Cambridge: Belknap Press of Harvard University Press, 1967) and *The Origins of American Politics* (New York: Alfred A. Knopf, 1968). Yet Bailyn loses sight of Locke in his welter of pamphleteers. He attempts to re-create a coherent body of thought by accumulating quotations from ephemeral tracts. Pamphlets (and editorials) can reflect a comprehensive intellectual system, but they cannot produce one. The medium of public polemic allows neither the time nor the space to lay out the sustained theorizing that can create a new mental horizon. The real use of this medium is in popularizing the thoughts of more powerful minds.

   In neglecting the centrality of Locke, Bailyn reveals a touching political prejudice. It is no accident that he seriously underestimates the issue of taxation. See *Ideological Origins*, p. 162, quoting Charles McIlwain's dismissal of the question as "a mere incident," and *Origins of American Politics*, p. 159, defending the stamp tax.

   It is also no accident that Bailyn has written the most sympathetic biography ever published in the United States of Thomas Hutchinson, royal governor of Massachusetts during the stamp tax controversy. See *The Ordeal of Thomas Hutchinson* (Cambridge: Belknap Press of Harvard University Press, 1974).

   After two centuries of scholarship and innumerable fads of interpretation, the most plausible statement of the issue leading to the American Revolution remains what the colonists said it was—No Taxation without Representation.

31. See, especially, Edmund S. and Helen M. Morgan, *The Stamp Act Crisis* (New York: Collier Books, 1963), p. 52.

32. William Edward Hartpole Lecky, *A History of England in the Eighteenth Century* (New York: D. Appleton & Co., 1891), pp. 72–73.

33. Robert A. Becker, *Revolution, Reform and the Politics of American Taxation, 1763–1783* (Baton Rouge: Louisiana State University Press, 1980), p. 34; Morgan, *Stamp Act*, pp. 36–37.

34. Morgan, *Stamp Act*, pp. 41–42, n. 16; p. 58.

35. Ibid., pp. 52, 79.

36. Thomas Whately, *The Regulation Lately Made Concerning the Colonies and the Taxes Imposed on Them, Considered* (London, 1765), in Edmund S. Morgan, ed., *Prologue to Revolution: Sources and Documents on the Stamp Act Crisis, 1764–1766* (Chapel Hill: University of North Carolina Press, 1959), p. 18.

37. Montesquieu, *The Spirit of the Laws*, trans. Thomas Nugent (New York: Hafner Publishing Co., 1949), Book XIII, chap. 9. Bailyn, curiously, endorses this view. He writes, "The stamp tax was not a crushing tax; it

was generally considered to be an innocuous and judicious form of taxation" (*Origins of American Politics*, p. 159).

38. Lecky, *History of England*, p. 127; Edmund S. Morgan, *The Birth of the Republic, 1763–89* (Chicago: University of Chicago Press, 1977), p. 33.
39. Morgan, *Prologue to Revolution*, p. 10. Notice the echo of David Hume's passage on tax incidence quoted in chapter 1.
40. "Virginia Memorial to the House of Lords," in ibid., p. 15.
41. Hart, *Commonwealth*, vol. 2, chap. 7, "Finance and Paper Money," by Davis Rich Dewey, pp. 192–220; William B. Weeden, *Economic and Social History of New England, 1620–1789*, vol. 2 (Boston: Houghton Mifflin and Co., 1890), pp. 473–92.
42. Becker, *Revolution*, pp. 39–40.
43. Whately, *Regulation*, p. 19.
44. Ibid.
45. "The Massachusetts Resolves, October 29, 1765," in Morgan, ed., *Prologue to Revolution*, p. 56.
46. *The Adams Papers: Papers of John Adams*, vol. 1, ed. Robert J. Taylor (Cambridge: Belknap Press of Harvard University Press, 1977), pp. 42–43.
47. *The Adams Papers: Diary and Autobiography of John Adams*, 4 vols., ed. L. H. Butterfield (New York: Athenaeum, 1964), 3:351.
48. Ibid., p. 352.
49. As the Congress debated, delegates began to ask Adams what plan of government he would recommend, and these questions threw him back on his previous learning. "I had read Harrington, Sydney, Hobbs, Nedham and Lock, but with very little Application to any particular Views: till these debates in Congress and these Interrogations in public and private, turned my thoughts to those Researches, which produced the Thoughts on Government, the Constitution of Massachusetts, and at length the Defence of the Constitutions of the United States and the Discourses on Davila" (ibid., pp. 358–59).
50. "Petition of Pittsfield, May, 1776," in Robert J. Taylor, ed., *Massachusetts, Colony to Commonwealth: Documents on the Formation of Its Constitution, 1775–1780* (Chapel Hill: University of North Carolina Press, 1961), p. 28.
51. (William Whiting), "Address to the Inhabitants of Berkshire" (1778), in ibid., pp. 101–05. Whiting observed that in Locke's doctrine, a state of society intervened between the anarchic state of nature and the forming of any particular constitution. Independence, he said, annihilated the constitution of the Bay Colony but it left the state of society intact. "Are you members of the political society of the state of Massachusetts-Bay? Or are you not?" he pointedly asked the Berkshire men. For them to deny this membership and yet insist on a say in framing the constitution, he continued, "is really no less preposterous than it would be for the savages of the wilderness to run together, and take upon them, in hideous yells, to frame, and enact, a constitution and form of government for the state of Massachusetts-Bay" (p. 103).

52. Commonwealth of Massachusetts, Constitution of 1780, Part the First, Article III; Part the Second, Chapter 5, Section 2.

53. *The Adams Papers: Adams Family Correspondence*, 4 vols., ed. L. H. Butterfield and Marc Friedlaender (Cambridge: Belknap Press of Harvard University Press, 1973), 3:226, n. 3.

54. Commonwealth of Massachusetts, Constitution of 1780, Part the First (Declaration of Rights), Article X.

55. Oscar and Mary Handlin, eds., *The Popular Sources of Political Authority: Documents on the Massachusetts Constitution of 1780* (Cambridge: Belknap Press of Harvard University Press, 1966), pp. 40–53.

56. O.P.Q., "To the Electors of Representatives for the Colony of Massachusetts Bay, May 18, 1776," in Handlin, *Popular Sources*, pp. 79–87. Also in Taylor, *Massachusetts, Colony to Commonwealth*, pp. 29–35.

57. O.P.Q., "To Electors".

58. "Essex County Convention, Ipswich, April 25, 26, 1776," in Handlin, *Popular Sources*, pp. 73–77; Taylor, *Massachusetts, Colony to Commonwealth*, pp. 38–39.

59. Handlin, *Popular Sources*, p. 74.

60. See, *inter alia*, returns from Greenwich, Ludlow, Monson, Pelham, Southwick, and Sunderland, in ibid., pp. 561, 566–67, 590–91, 603–04, 610–11.

61. Stephen E. Patterson, *Political Parties in Revolutionary Massachusetts* (Madison: University of Wisconsin Press, 1973), pp. 125–52; Handlin, *Popular Sources*, passim.

62. Hart, *Commonwealth*, vol. 3, chap. 12, "Economic and Commercial Conditions," by Davis Rich Dewey, pp. 345–48.

63. Ibid., p. 352.

64. Ibid., p. 351. In April 1781, Alexander Hamilton wrote to Robert Morris that Massachusetts "is one of the states where taxation has been carried furthest." In fiscal year 1781, the legislature borrowed heavily to cover a 30% deficit because taxes had been so heavy the preceding year that it felt unable to impose more. Alexander Hamilton to Robert Morris, April 1781, in *The Papers of Robert Morris, 1781–1784* (Pittsburgh: University of Pittsburgh Press, 1973), pp. 37–38, n. 7 on p. 59.

65. George Richards Minot, *History of the Insurrections in Massachusetts in 1786 and of the Rebellion Consequent Thereon* (reprint of 1788 first edition, New York: Da Capo Press, 1971), pp. 20–46.

66. Ibid., pp. 34–37; C. O. Parmenter, *History of Pelham, Mass. from 1738 to 1898* (Amherst: Press of Carpenter and Morehouse, 1898), pp. 367–69; John Fiske, *The Critical Period of American History* (Boston: Houghton, Mifflin, and Company, 1888), pp. 177–83.

67. Minot, *Insurrections*, pp. 9–11, 20–46.

68. On the other hand, one can give an alternative ethnic explanation of Shays' Rebellion. It is suggestive that Daniel Shays' hometown of Pelham was settled by Scotch-Irish immigrants in 1738. The Scotch Presbyterians came to America for different motives than did the seventeenth-century Puritans. Brought to Ireland to displace Catholics in Ulster, they

became dissatisfied with their conditions of land tenure and their forced tithing to the established Episcopal church. The final straw was the surge in British taxation during the Napoleonic Wars. On their arrival in the New World, they were more interested in economic and religious freedom than in the effort to found a religious commonwealth. See Parmenter, *Pelham*, pp. 7–13; George Bancroft, *History of the United States of America* (Port Washington, NY: Kennikat Press, 1967), pp. 27–29.

The bitter memories of these tax refugees lasted for generations. The grandson of an émigré from County Tyrone wrote in his autobiography: "The hardships experienced by my grandfather's family and my own parents became so thoroughly engrained in my nature, when a child, that I have always felt a strong opposition . . . to all measures rendering an increase of taxes necessary. It was the universal complaint which drove our people from their homes." The writer was Thomas Mellon, of Poverty Point, Pennsylvania, father of Andrew Mellon, secretary of the Treasury under Presidents Harding and Coolidge. Quoted in Harvey O'Connor, *Mellon's Millions* (New York: John Day Company, 1933), p. 3.

The Scotch-Irish dominated the frontier, producing figures like Andrew Jackson. They desired a much more limited government and taxation than did the more communal Puritan stock. In light of frontier support for tax-limitation movements, one could argue that the most significant ethnic conflict in American history has been that between the English and the Scotch-Irish.

69. Quoted in Herbert J. Storing, *The Complete Anti-Federalist*, 7 vols. (Chicago: University of Chicago Press, 1981), "What the Anti-Federalists Were For," 1:76.

4. Phase Two. Lessons of New York

1. Herbert D. A. Donovan, *The Barnburners: A Study of the Internal Movements in the Political History of New York State and of the Resulting Changes in Political Affiliation, 1830–1852* (New York: New York University Press, 1925), p. 37.
2. David Hume, *Essays Moral, Political and Literary* (London: Oxford University Press, 1963), p. 357.
3. Dixon Ryan Fox, *The Decline of Aristocracy in the Politics of New York, 1801–1840*, ed. Robert V. Remini (New York: Harper and Row, 1965), p. 282.
4. Thomas Hart Benton, *Thirty Years' View*, 2 vols. (New York: D. Appleton and Company, 1856), 2:700.
5. "I don't like the Jackson frolic very well, but I suppose we must have it," Hoffman wrote to Azariah Flagg in the 1820s. Fox, *Decline*, p. 283. Another member of this circle, William L. Marcy, immortalized another feature of Jacksonian politics in a line uttered in debate with Henry

Clay: "They saw nothing wrong in the rule, that to the victor belong the spoils of the enemy" (ibid., p. 284).

6. J. Hampden Dougherty, *Constitutional History of New York State from the Colonial Period to the Present Time* (New York: National Americana Society, 1911), pp. 129–33, 135, quoting Hon. Henry W. Hall, *An Historical Review of Waterway and Canal Construction in New York State* (Buffalo: Buffalo Historical Society, 1908).

7. Dougherty, *Constitutional History*, p. 138.

8. Ibid. One of Seward's biographers gives a disapproving account of his strategy in this crisis: "The undignified and enervating practice of appealing to the general government for relief from state and local misfortunes of various kinds was sadly common about 1840. Seward now made solemn and persistent efforts to justify an elaborate and expensive system of internal improvements by counting in as a permanent and reliable sinking fund the share of the proceeds claimed by New York from the sale of public lands." Seward also proposed to the secretary of war that the federal government give aid to the states by purchasing from them "the perpetual enjoyment of the right to use such public thoroughfares of the states." Frederic Bancroft, *The Life of William H. Seward* (New York: Harper & Bros., 1900), pp. 94–95. Cf. Glyndon G. Van Deusen, *William Seward* (New York: Oxford University Press, 1967), pp. 80–83. See also Jabez D. Hammond, *Life and Times of Silas Wright* (Syracuse: Hall & Dickson, 1848), p. 285.

9. David Malwyn Ellis et al., *A History of New York State* (Ithaca, NY: Cornell University Press, 1967), pp. 305–14.

10. David Malwyn Ellis, *Landlords and Farmers in the Hudson-Mohawk Region, 1790–1850* (Ithaca, NY: Cornell University Press, 1946), pp. 225–266.

11. Dougherty, *Constitutional History*, p. 147.

12. Ibid., p. 149; New York, Constitution of 1846, Article I, Section 12.

13. After the Panic of 1837, the Radicals steadfastly supported a state law prohibiting banks from issuing bills in denominations of less than five dollars. They defeated a popular attempt to repeal it, and the Whigs rode the issue to a triumph at the polls that November. The interesting point is that in upholding the small-note prohibition they were slavishly following Adam Smith. See Joseph Dorfman's Introductory Essay to William M. Gouge, *A Short History of Paper Money and Banking in the United States* (New York, 1833; reprint, New York: Augustus M. Kelley Publishers, 1968), pp. 8, 10.

14. Donovan, *Barnburners*, p. 47.

15. Ibid., p. 44.

16. See James Willard Hurst, *The Legitimacy of the Business Corporation in the Law of the United States, 1780–1970* (Charlottesville: University Press of Virginia, 1970), pp. 30–33.

17. Dougherty, *Constitutional History*, p. 149.

18. W. Attree and W. Bishop, eds., *Report of Debates and Proceedings of*

the *Convention for the Revision of the Constitution of the State of New York, 1846* (Albany: Albany Evening Argus, 1846), p. 945. See also William J. Quirk and Leon Wein, "A Short Constitutional History of Entities Commonly Known as Authorities," *Cornell Law Review* 56 (April 1971): 526–38; DeAlva Stanwood Alexander, *A Political History of the State of New York* (New York: Henry Holt & Co., 1906), pp. 103–13.

19. Attree and Bishop, *Report of Debates*, p. 944.

20. Ibid., p. 873.

21. Ibid., pp. 943–44. Cf. Chap. 2, n. 11.

22. Ibid., p. 944.

23. Ibid., p. 946. Loomis invoked the principles of Thomas Jefferson, stating: "The legislature and the people . . . never had the right to legislate for the future, to enthrall and bind down those who came after them, either by debt or any other system of legislation which would preserve them from a perfect freedom of action" (p. 944). The convention took Loomis seriously, adopting a constitutional provision requiring the legislature to submit to the people every twenty years the question of whether to hold a constitutional convention. New York, Constitution of 1846, Article XIV, Section 2.

24. Marvin Meyer dismisses this debate as "an *opera bouffe* affair of wooden swords and ketchup wounds." He uncritically accepts the Whig Alvah Worden's claim that "the difference between us had not been one of principle." *The Jacksonian Persuasion* (New York: Vintage Books, 1957), pp. 267–73. This interpretation seriously misreads the politics and principles of the debate, including Worden's own role, the damaging intraparty Democratic fight before the debate, which denied renomination to Governor William C. Bouck, and the Barnburner secession afterward. Meyer ignores Hoffman and Loomis's device of a public referendum on debt, Worden's attack on it, and the Whig attempt to outflank it.

   One could also ask why, if they opposed taxation, did the Barnburners reintroduce direct taxes after a seventeen-year lapse and why did they insist that taxes be voted to support new debt. The answer is twofold. First, organized as they were around the State Comptroller's Office, they were acutely aware of the deteriorating financial reserves of the state and recognized that the consequences of borrowing to cover expenses would lead to fiscal crisis and an even higher tax burden in the future, to cover not only current expenses but also accumulated deficits and interest. (At the time, interest rates on public debt were high.) Second, they considered the tax requirement to back debt to be another form of public control on the legislature. The representatives would be less inclined to spend if they had to answer immediately to their constituents instead of pushing the bill onto future generations.

25. Letter to Henry Stephens Randall, 23 May 1857, in Thomas Pinney, ed., *The Selected Letters of Thomas Babington Macaulay* (Cambridge: Cambridge University Press, 1982), pp. 284–86.

26. Donovan, *Burnburners*, p. 106.

27. John Walker Mauer, "Southern State Constitutions in the 1870s: A Case Study of Texas" (Ph.D. dissertation, Rice University, 1982), pp. 1–17.

28. James C. Mohr, *The Radical Republicans and Reform in New York during Reconstruction* (Ithaca, NY: Cornell University Press, 1973), pp. 1–20, 202–71. A parallel disaster over black suffrage befell the Radical Republicans in Ohio. Even though superseded by the Fifteenth Amendment, racial language in Ohio's suffrage article was an issue as late as 1912, when a constitutional amendment to remove it was soundly rejected by voters. See also James C. Mohr, ed., *Radical Republicans in the North: State Politics During Reconstruction* (Baltimore: Johns Hopkins University Press, 1976), pp. 66–82, 104–119, 50–66.

29. Clifton K. Yearley, *The Money Machines: The Breakdown and Reform of Governmental and Party Finance in the North, 1860–1920* (Albany: State University of New York Press, 1970), pp. 31–32; State of New York, *Proceedings and Debates of the Constitutional Convention of the State of New York Held in 1867 and 1868 in the City of Albany*, 7 vols. (Albany: Weed, Parsons and Co., 1868), 5:3761–62; Mohr, *Radical Republicans in New York*, p. 220, n. 64.

30. State of New York, *Proceedings and Debates, 1867 and 1868*, 5:3761.

31. Ibid.

32. Ibid., 5:3762.

33. Charles Z. Lincoln, *The Constitutional History of New York*, 6 vols. (Rochester, NY: Lawyer's Cooperative Publishing Co., 1906), 2:419. The vote on the constitution as a whole was 223,935 yes to 290,456 no; on Negro suffrage, 249,802 yes to 282,403 no; on uniform taxation, 183,812 yes to 273,260 no. A third referendum, on the article on the judiciary, was approved.

34. Donovan, *Barnburners*, p. 113. The exodus of Jacksonian Democrats to the new Republican Party is well described by Eric Foner in *Free Soil, Free Labor, Free Men: The Ideology of the Republican Party before the Civil War* (London: Oxford University Press, 1970), pp. 168–85. However, Foner misses the crucial points of fiscal policy that concern us here.

35. Jerome Mushkat, *The Reconstruction of the New York Democracy, 1861–1874* (Rutherford, NJ: Fairleigh Dickinson University Press, 1981), pp. 237–41.

36. Quoted in Thomas M. Cooley, *A Treatise on the Constitutional Limitations Which Rest Upon the Legislative Power of the States of the American Union* (Boston: Little, Brown and Company, 1868; reprint, New York: Da Capo Press, 1972), pp. 273–74.

37. Yearley, *Money Machines*, pp. 31–32.

38. Cooley, *Constitutional Limitations*, pp. 264–68.

39. Alexander B. Callow, Jr., *The Tweed Ring* (New York: Oxford University Press, 1970), pp. 245–46.

40. New York, *Record of the Constitutional Convention of the State of New York, 1915*, vol. 2 (Albany: J. B. Lyon Co., 1915), p. 1256.

5. The Fall and Rise of New York

1. Charles Z. Lincoln, *The Constitutional History of New York*, 6 vols. (Rochester, NY: Lawyer's Cooperative Publishing Co., 1906), 2:218–24; *Newell v. People*, 7 New York 9 (1852); Wade S. Smith, *The Appraisal of Municipal Credit Risk* (New York: Moody's Investor Services, 1979), p. 172.
2. Smith, *Appraisal*, p. 173, Table 13-2; *Municipal Market Developments* (monthly newsletter of the Public Securities Association, One World Trade Center, New York, 4 February 1981), Tables 2-A, 2-B.
3. Annmarie Hauck Walsh, *The Public's Business: The Politics and Practices of Government Corporations* (Cambridge: MIT Press, 1978), p. 24.
4. Ibid., p. 97.
5. Peter McClelland and Alan L. Magdovitz, *Crisis in the Making: The Political Economy of New York State Since 1945* (Cambridge: Cambridge University Press, 1981), pp. 219–25.
6. William J. Quirk and Leon Wein, "A Short Constitutional History of Entities Commonly Known as Authorities," *Cornell Law Review* 56 (April 1971): 561–75.
7. McClelland and Magdovitz, *Crisis in the Making*, p. 159–61; Quirk and Wein, "History of Authorities," p. 586.
8. Quirk and Wein, "History of Authorities," pp. 587–92; New York State Moreland Act Commission on the Urban Development Corporation and Other State Financing Agencies, *Restoring Credit and Confidence: A Reform Program for New York State and Its Public Authorities*, a report to the governor (New York: 31 March 1976), pp. 109–10.
9. Moreland Act Commission, *Restoring Credit*, pp. 119–20.
10. "The Collapse of the UDC," *The Wall Street Journal*, 7 April 1975; "Expert Criticizes UDC's Operations," *The New York Times*, 16 October 1975, p. 31.
11. Richard Karp, "Albany Maul: Rockefeller's Edifice Complex Will Cost Nearly $2 Billion," *Barron's*, 22 March 1976, p. 5.
12. Walsh, *Public's Business*, pp. 267–73.
13. In 1965, New York State's tax burden was 113.6% of the U.S. average, ranking twentieth. In 1975, the comparable figure was 135.5%. The next nearest outrider, Vermont, exceeded the U.S. average by only 125.8%. Advisory Commission of Intergovernmental Relations (ACIR), *Significant Features of Fiscal Federalism*, 1978–79 edition (Washington, D.C., May 1979), p. 35, Table 24.
14. Robert H. Connery and Gerald Benjamin, *Rockefeller of New York: Executive Power in the Statehouse* (Ithaca, NY: Cornell University Press, 1979), p. 189.
15. Ibid., pp. 191, 195; James Desmond, *Nelson Rockefeller, a Political Biography* (New York: Macmillan Co., 1964), pp. 203–08; Michael Kramer and Sam Roberts, *"I Never Wanted to be Vice President of Anything": An Investigative Biography of Nelson Rockefeller* (New York:

Basic Books, 1976), pp. 215–18; McClelland and Magdovitz, *Crisis in the Making*, pp. 166–73, 204–10.

16. Connery and Benjamin, *Rockefeller*, pp. 195–98. Rockefeller was not even the worst alternative. During the 1970 campaign, Democratic gubernatorial nominee Arthur Goldberg called for raising the top bracket on the personal income tax to 20% at $35,000. *The New York Times*, 22 October 1970, p. 23.

17. Connery and Benjamin, *Rockefeller*, pp. 193–94.

18. Kramer and Roberts, *"I Never Wanted to Be Vice President . . ."*, p. 336.

19. Connery and Benjamin, *Rockefeller*, p. 193; Kramer and Roberts, *"I Never Wanted to Be Vice President . . ."*, p. 335.

20. Connery and Benjamin, *Rockefeller*, p. 199.

21. Charles R. Morris, *The Cost of Good Intentions: New York City and the Liberal Experiment* (New York: W. W. Norton and Co., 1980), p. 17. Morris, a former member of Mayor Lindsay's administration, makes as good a case for John Lindsay as the facts will allow, and sometimes more, by generously sharing the blame with his predecessor and successor.

22. Ibid., pp. 136–37.

23. *The New York Times*, 29 November 1965, p. 44.

24. Ibid., 30 November 1965, p. 31; 29 November 1965, p. 44.

25. Ibid., 4 March 1966, p. 18.

26. New York City Business Tax Task Force, "Taxes and Tax Policy in New York City," (June 1980), p. C-5.

27. Connery and Benjamin, *Rockefeller*, pp. 199–210.

28. Peter Kihss, "Poor and Rich, Not Middle-Class: The Key to Lindsay Re-election," *The New York Times*, 6 November 1969, p. 37.

29. David Grossman, "The Lindsay Legacy: A Partisan Appraisal," *City Almanac* 8 (October 1973): 1–4, published by the Center for New York City Affairs of the New School for Social Research, New York City.

30. Kenneth A. Auletta, "The City Politic, Ford's Radical Solution," *New York Magazine* (10 November 1975): 8; William J. Quirk and Leon E. Wein, "Fiscal Lawlessness in New York: Reflections on Reading the Testimony Given Before the Moreland Act Commission on the Urban Development Corporation and Other State Financing Agencies" (New York, 1978, mimeographed), p. 1.

31. Morris, *Cost of Good Intentions*, pp. 144–46, 150–55.

32. Ibid., pp. 144–45, 150–54; Connery and Benjamin, *Rockefeller*, pp. 198–99.

33. Morris, *Cost of Good Intentions*, p. 155.

34. Moreland Act Commission, *Restoring Credit*, pp. 165–220.

35. "New York's Unwelcome Chickens," *The Wall Street Journal*, 21 January 1975.

36. "New York's Financial Gadfly," *The Wall Street Journal*, 4 May 1976, p. 22.

37. New York State, Office of the State Comptroller, Division of Audits and Accounts, *Audit Report on Review of New York City's Central Budgetary and Accounting Practices, Interim Report No. 3—Special and Miscellaneous Revenue Accounts*, Report No. NYC 31–76.

38. Securities and Exchange Commission (SEC), *Staff Report on Transactions in Securities of the City of New York*, vol. 1, *Chronology of Events, October 1, 1974–April 8, 1975* (26 August 1977), pp. 94–124, especially pp. 110–12. Cf. Morris, *Cost of Good Intentions*, pp. 226–28, which misses the importance of the Wein suit.

39. For the most flagrant example, see SEC, *Staff Report*, p. 144.

40. Ibid., *Chronology*, p. 173. "Notes taken at the meeting of [of fifteen banks and brokerage houses on March 12, 1975] by Jean Rousseau of Merrill Lynch reported that there was some discussion about 'poss(ible) criminal liability if we participate. . . .' "

41. *In re Municipal Securities*, U.S. District Court for the Southern District of New York, Docket No. M21-22. This is the so-called Friedlander case, which has already broken all records for size and complexity in municipal securities litigation. The depositions from the Clearinghouse banks include tables of their monthly holdings of New York City notes prior to default.

42. New York State, Office of the State Comptroller, Division of Audits and Accounts, *Audit Report on Review of New York City's Central Budgetary and Accounting Practices, Interim Report No. 1—Prior Year Accounts Receivable*, Report No. NYC-3-76; ibid., *Interim Report No. 2—Uncollected Real Estate Taxes*, Report No. NYC-26-76.

43. U.S. Department of Labor, Bureau of Labor Statistics, *Some Facts Relevant to the Current Economic Scene in New York*, prepared for the New York Region Office by Herbert Bienstock, Assistant Regional Director, 5 December 1975 (mimeographed).

44. ACIR, *Significant Features*, 1978–79 edition, pp. 46–47.

45. Ibid.

46. New York City, Temporary Commission on City Finances, *The City in Transition: Prospects and Policies for New York*, June 1977, pp. 196–98, 200–215. The commission concluded, "The City's tax policy, in short, was wasting assets important to the future of New York City by failing to recognize the long-term counter-productivity of raising taxes to the point where they drove out revenue-producing individuals and businesses" (ibid, p. 200). The commission recommended cutting city business taxes rather than its personal income tax, but it also endorsed the conclusion of the state's Special Task Force on Taxation that the state personal income tax be reduced one percentage point each year to a top rate of 10% (ibid, p. 215).

Interim reports of the commission were even more emphatic. The Ninth Report, *The Effects of Taxation on Manufacturing in New York City* (December 1976), concluded: "Unlike the city's non-manufacturing sector, manufacturing activities are particularly sensitive to local tax rates. . . . The reduction of manufacturing taxes proposed in this report would both halt the city's rapid decline in manufacturing employment and result in sharply increased tax revenues for the City of New York. . . . While the Commission's proposals may cost the city as much as $90 million within the first two years of implementation, by the end of the third year that entire amount will have been recovered" (pp. 2–3).

However, the Eleventh Interim Report, *The Effects of Personal Taxes in New York City: Some Proposals for a More Rational System* (14 February 1977), recommended a doubling of the commuter tax. It analyzed at length the excessive city and state tax burden, yet made the unwarranted assumption that raising the tax on nonresidents would drive their jobs back into the city rather than out of the region altogether. This report did, on the other hand, warn that the sales tax rate could not be raised further without producing economic loss.

47. Municipal Union/Financial Leaders Group, "Taxes in New York City" (position paper, 21 July 1977, mimeographed). The statement was signed by MUFL's principal leaders, Walter Wriston, chairman of Citibank, and Jack Bigel, consultant to the Municipal Labor Committee. It concluded: "Further cuts in taxes are needed in coming years as part of a full, well-thought-out plan necessary to hold, attract, and create the jobs that are the very foundation of the City's economic base" (ibid, p. 6). The text of the statement makes an interesting argument about the role of "factor mobility" in making the level of taxation a more important influence on the economy: "Lack of tax competitiveness is, we believe, becoming an increasingly important factor with respect to the economic difficulties of New York City.

"The locational options of American business have increased in recent decades. Improvements in communications and transportation and growth and economic maturation of other areas of the country and of other metropolitan areas throughout the nation have played a part in expanding these options. And a decline in the number of very small businesses, which have the greatest need to locate near complementary types of business as well as competitors, has reduced the very need to locate in an urban sector.

"New York's ability to extract a 'rent' in terms of relatively high taxes and other costs is suffering erosion as the need for individual businesses to remain located here is diminished" (ibid, p. 5).

Bigel, who was the target of red-baiting during the mid-fifties, later said he signed the statement not because he endorsed supply-side tax cuts but because Wriston had persuaded him it would send a positive signal to Washington and the national financial community. Interview with Jack Bigel, New York, March 1979. See also James Ring Adams, "The Muffle Men," *Empire State Report* (April 1979): 19–23.

48. *The New York Times*, 11 August 1977, quoted in Bruce Bartlett, *Reagonomics: Supply Side Economics in Action* (Westport, CT: Arlington House, 1981), p. 67.

49. Roy Bahl did study the connection between the changing economy and

the tax structure, but he took it the other way around. In a major Maxwell School research project in 1974, he analyzed the impact of the city's economic shift to services and government employment on its ability to raise tax revenue. Since these sectors paid fewer kinds of taxes, particularly property tax, than manufacturing and trade, the shift weakened the city's tax base. Bahl suggested an increase in the commuter tax as compensation, a result of his getting the tax-economy relationship backward. See Roy W. Bahl, Alan K. Campbell, and David Greytak, *Taxes, Expenditures and the Economic Base: Case Study of New York City* (New York: Praeger Publishers, 1974), pp. 143–50.

50. New York City, Office of Management and Budget, Presentation to Moody's Bond Rating Agency, November 1983.

51. ACIR, *Significant Features*, 1981–82 edition, pp. 38–39, Tables 22.1, 22.2.

52. New York City, Office of Management and Budget, *Report on Economic Conditions July–December 1983* (New York City: 15 March 1984), pp. 2–3, 45.

6. Phase Three. California the Golden

1. Carey McWilliams, *California: The Great Exception* (Santa Barbara, CA: Peregrine Smith, 1976), pp. 3, 4.

2. Owen Cochran Coy, *California Gold Days* (Los Angeles: Powell Publishing Co., 1929), pp. 17–64; John Walton Caughey, *The California Gold Rush* (Berkeley: University of California Press, 1948; paperback, 1975), pp. 1–38.

3. Coy, *Gold Days*, p. 59; Caughey, *Gold Rush*, pp. 19–20.

4. Coy, *Gold Days*, pp. 60–64, 317; Caughey, *Gold Rush*, pp. 41–44.

5. Quoted in Coy, *Gold Days*, p. 166.

6. Ibid., p. 168.

7. Walton Bean, *California: An Interpretive History*, 3rd ed. (New York: McGraw-Hill, 1978), p. 155; Gerald D. Nash, *State Government and Economic Development: A History of Administrative Policies in California, 1849–1933* (Berkeley: Institute of Governmental Studies, University of California, 1964), pp. 36–41. Following the recommendation of President Zachary Taylor in 1849, a Senate committee considered a bill to parcel the mining claims into small lots for sale, but it died under the opposition of U.S. Senator Thomas Hart Benton, well connected in California through his sons-in-law; Coy, *Gold Days*, p. 169.

8. Coy, *Gold Days*, pp. 169–83; Caughey, *Gold Rush*, pp. 225–31. A bill confirming titles to existing claims was finally maneuvered through the U.S. Congress in 1866. It also ratified local mining rules not in conflict with U.S. laws. Nash, *State Government*, pp. 39–40.

The spontaneous development of mining law in the California camps is the most striking, but not the unique expression of this tendency in American frontier life. James Willard Hurst records documents of the

Pike River (Wisconsin) Claimants Union, a voluntary association of squatters on unsurveyed federal land. Such "claims associations" elected officers to record claims and settle conflicts, acting only on the authority of the voluntary agreement of men who considered themselves, at least as far as land title was concerned, to be in a "state of nature." James Willard Hurst, *Law and the Conditions of Freedom in the Nineteenth-Century United States* (Madison, WI: University of Wisconsin Press, 1956), pp. 4–7. The phrase "state of nature" appears in the constitution of the Pike River Claimants Union (ibid., p. 4).

9. Coy, *Gold Days*, pp. 204–05; Caughey, *Gold Rush*, pp. 232–48; Bean, *California*, p. 125. Writing under the pseudonym Dame Shirley, the wife of a doctor living near the diggings described a particularly pathetic hanging in one of a fascinating series of letters and contrasted the cruelty of the miners with the "noble Vigilance Committee of San Francisco." She wrote of the Vigilantes: "In no case have they hung a man, who had not been proved beyond the shadow of a doubt, to have committed at least one robbery in which life had been endangered, if not absolutely taken." [Louise Amelia Knappe Smith Clappe], *The Shirley Letters from the California Mines, 1851–52* (New York: Alfred A. Knopf, 1949), p. 98.

10. Friedrich Gerstaecker, *California Gold Mines* (Oakland, CA: Biobooks, 1946), p. 9; Henry George, *Progress and Poverty* (New York: Robert Schalkenbach Foundation, 1971), pp. 144–45.

11. Bean, *California*, pp. 132–36; W. W. Robinson, *Land in California* (Berkeley: University of California Press, 1948; paperback, 1979), pp. 111–32; Leonard Pitt, *The Decline of the Californios: A Social History of the Spanish-Speaking Californians, 1846–1890* (Berkeley: University of California Press, 1966), pp. 83–103.

12. William Henry Ellison, *A Self-Governing Dominion: California, 1849–1860* (Berkeley: University of California Press, 1950), pp. 27–28, 32–37; Lately Thomas, *Between Two Empires: The Life Story of California's First Senator* (Boston: Houghton Mifflin Co., 1969), pp. 39–50.

13. Ellison, *Dominion*, pp. 167–91.

14. Bean, *California*, pp. 171–80.

15. California, Constitution of 1879, Article 19, Section 1. See also Carl Brent Swisher, *Motivation and Political Technique in the California Constitutional Convention, 1878–79*, Political Science Monograph Series (Claremont, CA: Pomona College, 1930; reprint, New York: Da Capo Press, 1969), pp. 5–16, 83–92; James Bryce, *The American Commonwealth*, 2 vols., (New York: Macmillan and Co., 1891), 2:385–408, with a reply from Denis Kearney, pp. 747–50. Bryce, in ibid., 1:683–724, reprints the California Constitution of 1879.

16. Henry George, *Progress and Poverty*, p. 272.

17. Ibid.

18. Ibid., p. 386.

19. Ibid., p. 387.

20. Ibid., p. 276.

21. Ibid., p. 409.
22. Ibid., p. 410.
23. Ibid., p. 428.
24. Ibid., p. 427.
25. Ibid., pp. 434–35.
26. Quoted in Coy, *Gold Days*, pp. 270–71.
27. Advisory Commission on Intergovernmental Relations, *Regional Growth, Historic Perspective*, Commission Report A-74 (Washington, D.C.: June 1980), pp. 9–12, n. 2, p. 27; McWilliams, *California*, p. 33; Caughey, *Gold Rush*, p. xv.
28. McWilliams, *California*, p. 25.
29. U.S. Department of Commerce, Bureau of the Census, *Historical Statistics of the United States: Colonial Times to 1957*, a Statistical Abstracts Supplement (Washington, D.C.: GPO, 1961), pp. 11–13; Ann E. Weidel, "Miners and Mining Camps: A Portrait of Gold Rush California" (unpublished paper, 11 December 1979, available from author, c/o Library, Security Pacific Bank, Los Angeles, California.)
30. Bureau of the Census, *Historical Statistics*, pp. 12–13.
31. Bryce, *American Commonwealth*, 2:385–86, 387–88.
32. McWilliams, *California*, p. 194.
33. Spencer C. Olin, Jr., *California's Prodigal Sons, Hiram Johnson and the Progressives, 1911–1917* (Berkeley: University of California Press, 1968), p. 26.
34. Hiram W. Johnson, "Inaugural Address," reprinted in Franklin Hichborn, *Story of the Session of the California Legislature of 1911* (San Francisco: Press of the James H. Barry Company, 1911), Appendix, p. 11.
35. Ibid., p. iii.
36. Ibid., p. v.
37. George E. Mowry, *The California Progressives* (Berkeley: University of California Press, 1951; Encounter Paperback, Chicago: Quadrangle Books, 1963), pp. 140–42; Hichborn, *Story of 1911*, pp. 93–101.
38. Mowry, *Progressives*, p. 140.
39. Leonard Pitt, ed., *California Controversies: Major Issues in the History of the State* (Glenview, IL: Scott, Foresman and Co., 1968), pp. 120–30.
40. Mowry, *Progressives*, pp. 148–49. The vote on the initiative and referendum measure was 168,744 yes to 52,093 no. The measure on impeachment of judges and elected officials passed by 157,596 yes to 49,345 no.
41. League to Protect the Initiative, *The Initiative and Referendum in Danger!* (Los Angeles and San Francisco, 1922), pp. 1–2.
42. Mansel G. Blackford, *The Politics of Business in California, 1890–1920* (Columbus, OH: Ohio State University Press, 1977), pp. 147–60.
43. Bean, *California*, pp. 344, 352–53; Advisory Commission on Intergovernmental Relations (ACIR), *Significant Features of Fiscal Federalism, 1979–80 edition* (Washington, D.C., October 1980), pp. 46–47.

44. California, State Legislature, Office of the Legislative Analyst, *Analysis of the Budget Bill for the Fiscal Year July 1, 1966 to June 30, 1967* (hereafter, *Budget Analysis*), (Sacramento, various years), pp. ix–x.

45. California, Office of the Governor, *Governor's Budget, 1967–68*, (Sacramento, February 1967), p. 7; Lou Cannon, *Ronnie & Jesse: A Political Odyssey* (Garden City, NY: Doubleday & Company, 1969), pp. 132–50.

46. Ronald Reagan, Press Conference, 24 January 1967 (Reagan Archives, Hoover Institution, Palo Alto, CA), p. 9.

47. Ibid., 7 February 1976, p. 12.

48. Ibid.

49. Ronald Reagan, Governor, State of California, *Tax Message* (n.p., 8 March 1967), p. 11.

50. Kent H. Steffgen, *Here's the Rest of Him* (Reno, NV: n.p., 1967), quoted in Cannon, *Ronnie*, p. 155. Steffgen was an associate of state Senator John Schmitz, the 1972 American Independent Party candidate for president, who, in 1982, became one of the first men in history to be expelled from the John Birch Society Council for making intemperate remarks.

51. Edmund G. (Pat) Brown, *Reagan and Reality: The Two Californias* (New York: Praeger Publishers, 1970), p. 72; cf. Edmund G. (Pat) Brown and Bill Brown, *Reagan: The Political Chameleon* (New York: Praeger Publishers, 1976).

52. *Budget Analysis, 1968–69; Budget Analysis, 1969–70*, p. A18.

53. Ibid., p. A50.

54. Telephone interview with Ronald Reagan, Sacramento, CA, May 1977; interview with John Vickerman, Chief Deputy Legislative Analyst, Sacramento, CA, 26 February 1982.

55. Robert Kuttner, *Revolt of the Haves: Tax Rebellions and Hard Times* (New York: Simon and Schuster, 1980), pp. 31–36.

56. Ibid., pp. 36–43; Frank Levy, "On Understanding Proposition 13," *The Public Interest* 56 (Summer 1979): 68–72; *The Los Angeles Times*, 19 February 1982, Part II, p. 1.

57. Interview with William Craig Stubblebine, Director, Center for the Study of Law Structures, Claremont McKenna College, Claremont, CA, 22 February 1982; Lewis K. Uhler, "Draft . . . July 17, 1972," p. 14, in File "Proposition 1" (Center for the Study of Law Structures, Claremont, CA).

58. William A. Niskanen to Lewis K. Uhler, 21 December 1972, File "Proposition I" (Center for the Study of Law Structures, Claremont, CA); Ronald Reagan, "Excerpts of Remarks to the . . . California Newspaper Publishers Association, San Francisco, February 9, 1973" (Reagan Archives, Hoover Institution, Palo Alto, CA), p. 6.

   The Proposition 1 literature did draw the distinction between the comprehensive approach and the single-tax limitation sought by the Watson amendment. See, e.g., the following question-and-answer segment from the "Blue Book," the main briefing book for Proposition 1: "6. Isn't your concept of a tax limitation the same as the Watson Amendment, which was defeated by the people at the polls in the last election?" "No. The Watson Amendment was an arbitrary fixed limitation on one tax without regard to income and other economic variations. The revenue control and tax limitation program is a flexible limit on the general power of the State to tax in relation to the income of the people." A Reasonable Program for . . . Revenue Control and Tax Reduction, Submitted to California Legislature, March 12, 1973 (Sacramento: n.p., 1973), p. 21.

59. Brown and Brown, Reagan, pp. 61–67; California, State Legislature Office of the Legislative Analyst, "Statement . . . on the Main Financial Issues of Proposition No. 1, presented to Assembly Select Committee on Agriculture, Food and Nutrition, Fresno, 31 October 1973," (mimeographed).

60. Bruce Keppel, "An Offer Californians Did Refuse," California Journal (December 1973): 400–03.

61. Interviews with Arthur Laffer, Los Angeles, May 1977, and New York City, April 1984, and Jude Wanniski, Morristown, NJ, November 1983.

62. A Reasonable Program, pp. 24–25.

63. William Howard Taft, Popular Government, Its Essence, Its Permanence and Its Perils (New Haven: Yale University Press, 1913), p. 54.

64. Michael S. Salkin and Dan Durning, "Housing Prices in California: Changes and Implications" (San Francisco: Economics Department, Bank of America, January 1982), p. 3.

65. California, Office of the Governor, Governor's Budget, 1977–78 (Sacramento, 10 January 1977), pp. A9–10; Levy, "On Understanding Proposition 13," pp. 82–85; Kuttner, Revolt of Haves, pp. 57–65.

66. California, State Legislature, Office of the Legislative Analyst, A Report on California's General Fund Surplus, December 1978, (Sacramento, December, 1978), p. 7; interviews with Governor Edmund G. (Jerry) Brown, Sacramento and Los Angeles, 1977–82.

67. James Ring Adams, "Jerry Brown Plays the Numbers," The Wall Street Journal, 31 March 1977, p. 22.

68. Kuttner, Revolt of Haves, p. 65.

69. Interview with Howard Jarvis, Los Angeles, 24 February 1982; interview with Paul Gann, Los Angeles, 25 February 1982; Sacramento, 27 February 1982; "State and Local Tax Limitation Initiative Constitutional Amendment," sponsored by People's Advocate, Inc.; "Citizens Petition to Lower Property Taxes," sponsored by United Organizations of Taxpayers, Howard Jarvis, Chairman. Howard Jarvis with Robert Pack, I'm Mad as Hell (New York: Times Books, 1979), pp. 32–54.

70. Kuttner, Revolt of Haves, p. 78.

71. California, State Legislature, Office of the Legislative Analyst, An Analysis of Proposition 13; the Jarvis-Gann Property Tax Initiative, Report No. 78-11 (Sacramento, May 1978), pp. S6–9.

72. Kuttner, Revolt of Haves, p. 78.

73. Eric Smith and Jack Citrin, "The Building of a Majority for Tax Limitation in California, 1968–79," Research Report No. 1, State Data Program (University of California, Berkeley, 1978, mimeographed).

74. James Ring Adams, "Coping With Proposition 13," *The Wall Street Journal*, 10 October 1978, p. 22; "The California Tax Derby," *The Wall Street Journal*, 29 August 1978, p. 16.

75. Alvin Rabushka and Pauline Ryan, *The Tax Revolt* (Palo Alto: Hoover Institution, Stanford University, 1982), pp. 149–51.

76. Personal interviews and file "Memorandum: How the Legal Services Corporation very substantially assisted the defeat of Proposition 9 on the California ballot in June 1980, by providing tens of thousands of dollars, and its entire California organization, for that purpose," 8 September 1983, with fourteen documents (prepared by new leadership of the Legal Services Corporation and in the possession of staff writers for *The Wall Street Journal* editorial page).

77. Rabushka and Ryan, *Tax Revolt*, pp. 176–83, 201–10, especially 210.

78. Conrad C. Jamison, "Before and After Proposition 13: Expenditure by State and Local Government in California" (Los Angeles: Security Pacific National Bank, March 1982, mimeographed), pp. A-8–10.

79. David O. Sears and Jack Citrin, *Tax Revolt: Something for Nothing in California* (Cambridge: Harvard University Press, 1982), pp. 118–19.

7. Louisiana and the Sunbelt

1. Conversation with Houston Chamber of Commerce officials, Houston, March 1978; Kirkpatrick Sale, *Power Shift: The Rise of the Southern Rim and Its Challenge to the Eastern Establishment* (New York: Vintage Books, 1976).

2. U.S. Department of Commerce, Bureau of Economic Analysis, "1982 State Per Capita Personal Income," press release BEA 83–47, September 6, 1983.

3. Idem., "Fourth Quarter 1981 State Nonfarm Personal Income and 1981 State Per Capita Personal Income," press release BEA 82-23, May 1982; U.S. Department of Labor, *Employment and Earnings* (Washington, D.C.: GPO, May 1982), Table "State and Area Unemployment Data." Unless otherwise noted, figures on personal income and employment are drawn from these two publication series.

4. Advisory Commission on Intergovernmental Relations (ACIR), *Significant Features of Fiscal Federalism*, 1981–82 edition (Washington, D.C., April 1983), Report M-135, pp. 38–39, Tables 22.1, 22.2.

5. For an earlier discussion of this point, see John B. Boles, ed., *Dixie Dateline: A Journalistic Portrait of the Contemporary South* (Houston: Rice University Studies, 1983), pp. 141–57 (Chap. 9, "The Sunbelt," by James Ring Adams).

6. A. J. Liebling, *The Earl of Louisiana* (New York: Ballantine Books, 1960), p. 87.

7. E. Merton Coulter, *The South During Reconstruction* (Baton Rouge: Louisiana State University Press, 1947), p. 156.

8. Ibid., p. 155. For the more sympathetic view, see Thomas D. Clark and

Albert D. Kirwan, *The South Since Appomattox* (New York: Oxford University Press, 1967), pp. 38–39.

9. Carl H. Moneyhon, *Republicanism in Reconstruction Texas* (Austin: University of Texas Press, 1980), pp. 162–63.

10. James W. Garner, *Reconstruction in Mississippi* (Baton Rouge: Louisiana State University Press, 1968), p. 297.

11. C. Vann Woodward, *Origins of the New South, 1877–1913* (Baton Rouge: Louisiana State University Press, 1951; paperback, 1966), pp. 65–66. For a more detailed account, stressing the diversity among the Reconstruction constitutions and their continuity with northern constitution-making, see John Walker Mauer, "Southern State Constitutions in the 1870s: A Case Study of Texas" (Ph.D. dissertation, Rice University, 1982).

12. Woodward, *Origins*, p. 59.

13. Ibid., p. 60.

14. Ibid., p. 61; Rupert Richardson, *Texas: The Lone Star State* (New York: Prentice-Hall, 1943), pp. 288–98.

15. Woodward, *Origins*, p. 62.

16. Interview with Edward J. Steimel, President, Louisiana Association of Business and Industry, Baton Rouge, May 1982.

17. Josiah Quincy, *Speeches Delivered in the Congress of the United States*, ed. Edmund Quincy (Boston: Little, Brown and Company, 1874), p. 216; Joe Gray Taylor, *Louisiana: A Bicentennial History* (New York: W. W. Norton & Co., 1976), p. 27.

18. Taylor, *Louisiana*, pp. 48–49.

19. Allan P. Sindler, *Huey Long's Louisiana: State Politics, 1920–1952* (Baltimore: Johns Hopkins Press, 1956), pp. 3–6.

20. Lawrence Goodwyn, *The Populist Moment: A Short History of the Agrarian Revolt in America* (Oxford: Oxford University Press, 1978), p. 195.

21. Liebling, *Earl*, p. 89.

22. T. Harry Williams, *Romance and Realism in Southern Politics* (Baton Rouge: Louisiana State University Press, 1966), p. 24.

23. Ella Lonn, *Reconstruction in Louisiana after 1868* (New York: G. P. Putnam's Sons, 1918), p. 18.

24. Ibid., pp. 83–85.

25. Williams, *Romance and Realism*, p. 30.

26. Ibid., p. 31.

27. Ibid., p. 42.

28. Constitution of the State of Louisiana, Adopted in Convention at the City of New Orleans, July 23, 1879 (Baton Rouge: Leon Jastremski, State Printer, 1884), Article 209, pp. 53–54. Cf. Mauer, "Southern State Constitutions," pp. 48–106.

29. Sindler, *Huey Long's Louisiana*, pp. 40–44; Constitution of the State of Louisiana Adopted in Convention at the City of Baton Rouge, June 18, 1921.

30. Louisiana, Constitution of 1921, Article 10, Section 21.

31. T. Harry Williams, *Huey Long* (New York: Alfred A. Knopf, 1969), p. 857.
32. ACIR, *Significant Features*, 1981–82 edition, p. 47.
33. Sindler, *Huey Long's Louisiana*, p. 61.
34. Ibid., pp. 54–71, 105.
35. Williams, *Huey Long*, p. 720.
36. Sindler, *Huey Long's Louisiana*, pp. 88–90, 132.
37. Williams, *Huey Long*, pp. 745–46.
38. Sindler, *Huey Long's Louisiana*, pp. 94–95.
39. Ibid., p. 106.
40. Williams, *Huey Long*, p. 876.
41. Sindler, *Huey Long's Louisiana*, pp. 128–32.
42. Ibid., p. 132.
43. Ibid., pp. 161, 172–73.
44. Ibid., p. 175.
45. Ibid., p. 178.
46. See Chap. 8, n. 46.
47. Ibid., pp. 186–97.
48. Ibid., pp. 208–09.
49. William D. Ross, "The Federal-State-Local Tax Structure in Louisiana," *National Tax Journal* 7 (Winter 1954)4: 371–76. Ross objected that the statistics of the day gave only state tax burdens, and in Louisiana local taxes were lower than average. Yet he admitted that the combined state-local burden was still the highest in the country. He claimed the burden looked more reasonable if severance taxes were excluded, but did not report those figures.
50. ACIR, *Significant Features*, 1981–82 edition, p. 47.
51. Thomas R. Beard, ed., *The Louisiana Economy* (Baton Rouge: Louisiana State University Press, 1969), pp. 197–200.
52. Louisiana Association of Business and Industry, *The Stalled Louisiana Economy* (Baton Rouge, May 1976).
53. James Ring Adams, "The Gusto of Louisiana Politics," *The Wall Street Journal*, 16 May 1979, p. 22.
54. Interviews with Representative Louis Jenkins, Baton Rouge, May 1982. The state spending limit was subsequently adopted as a statute.
55. *PAR's Voter's Guide to the 1974 Proposed Constitution* (Baton Rouge: Louisiana Public Affairs Research Council, 1974), pp. 27–28.
56. *Special Election on the Constitution, 20 April 1974*, PAR Analysis Number 198, April 1974 (Baton Rouge: Louisiana Public Affairs Research Council, 1974), pp. 1, 3. In another version of Chehardy's efforts, the convention adopted a resolution of tribute, and the delegated orator intoned, "He . . . believes that there should be constitutional barricades to prevent the destruction of initiative in the production of income and that, to do otherwise, would add another brick in the construction of the devil's workshop called idleness and discourage the taking of advantage of all idle hours for creative and productive labor."

(17 January 1974, copy provided by Lawrence A. Chehardy.) His son, Lawrence Edward, is continuing the family tradition, both as Jefferson Parish tax assessor and as author of constitutional amendments.

57. *ACIR, Significant Features,* 1981–82 edition, p. 61.
58. Ibid., p. 76.
59. Ibid., p. 34.
60. Louisiana Association of Business and Industry, *The Un-Stalled Louisiana Economy* (Baton Rouge, July 1981), pp. 1–2.
61. Ibid., p. 7.
62. Stuart P. Stevens, "The Healer Returneth: Fast Eddie Takes on Dull Dave," *The New Republic* 189, no. 18 (31 October 1983): 8–10.

8. Texas: The Jacksonian Nation-State

1. Mark E. Nackman, *A Nation Within a Nation: The Rise of Texas Nationalism* (Port Washington, NY: Kennikat Press, 1975), pp. 52–53.
2. Rupert Norval Richardson, *Texas: The Lone Star State* (New York: Prentice-Hall, 1943), p. 114. Smyth must have touched some element of the Texas psyche, considering how frequently he is quoted. See also D. W. Meinig, *Imperial Texas: An Interpretive Essay in Cultural Geography* (Austin: University of Texas Press, 1969), p. 34; T. R. Fehrenbach, *Lone Star: A History of Texas and the Texans* (New York: Collier Books, 1980), p. 166.
3. Fehrenbach, *Lone Star,* pp. 140, 165–66.
4. Llerena B. Friend, *Sam Houston: The Great Designer,* Texas History Paperback (Austin: University of Texas Press, 1969), pp. 3–23.
5. Ibid., p. 54.
6. Frederic Gaillardet, *Sketches of Early Texas and Louisiana,* trans., with an introduction and notes, by James L. Shepherd III, Texas History Paperbacks (Austin: University of Texas Press, 1966), pp. 57–59, 64–72.
7. Homer S. Thrall, *History of Texas* (n.p., 1878), pp. 316–20; Fehrenbach, *Lone Star,* pp. 252–61.
8. William M. Gouge, *The Fiscal History of Texas* (Philadelphia: Lippincott, Grambo, and Co., 1852; reprint, New York: Augustus M. Kelley, 1968), pp. 141–42.
9. Ibid., pp. 110–11.
10. Fehrenbach, *Lone Star,* pp. 276–78; Richardson, *Texas,* p. 185; Thrall, *History,* pp. 765, 787.
11. Charles William Ramsdell, *Reconstruction in Texas,* Texas History Paperbacks (New York: Columbia University Press, 1910; reprint, Austin: University of Texas Press, 1970), p. 309; Thrall, *History,* p. 787. The maximum tax rate may not necessarily have been applied in practice.
12. *Proceedings of a Mass Meeting of the City of Galveston Held August 18, 1871, to Take into Consideration the Governor's Proclamation Ordering Troops to Surround the Election Polls and to Consider the Op-*

pressive and Unconstitutional System of Taxation Adopted by the Last Legislature (Galveston: the "News" Steam Book and Job Office, 1871), p. 4.

13. A committee of seven appointed to memorialize the legislature included Andrew Jackson Hamilton, provisional governor from 1865 to 1866; James W. Throckmorton, governor from 1866 to 1867; and Elisha M. Pease, governor from 1867 to 1869, also from 1853 to 1857. The committee actually had eight members, adding Pease at the last minute.

14. *Proceedings of the Tax-Payers Convention, Convened at Austin, Texas, September 22, 1871* (n.p., 1871), pp. 24–25.

15. Carl H. Moneyhon, *Republicanism in Reconstruction Texas* (Austin: University of Texas Press, 1980), pp. 162–63. A. J. and Morgan Hamilton were earlier the leaders of the different sides in the *ab initio* controversy, inspired by the radical claim that Texas had ceased to be a legitimate sovereignty when it seceded from the Union and that therefore all state actions during that period, including marriage registration and title transfers, were null and void from their inception (*ab initio*). The Reconstruction state legislature ultimately passed a law reconfirming such routine works of the state, but the issue split the Texas Republican Party in 1868. The controversy reached the U.S. Supreme Court in the case of *Texas v. White* (7 Wallace 700, 10 L. Ed. 227 (1869)) and produced Chief Justice Salmon P. Chase's ringing reaffirmation of "an indestructible Union, composed of indestructible states." The postwar theoretical debate over the status of the rebel states has been dismissed by current historians as "protracted and turgid" (see David Donald, *The Politics of Reconstruction, 1863–1867* [Baton Rouge: Louisiana State University Press, 1965], pp. 54–56), a sure sign that important material is being overlooked. The split between A. J. and Morgan Hamilton suggests the inadequacy of all nontheoretical explanations for this controversy, except perhaps for sibling rivalry. For the *ab initio* controversy, see Charles William Ramsdell, *Reconstruction*, pp. 206–11.

16. Moneyhon, *Republicanism*, pp. 161–63, 166.

17. Fehrenbach, *Lone Star*, pp. 429–32.

18. Richardson, *Texas*, pp. 288–98; George D. Braden, *Citizen's Guide to the Texas Constitution* (Austin: Texas Advisory Commission on Intergovernmental Relations, 1972), p. 62. For the most complete text of the constitution, see *Texas Almanac and State Industrial Guide, 1982–83* edition (Dallas: A. H. Belo Corporation, 1981), pp. 442–89.

19. Braden, *Guide*, pp. 61–72; Janice C. May, "Texas Constitutional Revision," *National Civic Review* 66 (February 1977), reprinted in Ernest Crain et al., *The Challenge of Texas Politics: Text with Readings* (St. Paul, MN: West Publishing Co., 1980), pp. 54–61.

20. John Walker Mauer, "Southern State Constitutions in the 1870s: A Case Study of Texas" (Ph.D. dissertation, Rice University, 1982), pp. 3–23; *Texas Almanac*, p. 590.

21. Alwyn Barr, *Reconstruction to Reform: Texas Politics, 1876–1906*

(Austin: University of Texas Press, 1971), p. 59; Richardson, *Texas*, pp. 328–32.

22. Oran Milo Roberts, "The History and Burden of Taxation," *Bulletin of the University of Texas* (Austin, December 1889), pp. 1–16.

23. Ibid., p. 3.

24. Ibid., p. 4.

25. Ibid., p. 5.

26. Ibid., p. 5. See also Roberts's summation on page 12: "And better still, if the time should ever come when it shall be seen and acted on, that the true principle in a republic is that the labor materialized into permanent property shall be made to support the government mainly if not entirely, and not the labor itself in the effort of the acquisition of property, the vast majority of people, the millions who reach maturity of manhood and womanhood, and who must commence their life-work for their own self-elevation without property to assist them in it, would be encouraged to improve their condition in life, with the knowledge that the government did not impose any drawback upon their labor by taxing the necessaries of life."

27. Ibid., p. 5.

28. Ibid., p. 12.

29. Richardson, *Texas*, p. 332.

30. John Stricklin Spratt, *The Road to Spindletop: Economic Change in Texas, 1875–1901*, Texas History Paperbacks (Dallas: Southern Methodist University Press, 1955; reprint, Austin: University of Texas Press, 1970), pp. 277–83.

31. Ruth Sheldon Knowles, *The Greatest Gamblers: The Epic of American Oil Exploration* (Norman, OK: University of Oklahoma Press, 1978), pp. 23–43; Spratt, *Road to Spindletop*, pp. 274–76.

32. Knowles, *Greatest Gamblers*, pp. 35–40.

33. *Journals of the Convention Assembled at the City of Austin on the Fourth of July, 1845, for the Purpose of Framing a Constitution for the State of Texas*, preface by Mary Bell Hart (Austin: Miner & Cruger, Printers to the Convention, 1845; reprint, Austin: Shoal Creek Publishers, 1974), pp. 67–69, 173–77; C. Read Granberry and John T. Potter, "Some Texas Tax Trails," *Texas Quarterly* 7 (Winter 1964): 132–33.

34. Barr, *Reconstruction to Reform*, p. 59.

35. Peter Molyneaux, "Why a State Income Tax? An Analysis of a Revolutionary Proposal," *The Texas Monthly* (June 1929): 728–46; see also, "The Seven Years Ahead" and "Taxes and City Growth," same issue, pp. 721–27.

36. Peter Molyneaux, editorial, *The Texas Weekly* 9 (7 January 1933): 1–3.

37. Texas State Legislature, Legislative Committee on Organization and Economy, *A Plea for Reduction of Taxes and Bonds in Texas* (Austin, n.d.), p. 2.

38. Richardson, *Texas*, p. 465.

39. E. T. Miller, "The Historical Development of the Texas State Tax System," *The Southwestern Historical Quarterly* 55 (July 1951): 16–17;

David F. Prindle, *Petroleum Politics and the Texas Railroad Commission* (Austin: University of Texas Press, 1981), pp. 21–39.

40. George Fuermann, *Reluctant Empire* (Garden City, NY: Doubleday and Co., 1957), p. 266.

41. Granberry and Potter, "Tax Trails," pp. 138–39. Fuermann, *Reluctant Empire*, p. 266.

42. Texas, Comptroller of Public Accounts, *Annual Financial Report, 1981*, (Austin, 1982) pp. 3–5; idem, untitled twenty-year summary of revenues and expenditures (Austin, 1982, mimeographed).

43. Interview with Bob Bullock, Texas State Comptroller of Public Accounts, Austin, April 7, 1982.

44. Fehrenbach, *Lone Star*, p. 656.

45. Granberry and Potter, "Tax Trails," pp. 139–41.

46. Texas, Commission on State and Local Tax Policy, *Factual Reports*, vol. 1, *Our State Tax Policy: Its History: Its Future*; vol. 2, *State Tax Policy and the Individual*, pp. 1–10, 48–66; vol. 3, *State Tax Policy and Business*; vol. 4, *Effect of the 1959 Tax Bill on State Revenues*.

47. Texas State Legislature, Legislative Budget Office, *Legislative Tax Handbook, Fiscal Year Ended August 31, 1980* (Austin, 1981), pp. B38–41.

48. Thomas R. Plaut, *A Supply-Side Model of the Texas Economy and Economic and Population Forecasts to the Year 2000* (Austin: Bureau of Business Research, University of Texas, 1982), no. BF 82-2, Figure 3.

49. Texas, Legislative Budget Board, *Fiscal Size Up, 1982–1983* (Austin, 1982), pp. 3–5.

50. Janice C. May, Stuart A. MacCorkie, and Dick Smith, *Texas Government*, 8th ed. (New York: McGraw-Hill, 1980), pp. 257–65; Texas Research League, *Bulletin* 5 (Austin, 11 August 1978), pp. 1–6.

51. Interview with Thomas M. Kheel, Legislative Budget Director, Austin, April 7, 1982.

52. Interviews, Austin, April 1980.

9. Ohio: The Middle-aged "Middle Region"

1. James L. Bates, *Alfred Kelley, His Life and Work* (Columbus, OH: privately printed, 1888), p. 12.

2. Walter Prescott Webb, *The Great Frontier* (Austin: University of Texas Press, 1975), pp. 13–28.

3. Adam Smith, *The Wealth of Nations* (New York: The Modern Library, Random House, 1937), pp. 531–32.

4. Carl Wittke, ed., *The History of the State of Ohio*, vol. 1, *The Foundations of Ohio*, by Beverly W. Bond, Jr. (Columbus: Ohio State Archaeological and Historical Society, 1941), pp. 3–9, 166–68.

5. John Fiske, *The Critical Period of American History, 1783–1789* (Boston: Houghton Mifflin and Company, 1888), pp. 187–91.

6. Bond, *Foundations*, pp. 250–54; Fiske, *Critical Period*, pp. 191–96.

7. Fiske, *Critical Period*, pp. 203–07; Bond, *Foundations*, pp. 254–67; Montesquieu, *The Spirit of the Laws*, trans. Thomas Nugent (New York: Hafner Publishing Co., 1949), Book IX, Chap. 2.

8. Frederick Jackson Turner, *The Frontier in American History* (New York: Henry Holt and Company, 1958), p. 170.

9. Harlan Hatcher, *The Western Reserve: The Story of New Connecticut in Ohio* (Indianapolis: Bobbs-Merrill Company, 1949), pp. 27–35; Bond, *Foundations*, pp. 349–73.

10. Isaac Franklin Patterson, *The Constitutions of Ohio* (Cleveland: Arthur H. Clarke Company, 1912), pp. 15–16.

11. James P. Lawyer, Jr., *History of Ohio from the Glacial Period to the Present Time* (Columbus: Union Publishing Co., 1905), pp. 122–34, 145–46; George H. Crow and C. P. Smith, *My State—Ohio: An Authentic History of the Buckeye State* (Columbus: Ohio Teacher Service Bureau, 1935), pp. 387–90; Paul W. Miller, ed., *Brand Whitlock's The Buckeyes: A Story of Politics and Abolitionism in an Ohio Town, 1836–1845* (Athens, OH: Ohio University Press, 1977), pp. 26–43. A passage in this historical novel by Whitlock, the turn-of-the-century Progressive mayor of Toledo, portrays the development of Ohioanism in the protagonist during the 1840 campaign: "He was beginning to take a pride in Ohio too, now that he had a stake in the country. He was beginning to think of himself not so much as a Kentuckian as an Ohioan; not a Corn Cracker but a Buckeye, as Ohioans had begun to call themselves since they had been singing [Otway Curry's] spirited song in this present campaign" (p. 175).

12. Patterson, *Constitutions*, pp. 18–19. "In stopping the wild debauch of the treasury and tying the hands of the privileged interests the people became welded into a real commonwealth" (p. 19). Turner, *Frontier*, pp. ii, 157–59.

13. Crow and Smith, *My State*, pp. 397–412; Bond, *Foundations*, pp. 445–46.

14. Neal R. Pierce and John Keefe, *The Great Lakes States of America* (New York: W. W. Norton and Co., 1980), pp. 16–19, 301.

15. Enibius O. Randell and Daniel J. Ryan, *History of Ohio*, 4 vols. (New York: Century History Co., 1912), 3:351–54; Patterson, *Constitutions*, pp. 15–17, 20–23; Constitution of the State of Ohio, Article VIII, Sections 1, 2, 3, Sections 2a–2j.

16. Official Statement Relating to the Original Issuance of $70,000,000 State of Ohio Economic Development Bonds, Series 1982 (Columbus: Treasurer of State of Ohio, 1 May 1982), p. 52 (hereafter, Bond Prospectus).

17. Bates, *Kelley*, p. 143.

18. Randell and Ryan, *History*, p. 356; Crow and Smith, *My State*, p. 432.

19. Bates, *Kelley*, p. 143.

20. Charles B. Galbreath, *History of Ohio*, 3 vols. (Chicago: American Historical Society, 1925), 2:97–98; Paul R. Good, *A Digest of the Debates*

and Addresses Before the Fourth Ohio Constitutional Convention (Columbus, Paul R. Good, 1912), pp. 41–44.

21. Galbreath, *History*, 2:104–05; Crow and Smith, *My State*, p. 432; James K. Mercer, *Ohio Legislative History, 1909–1913* (Columbus: Press of the Edward T. Miller Co., 1913), pp. 466–67. The results of the convention were submitted to the voters in forty-two separate referendums. The item providing woman suffrage was defeated by nearly 90,000 votes, the largest negative margin of the lot. The voters also refused to delete the word "white" from the section defining the qualifications for the vote.

22. Crow and Smith, *My State*, pp. 433–36; Wittke, *History of the State of Ohio*, vol. 6, *Ohio in the Twentieth Century, 1900–1938*, ed. Harlow Lindley (Columbus: Ohio State Archaeological and Historical Society, 1942), pp. 49–51, 66–68, 74–77; *The Cleveland Plain Dealer*, 10 May 1933, p. 7.

23. "Argument for the Ten Mill Limitation Amendment," September 7, 1933, in file "Ten Mill Limitation Amendment, November, 1933" (Elections Division, Office of Secretary of State, Columbus, Ohio).

24. "Argument Against Initiated Constitutional Tax Limit Amendment," file (Office of Secretary of State, Columbus, Ohio).

25. Crow and Smith, *My State*, pp. 433–36; Lindley, *Ohio in the Twentieth Century*, pp. 66–68, 74–77.

26. Pierce and Keefe, *Great Lakes States*, pp. 303–07; Frederick D. Stocker, *The Rough Road to Tax Reform: The Ohio Experience*, Working Papers in Public Policy, No. 1 (Columbus: Division of Public Administration, College of Administrative Science, Ohio State University, March 1972), pp. 1–4.

27. Advisory Commission on Intergovernmental Relations (ACIR), *Significant Features of Fiscal Federalism*, 1980–81 edition (Washington, D.C., December 1981), pp. 65, 89, Tables 47, 68; *Bond Prospectus*, p. 52.

28. Ohio Bureau of Employment Services, "Employment, Hours and Earnings in Ohio," March 1982, Ohio Labor Market Information, p. 9. Robert Premus, "The Ohio Economy, Past, Present and Future" (n.d., mimeographed), pp. 17–20.

29. U.S. Department of Commerce, Bureau of Census, "Population of States"; emigration figures provided by Jack Brown, Ohio Department of Economic and Community Development, Columbus, April 1982.

30. Hatcher, *Western Reserve*, pp. 202–19.

31. Hugh Allen, *Rubber's Home Town: The Real-Life Story of Akron* (New York: Stratford House, 1949), pp. 116–32.

32. William Papier, "Research and Development in the Great Lakes States," *Bulletin of Business Research* 156, no. 5 (Columbus: Center for Business and Economic Research, Ohio State University, May 1971); " 'Push-Pull' and 'Brain Drain,' " *Personnel Administration* (Journal of the Society for Personnel Administration) (November–December 1968): 43–49. Mr. Papier is director of research for the Ohio Bureau of Employment Services.

33. Stocker, *Rough Road to Tax Reform*, pp. 10–25; Pierce and Keefe, *Great Lakes*, pp. 308–10.

34. Stocker, *Rough Road to Tax Reform*, pp. 18–25.

35. William Papier, "Employment Problems in Ohio," *Agenda for Management* (Journal of the Ohio University College of Business Administration) 1, no. 3 (Winter 1979): 5; Richard K. Vedder, "State and Local Fiscal Policy and Economic Development: The Case of Ohio" (report to Ohio's U.S. Representative Clarence J. Brown, R., 19 August 1981, mimeographed), p. 36. See also Richard K. Vedder, "Rich States, Poor States: How High Taxes Inhibit Growth," *Journal of Contemporary Studies* 5, no. 4 (Fall 1982): 19–32, esp. p. 22. Vedder's econometric study of Ohio is discussed in more detail in *State and Local Economic Development Strategy: A "Supply Side" Perspective*, Subcommittee on Monetary and Fiscal Policy, Joint Economic Committee, Congress of the United States (Washington, D.C.: GPO, 26 October 1981), pp. 23–24.

36. Vedder, "State and Local Fiscal Policy," p. 36.

37. Pierce and Keefe, *Great Lakes*, pp. 309–10.

38. Interview with Edward Kelly, Research Director, OPIC, Cleveland, Ohio, May 14, 1982; "Yes on Two," press packet of the Ohio Fair Tax Initiative Committee, 1980; Arthur A. Schwartz and Sherrod Brown, "Voter Participation in Constitutional Amendment and Legislation; Proposed Constitutional Amendments, Initiated Legislation, and Laws Challenged by Referendum, Submitted to the Electors" (Columbus: Ohio Secretary of State, 1982, mimeographed), p. 17. The vote on Issue Two, the Fair Tax Initiative, was 880,671 yes to 3,000,028 no.

39. Interview with Howard Collier, Director, Ohio Office of Management and Budget, Columbus, May 12, 1982; U.S. Department of Commerce, Bureau of Economic Analysis, "Fourth Quarter 1981 State Nonfarm Personal Income and 1981 State Per Capita Personal Income," *U.S. Department of Commerce News* (Washington, D.C., 9 May 1982), BEA 82-23.

40. Ohio Legislative Budget Office, "Summary Materials Describing the FY 1982 and FY 1983 GRF Budget Problem" (Columbus: 22 April 1982, mimeographed).

41. William Hershey, "Most Ohioans Polled Favor Budget Cuts over Tax Hike," *Akron Beacon* (12 May 1982), p. 1; Ohio Legislative Budget Committee and Office, "Summary of the Revenue and Appropriation Changes in Sub. S.B. 530 as Reported by House Ways and Means" (4 May 1982, mimeographed memo); interview with Waldo Bennett Rose, Assistant Minority Leader, Ohio House of Representatives, Columbus, May 12, 1982.

10. Michigan: Tax Revolts and Hard Times

1. Thomas McIntyre Cooley, *Michigan: A History of Governments* (Boston: Houghton Mifflin and Co., 1885), pp. 8, 26.

2. Ibid., pp. 71–72.
3. Ibid., pp. 211–27, 255; Willis F. Dunbar, *Michigan: A History of the Wolverine State* (Grand Rapids, MI: William B. Eerdmans Publishing Co., 1965), pp. 301–19.
4. Cooley, *Michigan*, pp. 254–58, 261–62.
5. Ibid., p. 272.
6. Ibid., p. 268.
7. Ibid., pp. 272–74.
8. Ibid., pp. 281–84; Reginald C. McGrane, *Foreign Bondholders and American State Debts* (New York: Macmillan Co., 1935), p. 144; Alexander Trotter, *Observations on the Financial Position and Credit of Such of the States of the North American Union as have Contracted Public Debts* (London: Longman, Orme, Brown, Green and Longmans, 1839), pp. 32–50, 343. Trotter wrote of Michigan: "This state may be destined to hold a high position among the United States, but, in the meantime, the works undertaken have involved it in a debt which is disproportioned to the number and resources of the inhabitants" (p. 343). This warning was prescient, observes McGrane, but it did not circulate in England in time to prevent heavy investment in Michigan's $5-million bond issue. McGrane, *Foreign Bondholders*, p. 150.
9. McGrane, *Foreign Bondholders*, pp. 144–55; Cooley, *Michigan*, pp. 283–91.
10. McGrane, *Foreign Bondholders*, pp. 155–67; Cooley, *Michigan*, pp. 287–91. For a jurist so identified with the protection of private property, Cooley is remarkably restrained in commenting on Michigan's course of conduct; see page 189. American state bonds did not reappear in the European market until March 1984 with the sale of an Alaska Housing Authority issue.
11. Trotter, *Observations*, p. 355.
12. Ibid.
13. McGrane, *Foreign Bondholders*, p. 158.
14. Ibid., pp. 161–62.
15. Michigan, Constitution of 1850, Article XIV, Sections 3 and 4. Standard language also allowed the state to contract debt "to repel invasion, suppress insurrection, defend the state in time of war."
16. Quoted in James C. Mohr, ed., *Radical Republicans in the North: State Politics During Reconstruction* (Baltimore: Johns Hopkins University Press, 1976). Chap. 7, "Michigan: Quickening Government in a Developing State," by George M. Blackburn, p. 122.
17. Cooley, *Michigan*, pp. 309–11; Dunbar, *Michigan*, pp. 281–85.
18. Dunbar, *Michigan*, pp. 551–64.
19. *Proceedings and Debates of the Constitutional Convention of the State of Michigan Convened in the City of Lansing, Tuesday, October 22, 1907*, vol. 1 (Lansing: Wynkoop, Hallenbeck, Crawford Co., State Printers, 1907), p. 651, col. 1. Delegate Victor M. Gore was citing William Edward Hartpole Lecky's *Democracy and Liberty*.
20. *Proceedings and Debates*, vol. 2, p. 1442. The 1908 constitution al-

lowed the legislature in joint convention to reject the amendment or propose an alternative. Said the Address to the People, "The consideration was potent with the Convention that public opinion is subject to sudden fluctuations that the cherished policies of one year may be discarded the next upon fuller information and maturer thought." See also Citizens Research Council of Michigan, *Taxation and the Referendum in Michigan* (Detroit and Lansing, March 1980), pp. 17–21.

21. Citizens Research Council, *Taxation and the Referendum*, p. 20. Nineteen were proposed, and seven succeeded.

22. David N. Rosenberger, "Historical Perspective on Constitutional Limitation of Property Taxes in Michigan," *Wayne Law Review* 24 (1978): 939–69; Michigan State Tax Commission, *Twenty-fourth Report, 1945–46* (Lansing: Franklin De Kleine Co., State Printers, 1947), pp. 58–63, Table XVI, p. 61.

23. Robert S. Ford, *Recent Developments in the Michigan Tax Structure*, New Series Bulletin, No. 4 (Ann Arbor: University of Michigan Bureau of Government, June 1936), pp. 11–14, Table VII.

24. See Chap. 9, p. 252.

25. Rosenberger, "Historical Perspective," pp. 940–41. Ford, *Recent Developments*, pp. 12–13.

26. The state showed a more determined resistance than most, however, to the drive for an income tax, which was originally intended to fill in the gaps of the general property tax. See Chap. 2. Constitutional initiatives for an income tax were defeated in 1922, 1924, and 1934. A petition was circulated in 1936 by real estate groups to repeal the general property tax altogether and substitute an income tax; that one lost, too. See Ford, *Recent Developments*, pp. 22, 24; Citizens Research Council, *Taxation and the Referendum*, p. A1. In a further artifact, the 1963 constitution retained a property qualification for voting on tax limit overrides (Article II, Section 6).

27. Ford, *Recent Developments*, pp. 18–24; Rosenberger, "Historical Perspective," pp. 944–45. Compare Ford, p. 23, n. 33 with William H. Chafe, "Flint and the Great Depression," in *Michigan Perspectives, People, Events, Issues*, ed. Alex S. Brown, John T. Houdek, and John H. Yzenbaard (Dubuque, IA: Kendall/Hunt Publishing Co., 1974), pp. 245–55. Chafe's article is reprinted from *Michigan History* 53 (Fall 1969), pp. 225–39. He finds that at the end of the 1930s the people of Flint had become accustomed to a much higher level of social services, even though one of its welfare administrators was saying that second-generation relief recipients should be sterilized (pp. 250, 255).

28. *Butcher v. Township of Grosse Isle*, 387 Mich. 42; 194 N.W. 2nd at 845 (1972).

29. Ibid., at 58–60, 194 N.W. 2nd at 851–52 and n. 3. Quoted in Rosenberger, "Historical Perspective," p. 960.

30. Carolyn Stieber, *The Politics of Change in Michigan* (East Lansing: Michigan State University Press, 1970), p. 8.

31. Ibid., pp. 15–22; Dunbar, *Michigan*, pp. 639–43.

32. Stieber, *Politics*, pp. 17–28. Legislators were ineligible to serve as delegates during their terms.
33. Michigan, Constitution of 1963, Article IX, Section 1 (budget); Section 15 (long-term debt); Section 7 (income tax). The constitution did, however, eliminate the 1850 prohibition against long-term debt and the dollar limit on budget notes.
34. Stieber, *Politics*, p. 80. The same bill introduced a corporate income tax of 5.6% and a financial-institution tax of 7%.
35. *Michigan Manual* (Lansing: State of Michigan Department of Management and Budget, 1981), p. 82.
36. Michigan State Senate, Senate Fiscal Agency, *Tax Proposals on the 1978 Ballot in Michigan* (Lansing, September 1978); Citizens Research Council of Michigan, "The Michigan Tax Limitation Amendment—1," *Council Comments* (Detroit and Lansing, 9 November 1981); idem, "The Michigan Tax Limitation Amendment, Current Status and Issues" (Detroit and Lansing, October 1981, mimeographed), p. 9.
37. Michigan State Senate, Senate Fiscal Agency, *A Report on Tisch II*, prepared by Theodore A. Ferris and Thomas L. Hickner (Lansing, October 1980). Tisch I had allowed an increase in the state income tax to replace lost property tax revenue. Tisch II did not.
38. "Mr. Headlee sounds good," Tisch said in an interview in his handcrafted living room, settling into a rolling cadence. "Mr. Headlee uses lots of cutsie pie one-liners. He has a little black book full of loose-leaf pages that he has used since he was president of the Junior Chamber of Commerce. He does well with any group, with any problem so long as he carries his little black book. He carries his lines with him in a loose-leaf black book." Interview, Laingsburg, Michigan, July 30, 1982.
39. Interviews with Governor James Blanchard, Lansing, 16 August 1983; James DeMar, Armada, 17 August 1983; Mick Steiner, Pontiac, 17 August 1983; Joe Cisneros, "State Tax Reformers Set Their Sights on '84," *The Oakland* (Michigan) *Press*, 18 July 1982, pp. A-1, A-8.

11. New England: The Oldest Frontier Revives

1. Raymond D. Gastil, *Cultural Regions of the United States* (Seattle: University of Washington Press, 1975), p. 151.
2. Lincoln Steffens, *The Autobiography of Lincoln Steffens*, 2 vols. (New York: Harcourt Brace Jovanovich, 1974), 2:472–73, 481.
3. John Gould, *Maine Lingo* (Camden, ME: Down East Magazine, 1975), p. 175 ("Maineiac"), 275 ("State of Maine (I)"). Mr. Gould observes that the insistence on the full title is embodied in the state constitution. "There was much pondering at the time of separation from Massachusetts as to the appropriate style and title, and most Mainers agreed they had no desire to be another damn commonwealth" (p. 275).
4. Frank B. Sanborn, *New Hampshire: An Epitome of Popular Government* (Boston: Houghton Mifflin and Co., 1904), pp. vii–viii.

5. Samuel Williams, *Vermont During the War for Independence* (Burlington, VT: Free Press Printing Co., 1944), facsimile reprint of three chapters from Williams's *Natural and Civil History of Vermont* (n.p., 1794), pp. 227–28, 233, 299; see also Frederic F. Van DeWater, *The Reluctant Republic: Vermont, 1724–1791* (Taftsville, VT: Countryman Press, 1974); Charles Miner Thompson, *Independent Vermont* (Boston: Houghton Mifflin Co., 1942).

    Williams describes Vermont on the eve of the Revolution: "The situation of the inhabitants at this time, seems to have approached nearly to what has been called by some, a state of nature. A large number of people were scattered over a large tract of country, in small settlements, at a great distance from each other, without any form of government, any established laws, or civil officers" (pp. 227–28). After the Declaration of Independence, they acted on this model: "The period was now come, when as they expressed it, they were reduced to a state of nature. Some form of government must be adopted. They had the same right to assume the powers of government, that the Congress had" (p. 233).

6. Advisory Commission on Intergovernmental Relations (ACIR), *Significant Features of Fiscal Federalism*, 1979–80 edition (Washington, D.C., October 1980), p. 56, Table 42; p. 74, Table 54; pp. 46–47, Tables, 35.1, 35.2.

7. Conversations with former governor Meldrim Thomson, Orford, NH; Professor Jack Menges, Hanover, NH, July 18, 1982.

8. Sanborn, *Epitome*, p. 15.

9. Maurice H. Robinson, "A History of Taxation in New Hampshire" (publications of the American Economic Association, Third Series, III, no. 3, August 1902), p. 7. This spirited woman was the former Elizabeth Hersie, from Hingham, Massachusetts.

10. Ibid., p. 37.

11. Ibid., p. 38.

12. Sanborn, *Epitome*, pp. 169–74, 204–05; Jere R. Daniell, *Colonial New Hampshire* (Millwood, NY: KTO Press, 1981), pp. 217–44.

13. Elizabeth Forbes Morison and Elting E. Morison, *New Hampshire: A Bicentennial History* (New York: W. W. Norton and Co., 1976), p. 81; Leon W. Anderson, *New Hampshire Constitution: Development of the Constitution over 200 Years* (Concord: New Hampshire Secretary of State, 1981), pp. 6–12; Thompson, *Independent Vermont*, pp. 346–49.

14. Anderson, *New Hampshire Constitution*, pp. 11–12.

15. Sanborn, *Epitome*, pp. 252–55; Donald B. Cole, *Jacksonian Democracy in New Hampshire, 1800–1851* (Cambridge: Harvard University Press, 1970).

16. Sanborn, *Epitome*, pp. 256–57.

17. Robinson, "History of Taxation," p. 96.

18. Ibid., p. 96.

19. Ibid., pp. 96–97.

20. Constitution of New Hampshire, Part the Second, Article the Fifth.
21. Colin D. Campbell and Rosemary G. Campbell, *A Comparative Study of the Fiscal Systems of New Hampshire and Vermont, 1940–1974* (Hampton, NH: Wheelabrator Foundation, 1976), p. 14.
22. Ibid., pp. 7, 17–20.
23. Ibid., p. 7; interview with Professor Colin D. Campbell, Hanover, NH, 18 July 1982. For Vermont's reply, see Dr. David K. Smith, "A Critique of the Campbell & Campbell Report" (Middlebury College, 12 July 1976, mimeographed).
24. David Hale, "Vermont in the Age of Reagan" (Chicago, December 1981, mimeographed). Also published as a four-part series in the *Burlington Free Press*, Burlington, VT, December 1981.
25. U.S. Department of Labor, *Employment and Earnings* (Washington, D.C.: GPO, May 1982).

12. Massachusetts: The Tax Revolt Continues

1. *Debates in the Massachusetts Constitutional Convention, 1917–1918*, vol. 3 (Boston: Wright and Potter Printing Co., 1920), pp. 780, 794. William S. Kinney stated that the income tax produced $13.5 million in 1917, against $6 million from the application of the general property tax to the same class of property in 1916. Another delegate asked where the revenue would come from if a contemplated tax cut went through. "That is the old cry that everybody interested in tax reform in Massachusetts has had to face for ten years," Kinney replied. The answer, other speakers made clear, was from the economic growth allowed by the lower tax rate (pp. 789–90).
2. Ibid., p. 778.
3. Unadjusted census and Bureau of Economic Analysis figures. By the ACIR's adjusted calculation, Massachusetts in 1965 was 2.3 percentage points *below* the U.S. average. Advisory Commission on Intergovernmental Relations (ACIR), *Significant Features of Fiscal Federalism*, 1981–82 edition (Washington, D.C., April 1983), pp. 38–39, Tables 22.1–22.3.
4. "No Last Hurrah: Reports of Boston's Demise Are Grossly Exaggerated" (transcript of interview with Boston Mayor Kevin White), *Barron's*, 21 November 1977, p. 16.
5. Colin D. Campbell and Edward G. Gagnon, *Rising Tax Burdens in Massachusetts, New Hampshire and Vermont, 1957–1976* (a report to Data General Corporation, Hanover, NH 1977), p. 12.
6. Charles W. Kadlec and Arthur B. Laffer, *An Analysis of Fiscal Policy and Economic Growth in Massachusetts* (Rolling Hills Estates, CA: A. B. Laffer Associates, April 16, 1981), pp. 56–59.
7. Campbell and Gagnon, *Tax Burdens*, p. 17, Table 12.
8. Ibid., p. 42, Appendix I.

9. Ibid, p. 25.

10. Massachusetts Department of Revenue, *Monthly Report of Tax Collections*, through June 30, 1975.

11. Governor Michael Dukakis, Press Release and Statement, May 2, 1975, p. 2.

12. Various interviews, Boston, September 1975.

13. See, for instance, John Kifner, "Massachusetts Raises Taxes Sharply Under Pressure of Banks," *The New York Times* (10 November 1975), p. 33; "Heeding a Lesson," in Review and Outlook, *The Wall Street Journal* (13 November 1975), p. 20.

14. Office of Governor Michael Dukakis, "Fact Sheet on Massachusetts Delegation Trip to New York," news advisory, November 13, 1975.

15. Ibid.; reporter's notes.

16. Kadlec and Laffer, *Analysis*, pp. 30–41; figures supplied by Massachusetts Department of Employment Security, August 1982.

17. U.S. Department of Commerce, Bureau of the Census, *Current Population Survey* (various years).

18. David Warsh, "The Supply-Sider Who's Read All Over," *The Boston Globe* (7 September 1982), pp. 1, 50. One of Brookes's first submissions compared the economies of Massachusetts and New Hampshire. Written in 1976, before Brookes had even heard of Arthur Laffer and before the "supply-side" label had been coined, it traced the dramatic difference in vigor to their tax burdens. From this seed grew the corpus of state-oriented supply-side writing. This article is summarized in Warren Brookes's remarkable book *The Economy in Mind* (New York: Universe Books, 1982), pp. 198–200. The article was originally submitted to *The Wall Street Journal* but, inexplicably, not used.

19. K. Heinz Muehlmann, *An Appraisal of the Economy of Massachusetts with Proposals for an Economic Strategy* (Boston: Massachusetts Department of Commerce and Development, December 1971), p. 2.

20. Massachusetts High Technology Council, "A New Social Contract for Massachusetts" (Boston, 1979[?]), p. 3. See also, Technical Marketing Associates, Inc., *High Technology Enterprise in Massachusetts—Its Role and Its Concerns* (Concord, MA, October 1979).

21. Warren Brookes, "Massachusetts Tax Relief: A Compromise with Clout," *The Boston Herald American* (22 June 1979).

22. James Ring Adams, "Taxachusetts Turns Around," *The Wall Street Journal* (5 February 1980), p. 22.

23. Raymond L. Bridgman, *The Massachusetts Constitutional Convention of 1917* (Boston, 1922), p. 49–51.

24. Constitution of Massachusetts, Article XVIII, Article LXXXI. Statutory petitions can be altered only on technical matters, and only with the consent of the majority of the first ten signers.

25. (James H. Powers), Legislative Research Council, *Limiting Taxation and Spending by State and Local Governments* (Boston: Commonwealth of Massachusetts, 10 June 1980), pp. 381–83. See also Sherry [Tvedt] Davis, "Enough Is Enough: The Origins of Proposition 2½" (master's thesis,

Massachusetts Institute of Technology, June 1981), pp. 27–35. A much condensed version of this interesting paper appears in Lawrence E. Susskind, ed., *Proposition 2½: Its Impact on Massachusetts* (Cambridge: Oelgeschlager, Gunn and Hain, 1983), pp. 3–11.

26. Davis, "Enough is Enough," pp. 39–45.

27. Ibid., pp. 43–46.

28. Interviews with Barbara Anderson, Howard Foley, K. Heinz Muehlmann, August 1982.

29. Subsequent corrective legislation allowed the tax base to grow with additional construction and lowered the 4% limit on special-district and county assessments on localities to 2½%.

30. Warren Brookes, "How the Legislature Destroyed the Initiative Petition Process," *The Boston Herald American* (11 July 1980), A15; Associated Industries of Massachusetts, "Legislature Stonewalls Constitutional Tax Reform," *Legislative Bulletin* 20, no. 20 (3 July 1980).

31. Massachusetts High Technology Council, minutes of meeting of Executive Committee of the Board of Directors, August 26, 1980; September 2, September 8, September 15, and September 30, 1980. A. V. d'Arbeloff, in a letter to the MHTC Board of Directors, September 2, 1980; Howard Foley, memo to MHTC members, September 30, 1980.

32. Dresner, Morris and Tortorello Research, "Proposition 2½: Why We Won?" (New York, November 1980).

33. Legislative Research Bureau, *Massachusetts Initiative Proposal for a Constitutional Amendment Limiting State and Local Taxation* (Boston, 16 July 1982), pp. 8–22.

34. Helen F. Ladd and Julie Boatright Wilson, "Proposition 2½: Explaining the Vote" (Program in City and Regional Planning, John F. Kennedy School of Government, Harvard University, April 1981), pp. 8–22, 28.

35. James Ring Adams, "Boston's Curious Financial Crisis," *The Wall Street Journal*, 12 August 1981.

36. Susskind, *Proposition 2½*, p. 8.

37. Warren T. Brookes, "Is Supply-Side Economics Dead? A Symposium," *The American Spectator* 16, no. 11 (November 1983): 12.

38. The Massachusetts High Technology Council has kept an elaborate chronology of this episode.

39. This initiative was ultimately kept off the ballot by State Attorney General Francis X. Bellotti, after its sponsors had collected 150,000 signatures. Bellotti, who has become a major barrier to the initiative process, made a questionable ruling that the initiative did not propose a "law," and he was upheld in a controversial Supreme Judicial Court decision. *Milton Paisner and Others vs. Attorney General and Others*, S.J.C. Docket No. 3314, December 14, 1983. "The Empire Strikes Back," *The Wall Street Journal*, 18 January 1984.

13. Revealing the Secrets of the Tax Revolt

1. Montesquieu, *Esprit des Lois*, Book XIII, Chap. 7 (my translation). Jean Baptiste Say echoed this argument in a strong defense of progressivity that was largely ignored by nineteenth century Americans. Jean Baptiste Say, *A Treatise on Political Economy; or The Production, Distribution and Consumption of Wealth*, trans. C. R. Prinsep, 3rd American Edition (Philadelphia: John Grigg, 1827), pp. 417–18.

2. *The Adams Papers: Adams Family Correspondence*, 4 vols., L. H. Butterfield and Marc Friedlander, eds. (Cambridge: Belknap Press of Harvard University Press, 1973), 3:226, n. 3. The editors quote Adams's recollection of this section: "As the Words flowed from my Pen, from the heart in reality rather than the head, in composing this paragraph, I could not help laughing, to myself alone in my Closet, at the Oddity of it. I expected it would be attacked in the Convention from all quarters, on the Score of Affectation, Pedantry, Hypocrisy, and above all Oeconomy." See also Chap. 3, p. 64.

3. Commonwealth of Massachusetts, Constitution of 1780, Part the Second, Chapter 5, Section 2.

4. John Locke, *The Second Treatise on Government*, Chapter XI, Section 140.

5. Elie Halévy, *The Growth of Philosophic Radicalism*, trans. Mary Morris (Boston, Beacon Press, 1955), p. 121.

INDEX

Abolitionist movement, 4, 87, 247
Accumulation phase of a fiscal
    crisis, 91, 92–111, 311–13
Adams, Charles Francis, 309
Adams, John, 30, 32, 61, 62, 63, 64,
    71, 318, 343–44
Adams, Sherman, 301
Advisory Commission on
    Intergovernmental Relations
    (ACIR), 17, 18, 22
Alabama, 180
Alaska, 117
Albany Evening Argus, 82
Allen, Ethan, 211, 293
Allen, O.K., 194, 195, 196
Anderson, Barbara, 326, 329, 330,
    332, 333
Andros, Sir Edmond, 52, 53, 55, 61
Anti-Rent movement, 78–79
Arkansas, 180
Articles of Confederation, 244, 245,
    268, 293
Associated Industries of
    Massachusetts (AIM), 317–18,
    325–27, 328, 330
Atkins, Chester G., 320
Auletta, Kenneth A., 107
Austerity phase of a fiscal crisis, 92,
    117–18
Austin, Stephen, 211–12
Authority bonds, 93–95, 96, 98, 106,
    112

Badillo, Herman, 119
Bagley, John, 274
Bahl, Roy, 119
Bank of the United States, 33, 216,
    270, 271, 272
Bank taxes, 118, 119–20, 149
"Barnburners," 74, 77, 80, 84, 87
Barr, Alwyn, 228
Barry, John, 273–74
Bascom, Ansel, 82
Beame, Abraham, 103, 112, 113–15,
    117, 118, 119, 120
Beauregard, P.G.T., 191
Behr, Peter, 165

Bell, Jeffrey, 23
Bellotti, Frances X., 325
Bickel, Alexander, 107
Biddle, E. R., 272
Biddle, Nicholas, 272
Black, Eugene F., 278–79
Blanchard, James, 285, 287
Bond Anticipation Notes (BANs),
    110
Boston Finance Commission, 325
Boston Globe, 312, 320–21
Boston Herald American, 317
Boyle, Robert, 55
Bracket creep, 7, 149, 151
Braden, George D., 222
Brake, D. Hale, 281
Brannan, Samuel, 126, 137
Braucher, Ron, 264
Bricker, John, 252
Brookes, Warren, 317, 320, 325,
    332–33
Brown, Clarence L., 263
Brown, Edmund G. (Pat), 144,
    145–47, 148, 150, 153, 157,
    174
Brown, Edmund G. Jr. (Jerry), 145,
    159, 161–62, 163, 166–67, 292,
    314
Brown, Richard, 43, 44
Bryan, William Jennings, 4
Bryce, Viscount James, 35, 36, 138
Buchanan, James, 160
Buell, Abel, 243
Bulger, William, 329
Bush, George, 254, 296
Business profits tax, *see* Corporate
    income tax
Butcher-Forde consulting firm,
    169
Butler, Benjamin, 189

California, 3–4, 8, 39, 124–78, 300,
    317, 346
    Constitution of, 130, 131–32, 141,
        142, 167, 170
    Gold Rush, 4, 125–29, 132, 133,
        135, 136, 137, 138

California (*cont.*)
origin of initiative and
    referendum in, 139–42
Proposition 1, 22, 156–60, 168,
    170, 203, 238, 282
Proposition 4 (1979), 168, 173–74
Proposition 4 (1980), 170–71
Proposition 9, 168–70
Proposition 13, 3, 8, 13, 15, 23,
    124–25, 156, 157, 160–61,
    164–67, 170–76, 237, 260,
    283, 340
SB 90, 152, 153, 154, 155, 157, 158
Watson initiatives, 155, 156, 157,
    161, 165
California Taxpayers' Association,
    230
Campbell, Colin D., 302, 303
Canada, 53, 247, 268
Canto, Victor A., 16, 17
Capital gains tax, 320
Carey, Hugh, 118, 119–21, 122, 320
Carman v. Alvord, 172
Carr, Waggoner, 232
Carter, Jimmy, 6
Case, Clifford, 23
Caughey, John Walton, 136
Celeste, Richard F., 242, 263, 264,
    287
Central Pacific Railroad, 131, 133,
    137, 139
Champion, Hale, 147
Charles I, King of England, 25,
    47–48, 297
Charles II, King of England, 52, 293
Chehardy, Lawrence A., 203–4
Chehardy, Lawrence E., 378
Chin, Young D., 13–15, 17, 320
Chrysler Corporation, 261
Cigarette tax, 301
Citizens for Limited Taxation (CLT),
    324–27, 328, 329, 330, 332,
    333
Claiborne, William C. C., 188
Cleaveland, Moses, 240, 245
Clements, William P., Jr., 221, 237,
    258
Clinton, DeWitt, 75
Cohen, Gerald M., 328
"Cohen amendment," 328, 329–30,
    333
Coke, Richard, 221, 222

Collapse phase of a discal crisis, 92,
    117–18, 315, 316
Collier, Howard, 261–62, 264
Connally, John, 179
Connecticut, 243, 245
Constitution, U.S., 176, 198, 341
Constitutions, state, 34, 37, 38, 39
California, 130, 131–32, 141, 142,
    167, 170
Illinois, 84
Iowa, 130
Louisiana, 187, 188, 191, 192–93,
    195, 198, 199–200, 203–5
Massachusetts, 30–31, 63–65,
    308–9, 322–23, 324
Massachusetts Bay Colony, 63–65,
    318, 343
Michigan, 269, 274, 275–76, 278,
    281, 287
New Hampshire, 31, 298
New York, 81, 83, 84, 87, 90,
    94–95, 108, 122–23, 130,
    248, 249, 345
Ohio, 247, 248, 249, 250–51, 258
Pennsylvania, 84
Rhode Island, 34
taxation and debt limitations
    written into, 39, 81, 83–85,
    90, 93, 122–23, 130, 167,
    192–93, 199–200, 203,
    221–22, 237–38, 248,
    250–51, 253, 274, 275–76,
    277, 278, 281, 284, 308–9,
    345
Tennessee, 23
Texas, 214, 216, 221–22, 228,
    237–38
Cooley, Thomas McIntyre, 34, 37,
    88–89, 268, 270, 271
Coolidge, Calvin, 338
Coons, John, 153
Corporate franchise tax, 118, 119–20,
    149, 157, 251, 258, 262
Corporate income tax, 36, 339–40
in California, 144, 152
in Massachusetts, 315
in New Hampshire, 300, 301, 305
in New York City, 104, 108, 111,
    120
in New York State, 102
see also Inventory tax; Severance
    taxes

Coulter, E. Merton, 184
Council of Economic Advisors, 9, 160
Cranston, Alan, 285
Crocker, Charles, 131
Cromwell, Oliver, 48
Cuomo, Mario, 122

Daniel, W. Lee, 233, 236
d'Arbeloff, Alexander, 327
Dart, Justin, 159
Davis, Edmund J., 185, 218, 219, 220–21, 222
Davis, Jimmie, 199
Davoren, John F. X., 311
Deaver, Michael, 159
Declaration of Independence, 29, 30, 63, 64, 341
DeMar, Jim, 286, 288
Descartes, René, 55
Deukmejian, George, 173
Direct democracy, see Initiatives and referendum
Direct Legislation League, 140
DiSalle, Michael V., 253–54
Discovery phase of a fiscal crisis, 91, 98, 112–17, 313–15, 316
Dukakis, Michael, 313–14, 315, 316, 317, 319, 321, 330, 333

Edwards, Edwin W., 203, 206
Eisenhower Administration, 232, 301
Emergency Financial Control Board, 117
England, 25, 47–49, 268, 293
    taxation of American colonies and, 51–52, 53, 56–59, 60–61, 297–98, 344–45
Erie Canal, 73, 75–76, 80, 87, 91–93, 240, 269
Essay concerning Human Understanding, An (Locke), 29, 55
Essays Moral, Political, and Literary (Hume), 28
Ewing, Thomas, 127
Excise taxes, 251

"Fair Tax Initiative," 260
Feder, Donald, 324, 325
Federalist, The (Hamilton), 31, 176

Federal Reserve Bank, 112
Federal taxes, 5, 6, 8, 204, 225
Fenton, Reuben, 85
Ferguson, James, 230, 233
Field, Stephen J., 128
First National Bank of Boston, 315
Fiscal crises, phases of, 91–123, 311–15, 316, 317, 321–22
Fiscal limitations, see Constitutions, state; Initiatives and referendum; Representation, taxation linked with; Tax Revolt
Flagg, Azariah C., 80
Florida, 181, 185
Foley, Howard, 317, 318, 319, 325, 327, 328, 330
Ford, Gerald R., 6, 117, 159
Ford Motor Company, 160, 275, 279, 282
Fox, Dixon Ryan, 74
France, 267–68
Free-Soil Democrats, 87
Friedman, Milton, 160, 169, 175, 176, 338
Frost, Robert, 299

Galbreath, Charles B., 251
Gallen, Hugh, 305
Gann, Paul, 160–61, 164–66, 168, 171, 172, 173, 174, 260, 283, 285–86, 333
Geddes, Jenny, 48
General Motors, 275, 277, 279
General property taxes, 13, 34, 35–36, 37, 39, 64, 70, 341
    in California, 142–44, 300
    in Massachusetts, 308–9
    in Michigan, 276–77
    in New Hampshire, 299–300
    New York debate on, 85–86
    in Ohio, 249–50, 251
    origins of, 48–50
    in Texas, 214, 221–22, 223, 224, 228, 237–38
    see also Real estate taxes
Genetski, Robert, 13–15, 16, 17, 18, 320
George, Henry, 125, 132–35, 136, 142, 224–25
George II, King of England, 297
Georgia, 181, 243
Gerstaecker, Friedrich, 129

Gilder, George, 9
Gilligan, John J., 258, 259–60
Gilman, Moses, 297
Goldin, Harrison, 114
Goodrich, Benjamin Franklin,
     256–57
Gouge, William, 216
Great Depression, 39, 251, 276, 300,
     338
Greenback Party, 4, 228
Grenville, George, 56–58, 60
Gwin, William M., 130

Halévy, Elie, 345
Hamilton, Alexander, 31, 32
Hamilton, Andrew Jackson, 219
Hamilton, Morgan, 219–20
Harding, Warren G., 338
Harriman, W. Averell, 101
Harrison, William Henry, 246
Harris Trust and Savings Bank, 13,
     15, 320
Hawaii, 4–5, 209
Haynes, John Randolph, 140, 141,
     142
Headlee, Richard, 23, 283–84, 285,
     333
Higgins, Paltillo, 226–27
Hightower, Jim, 236–37
Hill, Richard D., 315
"History and Burden of Taxation,
     The," 223
History of the Colony and Province
     of Massachusetts Bay
     (Hutchinson), 59
Hobbes, Thomas, 25, 55
Hoffman, Michael, 73–75, 77, 80, 81,
     82–83, 87, 92
Honig, William, 173
Hoover, Herbert, 6
Hopkins, Harry, 107
Hopkins, Mark, 131
Hopkins, Stephen, 45, 46, 47
Horton, Raymond D., 119
Housing Finance Agency (HFA), 96,
     97
Houston, Sam, 212, 213–15, 216, 217
Howell, P. A., 252–53
Hume, David, 22, 28–29, 31, 32, 46,
     57
"Hunkers," 77, 80
Hunt, Washington, 92–93

Huntington, Collis P., 131
Hutchinson, Thomas, 59
Hutt, W. W., 9
Hyatt, Gregory, 325–26

Ibn Khaldun, 25, 27
Illinois, 84, 222, 248
Impact: 2½ Project, 332
"Incidence," defined, 22
Income tax, see Corporate income
     tax; Personal income tax
Indiana, 248
Inheritance tax, 251
Initiatives and referendum, 38, 39,
     123, 130, 139–42, 156–57, 175,
     176, 198, 238, 345–46
  in California, see California
  in Massachusetts, 3–4, 307,
     322–23, 325–34
  in Michigan, 267, 276, 277, 278,
     281, 282–84, 286, 288
  New York constitutional
     provisions for referendum,
     81–84, 87, 90, 92–93, 96,
     170, 345
  in Ohio, 242, 250, 251, 252, 258,
     259, 260, 263, 264–65
Inquiry into the Nature and Causes
     of the Wealth of Nations, The
     (Smith), 29–30
Internal Revenue Service, 7
Inventory taxes, 156, 168, 300
Iowa, 130

Jackson, Andrew, 33, 74, 130, 213,
     214, 216, 224, 269, 270, 271,
     338
Jacksonian Democracy, 24, 29,
     33–34, 38–39, 183, 211–12,
     299, 344, 345
James II, King of England, 52, 53
Jarvis, Howard, 8, 160, 164–66, 167,
     168–69, 171, 172, 173, 174,
     260, 283, 284
Jefferson, Thomas, 30, 32, 224, 244,
     338
Jenkins, Louis (Woody), 203
Johnson, Grove, 141, 158
Johnson, Hiram, 95, 139–41, 142, 144
Johnson, Milbank, 230
Jones, Sam Houston, 196, 197–98
Judah, Theodore D., 131

Kadlec, Charles W., 10, 13
Kantor, Michael, 169
Kearney, Denis, 131
Keayne, Robert, 46
Kelley, Alfred, 240, 241, 249, 250, 251
Kelly, Francis, 292
Kemp-Roth bill, 159, 160
Kentucky, 180, 247
Keynesian economics, 9, 10, 22, 338
King, Edward F., 319, 324, 325
"King amendment," 324–25, 330
King, Edward J., 319–21, 325, 327, 330
King, John, 301
King Philip's War, 51, 53
Knight, Goodwin, 144
Koch, Edward I., 118, 119, 121–22, 180
Kuttner, Robert, 165, 166, 174

Laffer, Arthur, 9, 10, 11, 13, 16, 25, 125, 159–60, 169, 170, 317
Laffer Curve, 11–12, 13, 16, 17, 28, 56, 66, 320
Lama, Alfred J., 95–96, 105
Lamar, Mirabeau Buonaparte, 214, 215, 217
Lausche, Frank J., 253
Law of Markets, 10, 11
League to Protect the Initiative, 142
Leche, Richard W., 197
Lehrman, Lewis, 23, 122
Liebling, A. J., 183, 189
Lincoln, Abraham, 74, 76–77, 247
Lincoln, Benjamin, 70
Lindsay, John V., 103–12, 113, 115, 145, 286, 312, 313
Local taxes, 7, 8, 36, 204; see also New York City; Real estate taxes
Locke, John, 25–27, 28, 29, 30–31, 32, 34–35, 37, 38, 44, 46, 83, 84, 127–28, 277, 334, 341–44
    influence on Massachusetts Bay Colony, 54–55, 61, 64, 345
Logue, Edward J., 98
Long, Earl, 194–95, 199, 200, 206
Long, Huey, 4, 95, 188, 189, 191, 192, 193–97, 198, 199, 206
Loomis, Arphaxed, 77, 80, 81, 83, 87
Louisiana, 179–207, 267, 341

Constitution of, 187, 188, 191, 192–93, 195, 198, 199–200, 203–5
    under Huey Long, 193–96
    oil and gas taxes in, 192, 194, 196, 197, 198, 199, 200, 203, 205–6
    political history of, 187–89, 193–200
    Reconstruction period in, 183–85, 189–92
    Redeemers and Retrenchers in, 185–86, 191–92
Louisiana Association of Business and Industry (LABI), 202
Lucas, Anthony, 227

McGivern, Owen, 119
"McGivern Commission," 118–19, 120
McKennon, Robert, 199
McLane, Malcolm, 302
McNelly, Leander H., 212–13
McWilliams, Carey, 124, 136, 138, 163
Magna Carta, 52, 187
Maine, 292, 293
Manchester Union Leader, The, 302
Marshall, James W., 126
Marshall, John, 37
Maryland, 244
Mason, Richard B., 127, 128
Mason, Steven, 272
Mason, Thomas, 297
Massachusetts, 3–4, 8, 13, 38, 117, 243, 254, 265, 292–93, 307–34, 338–39
    Constitution of, 30–31, 63–65, 308–9, 322–23, 324
    fiscal crisis in, 311–17, 321–22
    Proposition 2½, 3–4, 307, 325–33, 340
    Shays' Rebellion, 44, 68–71
    Tax Revolt in, 322–34
    see also Massachusetts Bay Colony
Massachusetts Arts Council, 314
Massachusetts Bay Colony, 43–72, 342–43, 345
    general property tax originating in, 48–50
    Locke's influence on, 54–55, 61, 64

Massachusetts Bay Colony (*cont.*)
   Massachusetts Constitution of
      1780, 63, 67, 318, 343
   taxation linked with
      representation in, 43–44, 47,
      53, 54, 55, 58, 60–61, 65,
      66–67, 70–71
Massachusetts High Technology
   Council, 317, 319–20, 325–28,
   329, 330, 332, 333
Massachusetts Taxpayers
   Foundation, 319–32
Mather, Increase, 53, 55
Matthews, Nathan, 48, 49
Mauer, John Walker, 222
Mellon, Andrew, 338
Menges, Jack, 294–96, 301
Merriam, Frank, 144
Michigan, 23, 88, 246, 266–88, 339,
   341
   Constitution of, 269, 274, 275–76,
      278, 281, 287
   history of, 267–79
   Proposal A, 285
   Proposal C (Headlee amendment),
      282–84
   Tax Revolts in, 266–67, 279–88
   Tisch amendment, 283–84, 285,
      286
   "Voter's Choice" amendment, 288
Miller, Perry, 53–54
Miller, William, 78
Milliken, William, 282, 285, 286–87
Minot, George Richards, 70–71
Mississippi, 180, 185
Mitchell, John, 96, 98, 107–8
Mitchell, MacNeil, 95–97, 105
Molyneaux, Peter, 229–30
Money, issuing paper, 59, 67–68, 270
Montesquieu, Baron de La Brède et
   de, 27–28, 29, 31, 32, 57, 82,
   230, 244–45, 342
Moody, Dan, 229
Morality of Consent, The (Bickel),
   107
"Moral obligation" bond, 95, 96,
   107–8, 113–14
Morgan, Edmund, 56–7
Morris, Charles, 111
Morris, Gouverneur, 75
Morris Canal and Banking Company,
   272

Morrison, Delesseps S., 188
Moses, Robert, 94, 95
Municipal Assistance Corporation,
   117
Muehlmann, K. Heinz, 317–18, 325,
   327, 330
Muqaddimah (Ibn Khaldun), 25, 27
Muther, Walter, 328

National Reform movement, 79
National Tax Limitation Committee,
   156
Native American Party, 78, 79
Navigation Acts, 51
Nebraska, 302
Nevada, 300
New Hampshire, 18, 37, 254,
   291–306, 316
   Constitution of, 31, 298
New Jersey, 23, 120
New Orleans Times, 189
New Republic, The, 206
Newton, Sir Issac, 55
New York and Erie Railroad
   Company, 77
New York City, 75–76, 78, 80, 85–86
   fiscal crisis in, 102–21, 122, 313
   limitations on indebtedness of,
      88–90
New York State, 8, 13, 23, 37, 103,
   112, 148, 180, 243, 245, 293,
   316, 317, 340, 345
   colony of, 58
   constitutional convention of 1846,
      77, 79–84, 92
   constitutional convention of 1867,
      85
   Constitution of, 81, 83, 84, 87, 90,
      93, 94–95, 108, 122–23, 130
   fiscal crisis of 1975 in, 91–102,
      107, 118–23, 313
   phase two of the Tax Revolt in,
      73–90, 345
   Stop and Tax law of, 77, 92
New York Tribune, 220
Niskanen, William A., 160, 282
Nixon, Richard, 9, 233, 311, 338
"Nuisance" taxes, 111

Occupation tax, 224
Ohio, 240–65, 304, 339, 341
   Constitution of, 247, 248, 249,

250–1, 258
failed Tax Revolt in, 264–65
history of, 243–52, 269
reasons for stagnation of, 254–62,
    265
"Ohioans to Stop Excessive
    Taxation" (S.E.T.), 263–64,
    265
Ohio-Erie Canal, 248, 250, 256
Ohio Public Interest Campaign
    (OPIC), 260
Oklahoma, 181
Olds, Ransom E., 275
"O.P.Q.," 66, 70

Paine, Thomas, 6
Panic of 1837, 33, 76, 215
Parker, John M., 192
Parliament of England, 48, 57, 58,
    59, 60, 61, 67, 344
Pennsylvania, 84, 222, 243, 316
Pennsylvania Bank of the United
    States, 272
Personal income tax, 6–7, 21, 36,
    204, 225, 302, 339–40
    in California, 144, 149–50, 151,
        157, 168
    in Louisiana, 192–93, 195, 198,
        203, 204, 205–6
    in Massachusetts, 308–9, 313, 315,
        320
    in Michigan, 281–82, 286, 287,
        288
    Nebraska, 302
    in New York City, 104, 108, 111,
        121
    in New York State, 99, 101, 102,
        118, 120, 195
    in Ohio, 251, 252, 253, 258–59,
        260, 262, 263
    in Texas, 222, 228–30
    in Vermont, 294, 300, 303
Peterson, Walter, 301–2
Phillips, George, 43, 44
Plymouth Colony, 45, 46–47, 51
Poll taxes, 214
Populists, 4, 188–89, 192, 236–39
Port Authority of New York and
    New Jersey, 94, 112
Powell, Wesley, 301
Power Shift (Sale), 179
Pressman, Joel, 331

Priolo, Paul, 165
Progress and Poverty (George),
    132–33, 134–35
Progressive movement, 4, 39,
    139–41, 142, 251, 275, 276
Progressive taxation, 65, 104, 149,
    192, 195, 198, 234, 258, 259,
    342
Property tax, see General property
    tax; Real estate taxes
Proportional taxation, 35, 38, 54, 65,
    84, 104, 192, 195, 300, 308–9,
    313, 324, 342
Proposal A (Michigan), 285
Proposal C (Michigan), 282–83
Proposition 1 (California), 22,
    156–60, 168, 170, 203, 238,
    282
Proposition 2½ (Massachusetts),
    3–4, 307, 325–33, 340
Proposition 4 (California):
    1979, 173–79
    1980, 170–71
Proposition 9 (California), 168–70
Proposition 13 (California), 3, 8, 13,
    15, 23, 124–25' 156, 157,
    160–61, 164–67, 170–76, 237,
    260, 283, 340
Public Affairs Research Council, 204

Quincy, Josiah, 187–88
Quirk, William J., 113

Ranson, David, 9
Reagan, Ronald, 3, 4, 261, 285, 296,
    328
    as California's governor, 22, 125,
        144–45, 147–58, 161, 163,
        165, 174, 203, 340
    Proposition 1 and, 22, 156–60,
        165, 203, 238
    tax cuts of, 6, 32, 151–52, 153, 154,
        156
Real estate taxes, 36, 89
    in California, 125, 130, 153–55,
        161–62, 164–67
    in Louisiana, 189–90, 191–92, 195,
        197, 204
    in Massachusetts, 307, 308, 313,
        320, 323, 324, 325, 326–32
    in Michigan, 283, 284
    in New Hampshire, 303

Real estate taxes (*cont.*)
  in New York City, 103, 111, 115,
    118, 120–21
  in Ohio, 252–53
  see also General property taxes
Recall provisions, 140, 141, 287–88
Recovery phase of a fiscal crisis, 92,
    118–23, 321–22
Referendum, *see* Initiatives and
    referendum
Representation, taxation linked
    with, 28, 43–72, 74, 334,
    344–45
Revenue Anticipation Notes (RANs),
    110
Revenue bonds, 93, 95, 170
Rhode Island, 34, 316
Rhodes, James, 254, 258, 260, 262,
    263
Richardson, Rupert, 217
Ring, William, 45
Roberts, Oran M., 223–26, 228
Roberts, Paul Craig, 9
Robinson, Maurice, 299–300
Rockefeller, David, 117
Rockefeller, Nelson, 91, 95–102, 106,
    107, 108, 110–11, 115, 145, 313,
    340
Rohatyn, Felix, 182
Romney, George, 281
Roosevelt, Franklin D., 144, 195

Sale, Kirkpatrick, 179
Sales tax:
  in California, 144, 149, 152, 153,
    157
  in Louisiana, 195–96, 197, 198,
    199
  in Massachusetts, 313, 315
  in Michigan, 277, 279–81
  in Nebraska, 302
  in New York City, 103, 111
  in New York State, 101, 103, 118,
    121
  in Ohio, 252, 253, 262
  in Texas, 210, 230, 231, 233–34,
    235
  in Vermont, 294, 303
Salingey, M. de, 215–16
Santa Anna, Antonio López de, 211,
    212
Santa Fe Railroad, 137

Sargent, Francis, 308, 312, 313, 314
Say, Jean Baptiste, 10, 11, 33, 35,
    299, 341
Schmidt, Helmut, 117
Schools, taxes to support, 50,
    340–41, 342–43
  in California, 152, 153, 154, 173
  in Michigan, 275
  in Ohio, 258, 259
  in the South, 186, 193, 194, 197,
    218, 219, 220
  Vermont–New Hampshire
    comparison, 303
Schwulst, Earl B., 103, 104
Second Treatise (Locke), 26–27, 30,
    83
Serrano v. Priest, 153
Severance taxes:
  in Louisiana, 182, 192, 194, 197,
    198, 199, 200, 203, 205
  in Ohio, 251, 258
  in Texas, 210, 231–33
Seward, William, 76–77, 87, 91, 92
Shaker, William, 282
Shannon, John D., 17, 18
Share Our Wealth Society, 195, 197
Shays' Rebellion, 44, 68–71
Shepard, William, 69, 70
Shreveport Evening News, 188–89
Simon, William, 118
"Sin taxes," 301
Smith, Adam, 10, 28, 29–30, 31, 32,
    34 ,35, 46, 57, 81, 230, 241,
    299, 341, 342, 344
Smyth, George, 208–9, 213, 228
Social contract, 25–26, 34, 35, 38,
    44, 46, 54, 64, 277, 341, 342
  see also Locke, John
"Social Contract" in Massachusetts,
    319–20, 325, 332
Social Security tax, 6
South Dakota, 200
Southern Pacific Railroad, 137, 139,
    141
Stabilization Revenue Corporation
    (SRC), 113–14, 117
Stalled Economy, The, 202
Stamp Act (1765), 56, 57, 60, 61
Standard Oil, 192, 194, 196, 197, 227
Stanford, Leland, 131
Stanton, Elizabeth Cady, 73
Stanton, Henry, 73

State taxes, 7–8, 13–23, 36
  Adam Smith's influences on
    systems of, 29
  economic health and, 20–21,
    101–2, 116–17, 204–5,
    206–7, 210, 226, 265,
    304–6, 315–16, 321–22,
    332–33, 339–40
  in Jacksonian era, 33–34, 38–39
  see also individual states and
    types of taxes
Stein, Herbert, 9
Sterling, Ross, 231
Stock-in-trade tax, see Inventory tax
Stock transfer tax, 103, 120
Stubblebine, William Craig, 160,
  168, 169, 282
Sugar Act (1764), 56–57
Sugarman, Stephen, 153
Sunbelt, 179–86
  see also individual states
Sununu, John, 305
Supply-side economics, 5, 9–12, 15,
  23, 134–35, 148, 159, 193, 263,
  308, 316, 334, 338–41, 346
  antecedents of, 24–39, 66, 70
  Jacksonian Democracy and, 24,
    29, 33–34
  in Massachusetts, 317–22, 332–33
  in New York, 1$0–23
  Reagan's conversion to, 159–60
  see also Tax Revolt
Sutter, John, 126, 137

Taft, William Howard, 160
Tax Anticipation Notes (TANs),
  109–10, 114
Taxation, see types of taxes, e.g.
  Personal income tax; Sales tax;
    and individual states
Taxatiol linked to representation,
  28, 43–72, 74, 334, 344–45
Tax burden, 13, 17, 18, 20, 21–22
Tax Killer, The, 250
"Taxpayers United," 282
Tax Reduction Task Force, 157–58,
  160
Tax Revolt:
  applications and limitations of,
    179–288
  the first general, 51–54
  implications of, 335–46

phase one, 38, 43–72, 74, 344–45
phase two, 38, 73–90, 345
phase three, 39, 124–78, 345–46
philosophy and antecedents of,
  24–39, 341–44
supply-side movement and the
  states, 3–23
three waves of, 37–39, 344–46
vindication of, 289–334
Taylor, Bayard, 135–36
Temple, Arthur, 237
Tennessee, 22–23, 180, 213, 238
Texas, 4, 5, 180, 182, 185, 187,
  208–39, 254, 294, 332
  agrarian-corporate division in,
    234–39
  antibank sentiment in, 215–16
  before joining the Union, 211–17
  Constitution of, 214, 216, 221–22,
    228, 237–38
  1870s tax revolt in, 218–21
  oil's role in, 226–27, 231–33, 238,
    239
  shaping of modern tax system in,
    228–34
Texas Commission on State and
  Local Tax Policy, 234
Texas Observer, 237
Texas Railroad Commission, 237
Thomson, Meldrim, 302, 305
Tilden, Samuel, 80–81, 87
Tisch, Robert, 283–86
Tocqueville, Alexis de, 15, 50, 230,
  273, 346
Townshend, Charles, 57, 298
Townshend duties (1765), 56, 57–58
Traité d'economie politique (Say),
  10, 33
Treatise of Human Nature, A
  (Hume), 29
Treatise on the Constitutional
  Limitations Which Rest Upon
  the Legislative Power of the
  States of the American Union
  (Cooley), 34
Treen, David, 205–6
Triborough Bridge and Tunnel
  Authority (TBTA), 94
Trotter, Alexander, 273
Ture, Norman, 160
Turner, Frederick Jackson, 245, 246
Tweed, William Marcy, 89

Uhler, Lewis K., 156, 160, 282
Uniform taxation, 35, 38, 84, 85, 86,
    249–50, 341–42
University of Southern California
    Graduate School of Business
    Administration, 16
Unruh, Jesse, 150
Urban Development Corporation
    (UDC), 97–98, 105, 107, 112

Vallandigham, Clement Laird, 247
Van Buren, Martin, 74, 80–81
Van Rensselaer, Stephen, 78
Vedder, Richard, 259
Vermont, 4, 200, 209, 292, 293,
    294–96, 298, 300, 301, 302–3,
    304–5
Virginia, 58, 181, 243, 245, 247
Virtual representation, 58, 60, 67,
    344, 345
Volpe, John A., 311, 312, 313
"Voter's Choice" amendment
    (Michigan), 288

Wagner, Robert F., 102–3, 105, 106,
    111
Wainwright & Co. Economics, H. C.,
    7, 317
Walker, Jimmy, 115
Wall Street Journal, The, 9, 159, 315
Wanniski, Jude, 9, 11, 159
Warmoth, Henry C., 190
Warren, Earl, 144
Warren, Marcy Otis, 71–72

Washington, George, 32, 69
Washington Post, 311
Watson, Philip E., 155, 156, 157, 161,
    164
Webb, Robert I., 16, 17
Webb, Walter Prescott, 240–41, 292
"Wedge, the," 11, 16, 21–22
Wein, Leon E., 113
Weinberger, Caspar, 152
Wentworth, John, 297, 298
Western Center on Law and Poverty,
    169
West Virginia, 180
Whately, Thomas, 57, 60
Wheelabrator-Frye Corporation, 302
White, George, 251–52, 253
White, Kevin H., 311, 331
White, Mark, 237
White and Case, 114, 115
William of Orange, 45, 52
Williams, G. Mennen, 279
Williams, T. Harry, 190–91
"Windfall profits tax," 6
Winthrop, John, 43–44, 47
Wisconsin, 200
Wise, John, 52
Wood, Dawson, Love & Sabatine, 114
Woodward, Augustus, 275
Worden, Alvah, 81–82
Wright, Silas, 75, 79

Yearley, Clifton K., 86, 88
Younger, Evelle, 167